STALIN
1939–1953

SIMON SEBAG MONTEFIORE

PHOENIX

A PHOENIX PAPERBACK

This edition produced for The Book People Ltd,
Hall Wood Avenue, Haydock, St Helens WA11 9UL

First published in Great Britain in 2003
by Weidenfeld & Nicolson
Paperback edition published in 2004
by Phoenix,
an imprint of Orion Books Ltd,
Orion House, 5 Upper St Martin's Lane,
London WC2H 9EA

An Hachette UK company

A CIP catalogue record for this book
is available from the British Library.

ISBN 978-1-4072-2147-2

Typeset by Selwood Systems, Midsomer Norton

Printed and bound in Great Britain by
Clays Ltd, St Ives plc

The Orion Publishing Group's policy is to use papers that
are natural, renewable and recyclable products and
made from wood grown in sustainable forests. The logging
and manufacturing processes are expected to conform to
the environmental regulations of the country of origin.

www.orionbooks.co.uk

Contents

Part Nine: The Dangerous Game of Succession, 1945–1949

Part Ten: The Lame Tiger, 1949–1953

STALIN'S FAMILY

DJUGASHVILIS

SVANIDZES

ALLILUYEVS

N.B This genealogy is selected to include the main characters described in the book. Marriages and children after Stalin's death are not included.

Vissarion 'Beso' Djugashvili 1850–1910 = m. 1870 Ekaterina 'Keke' Geladze 1858–1937

JOSEPH STALIN 1878–1953

Ekaterina 'Kato' Svanidze 1885–1907

Alexander 'Alyosha' Svanidze 1884–1941 = Maria Korona 1889–1942

Mariko Svanidze 1884?–1942

Sashiko Svanidze ?

Tolya d. 1941

John Reed 'Johnik' 1927–1990

Zoya Gunina 1908–1957 = Yakov 'Yasha' 1907–1943 = Julia Meltzer ?–1967

Gulia 1939–

Nadezhda 'Nadya' Alliluyeva 1901–1932

Vasily 1921–1962 = m. 1940 1. Galina Bourdonovskaya d. 1990 = m. 1946 2. 'Katya' Timoshenko d. 1983 = m. 1930 3. Kapitolina Vasilieva

Alexander 1941–

Nadezhda 1943–

Svetlana 1926– = m. 1945 1. Grigory Morozov 1921–2002 = m. 1948 2. Yury Zhdanov 1918–

Joseph Morozov 1945–

Katya Zhdanov 1950–

Vasily 1949–72

Svetlana 1947–90

Sergei Alliluyev 1866–1945 = m. 1893 Olga Fedorenko 1877–1951

Pavel 1894–1938 = Yevgenia 'Zhenya' Zemlyanitsyn 1898–1974

Anna 1896–1964 = Stanislav Redens 1893–1940

Fyodor 1898–1955

Kira 1919–

Sergei 1928–

Alexander 1931–

Leonid 1928–

Vladimir* 1935–

Vladimir Redens was adopted by Fyodor Alliluyev in 1948 and changed his name to Alliluyev.

The Soviet Union under Stalin 1929–1953

Territory won in Finnish War 1940

Territories added 1939/1940 after
Molotov–Ribbentrop Pact

German and Czech territory
annexed by USSR in 1945

Extent of the German invasion
January – July 1942

SWEDEN

FINLAND

Leningrad

ESTONIA

Baltic Sea

LATVIA

LITHUANIA

• Minsk
BELORUSSIA

• Smolensk

• Moscow

SOVIET
UNION

• Gorky (Nizhny-Novgorod)

• Kuibyshev
(Samara)

POLAND

CZECHOSLOVAKIA

HUNGARY

Kursk

• Kiev

Kharkov

UKRAINE

Rostov-on-Don

• Stalingrad (Tsaritsyn)

RUMANIA

YUGOSLAVIA

BULGARIA

Kerch

Yalta

Black Sea

Caspian
Sea

GEORGIA
Tbilisi •

Baku

ARMENIA AZERBAIJAN

GREECE

TURKEY

IRAN

Teheran
•

Mediterranean Sea

Selected cities named after Stalin's comrades:

Molotov (Perm)
Zhdanov (Mariupol)
Kalinin (Tver)
Voroshilov (Lugansk)
Ordzhonikidze (Vladikafkaz)
Kirov (Viatka)
Gorky (Nizhny-Novgorod)

Kuibyshev (Samara)
Vorashilovsk (Stavropol)
Stalingrad (Tsaritsyn)
Stalino (Yuzhovka)
Stalinabad (Dushanbe)
Kirovabad (Elizavetpol)

Stalingrad

Rostov-on-Don

Volga

Stavropol
(Voroshilovsk)

Maikop

Sochi
Gagra   ABKHAZIA
New Athos (Novy Afon)
Sukhumi

Grozny

Ordzhonikidze
(Vladikafkaz)

Caspian Sea

Black Sea

GEORGIA   C A U C A S U S

Batumi

Gori
Borzhomi
(Borjomi)   Tiflis
(Tbilisi)

ARMENIA

TURKEY

Yerevan

AZERBAIJAN   Baku

NAXCIVAN

IRAN

The Soviet Caucasus Under Stalin
1929–1953

Furthest southern advance of the German troops
by November 1942

List of Characters

Joseph Stalin born Djugashvili known as 'Soso' and 'Koba'. Secretary of Bolshevik Party 1922–1953 and Premier 1941–53. Marshal. Generalissimo

Family

Keke Djugashvili, Stalin's mother

Kato Svanidze, Stalin's first wife

Yakov Djugashvili, son of Stalin's first marriage to Kato Svanidze. Captured by Germans

Nadya Alliluyeva, Stalin's second wife

Vasily Stalin, Stalin's son by Nadya Alliluyeva, pilot, General

Svetlana Stalin now known as Alliluyeva, Stalin's daughter

Artyom Sergeev, Stalin and Nadya's adopted son

Sergei Alliluyev, Nadya's father

Olga Alliluyeva, Nadya's mother

Pavel Alliluyev, Nadya's brother, Red Army Commissar married to

Zhenya Alliluyeva, Nadya's sister-in-law, actress, mother of Kira

Alyosha Svanidze, brother of Kato, Georgian, Stalin's brother-in-law, banking official married to

Maria Svanidze, diarist, Jewish Georgian opera singer

Stanislas Redens, Nadya's brother-in-law, secret policeman, married to Anna Redens, Nadya's elder sister

Allies

Victor Abakumov, secret policeman, head of Smersh, MGB Minister

Andrei Andreyev, Politburo member, CC Secretary, married to

Dora Khazan, Nadya's best friend, Deputy Textiles Minister, mother of Natasha Andreyeva

Lavrenti Beria, 'Uncle Lara', secret policeman, NKVD boss, Politburo member in charge of nuclear bomb, married to

Nina Beria, scientist, Stalin treated her 'like a daughter', mother of Sergo Beria, scientist, married to

Martha Peshkova Beria, granddaughter of Gorky, daughter-in-law
of Beria

Semyon Budyonny, cavalryman, Marshal, one of the Tsaritsyn
Group

Nikolai Bulganin, 'the Plumber', Chekist, Mayor of Moscow,
Politburo member, Defence Minister, heir apparent

Candide Charkviani, Georgian Party chief and Stalin's confidant

Semyon Ignatiev, MGB Minister, master of the Doctors' Plot

Lazar Kaganovich, 'Iron Lazar' and 'the Locomotive', Jewish Old
Bolshevik, Stalin's deputy early 1930s, Railways chief, Politburo
member

Mikhail Kalinin, 'Papa', the 'Village Elder', Soviet President, peasant/
worker

Nikita Khrushchev, Moscow, then Ukrainian First Secretary,
Politburo member

Sergei Kirov, Leningrad chief, CC Secretary, Politburo member and
Stalin's close friend

Valerian Kuibyshev, economic chief and poet, Politburo member

Alexei (A. A.) Kuznetsov, Zhdanov's deputy in Leningrad; post-
WW2, CC Secretary and curator of MGB, Stalin's heir apparent
as Secretary

Nestor Lakoba, Abkhazian boss

Georgi Malenkov, nicknamed 'Melanie' or 'Malanya', CC
Secretary, allied to Beria

Lev Mekhlis, 'the Gloomy Demon' and 'Shark', Jewish, Stalin's
secretary, then *Pravda* editor, political chief of Red Army

Akaki Mgeladze, Abkhazian, then Georgian boss; Stalin called him
'Wolf'

Anastas Mikoyan, Armenian Old Bolshevik, Politburo member,
Trade and Supply Minister

Vyacheslav Molotov, known as 'Iron-Arse', and 'our Vecha',
Politburo member, Premier, Foreign Minister, married to

Polina Molotova née Karpovskaya, known as Comrade
Zhemchuzhina, 'the Pearl', Jewish, Fishery Commissar, perfume
boss

Grigory Ordzhonikidze, known as Comrade Sergo and as 'Stalin's
Arse', Politburo member, Heavy Industry chief

Karl Pauker, ex-barber of Budapest Opera, Stalin's bodyguard and
head of Security

Alexander Poskrebyshev, ex-medical orderly, Stalin's *chef de
cabinet*, married to

Bronka Metalikova Poskrebysheva, doctor, Jewish

Mikhail Riumin, 'Little Misha', 'the Midget', MGB Deputy Minister and manager of the Doctors' Plot

Nikolai Vlasik, Stalin's bodyguard and head of Guards Directorate

Klim Voroshilov, First Marshal, Politburo member, Defence Commissar, veteran of Tsaritsyn married to

Ekaterina Voroshilova, diarist

Nikolai Voznesensky, Leningrad economist, Politburo member, Deputy Premier, Stalin's anointed heir as Premier

Genrikh Yagoda, NKVD chief, Jewish, in love with Timosha Gorky

Abel Yenukidze, 'Uncle Abel', Secretary of Central Executive Committee, Georgian, bon viveur, Nadya's godfather

Nikolai Yezhov, 'Blackberry' or 'Kolya', NKVD boss, married to

Yevgenia Yezhova, editor, socialite, Jewess

Andrei Zhdanov, 'the Pianist', Politburo member, Leningrad boss, CC Secretary, Naval chief, Stalin's friend and heir apparent, father of

Yury Zhdanov, CC Science Dept chief, married Svetlana Stalin

Generals

Grigory Kulik, Marshal, Artillery chief, womaniser and bungler, veteran of Tsaritsyn

Boris Shaposhnikov, Marshal, Chief of Staff, Stalin's favourite staff officer

Semyon Timoshenko, Marshal, victor of Finland, Defence Commissar, veteran of Tsaritsyn; his daughter married Vasily Stalin

Alexander Vasilevsky, Marshal, Chief of Staff, priest's son

Georgi Zhukov, Marshal, Deputy Commander-in-Chief, Stalin's best general

Enemies and Former Allies

Nikolai Bukharin, 'darling of the Party', 'Bukharchik', theorist, Politburo member, Stalin's co-ruler 1925–9, friend of Nadya, Rightist. Chief defendant in last show trial

Lev Kamenev, Leftist Politburo member, defeated Trotsky with Stalin, with whom ruled 1924–5, Jewish. Defendant in first show trial

Alexei Rykov, 'Rykvodka', Rightist Politburo member, Premier and co-ruler with Stalin and Bukharin 1925–8. Defendant in last show trial

Leon Trotsky, genius of the Revolution, Jewish, War Commissar and creator of Red Army, 'operetta commander' in Stalin's words

Grigory Zinoviev, Leftist Politburo member, Leningrad boss, Jewish. Triumvirate with Stalin and Kamenev 1924–5. Defendant in first show trial

'Engineers of the Human Soul'

Anna Akhmatova, poet, 'harlot-nun,' said Zhdanov

Isaac Babel, author of *Red Cavalry* and friend of Eisenstein, Mandelstam

Demian Bedny, 'the proletarian poet', boon companion of Stalin

Mikhail Bulgakov, novelist and playwright, Stalin saw his *Days of the Turbins* fifteen times

Ilya Ehrenburg, Jewish writer and European literary figure

Sergei Eisenstein, Russia's greatest film director

Maxim Gorky, Russia's most famous novelist, close to Stalin

Ivan Kozlovsky, Stalin's court tenor

Osip Mandelstam, poet: 'Isolate but preserve,' said Stalin

Boris Pasternak, poet, 'cloud dweller', said Stalin

Mikhail Sholokhov, novelist of Cossacks and collectivization

Konstantin Simonov, poet and editor, friend of Vasily Stalin, favourite of Stalin

Part Six

'The Great Game': Hitler and Stalin,
1939–1941

The Carve-up of Europe: Molotov, Ribbentrop and Stalin's Jewish Question

When Stalin concentrated on diplomacy, he first aimed his guns at his own diplomats. On the night of 3 May 1939, NKVD troops surrounded the Foreign Commissariat, bringing home the urgency of the countdown to war and the coming revolution of alliances. Molotov, Beria and Malenkov arrived to inform Maxim 'Papasha' Litvinov, the worldly rambunctious champion of European peace through 'collective security', that he had been sacked. This was not a surprise to Litvinov: Stalin would pat his Foreign Commissar and say, 'You see, we can reach agreement.'

'Not for long,' Papasha Litvinov replied.

The new Foreign Commissar was Molotov, already the Premier. Stalin emerged from the Terror more paranoid and more confident, a state of mind that made him, if anything, less equipped to analyse the dangerous international situation. Mikoyan noticed this new Stalin 'was an utterly changed person – absolutely suspicious, ruthless and boundlessly self-confident, often speaking of himself in the third person. I think he went barmy.' Kaganovich recalled that he hardly ever called together the Politburo now, deciding most things informally. Stalin does not 'know the West', thought Litvinov. 'If our opponents were a bunch of shahs and sheikhs, he'd outwit them.' Nor were his two main advisers, Molotov and Zhdanov, any better qualified. Stalin educated himself by reading history, particularly Bismarck's memoirs, but he did not realize that the Iron Chancellor was a conventional statesman compared to Hitler. Henceforth Stalin quoted Talleyrand and Bismarck liberally.

Molotov always said that Bolshevik politics was the best training for diplomacy and regarded himself as a politician not a diplomat but he was proud of his new career: 'Everything was in Stalin's fist, in my fist,' he said. But he worked in his tireless, methodical way under immense pressure, arguing ideas through with Stalin, while terrorizing his staff in 'blind rages'. Yet in his letters to his wife Polina, he revealed the vainglory and passion within: 'We live under constant pressure not to miss something ... I so miss you and our daughter, I want to hold you in my arms, to my breast with all your sweetness and charm ...' More direct and less intellectual than Stalin, he told Polina that he was starting to read, not about Talleyrand, but about Hitler. Apart from the smouldering desire for Polina, the most amusing part of these letters was the unabashed delight Molotov took in his new fame. 'I can tell you, without boasting,' he boasted, 'that our opposite numbers feel ... they deal with people that know their stuff.'

Stalin and Molotov developed into an international double act of increasing subtlety, masters of the old 'good cop, bad cop' routine. Stalin was always more radical and reckless, Molotov the stolid analyst of the possible, but neither saw any contradiction between imperial expansionism and their Marxist crusade: on the contrary, the former was the best way to empower the latter.

Europe in early 1939 was, in Stalin's own words, a 'poker game' with three players, in which each hoped to persuade the other two to destroy one another and leave the third to take the winnings. The three players were the Fascists of Adolf Hitler's Nazi Germany, the Capitalists of Neville Chamberlain's Britain allied with Daladier's France – and the Bolsheviks. Though the Georgian admired the flamboyant brutality of the Austrian, he appreciated the danger of a resurgent Germany militarily, and the hostility of Fascism.

Stalin regarded the Western democracies as at least as dangerous as Germany. He had matured politically during their intervention during the Civil War. He instinctively felt he could work with Hitler. As soon as the 'Austrian corporal' took power, Stalin began probing gently, advised by Karl Radek, his German expert, and using as personal emissaries, Abel Yenukidze and David Kandelaki. The sensitivity of these discussions was absolute since Stalin was simultaneously shooting thousands as German agents, with the country in a frenzy of Prussophobic war preparations. The legates were shot.

Hitler kept Stalin at arm's length as long as the democracies continued to appease him. But the Munich agreement convinced Stalin that the West was not serious about stopping Hitler. On the contrary, Stalin was sure that they were willing to let Hitler destroy Soviet Russia. Munich rendered Litvinov's 'collective security' bankrupt. Stalin warned the West that the Soviet Union would not be left to 'pick their chestnuts out of the fire'. The way forward was a division of the world into 'spheres'. This was an oblique signal to Germany that he would deal with whoever would deal with him. Berlin noted the change. Afterwards, at the Plenum, Stalin attacked Litvinov:

'Does that mean you regard me as an Enemy of the People?' asked plucky Litvinov. Stalin hesitated as he left the hall: 'No, we don't consider Papasha an Enemy. Papasha's an honest revolutionary.'*

Meanwhile, Molotov and Beria were terrorizing a meeting of their worldly diplomats, many of them Jewish Bolsheviks at home in the great capitals of Europe. Beria glanced around at them:

'Nazarov,' he said. 'Why did they arrest your father?'

'Lavrenti Pavlovich, you no doubt know better than I.'

'You and I will talk about that later,' laughed Beria.

The Foreign Commissariat was almost next door to the Lubianka and the two ministries were nicknamed 'the Neighbours'. Molotov's deputy, Vladimir Dekanozov, forty-one, another of Beria's intelligent Caucasian henchmen, supervised the purge of diplomats. This red-haired midget, with a taste for English movies (he called his son Reginald) and teenage girls, was a failed medical student who had known Beria since university when they both joined the Cheka. He was a Russified Georgian. Molotov joked that he was an Armenian pretending to be Georgian to please Stalin, who nicknamed him 'Slow Kartvelian' after his region of origin. At Kuntsevo, Stalin mocked his ugliness. When he appeared at the door, Stalin said sarcastically to general laughter:

'Such a handsome man! Look at him! I've never seen anything like it!'

The press officer of the Foreign Commissariat, Yevgeni Gnedin, himself a piece of revolutionary history as the son of Parvus,

---

* This sort of courage counted for something with Stalin. Litvinov, who was three years older than Stalin, could never curb his tongue. That cosmopolitan curmudgeon complained to his friends of Stalin's 'narrow-mindedness, smugness, ambitions and rigidity' while he called Molotov 'a halfwit', Beria 'a careerist' and Malenkov 'short-sighted'. Molotov said that Litvinov remained 'amongst the living only by chance' yet Stalin always just preserved him, despite Molotov's hatred for a much more impressive diplomat, because he was so respected in the West that he might be useful again. There was a story that Litvinov had saved Stalin from being beaten up by dockers in London in 1907: 'I haven't forgotten that time in London,' Stalin used to say.

Lenin's financier and middle man with Kaiserine Germany, was arrested by Dekanozov and taken to Beria's office where he was ordered to confess to spying. When he refused, Beria ordered him to lie on the floor while the Caucasian 'giant' Kobulov beat him on the skull with blackjacks. Gnedin was a 'lucky stiff'. In July, Beria ordered Prince Tsereteli to kill the Soviet Ambassador to China, Bovkun-Luganets, and his wife, in cold blood in a faked car accident (the method of killing those too eminent to just disappear).*

Stalin's diplomatic Terror was designed to appeal to Hitler: 'Purge the ministry of Jews,' he said. 'Clean out the "synagogue."' 'Thank God for these words,' Molotov (married to a Jewess) explained. 'Jews formed an absolute majority and many ambassadors ...'

Stalin was an anti-Semite by most definitions but until after the war, it was more a Russian mannerism than a dangerous obsession. He was never a biological racist like the Nazis. However, he disliked any nationality that threatened loyalty to the multinational USSR. He embraced the Russian people not because he rejected his own Georgian origins but for precisely the same reason: the Russians were the foundations and cement of the Soviet Union. But after the war, the creation of Israel, the increased self-consciousness among Soviet Jews and the Cold War with America combined with his old prejudice to turn Stalin into a murderous anti-Semite.

Stalin and his Jewish comrades like Kaganovich were proudly internationalist. Stalin, however, openly enjoyed jokes about national stereotypes. He certainly carried all the traditional Georgian prejudices against the Moslem peoples of the Caucasus whom he was to deport. He also persecuted Germans. He enjoyed the Jewish jokes told by Pauker (himself a Jew) and Kobulov, and was amused when Beria called Kaganovich 'the Israelite'. But he also enjoyed jokes about Armenians and Germans, and shared the Russian loathing for Poles: until the forties, Stalin was as Polonophobic as he was anti-Semitic.

He was always suspicious because the Jews lacked a homeland which made them 'mystical, intangible, otherworldly'. Yet Kaganovich insisted that Stalin's view was formed by the

---

* They planned to do the same to Litvinov but his English wife, Ivy, was terrified of imminent arrest and when she confided this to some American friends, the letter ended up on Stalin's desk. He phoned Papasha: 'You've an extremely courageous and outspoken wife. You should tell her to calm herself. She's not threatened.'

Jewishness of his enemies – Trotsky, Zinoviev and Kamenev. On the other hand, most of the women around him and many of his closest collaborators, from Yagoda to Mekhlis, were Jewish. The difference is obvious: he hated the intellectual Trotsky but had no problem with the cobbler Kaganovich.

Stalin was aware that his regime had to stand against anti-Semitism and we find in his own notes a reminder to give a speech about it: he called it 'cannibalism', made it a criminal offence, and regularly criticized anti-Semites. Stalin founded a Jewish homeland, Birobizhan, on the inhospitable Chinese border but boasted, 'The Tsar gave the Jews no land, but we will.'

Yet nationality always mattered in Soviet politics, however internationalist the Party claimed to be. There were a high proportion of Jews, along with Georgians, Poles and Letts, in the Party because these were among the persecuted minorities of Tsarist Russia. In 1937, 5.7 per cent of the Party were Jews yet they formed a majority in the Government. Lenin himself (who was partly Jewish by ancestry) said that if the Commissar was Jewish, the deputy should be Russian: Stalin followed this rule.*

Yet Stalin was 'sensitive' about Kaganovich's Judaism. At Kuntsevo dinners, Beria tried to bully Kaganovich into drinking more but Stalin stopped him:

'Leave him alone ... Jews don't know how to drink.' Once, Stalin asked Kaganovich why he looked so miserable during Jewish jokes: 'Take Mikoyan – we laugh at Armenians and Mikoyan laughs too.'

'You see, Comrade Stalin, suffering has affected the Jewish character so we're like a mimosa flower. Touch it and it closes immediately.' It happened that the mimosa, that super-sensitive flower that flinches like an animal, was Stalin's favourite. He never again allowed such jokes in front of Kaganovich.

None the less, there was increasing anti-Semitism during the thirties: even in public, Stalin asked if a man was a *'natsmen'* – a euphemism for Jewish based on the fifth point on Soviet personnel forms which covered 'nationality'. When Molotov remembered Kamenev, he said he 'did not look like a Jew except when you looked into his eyes'.

---

* The first three Soviet Premiers were Russians. On Lenin's death, Rykov succeeded him as PredSovnarkom even though Kamenev, a Jew, usually chaired the meetings. In 1930, Rykov was succeeded by Molotov. But Stalin refused the Premiership as much for political as for racial reasons.

The Jews at Stalin's court felt they had to be more Russian than the Russians, more Bolshevik than the Bolsheviks. Kaganovich despised Yiddish culture, asking Solomon Mikhoels, the Yiddish actor: 'Why do you disparage the people?' When the Politburo debated whether to blow up the Temple of the Saviour, one of the acts of vandalism in the creation of Stalinist Moscow, Stalin, Kirov and the others supported it but Kaganovich said, 'The Black Hundreds [the anti-Semitic gangs of 1905] will blame it on me!' Similarly, Mehklis reacted to Stalin's swearing about Trotsky's 'Yids': 'I'm a Communist not a Jew.' More honestly, he explained his own rabidity: 'You should realize that there is only one way of fighting [anti-Semitism] – to be brave; if you're a Jew, to be the most honest, pure as crystal, a model person, especially in human dignity.'

Stalin realized that, while he had to be seen to oppose anti-Semitism, his Jews were one obstacle to rapprochement with Hitler, particularly Litvinov (Wallach). Many Jewish Bolsheviks used Russian pseudonyms. As early as 1936, Stalin ordered Mekhlis at *Pravda* to use these pseudonyms: 'No need to excite Hitler!' This atmosphere sharpened at the Plenum in early 1939 when Yakovlev attacked Khrushchev for promoting a cult of personality using his full name and patronymic, a sign of respect. Khrushchev, himself anti-Semitic, replied that perhaps Yakovlev should use his real name, Epstein. Mekhlis intervened to support Khrushchev, explaining that Yakovlev, being a Jew, could not understand this.

The removal of the Jews was a signal to Hitler – but Stalin always sent double messages: Molotov appointed Solomon Lozovsky, a Jew, as one of his deputies.

* * *

The European poker game was played out with swift moves, secret talks and cold hearts. The stakes were vast. The dictators proved much more adept at this fast-moving game than the democracies who had started to play in earnest much too late. As the fighting intensified against the Japanese, Hitler was raising the ante, having consumed Austria and Czechoslovakia, by turning his panzers towards Poland. Belatedly, the Western democracies realized he had to be stopped: on 31 March, Britain and France guaranteed the Polish borders. They needed Russia to join them but failed to place themselves in Stalin's seat and did not understand his sense of weakness and isolation. Ironically the

Polish guarantee increased Stalin's doubts about the depth of this British commitment: if Hitler invaded Poland, what was to stop 'perfidious Albion' from using the guarantee as a mere bargaining chip to negotiate another Munich-style deal, leaving Hitler on his borders?

Stalin therefore required a contractual military alliance with the West if he was not to turn to Hitler. On 29 June, Zhdanov backed the German option in a *Pravda* article in which he stated his 'personal opinion' that 'I permit myself to express ... although not all my friends share it ... They still think that in beginning negotiations with the USSR, the English and French Governments have serious intentions ... I believe the English and French Governments have no wish for a treaty of equality with the USSR ...' The vulnerability of Leningrad made a free hand in the Baltic States necessary: that was the price of what Zhdanov called 'equality'. Zhdanov's son Yury remembers Stalin and his father reading a specially translated *Mein Kampf* and endlessly discussing the pros and cons of a German alliance. Stalin read in D'Abernon's *Ambassador of the World* that if Germany and Russia were allies, 'the dangerous power of the east' would overshadow Britain. 'Yes!' Stalin noted approvingly in the margin.

Britain and France had despatched a hapless and ludicrously low-level delegation to Moscow by slow steamship to offer an alliance but no guarantee of Soviet frontiers and no freedom of action in the Baltics. When Admiral Sir Reginald Aylmer Ranfurly Plunkett-Ernle-Erle-Drax (author of a book called *Handbook on Solar Heating*) and General Joseph Doumenc, arrived in Leningrad on the night of 9–10 August, the German–Russian flirtation was getting serious. The Admiral and the General took the train to Moscow and were taken to meet Voroshilov and Molotov.

Stalin was unimpressed with the quadruple-barrelled Admiral when he discussed the delegations with Molotov and Beria: 'They're not being serious. These people can't have the proper authority. London and Paris are playing poker again ...'

'Still the talks should go ahead,' said Molotov.

'Well if they must, they must.' This was now turning into an auction for Stalin's favours but with only one serious bidder. In Germany, meanwhile, Hitler decided to invade Poland on 26 August: suddenly, the agreement with Stalin was desperately necessary. The meetings with the Western powers only got started on 12 August but the gap between what the West was willing to offer and the price Stalin demanded, was unbridgeable. That day, the Russians signalled to the Germans that they were ready to start negotiations, even on the dismemberment of Poland. On the 14th, Hitler decided to send Ribbentrop, his Foreign Minister, to Moscow. On the 15th, the German Ambassador Count Friedrich Werner von der Schulenburg requested a meeting with Molotov, who, rushing to check with Stalin, reported that Russia was ready. When this news reached Ribbentrop, he hurried to tell Hitler at the Bergdorf. On the 17th, Voroshilov proposed a treaty of mutual military assistance to the British and French but added that there was no point in continuing the discussion until they had persuaded the Poles and Romanians to allow the passage of Soviet troops in the event of a German attack. But Drax had not yet received orders from London.

'Enough of these games!' Stalin told Molotov. 'The English and French wanted us for farmhands and at no cost!' On the afternoon of Saturday the 19th, Molotov hurriedly summoned Schulenburg, handing him a draft non-aggression pact that was more formal than the German version but contained nothing objectionable. Having signed the trade treaty that Stalin had specified was necessary before the real business could begin, the Germans, whose deadline was fast approaching, waited with a gambler's anticipation. Hitler shrewdly decided to cut the Gordian knot of mutual trust and prestige by personally addressing Stalin in a telegram dated 20 August: 'Dear Mr Stalin.' Stalin, Molotov and Voroshilov agreed the reply:

> To Chancellor of Germany A. Hitler. Thank you for your letter. I hope the German–Soviet agreement of non-aggression will be a turning point towards serious improvement of political relations between our countries ... The Soviet government has instructed me to inform you that it agrees to Mr Ribbentrop visiting Moscow on 23 August.
> J. Stalin.

Far to the east, that Sunday the 20th, Georgi Zhukov, commander of the Soviet army on the Khalkin-Gol River, launched a formidable cannonade against the Japanese, then attacked across the front. By the 23rd, the Japanese were defeated with losses as high as 61,000 men, a bloody nose that was enough to dissuade them from attacking Russia again.

At 3 p.m. on Monday the 21st, Molotov received Schulenburg who passed on Hitler's request for a meeting on the 23rd. Two hours later, he and Stalin agreed to the historic visit of Ribbentrop. Suddenly the two dictators were no longer holding back but hurtling towards one another, arms outstretched. At 7 p.m. next day, Voroshilov dismissed the British and French: 'Let's wait until everything has been cleared up …'*

Stalin's reply reached Hitler at eight-thirty that evening: 'Marvellous! I congratulate you' declaimed Hitler, adding, with the flashiness of the entertainer: 'I have the world in my pocket.'

That night, Voroshilov was leading a vital delegation of the Soviet leadership on a duck-shooting expedition into the countryside. Khrushchev had just arrived from Kiev. Before setting off to shoot duck, Khrushchev dined with Stalin at the dacha. It was then that Stalin, 'who smiled and watched me closely', informed him that Ribbentrop was arriving imminently. Khrushchev, who knew nothing about the negotiations, was 'dumbfounded. I stared back at him, thinking he was joking.'

'Why should Ribbentrop want to see us?' blurted out Khrushchev. 'Is he defecting?' Then he remembered that he was going hunting with Voroshilov on the great day. Should he cancel?

'Go right ahead. There'll be nothing for you to do … Molotov and I will meet Ribbentrop. When you return, I'll let you know what Hitler has in mind …' After dinner, Khrushchev and Malenkov set off to meet Voroshilov at his hunting reserve while Stalin remained at the dacha to consider tomorrow. Unless he was

---

* The comedy of these negotiations was neatly encapsulated in the question of the Order of the Bath. Drax had arrived without the relevant credentials, a mistake that told Stalin all he needed to know about Western commitment. At the very moment the credentials finally arrived, they had become utterly irrelevant. When Sir Reginald proudly read out his official titles and arrived at this noble order, the Soviet interpreter declaimed: 'Order of the Bath-tub.' Marshal Voroshilov, displaying both his overwhelming characteristics – childlike naïvety and heroic bungling capacity – interrupted to ask: 'Bathtub?' 'In the reign of our early kings,' Drax droned, 'our knights used to travel round Europe on horseback, slaying dragons and rescuing maidens in distress. They would return home travel-stained and grimy and report … to the King [who] would sometimes offer a knight a luxury … A bath in the royal bathroom.' The Western democracies could not deliver the 'price' of a Soviet alliance, namely to back up the Polish guarantee and deliver the Baltic States into Stalin's sphere of influence. Perhaps they were right since this would still not guarantee stopping Hitler, while there seemed little point in saving Poland from the Huns to deliver her to the Tatars.

in a very good mood, he thought 'hunting was a waste of time'.*
Perhaps it was that night that Stalin, reading Vipper's *History of
Ancient Greece*, marked the passage about the benefits of dictators
working closely together.

On Tuesday, 22 August, all the magnates visited the Little
Corner some time during the day. If the details were secret, the
policy was not. Its architects were Stalin assisted by Molotov and
Zhdanov but there was no party against it. Even Khrushchev and
Mikoyan, in their memoirs designed to blacken Stalin wherever
possible, admitted that there was no choice. These Leninists, as
Kaganovich put it, understood this was a Brest-Litovsk in reverse.

That evening, as the duck-shooters set off into the marshes of
Zavidovo, seventy-miles north-west of Moscow, the tall,
pompous, ex-champagne salesman Ribbentrop set off in Hitler's
Condor aeroplane, Immelman III, with a delegation of thirty. At
1 p.m. on 23 August, Ribbentrop arrived and descended from the
Condor in a leather coat, black jacket and striped trousers,
impressed to find the airport emblazoned with swastikas. An
orchestra played the German national anthem. Ribbentrop was
then guided into a bullet-proof black ZiS (a Soviet Buick) by
Vlasik. They sped into town for a short stop at the German
Embassy for caviar and champagne. At three, Ribbentrop, due to
meet Molotov, was driven through the Spassky Gate to the Little
Corner. Ribbentrop was greeted by Poskrebyshev in military
uniform and led up the stairs through anterooms, into a long
rectangular room where they found Stalin, in Party tunic and
baggy trousers tucked into boots, and Molotov in a dark suit,
standing together.

When they sat down at the table, the Russians, with their
interpreter V. N. Pavlov, on one side, the Germans on the other,

---

* Khrushchev's memoirs have left a confusing impression about the Politburo and the
Pact. Molotov, Premier and Foreign Minister, was the front man in this diplomatic
game and Stalin was clearly the engine behind it. It is usually stated that the
Politburo, including Voroshilov, knew nothing about the negotiations until
Ribbentrop's arrival was imminent but Politburo papers had always been confined to
the 'Five' or the 'Seven' – and not distributed to regional leaders such as the Ukrainian
First Secretary. The messages between Stalin and Hitler were discussed with Molotov,
Voroshilov and Beria, who was in charge of intelligence and had to know. Zhdanov,
with his Leningrad and Baltic viewpoint, his knowledge of German culture and his
publicly stated suspicion of Western intentions, had been closely linked to this whole
policy and may have been its co-architect with Stalin. The commercial aspects could
not be negotiated without Mikoyan. Zhdanov was in and out of Stalin's office that
week and he told his son that he was kept informed of the negotiations.

Ribbentrop declared: 'Germany demands nothing from Russia – only peace and trade.' Stalin offered Molotov the floor as Premier.

'No, no, Joseph Vissarionovich, you do the talking. I'm sure you'll do a better job than I.' They swiftly agreed to the terms of their pact which was designed to divide Poland and eastern Europe into spheres of influence – Stalin got Eastern Poland, Latvia, Estonia, Finland and Bessarabia in Romania, though Hitler kept Lithuania. But when Ribbentrop proposed a paean to German–Soviet friendship, Stalin snorted:

'Don't you think we have to pay a little more attention to public opinion in our two countries? For many years now, we have been pouring buckets of shit over each other's heads and our propaganda boys could not do enough in that direction. Now all of a sudden, are we to make our peoples believe all is forgotten and forgiven? Things don't work so fast.' With so much agreed so fast, Ribbentrop returned to the Embassy to telegraph Hitler.

At 10 p.m, he arrived back at the Little Corner, accompanied by a much larger delegation and two photographers. When Ribbentrop announced that Hitler approved the terms, 'a sudden tremor seemed to go through Stalin and he did not immediately grasp the hand proffered by his partner. It was as if he had first to overcome a moment of fear.' Stalin ordered vodka and toasted:

'I know how much the German nation loves its Führer. He's a good chap. I'd like to to drink his health.' Molotov then toasted Ribbentrop who toasted Stalin. One of the young Germans, a six-foot SS officer named Richard Schulze, noticed Stalin was drinking his vodka from a special flask and managed to fill his glass from it, only to discover it contained water. Stalin smiled faintly as Schulze drank it, not the last guest to sample this little secret.

By 2 a.m. on 24 August, the treaty was ready. The photographers – the Germans with up-to-date equipment, the Russians with ancient wooden tripod and wood-and-brass camera – were escorted into the room. The Red Army Chief of Staff, the ailing Shaposhnikov, respected by Stalin, took notes in a small notebook. When it came to the photograph, Stalin noticed the towering SS man who had sampled his flask and beckoned him into the picture where he positioned him between Ribbentrop and Shaposhnikov. Molotov signed.

A maid brought in champagne and snacks. When one of the German photographers flashed as Stalin and Ribbentrop raised their glasses, the former shook his finger and told him he did not want such a photograph published. The photographer offered to hand over his film but Stalin said he could trust the word of a German. At 3 a.m., as the excited leaders parted, Stalin told Ribbentrop: 'I can guarantee on my word of honour that the Soviet Union will not betray its partner.'

Stalin headed to Kuntsevo where the hunters awaited. Voroshilov, Khrushchev, Malenkov and Bulganin had already brought their ducks to be cooked in Stalin's kitchen. When Stalin and Molotov arrived jubilantly with a copy of their treaty, Khrushchev boasted about out-shooting Voroshilov, the vaunted 'First Marksman', before the laughing *Vozhd* told them how they had signed the world-shattering Molotov-Ribbentrop Pact: 'Stalin seemed very pleased with himself' but he was under no illusions about his new friendship. As they feasted on duck, Stalin boasted:

'Of course it's all a game to see who can fool whom. I know what Hitler's up to. He thinks he's outsmarted me but actually it's I who's tricked him.' War, he explained, 'would pass us by a little longer'.* Zhdanov mocked Ribbentrop's pear-shaped figure:

'He's got the biggest and broadest pair of hips in all of Europe,' he announced as the magnates laughed about Ribbentrop's preposterous girdle: 'Those hips! Those hips!'

The 'Great Game', as Molotov called the tournament of nerves between Stalin and Hitler, had begun.

* * *

At 2 a.m. on 1 September, Poskrebyshev handed Stalin a telegram from Berlin informing him that early that evening 'Polish' troops (in fact German security forces in disguise) had attacked the German radio station in Gleiwitz. Stalin left for the dacha and went to bed. A few hours later, Poskrebyshev called again: Germany had invaded Poland. Stalin monitored the campaign as Britain and France declared war on Germany, honouring their guarantees. 'We see nothing wrong in their having a good hard fight and weakening each other,' he told Molotov and Zhdanov. Stalin planned the Soviet invasion of Poland with Voroshilov,

---

* Across Europe at the Berghof, Hitler had heard the news at dinner, calling for silence and announcing it to his guests whom he then led out on to the balcony, whence they watched with awe as the northern lights illuminated the sky and the Unterberg mountains in an unnatural bath of blood-red light, dyeing the faces of the spectators incarnadine. 'Looks like a great deal of blood,' said Hitler to an adjutant. 'This time we won't bring it off without violence.'

Shaposhnikov and Kulik, who was to command the front along with Mekhlis, but waited until he had secured an end to the war with Japan first. At 2 a.m on 17 September, Stalin accompanied by Molotov and Voroshilov, told Schulenburg: 'At 6 a.m, four hours from now, the Red Army will cross into Poland.' Premier Molotov took to the radio to announce the 'sacred duty to proffer help to ... Ukrainian and Belorussian brothers'. Mekhlis claimed to Stalin that the West Ukrainians welcomed the Soviet troops 'like true liberators' with 'apples, pies, drinking water ... Many weep with joy.'

Khrushchev, Ukrainian First Secretary, donned a military uniform and, accompanied by his NKVD boss, Ivan Serov, joined the forces of Semyon Timoshenko, commander of the Kiev Military District. Timoshenko was a tough, shaven-headed veteran of the First Cavalry Army in Tsaritsyn; he was a competent officer, yet in the Terror, he had both denounced Budyonny and been denounced himself. Khrushchev claimed to have saved his life. Khrushchev's advance into Poland was an adventure for him, but even more so for his wife, Nina Petrovna who, also sporting military uniform and a pistol, liberated her own parents who had remained in Poland since 1920. Khrushchev, ensconced in Lvov, celebrated at the sight of her and her parents but lost his temper when he saw her pistol.*

If the invasion was joyous for the Khrushchevs, it unleashed depredations on the Polish population every bit as cruel and tragic as those of the Nazis. Khrushchev ruthlessly suppressed any sections of the population who might oppose Soviet power: priests, officers, noblemen, intellectuals were kidnapped, murdered and deported to eliminate the very existence of Poland. By November 1940, one tenth of the population or 1.17 million innocents had been deported. Thirty per cent of them were dead by 1941; 60,000 were arrested and 50,000 shot. The Soviets behaved like conquerors. When some soldiers were arrested for stealing treasures from a Prince Radziwill, Vyshinsky consulted Stalin.

'If there's no ill-will,' he wrote on the note, 'they can be pardoned. J.St.'

---

* There was a priceless moment when Nina's parents arrived in Khrushchev's apartment and marvelled at the running water: 'Hey Mother, look at this,' shouted the father. 'The water comes out of a pipe.' When the parents saw the impressive, lantern-jawed Timoshenko beside the small fat Khrushchev, they asked if the former was their son-in-law.

At 5 p.m. on Wednesday 27 September, Ribbentrop flew back to negotiate the notorious protocols, so secret that Molotov was still denying their existence thirty years later. By 10 p.m., he was at the Kremlin in talks with Stalin and Molotov around the green baize table. Stalin wanted Lithuania. Ribbentrop telegraphed Hitler for his permission so the talks were delayed until 3 p.m. the next day. But Hitler's message had not arrived by the time Ribbentrop returned to negotiate the cartological details.

That night, while Stalin held a gala dinner for the Germans to celebrate the carve-up of Europe, the Russians were meeting the unfortunate Estonian Foreign Minister to force him to allow Soviet troops into his country, the first step to outright annexation. The Nazis were greeted at the door of the Great Kremlin Palace, led through the dull wooden Congress Hall which looked like a giant schoolroom, and then dazzled by the scarlet and gold reception room where Stalin, Molotov and the Politburo, including Jewish Kaganovich, awaited them. Stalin's manner was 'simple and unpretentious', beaming with 'paternal benevolence' that could turn to 'icy coldness' as he 'rapped out orders', though he used a 'jocular and kind manner with his junior assistants'. The Germans noticed how respectful the Russians were to Stalin: Commissar Tevosian, the 'lucky stiff' who had narrowly avoided execution in 1938, rose 'like a schoolboy' whenever Stalin addressed him. The fear surrounding Stalin had become intense since 1937. But he was cordial with Voroshilov, friendly with Beria and Mikoyan, matter-of-fact with Kaganovich, chatty with Malenkov. Only Molotov 'would talk to his chief as one comrade to another'.

Their swagger was so raffish that Ribbentrop said he felt as at ease as he did among old Nazi comrades. While the guests were chatting, Stalin went into the sumptuous Andreevsky Hall to check the seating plan, which he enjoyed doing, even at Kuntsevo.* The twenty-two guests were dwarfed by the grandeur of the hall, the colossal flower arrangements, the imperial gold cutlery and, even more, by the twenty-four courses that included caviar, all manner of fishes and meats, and lashings of pepper vodka and Crimean champagne. The white-clad waiters were the

---

* Stalin was filmed checking places at Kuntsevo by Vlasik. Hitler too was a punctilious checker of dinner placement. Both men appreciated the importance of personal pride in matters of State.

same staff from the Metropol Hotel who would serve Churchill and Roosevelt at Yalta. Before anyone could eat, Molotov started to propose toasts to each guest. Stalin stalked over to clink glasses. It was an exhausting rigmarole that would become one of the diplomatic tribulations of the war. When Molotov had run through every guest, the Germans sighed with relief until he announced: 'Now we'll drink to all members of the delegations who couldn't attend this dinner.' Stalin took over, joking:

'Let us drink to the new anti-Comintern Stalin' and he winked at Molotov. Then he toasted Kaganovich, 'our People's Commissar of Railways'. Stalin could have toasted the Jewish magnate across the table but he deliberately rose and circled the table to clink glasses so that Ribbentrop had to follow suit and drink to a Jew, an irony that amused Stalin. Forty years on, Kaganovich was still telling the story to his grandchildren. When Molotov embarked on another toast to his *Vozhd*, Stalin chuckled:

'If Molotov really wants to drink, no one objects but he really shouldn't use me as an excuse.' Stalin himself drank almost nothing and when Ribbentrop noticed how well he was bearing the toasts, he cheerfully revealed that he was drinking white wine. But Beria, who had transformed the Georgian tradition of forced hospitality into a despotic trial of submission, delighted in making his guests drink. The German diplomat Hilger, who wrote vivid memoirs of the evening, refused another vodka. Beria insisted, drawing the attention of Stalin himself who was sitting opposite them.

'What's the argument about?' he asked, adding, 'Well if you don't want to drink, no one can force you.'

'Not even the chief of the NKVD himself?' smiled the German.

'Here at this table,' replied Stalin, 'even the NKVD chief has no more say than anyone else.' At the end of the dinner, Stalin and Molotov excused themselves as the Germans were despatched off to the Bolshoi to watch *Swan Lake*. As he left, Stalin whispered to Kaganovich, 'We must win time.' They then walked upstairs where the Estonian Foreign Minister miserably waited for Stalin to emasculate his little Baltic nation. Molotov demanded a Soviet garrison of 35,000 troops, more than the entire Estonian army.

'Come on, Molotov, you're rather harsh on our friends,' said Stalin, suggesting 25,000 but the effect was much the same. Having swallowed a country during the first act of *Swan Lake*, Stalin returned to the Germans at midnight for a final session during which Hitler telephoned his agreement to the Lithuanian concession.

'Hitler knows his business,' muttered Stalin. Ribbentrop was so excited that he declared the two countries must never fight again:

'This ought to be the case,' replied Stalin, shocking Ribbentrop who asked for it to be retranslated. When the German suggested Russia join a military alliance against the West, Stalin just said,

'I shall never allow Germany to become weak.' He obviously believed that Germany would be restrained in the West by Britain and France. When the maps were finally ready in the early hours, Stalin signed them in blue crayon, with a massive signature ten inches long, an inch high, and a tail eighteen inches long. 'Is my signature clear enough for you?'

By 3 October, all three Baltic States had agreed to Soviet garrisons. Stalin and Molotov turned their guns and threats on the fourth Baltic country in their sphere of influence, Finland, which they expected to buckle like the others.

The Murder of the Wives

As the world watched Stalin and Hitler carve up the East, the *Vozhd* was probing the submission of his comrades by investigating and sometimes killing their wives. His fragile trust in women was irreparably undermined by Nadya's suicide but this had been exacerbated by his own destruction of the wives of Enemies. As Khrushchev said, he became interested in other men's wives for the unusual reason that they were possible spies rather than mistresses.

Stalin had always shown a minute interest in the wives. When he received the 1939 census, he ticked the names of some magnates' wives and children in red pen. The meaning of the ticks was a mystery but it is tempting to regard everything about him as sinister. Maybe he was just working out how many cars the family needed. Wives now sat apart from their husbands at Kremlin dinners. Stalin's attitude to old favourites, Polina and Dora, had become malicious and suspicious, partly reflecting their relationship with Nadya. But he had always been obsessed with wives knowing too much. As early as 1930, he suggested to Molotov that some comrade's wife 'should be checked ... she could not help but know about the outrageous goings-on at their house.' This burning suspicion of uxoriousness partly derived from Stalin's dislike of anything that interfered with blind devotion to the Party and himself. 'Stalin did not recognize personal relations,' said Kaganovich. 'The love of one person for another did not exist.' He saw the wives as hostages for his comrades' good behaviour and punishment for bad: 'No one who contradicts Stalin,' Beria told Nina, 'keeps his wife.' But the slaughter of wives coincided with Beria's arrival.

Polina Molotova, the First Lady, was in danger. She was now Commissar of Fishing, a CC candidate member and mistress of her perfume empire. Yet Beria now started investigating her, discovering 'vandals' and 'saboteurs' secreted in her staff. She had 'unknowingly facilitated their espionage'.* Stalin may have been sending another anti-Semitic signal to Hitler.

On 10 August, when Stalin and Molotov were plotting their diplomatic somersaults, the Politburo indicted Polina. Stalin proposed her expulsion from the Central Committee. Molotov bravely abstained, showing his ability to disagree with Stalin, confidence – and love of Polina. On 24 October, she was relieved of her Commissariat, reprimanded for 'levity and hastiness' but declared innocent of 'calumnies'. Promoted to run Soviet haberdashery, she returned to her accustomed magnificence: her daughter Svetlana was already notorious as the ultimate Soviet 'princess' in her furs and French fashions but the family was constantly watched.† Stalin forgot neither Molotov's defiance nor Polina's sins, which would return to haunt her. Stalin and Beria had considered kidnapping and murdering her. She was lucky to be alive.

On 25 October 1938, Beria arrested President Kalinin's wife. In a land where the Head of State's wife was in prison, no one was safe from the Party. The ineffectual Kalinin, who had not dared resist Stalin since the warnings of 1930 and balletomanic romantic entanglements, though he seethed about his ill treatment, actually lived with another woman, his aristocratic housekeeper, Alexandra Gorchakova. His wife, a snub-nosed Estonian, Ekaterina Ivanovna, set off with a lady friend to arrange an anti-illiteracy campaign in the Far East. When she and this possibly Sapphic lady-friend returned to Kalinin's apartment, they were bugged grumbling about Stalin's blood lust. The lady friend was executed, Kalinina sent into exile, like Budyonny's wife before her. When petitioners asked for the President's help, Kalinin used the same excuse as Stalin himself: 'My dear chap, I'm in the same position! I can't even help my own wife – there's no way I can help yours!' Not everyone was as lucky as Molotova and Kalinina.

---

*Polina had an Achilles heel: not only was she Jewish but her brother Karp was a successful businessman in the USA. Indeed, in the mid-thirties, Stalin had even encouraged the US Ambassador Davies to do business in Moscow using Karp, a rare example of his nepotism.

†Take the case of Molotov's fitness instructor, a role that reveals a whole new side of the Foreign Commissar. A few months later, Vlasik, who did nothing without Stalin's knowledge, wrote to Molotov to inform him that Olga Rostovtseva, the fitness lady, was boasting about her closeness to the family: 'We know of cases not only where she talks about her sports instruction ... but also about your family and apartments ...'

In April 1937, Dr Bronka Poskrebysheva, twenty-seven, pretty wife of the *chef de cabinet*, rang Stalin and asked to see him alone at Kuntsevo, putting on her best dress, perhaps the polkadot which appears in all her family photographs. Her husband did not know about this appointment and would have been furious if he had. Vlasik alone knew of this secret meeting. She came to ask for the release of her arrested brother Metalikov, the Kremlin doctor, indirectly related through his wife to Trotsky. After Stalin's death, Vlasik revealed it to the family and hinted, according to Poskrebyshev and Bronka's daughter Natalya, that the two started an affair. This is unlikely since Stalin hated women pleading for relatives though one of the tragedies of Soviet life at this time was that women did beg potentates for the lives of their loved ones, offering anything they could, even their bodies. Bronka's mission failed.* She was terrified of being tarred with the Trotskyite brush.

Before his promotion to Moscow, Beria had groped Bronka at Kuntsevo and she slapped him. 'I won't forget it,' he said. But Bronka did not give up. On 27 April 1939, she called Beria and asked if she could come to discuss her brother. She was never seen again.

Poskrebyshev waited until midnight, then called Beria at home, who revealed that she was in custody but would not discuss it. In the morning, without having slept at all, Poskrebyshev complained to Stalin who said,

'It doesn't depend on me. I can do nothing. Only the NKVD can sort it out,' a line that could not have convinced Poskrebyshev. Stalin phoned Beria who reminded him of Bronka's Trotskyite connections. The three met, possibly around midnight on 3 May, when Beria was next in the Little Corner. Beria produced a confession implicating Bronka. Poskrebyshev begged Stalin to release her, using the most unBolshevik argument which would have moved anyone but these flinthearts: 'What am I to do with my girls? What will happen to them?' and then thinking of his wife's child by her first marriage: 'Will Galia go to an orphanage?'

*In a story that is criss-crossed with emotional distortions, perhaps the strangest cut of all is that Natalya Poskrebysheva, who was born nine months after her mother's visit to Stalin, believes she may be Stalin's daughter not only because of Vlasik's story but also because she once met the daughter of Mikhail Suslov, the ideological boss for most of Brezhnev's reign, who said: 'Everyone knows your real father is lying in the Mausoleum next to Lenin.' This was when Stalin still rested in the Mausoleum. 'Do I look like somebody?' Miss Poskrebysheva asked the author. 'Like Svetlana Stalin?' It is ironic that she believes her mother's murderer, Stalin, was her father because she in fact looks the image of Poskrebyshev.

'Don't worry, we'll find you another wife,' Stalin supposedly replied. This was typical Stalin, the man who had threatened Krupskaya that if she did not obey the Party, they would appoint someone else as Lenin's widow. By the standards of the time, Poskrebyshev made a fuss but he could do no more. After two years, Bronka was shot aged just thirty-one as the Germans approached Moscow.*

Her daughter Natalya was told she had died naturally. Poskrebyshev brought up the girls himself with loving devotion. He kept photographs of Bronka around the house. When Natalya pointed at one of the photos and said 'Mama,' Poskrebyshev burst into tears and ran out of the room. It was typical of the tragedies of the time that Natalya only discovered her mother had been shot when she was told at school by the daughter of Kozlovsky the singer. She sobbed in the lavatories. Poskrebyshev remarried.

Bronka's destruction did not affect Poskrebyshev's relationship with Stalin or Beria: the Party was just. Stalin took a solicitious interest in Bronka's daughter:

'How's Natasha?' he often asked his *chef de cabinet*. 'Is she plump and sweet?' Years later when she could not do her homework, she called her father to ask his help. Someone else answered.

'Can I speak to my father?' she asked.

'He's not here,' replied Stalin. 'What's the problem?' – and he solved her mathematical questions. The only awkwardness in Poskrebyshev's apparent friendship with Beria was when the latter hugged little Natalya and sighed:

'You're going to be as beautiful as your mother.' Poskrebyshev 'turned green', struggled to control his emotions, and rasped:

'Natalya, go and play.'

* * *

Before he turned to wantonly kill another of his friend's wives, Stalin capriciously saved two old friends from death. Sergo Kavtaradze was an Old Bolshevik Leftist, who had known Stalin since the turn of the century. He was an intelligent cosmopolitan Georgian married to Princess Sofia Vachnadze, whose godmother had been Empress Maria Fyodorovna, Nicholas II's mother. They

---

* Her body was buried in a mass grave near Moscow while her brother is in one of the pits at the Donskoi Cemetery along with many others. Dr Metalikov's daughter raised a monument to them in the Novodevichy Cemetery.

were an unusual couple. Kavtaradze consistently joined the oppositions yet Stalin always forgave him. Arrested in the late twenties, Stalin brought him back and ordered Kaganovich to help him. He was arrested again in late 1936, appearing on Yezhov's death-lists. His wife was also arrested. His daughter Maya, then eleven, thought both parents were already dead but she courageously wrote to Stalin to beg for their lives, signing her letters: 'Pioneer Maya Kavtaradze'. Both Kavtaradzes were tortured but because Stalin had put a dash next to his old friend's name on the death-list, their lives were spared. Now, in late 1939, 'Pioneer Kavtaradze's' letters reminded Stalin to ask Beria if his old friend was still alive.

In the Lubianka, Kavtaradze was suddenly shaved by a barber, given a comfortable room, and a menu from which he could order any food he liked. Delivered to the Hotel Lux, he found his wife was there, a frail shadow of her former self – but alive. Their daughter arrived from Tiflis. Soon afterwards, Kavtaradze was called: 'Comrade Stalin is waiting for you. If you're ready, a car will pick you up in half an hour.' He was taken to Kuntsevo where Koba greeted him in the study: 'Hello Sergo,' he said as if Kavtaradze had not been found guilty of involvement in a plot to kill him. 'Where've you been?'

'Sitting [in prison].'

'Oh you found time to sit?' The Russian slang for being in prison is *sidet* – to sit – hence Stalin's joke, a line he used frequently. After dinner, Stalin turned to him anxiously: 'Nevertheless, you all wanted to kill me?'

'Do you really think so?' Kavtaradze replied. Stalin just grinned. Afterwards, when he got home, Kavtaradze whispered to his wife: 'Stalin's sick.' A few weeks later, the family received a bizarre and revealing visitation.*

The Kavtaradzes had some friends to dinner when the telephone rang at 11 p.m. Kavtaradze said he had to rush out and

---

* This is often mentioned in Stalin biographies but never with the testimony of any of the five people present. The following is based on the author's interview with Maya Kavtaradze, the last of those five still alive whose story has never before been published. Now seventy-six and living in her father's huge, antique-filled apartment in Tbilisi, she has generously allowed the author to use her father's unpublished memoirs which are an invaluable source. In 1940, Kavtaradze was appointed to the State Publishing House and then as Deputy Foreign Commissar in charge of the Near East for the whole war. Since the Foreign Commissarat was just next door to the Lubianka, Kavtaradze used to joke: 'I crossed the road.' Kavtaradze was Soviet Ambassador to Romania after the war and died in 1971.

left without an explanation. His wife and their daughter Maya, fourteen, went to bed. At 6 a.m. Kavtaradze staggered into their three-room apartment on Gorky Street, still dizzy from drinking. 'Where've you been?' his wife scolded him.

'We've guests,' he announced.

'You're drunk!' Then she heard footsteps: Stalin and Beria tipsily walked in and sat down at the kitchen table. Vlasik stood guard at the front-door. While Kavtaradze poured out drinks, his wife rushed into Maya's room:

'Wake up!' she whispered.

'What's wrong?' asked the schoolgirl. 'They've come to arrest us at night?'

'No, Stalin's come.'

'I won't meet him,' retorted Maya who understandably hated him.

'You must,' replied her mother. 'He's a historical personage.' So Maya got dressed and came into the kitchen. As soon as she appeared, Stalin beamed:

'Ah, it's you – "Pioneer Kavtaradze."' He recalled her letters appealing for her parents. 'Sit on my lap.' She sat on Stalin's knee. 'Do you spoil her?'

Maya was charmed: 'He was so kind, so gentle – he kissed me on the cheek and I looked into his honey-coloured, hazel, gleaming eyes,' she recalls, 'but I was so anxious.'

'We've no food!' the little girl exclaimed.

'Don't worry,' said Beria. Ten minutes later, Georgian food was delivered from the famous Aragvi restaurant. Stalin looked closely at Kavtaradze's wife, the princess born at the imperial court. Her hair was white:

'We tortured you too much,' Stalin said.

'Whoever mentions the past, let him lose his eyes,' she answered shrewdly, using the proverb Stalin had used to Bukharin. He asked Beria about Kavtaradze's brother, also arrested, but they were too late: he had already died, like so many others, en route to Magadan.

Kavtaradze started singing a Georgian song but he was out of tune.

'Don't, Tojo', said Stalin, who nicknamed Kavtaradze, with his Oriental eyes, after the Japanese General Tojo. He started to sing himself 'in a sweet tenor'. Maya was 'shocked – there he was short and pock-marked. Now he was singing!' Then he announced: 'I want to see the apartment,' and inspected it carefully. The feast continued until 10 a.m. and Maya missed school that day.

Stalin appointed Kavtaradze to a publishing job that involved another prisoner, Shalva Nutsibidze, a celebrated Georgian philosopher. As a young man, Nutsibidze had once met Stalin. While in jail, Nutsibidze started translating the Georgian epic poem by Rustaveli, *The Knight in the Panther Skin*, into Russian. Every day, his work was taken from him and returned marked with the pen of an anonymous editor. Kobulov tortured him, tearing off his fingernails. Then he suddenly became friendly, telling the prisoner that during a recent meeting, Stalin had asked Beria if he knew what kind of bird the thrush was:

'Ever heard of a thrush singing in his cage?' Beria shook his head. 'It's the same with poets,' Stalin explained. 'A poet can't sing in a cell. If we wish to have Rustaveli perfectly translated, free the thrush.' Nutsibidze was released and, on 20 October 1940, Kavtaradze picked him up in a limousine and the two 'lucky stiffs' drove to the Little Corner to report to Poskrebyshev on the Rustaveli translation. When they were shown into the office, Stalin was smiling at them:

'You're Professor Nutsibidze?' he said. 'You've been offended a bit but let's not rake up the past,' and then he started to rave about the 'magnificent translation of Rustaveli'. Sitting the two men down, Stalin handed the astounded professor a leather-bound draft of the translation, adding, 'I've translated one couplet. Let's see how you like it.' Stalin recited it. 'If you really do like it, I give it to you as a present. Use it in your translation, but don't mention my name. I take great pleasure in being your editor.' He then invited the two to dinner where they reminisced about the old days in Georgia. After many horns of wine, Nutsibidze recalled the political meeting where he had first met Stalin, declaiming his speech from memory. Stalin was delighted:

'Extraordinary talent goes hand in hand with extraordinary memory!'* He came round the table and kissed Nutsibidze on the forehead.

* * *

They were particularly fortunate 'stiffs' because after the Ribbentrop Pact, Stalin liquidated the backlog of Yezhov cases,

---

* For the rest of his career, whenever Nutsibidze was challenged, he would point to his forehead and say, 'Stalin kissed me here.' The Rustaveli edition was expensively published and Stalin's name was never mentioned. Stalin ensured that Nutsibidze was allowed to live for the rest of his life in a large mansion in Tiflis still owned by the family. The author is most grateful to the Professor's stepson Zakro Megrelishvili for the extracts from his mother's autobiography.

including Blackberry himself who confessed to being an English, Japanese and Polish spy. But he also denounced his wife's literary lovers. Thus the indelible mark of Yevgenia's kisses proved fatal long after her own exit. Sholokhov was protected by the penumbra of Stalin himself but Isaac Babel was arrested, telling his young wife: 'Please see our girl grows up happy.'

On 16 January 1940, Stalin signed 346 death sentences, a list of the tragic flotsam of Terror that combined monsters with innocents, including some of the outstanding talents of the arts, such as Babel, theatre director Meyerhold, and Yezhova's lover, the journalist Koltsov (on whom Karpov in Hemingway's *For Whom the Bell Tolls* is based), as well as Yezhov himself with his innocent brother, nephews and socialite mistress, Glikina, and the fallen magnate Eikhe. Most (though not Yezhov) were mercilessly tortured with the relish that Beria and Kobulov brought to their work at Sukhanov prison, Beria's special realm which, ironically, had once been the St Catherine's Nunnery.

'The investigators began to use force on me, a sick sixty-five-year-old man,' Meyerhold wrote to Molotov. 'I was made to lie face down and then beaten on the soles of my feet and my spine with a rubber strap. They sat me on a chair and beat my feet from above ... For the next few days when those parts of my legs were covered with extensive internal haemorrhaging, they again beat the red, blue and yellow bruises and the pain was so intense it felt as if boiling water was poured on ... I howled and wept from pain. They beat my back ... punched my face, swinging their fists from a great height ... The intolerable physical and emotional pain caused my eyes to weep unending streams of tears ...'

Over the next few days, Stalin's hanging judge Ulrikh sentenced all to 'the highest measure of punishment' in perfunctory trials at Lefortovo prison before attending a Kremlin gala, starring the tenor Kozlovsky and the ballerina Lepeshinskaya. Babel was condemned as an 'agent of French and Austrian intelligence ... linked to the wife of Enemy of the People Yezhov'. At 1.30 a.m. on 27 January 1940, Babel was shot and cremated.

Eikhe was subjected to one last session of 'French wrestling' at Sukhanov prison. Beria and Rodos 'brutally beat Eikhe with rubber rods; he fell but they picked him up and went on beating him. Beria kept asking him, 'Will you confess to being a spy?' Eikhe refused. 'One of Eikhe's eyes had been gouged out and blood was streaming out of it but he went on repeating "I won't confess." When Beria had convinced himself he could not get a confession ... he ordered them to lead him away to be shot.'

It was now Yezhov's turn. On 1 February, Beria called his predecessor to his office at Sukhanovka to propose that if he confessed at his trial, Stalin would spare him. To his meagre credit, Yezhov refused: 'It's better to leave this earth as an honourable man.'

On 2 February, Ulrikh tried him in Beria's office. Yezhov read out his last statement to Stalin, dedicated to the sacred order of Bolshevik chivalry. He denied all charges of spying for what he called 'Polish landowners ... English lords and Japanese samurai' but 'I do not deny I drank heavily but I worked like a horse. My fate is obvious,' but he asked 'one thing: shoot me quietly, without putting me through any agony.' Then he requested that his mother be looked after, 'my daughter taken care of' and his innocent nephews spared. He finished with the sort of flourish that one might expect to find from a knight to his king at the time of the Round Table: 'Tell Stalin that I shall die with his name on my lips.'

He faced the *Vishka* less courageously than many of his victims. When Ulrikh pronounced the sentence, Yezhov toppled over but was caught by his guards, loaded into a Black Crow in the early hours of 3 February and driven to his special execution yard with the sloping floor and hosing facilities at Varsonofyevsky Lane. There Beria, the Deputy Procurator (N. P. Afanasev) and executioner, Blokhin, awaited him. Yezhov, according to Afanasev, hiccuped and wept. Finally his legs collapsed and they dragged him by the hands. That day, Stalin met Beria and Mikoyan for three hours, probably discussing economic matters, but there is no doubt that he would have wished to know the details of Blackberry's conduct at the supreme moment.

The ashes of these men, Yezhov the criminal, Babel the genius, were dumped into a pit marked 'Common Grave Number One – unclaimed ashes 1930–42 inclusive' at old Donskoi Cemetery. Just twenty paces away there is a gravestone that reads: 'Khayutina, Yevgenia Solomonovna 1904–1938'. Yezhov, Yevgenia and Babel lie close.*

---

* In the nineties, a monument was raised there that reads: 'Here lie buried the remains of the innocent, tortured and executed victims of political repressions. May they never be forgotten.' Antonina Babel did not find out that her husband had been executed until 1954 when he was rehabilitated. She spent many years living in America. Her heart-rending memoirs stand with those of Nadezhda Mandelstam and Anna Larina as classics.

Yezhov's eminence was eradicated from the memories of the time. Henceforth he was portrayed as a blood-crazed renegade killing innocents against Stalin's wishes. The era was named the *Yezhovshchina*, Yezhov's time, a word that Stalin probably coined for he was soon using it himself. Yagoda and Yezhov were both 'scum', thought Stalin. Yezhov was 'a rat who killed many innocent people', Stalin told Yakovlev, the aircraft designer. 'We had to shoot him,' he confided to Kavtaradze. But after the war, Stalin admitted: 'One can't believe a lot of the evidence from 1937. Yezhov couldn't run the NKVD properly and anti-Soviet elements penetrated it. They destroyed some honest people, our best cadres.'

Looking back, he also questioned Beria's Terror: 'Beria runs too many cases and everyone confesses.' But Stalin was always aware that the NKVD invented evidence: he jested and grumbled about it but often he chose to believe it because he had already decided who was an Enemy. More often, he had created it himself. 'Meyerhold was a huge talent,' Stalin reflected in 1950, but 'our Chekists don't understand artists who all have faults. The Chekists collect them and then destroy good people. I doubt Meyerhold was an Enemy of the People.' He protested too much. Stalin had carefully followed their careers. He disapproved of 'frivolous' Babel and his *Red Cavalry* 'of which he knows nothing' – and he signed the death-lists: no ruler has supervised his secret police as intimately as he.

Now Beria, cleaning the Augean stables of Yezhov's detritus, brought Stalin the death sentence for Blokhin the executioner himself. Stalin refused Beria's request, saying that this '*chernaya rabota*' – black work – was a difficult job but very important for the Party. Blokhin was spared to kill thousands more. Stalin's brother-in-law Stanislas Redens (implicated by Yezhov), was shot on 12 February, 1940.* His wife Anna was still convinced he would return and often called Stalin and Beria to inquire. Finally Beria told her to forget her marriage. After all, it had never been registered ...

---

* There was one strange mercy: Redens's widow and children did not share the tragedy of the families of other Enemies though they later suffered too. For the moment, they spent their weekends at Zubalovo with Svetlana and their life carried on as if nothing had happened. Indeed, Anna continued to ring Stalin and berate him about Svetlana's clothes or Vasily's drinking. Soon they were even reconciled.

Molotov Cocktails:
The Winter War and Kulik's Wife

Stalin was in high spirits after the Ribbentrop Pact but he remained dangerously paranoid, especially to the wives of his friends. In November 1939, the phone rang at the dacha of Kulik, the bungling Deputy Defence Commissar who had commanded the Polish invasion. He and his long-legged, green-eyed wife, Kira Simonich, said to be the finest looking in Stalin's circle, were holding his birthday party attended by an *Almanac de Gotha* of the élite, from Voroshilov and the worker-peasant-Count Alexei Tolstoy, to the omnipresent court singer, Kozlovsky, and a flurry of ballerinas. Kulik answered it:

'Quiet!' he hissed. 'It's Stalin!' He listened. 'What am I doing? I'm celebrating my birthday with friends.'

'Wait for me,' replied Stalin who soon arrived with Vlasik and a case of wine. He greeted everyone and then sat at the table, where he drank his own wine while Kozlovsky sang Stalin's favourite songs, particularly the Duke's aria from *Rigoletto*.

Kira Kulik approached Stalin, chatting to him like an old friend. The most unlikely member of Stalin's circle was born Kira Simonich, the daughter of a count of Serbian origins who had run Tsarist intelligence in Finland then been shot by the Cheka in 1919. After the Revolution she had married a Jewish merchant exiled to Siberia: she went with him and they then managed to settle in the south where she met Grigory Kulik, the stocky, 'always half-drunk' *bon vivant* who had commanded Stalin's artillery at Tsaritsyn, but whose knowledge of military technology was frozen in 1918. The Countess was his second wife: they fell in love on the spot, leaving their respective spouses – but she was trebly tainted, for she was an aristocrat with links to Tsarist intelligence and the ex-wife of an arrested Jewish merchant. Like Bronka, Kira Kulik chatted to Stalin informally and 'shone at Kremlin parties', recalled one lady who was often there herself. 'She was very beautiful. Tukhachevsky, Voroshilov, Zhdanov,

Yagoda, Yezhov, Beria all paid court to her.' Naturally there were rumours that Stalin himself had made her his mistress.

Now, by the piano at the party, Kulik and other young women surrounded him: 'We drink your health, Joseph Vissarionovich,' said a famous ballerina, 'and let me kiss you in the name of all women.' He kissed her in return, and toasted her. But then Kira Kulik made a mistake.

When she was alone by the piano with just Stalin, she asked him to free her brother, a former Tsarist officer, from the camps. Stalin listened affably, then put on the gramophone, playing his favourites. Everyone danced except Stalin.* Stalin gave Kulik a book inscribed 'To my old friend. J Stalin' but Kira's approach, presuming on her familiarity and prettiness, set a mantrap in his suspicious mind.

* * *

Days later, Kulik ordered the artillery barrage that commenced the Soviet invasion of Finland, the fourth country in their sphere of influence, which like the Baltic States had been part of the Russian Empire until 1918 and which now threatened Leningrad.

On 12 October, a Finnish delegation met Stalin and Molotov in the Kremlin to hear the Soviet demands for the cession of a naval base at Hango. The Finns refused the Soviet demands, much to Stalin's surprise. 'This cannot continue for long without the danger of accidents,' he said. The Finns replied that they needed a five-sixths majority in their Parliament. Stalin laughed: 'You're sure to get 99 per cent!'

'And our votes into the bargain,' joked Molotov. Their last meeting ended with less humour: 'We civilians,' threatened Molotov, 'can see no further ... Now it's the turn of the military ...'

During dinner with Beria and Khrushchev at his flat, Stalin sent Finland his ultimatum. Molotov and Zhdanov, who was in charge of Baltic policy, the navy, and the defence of Leningrad, backed him. Mikoyan told a German diplomat that he had warned the Finns: 'You should be careful not to push the Russians too far. They have deep feelings in regard to this part of the world and ... I can only tell you that we Caucasians in the Politburo are having a great deal of difficulty restraining the Russians.' When the

* Kozlovsky always sang the same songs at all Kremlin receptions. When he put some other songs into the repertoire, he arrived at the Kremlin to find the same programme as usual. 'Comrade Stalin likes this repertoire. He likes to hear the same things as usual.'

ultimatum ran out, they were still drinking in the Kremlin. 'Let's get started today,' said Stalin, sending Kulik to command the bombardment. The very presence of Kulik at any military engagement seemed to guarantee disaster.

On 30 November, five Soviet armies attacked along the 800-mile border. Their frontal assaults on the Mannerheim Line were foiled by the ingenious Finns, who, dressed like ghosts in white suits, were slaughtering the Russians. The forests were decorated with frozen pyramids of Soviet corpses. The Finns used 70,000 empty bottles, filled with gasoline, against the Russian tanks – the first 'Molotov cocktails', one part of his cult of personality that the vain Premier surely did not appreciate. By mid-December, Stalin had lost about 25,000 men. He amateurishly planned the Winter War like a local exercise, ignoring the Chief of Staff Shaposhnikov's professional plan. When Kulik's artillery deputy, Voronov, later a famous marshal, asked how much time was allotted for this operation, he was told, 'Between ten and twelve days.' Voronov thought it would take two or three months. Kulik greeted this with 'derisive gibes' and ordered him to work on a maximum of twelve days. Stalin and Zhdanov were so confident they created a crude puppet government of Finnish Communists. After 9 December, the Ninth Army was decimated around the destroyed village of Suomussalmi.

Stalin's military amateurs reacted with spasms of executions and recriminations. 'I regard a radical purge ... as essential,' Voroshilov warned the 44th Division. The need for the reform of the Red Army was plain to the cabinets of Europe. Yet Stalin's first solution was to despatch the 'gloomy demon' Mekhlis, now at the height of his power, to the front:

'I'm so absorbed in the work that I don't even notice the days pass. I sleep only 2–3 hours,' he told his wife. 'Yesterday it was minus 35 degrees below freezing ... I feel very well ... I have only one dream – to destroy the White Guards of Finland. We'll do it. Victory's not far off.'* On the 26th, Stalin finally appointed Timoshenko to command the North-Western Front and restore

* Bowing before the imperial status of his leader, Mekhlis was obsessed too with delivering a victory for Stalin on his birthday on 21 December 1939: 'I want to celebrate it with full defeat of Finnish White Guards!' When the great day arrived Mekhlis told his family: 'I'm saluting you. 60th birthday of JV. Celebrate it in the family!' Back at the Kremlin that night, Stalin celebrated his birthday with his courtiers, partying until 8 a.m. in the morning: 'An unforgettable night!' Dmitrov recorded in his diary.

order to his frayed forces who were now dying of hunger. Even Beria took a more humane stand, reporting to Voroshilov the lack of provisions: '139th Division's in difficulties ... no fodder at all ... no fuel ... Troops scattering.' Stalin sensed the army was concealing the scale of the disaster. Trusting only Mekhlis, he wrote:

'The White Finns published their operations report that claims "the annihilation of the 44th Division ... 1,000 Red Army soldiers as prisoners, 102 guns, 1,170 horses and 43 tanks." Tell me first – is this true? Second – where is the Military Council and Chief of Staff of the 44th Division? How do they explain their shameful conduct? Why did they desert their division? Third, why does the Military Council of the 9th Army not inform us ...? We expect an answer. Stalin.'

Mekhlis arrived in Suomussalmi to find chaotic scenes which he made worse. He confirmed the losses and shot the whole command: 'the trial of Vinogradov, Volkov and chief of Political Department took place in the open air in the presence of the division ... The sentence of shooting was performed publicly ... The exposure of traitors and cowards continues.' On 10 December, Mekhlis himself was almost killed when his car was ambushed, as he proudly recounted to Stalin: unlike many of Stalin's commissars, Mekhlis was personally courageous, if not suicidally reckless, under fire, partly because, as a Jew, he wanted to be 'purer than crystal'. Indeed, he took command of fleeing companies and led them at the enemy. Mekhlis and Kulik did not conceal the mess: 'We lack bread in the army,' Mekhlis reported. Kulik agreed: 'rigidity and bureaucracy are everywhere.' When Kulik rushed into a Politburo meeting to report yet more defeats, Stalin lectured him: 'You're lapsing into panic ... The pagan Greek priests were intelligent ... When they got disturbing reports, they'd adjourn to their bathhouses, take baths, wash themselves clean and only afterwards assess events and take decisions ...'

Stalin was saddened by these disasters: 'The snows are deep. Our troops are on the march ... full of spirit ... Suddenly there's a burst of automatic fire and our men fall to the ground.' At times, he looked helplessly depressed. Khrushchev saw him lying on a couch, despondent, a rehearsal of his collapse in the early days of the Nazi invasion. The pressure made Stalin ill with his usual streptococcus and staphylococcus, a temperature of 38°C and an agonizing sore throat. On 1 February, his health improved as

Timoshenko probed Finnish defences, launching his great offensive on the 11th. Soviet superiority finally took its toll on the plucky Finns. When the doctors re-examined Stalin, he showed them the maps: 'We'll take Vyborg today.' The Finns sued for peace. On 12 March, Zhdanov signed a treaty in which Finland ceded Hango, the Karelian Isthmus, and the north-eastern shore of Ladoga, 22,000 square miles, to insulate Leningrad. Finland lost around 48,000 soldiers, Stalin over 125,000.

'The Red Army was good for nothing,' Stalin later told Churchill and Roosevelt. Stalin was incandescent and he was not alone: Khrushchev later blamed Voroshilov's 'criminal negligence', sneering that he spent more time in the studio of Gerasimov, the court painter, than in the Defence Commissariat. At Kuntsevo, Stalin's anger boiled over. He started shouting at Voroshilov, who gave as good as he got. Turning red as a turkeycock, Voroshilov shrieked at Stalin,

'You have yourself to blame for all of this. You're the one who annihilated the old guard of our army, you had our best generals killed.' Stalin rebuffed him, at which Voroshilov 'picked up a platter of roast suckling pig and smashed it on the table'. Khrushchev admitted, 'It was the only time in my life I witnessed such an outburst.' Voroshilov alone could have got away with it.

On 28 March 1940, Voroshilov, who became Stalin's 'whipping boy' for the Finnish disasters, confessed, at the Central Committee, 'I have to say neither I nor General Staff ... had any idea of the peculiarities and difficulties involved in this war.' Mekhlis, who hated Voroshilov and coveted his job, declared: he 'cannot simply leave his post – he must be severely punished.' But Stalin could not afford to destroy Voroshilov.

'Mekhlis made a hysterical speech,' he said, restraining his creature. Instead he held a uniquely frank, sometimes comical, Supreme Military Council in mid-April. One commander admitted that the army had been surprised to find forests in Finland, at which Stalin sneered: 'It's time our army knew there were forests there ... In Peter's time, there were forests. Elizabeth ... Catherine ... Alexander found forests! And now! That's four times!' (Laughter) He was even more indignant when Mekhlis revealed that the Finns often attacked during the Red Army's afternoon nap. 'Afternoon nap?!' spat Stalin.

'An hour's nap,' confirmed Kulik.

'People have afternoon naps in rest homes!' growled Stalin, who

went on to defend the campaign itself: 'Could we have avoided
the war? I think the war was inevitable ... A delay of a couple of
months would have meant a delay of twenty years.' He won more
territory there than Peter the Great but he warned against the
'cult of the traditions of the Civil War. It brings to mind the Red
Indians who fought with clubs against rifles ... and were all
killed.' On 6 May, Voroshilov was sacked as Defence Commissar
and succeeded by Timoshenko.* Shaposhnikov was sacked as
Chief of Staff even though Stalin admitted he had been right in
the first place, 'but only we know that!' He raised military morale,
restoring the rank of General and the single command by soldiers,
whose tasks had been made incomparably harder by sharing
control with interfering commissars. He freed 11,178 purged
officers who officially returned 'from a long and dangerous
mission'. Stalin asked one of them, Konstantin Rokossovsky,
perhaps noticing his lack of fingernails, 'Were you tortured in
prison?'

'Yes, Comrade Stalin.'

'There're too many yesmen in this country,' sighed Stalin. But
some did not come back: 'Where's your Serdich?' Stalin asked
Budyonny about a mutual friend.

'Executed!' reported the Marshal.

'Pity! I wanted to make him Ambassador to Yugoslavia ...'

Stalin attacked his military 'Red Indians' but then turned to his
own tribe of primitive braves who remained obsessed with cavalry
and oblivious to modern warfare. Budyonny and Kulik believed
tanks could never replace horses. 'You won't convince me,'
Budyonny had recently declared. 'As soon as war comes, everyone
will shout, "Send for the cavalry!"' Stalin and Voroshilov had
abolished special tank corps. Fortunately, Timoshenko now
persuaded the *Vozhd* to reverse his folly.

None the less, Mikoyan called the dominance of these
incompetents 'the triumph of the First Cavalry Army' since they
were veterans of Stalin's favoured Civil War unit. Despite the

---

* A muscular paragon of peasant masculinity, typical of Stalin's cavalrymen,
Timoshenko had been a divisional commander in the Polish War of 1920: he appears
as the 'captivating Savitsky' in the *Red Cavalry* stories of Isaac Babel who praises the
'beauty of his giant's body', the power of his decorated chest 'cleaving the hut as a
standard cleaves the sky' and his long cavalryman's legs which were 'like girls
sheathed to the neck of shining jackboots'. The less poetical Mikoyan simply calls
him a 'brave peasant'.

tossing of the suckling pig, Voroshilov was promoted to Deputy Premier for 'cultural matters' which Mikoyan regarded as a joke, given the Marshal's love of being painted.

Mekhlis, who also became Deputy Premier, fancied himself a great captain: he harassed Timoshenko to ask Stalin to reappoint him as Deputy Defence Commissar. Stalin mocked Timoshenko's naïvety: 'We want to help him but he doesn't understand. He wants us to leave him Mekhlis. But after three months, Mekhlis will chuck him out. Mekhlis wants to be Defence Commissar himself.' Mekhlis enjoyed Stalin's 'unbounded confidence'. Kulik, the buffoonish artillery chief, who encouraged his subordinates by shrieking 'Prison or medal', was an ignorant Blimp. He despised anti-tank artillery: 'What rubbish – no rumble, no shell-holes ...' He denounced the invaluable new Katyusha rockets: 'What the hell do we need rocket artillery for? The main thing is the horse-drawn gun.' He delayed the production of the outstanding T-34 tank. Khrushchev, whom Stalin liked for his cheek, questioned Kulik's credentials.

'You don't even know Kulik,' roared Stalin. 'I know him from the Civil War when he commanded the artillery in Tsaritsyn. He understands artillery.'

'But how many cannons did you have there? Two or three? And now he's in charge of all the artillery in the land?' Stalin told Khrushchev to mind his own business. Higher than all of them, Zhdanov was now Stalin's artillery and naval expert. 'There were competent people,' wrote Mikoyan, 'but Stalin was increasingly distrustful of people so trust was more important than anything.' Stalin wavered, meandered and reversed his own decisions. It is remarkable any correct decisions were made at all.

* * *

In May, Stalin ordered the kidnapping of Kulik's wife, Kira at whose house he had been a guest in November. In the name of the *Instantsiya*, Beria commissioned 'the Theoretician' Merkulov to arrange it. On 5 May, Kobulov, the prince-assassin Tsereteli and a favoured torturer Vladzimirsky trailed Kira on her way to the dentist, then bundled the beauty into a car and took her to the Lubianka. Stalin and Beria evidently shared a playful sadism and perverse taste for these depraved games. The reason for the kidnapping is a mystery because no charges were made against her, but Mekhlis built a file against the Kuliks which catalogues Kira's nobility as well as Grigory's drunken indiscretions, incompetence, anti-Semitism, Social Revolutionary past, complaints about the Terror, and connections with Trotskyites. Was she kidnapped for appealing to Stalin or was she denounced by her latest lover, another victim of prudery? The most suspicious mark against her in Stalin's eyes, may have been Kulik's dangerous tendency to give 'orders in front of' his various wives.*

Two days after Kira's kidnapping, on 7 May, Stalin promoted her husband to Marshal, along with Timoshenko and Shaposhnikov, in what can only be called a stroke of ironical sadism. Next day, Kulik's delight at his Marshalate was tempered by worry about his wife. He called Beria, who invited him to the Lubianka. While Kulik sipped tea in his office, Beria called Stalin:

'Marshal Kulik's sitting in front of me. No, he doesn't know any details. She left and that's all. Certainly, Comrade Stalin, we'll announce an all-Union search and do everything possible to find her.' They both knew that Kira was in the cells beneath Beria's office. A month later, Countess Simonich-Kulik, mother of an eight-year-old daughter, was moved to Beria's special prison, the Sukhanovka, where Blokhin murdered her in cold blood with a shot to the head. Kobulov complained that Blokhin killed her before he arrived. Stalin perhaps took comfort or pleasure in the promotion of cronies such as Kulik while knowing, as they did not, the fate of their beloveds.

The public search for Kira Kulik continued for twelve years but the Marshal himself had long since realized that her dubious connections had destroyed her. He soon married again.

* * *

Meanwhile Stalin and his magnates debated the fate of the Polish officers, arrested or captured in September 1939 and held in three camps, one of which was close to Katyn Forest. When Stalin was undecided about an issue, there was surprisingly frank discussion. Kulik, commander of the Polish front, proposed freeing all the Poles. Voroshilov agreed but Mekhlis was adamant there were Enemies among them. Stalin stopped the release but Kulik persisted. Stalin compromised. The Poles were released – except for about 26,000 officers whose destiny was finally decided at the Politburo on 5 March 1940.

---

* No papers of formal charges were ever filed so the kidnapping was illegal even by Bolshevik standards. When Beria was arrested after Stalin's death, this kidnapping and murder was one of the crimes on the indictment.

Beria's son claimed that his father argued against a massacre, not out of philanthropy, but because the Poles might be useful later. There is no evidence for this, except that Beria often took a practical rather than ideological approach. If so, Beria lost the argument. He dutifully reported that the 14,700 officers, landowners and policemen and 11,000 'counter-Revolutionary' landowners, were 'spies and saboteurs ... hardened ... enemies of Soviet power' who should be 'tried by ... Comrades Merkulov, Kobulov and Bashtakov'. Stalin scrawled his signature first and underlined it, followed by Voroshilov, Molotov and Mikoyan. Kalinin and Kaganovich were canvassed by phone and voted 'For'.

This massacre was a chunk of 'black work' for the NKVD who were accustomed to the *Vishka* of a few victims at a time, but there was a man for the task: Blokhin travelled down to the Ostachkov camp where he and two other Chekists outfitted a hut with padded, soundproofed walls and decided on a Stakhanovite quota of 250 shootings a night. He brought a butcher's leather apron and cap which he put on when he began one of the most prolific acts of mass murder by one individual, killing 7,000 in precisely twenty-eight nights, using a German Walther pistol to prevent future exposure. The bodies were buried in various places – but the 4,500 in the Kozelsk camp were interred in Katyn Forest.*

* * *

That June, the *Führer* unleashed his *Blitzkrieg* against the Low Countries and France. Stalin still had a profound respect for the power of France and Britain, whom he counted on holding up Hitler in the West. On 17 June 1940, France sued for peace, a shock that should have made Stalin reassess his alliance with Hitler though it was also now the only game in town. Molotov congratulated Schulenburg 'warmly' but through gritted teeth, 'on the splendid success of the German *Wehrmacht*'. A rattled Stalin 'cursed' the Allies:

'Couldn't they put up any resistance at all?' he asked Khrushchev. 'Now Hitler's going to beat our brains in!'

---

* In November 1941, the Polish Ambassador Stanislaw Kot quizzed Stalin on the whereabouts of these men. Stalin made a show of setting up a phone call to Beria and changed the subject. In December 1941, he told General Anders they had escaped to Mongolia. As we have seen, these sort of sniggering acts of concern were part of his game with Beria. Mikoyan's son Stepan wrote graciously that his father's signature on this order was 'the heaviest burden for our family'.

Stalin rushed to consume the Baltic States and Bessarabia, part of Romania. As troops moved across the borders, Soviet bombers flew Stalin's proconsuls to their fiefdoms: Dekanozov to Lithuania, Deputy Premier (the former 'shoot the mad dogs' Procurator) Vyshinsky to Latvia, and Zhdanov to Estonia. Zhdanov drove through the Estonian capital, Tallinn, in an armoured car flanked by two tanks and then nominated a puppet 'Prime Minister', lecturing the Estonians 'that everything will be done in accordance with democratic parliamentary rules ... We're not Germans!' For some Baltic citizens, they were worse. A total of 34,250 Latvians, almost 60,000 Estonians and 75,000 Lithuanians were murdered or deported. 'Comrade Beria,' said Stalin, 'will take care of the accommodation of our Baltic guests.' The NKVD put icing on Stalin's cake on 20 August, when Beria's agent Ramon Mercader shattered Trotsky's skull with an icepick. Trotsky might have undermined Stalin's foreign policy but really his death simply closed the chapter of the Great Terror. Vengeance was Stalin's.

Stalin had seized a buffer zone from the Baltic to the Black Sea but he now started to receive intelligence of Hitler's intention to attack the USSR. He redoubled his attentions to the Germans. Yet he also laughed at the Nazis with Zhdanov by putting on Wagner's *Flight of the Valkyries* directed by the Jewish Eisenstein.

'And who's singing Wotan?' Zhdanov joked with Stalin. 'A Jewish singer.' These Hebraic Wagnerians did not restrain Hitler from gradually moving troops eastwards. Stalin instinctively distrusted the intelligence from the new chief of GRU, military intelligence, General Filip Golikov, an untried mediocrity, and from the NKVD under Beria and Merkulov. He regarded Golikov as 'inexperienced, naïve. A spy should be like the devil; no one should trust him not even himself.' Merkulov, head of the NKVD Foreign Department, was 'dextrous' but still scared in case 'someone will be offended'. It was understandable they were afraid of offending 'someone'. All their predecessors had been murdered.*

Stalin and Molotov's suspicions of their own spies reflected their origins in the murky Bolshevik underground where many

---

* At the Eighteenth Party Conference in February 1941, Stalin divided Beria's NKVD into two commissariats. Beria retained the NKVD while State Security (NKGB) was hived off under his protégé Merkulov. This was not yet a direct demotion for Beria: he was promoted to Deputy Premier and remained overlord or *curator* of both 'Organs'.

comrades (including the *Vozhd* himself) were double or treble agents. They evaluated the motives of others by the standards of their own paranoid criminality: 'I think one can never trust intelligence,' Molotov admitted years later. 'One has to listen ... but check on them ... There are endless provocateurs on both sides.' This was ironic because Stalin possessed the world's best intelligence network: his spies worked for Marx not Mammon. Yet the more he knew, the less he trusted: 'his knowledge', writes one historian, 'only added to his sorrow and isolation.' However insistent the facts of the German military build-up, the Soviet spymasters were under pressure to provide the information that Stalin wanted: 'We never went out looking for information at random,' recalled one spy. 'Orders to look for specific things would come from above.'

Stalin reacted to this uneasiness by aggressively pushing the traditional Russian interests in the Balkans which in itself alarmed Hitler, who was weighing up whether to attack his ally. He decided to invite Molotov to Berlin to sidetrack the Soviets into a push for the Indian Ocean. The night before Molotov left, he sat up late with Stalin and Beria, debating how to maintain the Pact. In his handwritten directive, Stalin instructed Molotov to insist on explanations for the presence of German troops in Romania and Finland, discover Hitler's real interests and assert Russian interests in the Balkans and Dardanelles. Molotov meanwhile told his wife, 'my pleasure honey', that he was studying Hitler: 'I've been reading Rauschning's *Hitler Spoke to Me* ... Rauschning explains much that H is carrying out now ... and in the future.'

Molotov Meets Hitler:
Brinkmanship and Delusion

Molotov set off late on 10 November 1940 from the Belorussia Station with a pistol in his pocket and a delegation of sixty which included Beria's two protégés, Dekanozov, Deputy Foreign Commissar, and Merkulov, sixteen secret policemen, three servants and a doctor. This was Molotov's second trip to Europe. In 1922, he and Polina had visited Italy in the early days of Fascism. Now he was to observe Fascism at its apogee.

At 11.05 a.m., Molotov's train pulled into Berlin's Anhalter Station, which was festooned with flowers sinisterly illuminated with searchlights and Soviet flags hidden behind swastikas. Molotov dismounted in a dark coat with his grey Homburg hat and was greeted by Ribbentrop and Field Marshal Keitel. He spent longest shaking hands with Reichsführer-SS Himmler. The band deliberately played the *Internationale* at double time in case any ex-Communist passers-by joined in.

Molotov sped off in an open Mercedes with outriders to his luxurious hotel, the Schloss Bellevue, once an imperial palace, on the Tiergarten where the Soviets were dazzled by the 'tapestries and paintings', the 'finest porcelain standing round exquisitely carved cabinets' and, above all, the 'gold-braided livery' of the staff. Molotov's entire delegation wore identical dark blue suits, grey ties, and cheap felt hats, obviously ordered in bulk. Since some wore the hats like berets, some on the back of their heads like cowboys and some low over the eyes like Mafiosi, it was clear that many had never worn Western headgear before. The tepidity of the visit became obvious when Molotov met Ribbentrop in Bismarck's old office and gave little away. 'A rather frosty smile glided over his intelligent, chess-player's face,' noticed a German diplomat who was amused that, in the gilded Bismarckian chairs, little Dekanozov's feet barely touched the floor. When Ribbentrop encouraged Russia to seek an outlet for her energies in warm oceans, Molotov asked: 'Which sea are you talking about?'

After lunch at the Bellevue, the open Mercedes drove Molotov to the Chancellery, where he was led through bronze doors, guarded by heel-clicking SS men, into Hitler's magnificent study. Two blond SS giants threw open the doors and formed an archway with impeccable Nazi salutes through which this plain, stalwart Russian marched towards Hitler's gargantuan desk at the far end. Hitler hesitated, then walked jerkily to greet the Russians with 'small, rapid steps'. He stopped and made a Nazi salute before shaking hands with Molotov and the others with a 'cold and moist' palm, while his 'feverish eyes' burned into them 'like gimlets'. Hitler's theatrical rigmarole to terrorize and impress his guests did not affect Molotov, who regarded himself as a Marxist-Leninist and therefore superior to everyone else, particularly Fascists: 'There was nothing remarkable in his appearance.' Molotov and Hitler were exactly the same height – 'medium' as the small Russian put it. But Hitler 'was very smug ... and vain. He was clever but narrow-minded and obtuse because of his egotism and the absurdity of his primordial idea.'

Hitler showed Molotov to a lounge area where he, Dekanozov and the interpreters sat on the sofa while Hitler occupied his usual armchair, whence he treated them to a long soliloquy about his defeat of Britain, generosity to Stalin, and disinterest in the Balkans, none of which was true. Molotov retorted with a series of polite, but awkward questions on the relationship between the two powers, pinpointing precisely Finland, Romania, Bulgaria. 'I kept pushing him for greater detail. "You've got to have a warm-water port. Iran, India – that's your future." And I said, "Why that's an interesting idea, how do you see it?"' Hitler ended the meeting without providing the answer.

That night, Ribbentrop hosted a reception for Molotov at the Kaiserhof Hotel attended by Reichsmarschall Göring, sporting a preposterous sartorial creation of silver thread and jewels, and Deputy Führer Hess. The Russian interpreter Berezhkov, observing Molotov talking to Göring, could not imagine two more different men. A telegram from Stalin awaited him, insisting again on the Balkans and Straits. The next morning, Molotov sent Stalin a telegram: 'I'm leaving for lunch and talk with Hitler. I will press him on the Black Sea, the Straits and Bulgaria.' First he called on Göring at the Air Ministry where he asked Hitler's 'paladin' more embarrassing questions which the Reichsmarschall simply doused with his pinguid heartiness. He then visited Hess.

'Do you have a Party programme?' he asked the Deputy Führer, knowing the Nazis did not. 'Do you have Party rules? And do you have a Constitution?' The Bolshevik ideologue was contemptuous: 'How could it be a Party without a programme?'

At 2 p.m., Hitler received Molotov, Merkulov and Dekanozov for a dinner with Goebbels and Ribbentrop. The Russians were disappointed by Hitler's austere menu that read simply: '*Kraftbruhe, Fasan, Obstsalat*' – beef tea, pheasant and fruit salad.

'The war is on so I don't drink coffee,' Hitler explained, 'because my people don't drink coffee either. I don't smoke, I don't drink liquor.' Molotov added later: 'It goes without saying that I was abstaining from nothing.'

Their second meeting, after the meal, lasted for a 'bad-tempered' three hours. Molotov pressed Hitler for answers. Hitler accused Russia of greed. Nothing dented the stolid persistence of 'Iron-Arse'. Molotov obeyed Stalin's telegraphed instructions to explain that 'all events from the Crimean War ... to the landing of foreign troops during the Intervention [Civil War] mean Soviet security cannot be settled without ... the Straits.'

Hitler almost lost his temper about his troops in Finland and Romania: 'That's a trifle!'

Molotov tartly commented that there was no need to speak roughly. But how could they agree on big issues when they failed to do so on small ones? Molotov noticed that Hitler 'became agitated. I persisted. I wore him down.'

Hitler drew out his handkerchief, wiped the sweat off his upper lip and saw his guest to the door.

'I'm sure history will remember Stalin's name forever,' he said.

'I don't doubt it,' replied Molotov.

'So we should meet ...' suggested Hitler vaguely, a meeting that never happened. 'But I hope it will remember me too,' he added with mock-modesty, for he had just two days earlier signed his Directive No. 18 that moved the Soviet invasion to the top of his agenda, an enterprise that would guarantee his place in history.

'I don't doubt it.'

Göring, Hess and Ribbentrop were the star guests at Molotov's banquet, with caviar and vodka at the grand but faded Soviet Embassy, which was interrupted by the RAF.

'Our British friends are complaining they have not been invited to the party,' joked Ribbentrop as Göring stampeded like a bejewelled, scented bison through the crowd, out to his Mercedes.

There was no air-raid shelter at the Embassy so most of the Russians were driven back to the hotel. Several got lost and Molotov was shepherded to Ribbentrop's private bunker. Here, to the music of the RAF bombs, and the cackle of AA-guns, the stuttering Russian sliced through the German's florid promises. If, as Hitler said, Germany was waging a life-and-death struggle against England, Molotov suggested this must mean that Germany was fighting 'for life' and England 'for death'. Britain was 'finished', answered Ribbentrop.

'If that's so, then why are we in this shelter and whose bombs are those falling?' Molotov responded.

Molotov departed next morning, having, as he told Stalin, achieved 'nothing to boast of but ... it does clarify the present mood of Hitler.'

* * *

Stalin congratulated Molotov on his defiance of Hitler: 'How,' he asked, 'did he put up with you telling him all this?' The answer was that Hitler did not: Molotov's obstinate Balkan ambitions convinced Hitler that Stalin would soon challenge his European hegemony. Having wavered over attacking Russia, he now accelerated his plans. On 4 December, Operation Barbarossa was set for May 1941.

A few days later, Yakovlev, the aircraft designer, who had been with Molotov in Berlin, bumped into the Foreign Commissar in Stalin's anteroom:

'Ah, here is the German!' joked Molotov. 'We'll both have to repent!'

'For what?' asked Yakovlev nervously.

'Well, did we dine with Hitler? We did. Did we shake hands with Goebbels? We did. We shall have to repent.' The Bolsheviks lived in a world of sin and repentance. When Stalin received Yakovlev, he ordered him to study Nazi planes:

'Learn how to beat them.'

On 29 December 1940, eleven days after Hitler signed Directive No. 21 on Operation Barbarossa, Stalin's spies alerted him to its existence. Stalin knew the USSR would not be ready for war until 1943 and hoped to delay it by frantic rearming and aggressive brinkmanship in the Balkans – but without provoking Hitler. The Führer, on the other hand, realized the urgency of his enterprise and that he had to secure the Balkans before he could attack Russia.

Stalin's panic to produce the best weapons and create the best strategy created a new Terror around him. The countdown to war redoubled the unreal miasma of fear and ignorance at the heart of the Soviet power. At a Kremlin lunch attended by all the magnates, they were just standing to leave when Stalin suddenly tore into them, complaining of the symptoms of his own dictatorship. 'I am the ONLY one dealing with all these problems. None of you could be bothered with them. I am out there by MYSELF. Look at me: I am capable of learning ... every day.' Kalinin alone dared reply:

'Somehow there's never enough time!' at which Stalin retorted furiously:

'People are thoughtless ... THEY'LL HEAR ME OUT AND GO ON JUST AS BEFORE. But I'll show you, if ever I lose my patience. You know very well I can do that. I'll hit the fatsos so hard you'll hear the crack for miles around!' He addressed himself especially to Kaganovich and Beria, who knew 'very well' how hard Stalin could hit 'the fatsos'. By the end, there were 'tears in Voroshilov's eyes'. The more Stalin realized the parlous condition of his military, the more he floundered, both convinced of his own infallibility and oblivious of his technical ignorance. He supervised every detail of every weapon. His meetings became ever more disturbing, his conduct, thought Mikoyan, ever more 'unhinged'.

There was a clear etiquette: it was deadly to disagree too much but, amazingly, his managers and generals stubbornly defended their expertise. 'I would have been more afraid if I'd known more,' said one commissar later. Silence was often a virtue and veterans advised neophytes on how to behave and survive.

When Stalin sent the Naval Commissar, Nikolai Kuznetsov, to inspect the Far East, the Admiral complained to Zhdanov, the naval overlord, that he was too busy with his new job.

'The papers can wait,' replied Zhdanov. 'I advise you not to say a word about them to Comrade Stalin.'*

When a new official arrived who had never attended a Stalin meeting, he called out 'Joseph Vissarionovich' when he wanted to speak. 'Stalin looked in my direction and again I saw ... an

---

* When Admiral Kuznetsov got to know him on their trip to the Far East, Zhdanov chatted about how much he enjoyed working with the navy. 'I'd love to go [on a cruiser]. But it's not always so easy to get away,' he said, adding with a smile, 'I am more a river man than a seaman. A freshwater sailor as they say. But I love ships.' Kuznetsov admired Zhdanov who 'did a great deal for the Navy'. But he was less helpful to other services.

unfriendly expression on his face. Suddenly a whisper from the man sitting behind me explained everything: "Never call him by his name and patronymic. He only allows a very narrow circle of intimates to do that. To all of us, he is Stalin. Comrade Stalin." ' It was shrewder to keep silent. Kuznetsov was about to object to building a fleet of heavy cruisers when another official whispered kindly:

'Watch your step! Don't insist!'

* * *

On 23 December 1940 Stalin called meetings of the high command which might have been a good idea had they not been paralysed with fear. Marshal Timoshenko and his most dynamic general, Georgi Zhukov, who commanded the Kiev Military District, criticized the glaring weaknesses of Soviet strategy and proposed a return to the forbidden 'deep operations' devised by the gifted Tukhachevsky. The powerful Zhdanov, Stalin's chief adviser on everything from howitzers to ships, Finland to culture, sat in on the meetings and reported back to Stalin, who next day summoned the generals. The insomniac Stalin, who was so accustomed to nocturnal life that he could only sleep after 4 a.m., confessed that he had not slept at all the night before. Timoshenko replied nervously that Stalin had approved his speech:

'You don't really think I have time to read every paper which is tossed at me,' replied Stalin, who at least ordered new plans and urgent war games. However, these merely exposed Soviet weakness, which rattled Stalin so much that on 13 January 1941 he summoned the generals without giving them time to prepare. The Chief of Staff, Meretskov, stumbled as he tried to report until Stalin interrupted:

'Well, who finally won?' Meretskov was afraid to speak, which only enraged Stalin even more. 'Here among ourselves ... we have to talk in terms of our real capabilities.' Finally Stalin exploded: 'The trouble is we don't have a proper Chief of Staff.' He there and then dismissed Meretskov. The meeting deteriorated further when Kulik declared that tanks were overrated; horse-drawn guns were the future. It was staggering that after two Panzer *Blitzkrieg* and only six months before the Nazi invasion, the Soviets were even debating such a thing. It was Stalin's fault that Kulik had been over-promoted but, typically, he blamed someone else:

'Comrade Timoshenko, as long as there's such confusion ... no mechanization of the army can take place at all.' Timoshenko retorted that only Kulik was confused. Stalin turned on his friend:

'Kulik comes out against the engine. It's as if he had come out against the tractor and supported the wooden plough ... Modern warfare will be a war of engines.'

The next afternoon, General Zhukov, forty-five, was rushed to the Little Corner, where Stalin appointed him Chief of Staff. Zhukov tried to refuse. Stalin, impressed by Zhukov's victory over the Japanese at Khalkin-Gol, insisted. The quintessential fighting general who would become the greatest captain of the Second World War was another Civil War cavalryman and a protégé of Budyonny since the late twenties. The son of an impoverished shoemaker, this convinced Communist had just managed to survive the Terror with Budyonny's help. Short, squat, indefatigable, with blunt features and a prehensile jaw, Georgi Zhukov shared Stalin's ruthless brutality, combining savage reprisals and Roman discipline with carelessness about losses. However, he lacked Stalin's deviousness and sadism. He was emotional and brave, often daring to disagree with Stalin who, sensing his gifts, indulged him.

A few days later, at Kuntsevo, Timoshenko and Zhukov tried to persuade Stalin to mobilize, convinced that Hitler would invade. Timoshenko advised him on handling Stalin: 'He won't listen to a long lecture ... just ten minutes.' Stalin was dining with Molotov, Zhdanov and Voroshilov, along with Mekhlis and Kulik. Zhukov spoke up: should not they bolster defences along the Western frontier?

'Are you eager to fight the Germans?' Molotov asked harshly.

'Wait a minute,' Stalin calmed the stuttering Premier. He lectured Zhukov on the Germans: 'They fear us. In secret, I will tell you that our ambassador had a serious conversation with Hitler personally and Hitler said to him, 'Please don't worry about the concentration of our forces in Poland. Our forces are re-training ...' The generals then joined the magnates for Ukrainian *borscht* soup, buckwheat porridge, then stewed meat, with stewed and fresh fruit for pudding, washed down with brandy and Georgian *Khvanchkara* wine.

* * *

Kulik's imbecilic advice unleashed another paroxysm of terror that would bring death to a Politburo family. On hearing that the Germans were increasing the thickness of their armour, he demanded stopping all production of conventional guns and switching to 107mm howitzers from World War I. The Armaments Commissar, Boris Vannikov, a formidable Jewish super-manager, who had studied at Baku Polytechnic with Beria, sensibly opposed Kulik but lacked his access to Stalin. Kulik won Zhdanov's backing. On 1 March, Stalin summoned Vannikov: 'What objections do you have? Comrade Kulik said you don't agree with him.' Vannikov explained that it was unlikely the Germans had updated their armour as swiftly as Kulik suggested: the 76mm remained the best. Then Zhdanov entered the office.

'Look here,' Stalin said to him, 'Vannikov doesn't want to make the 107mm gun ... But these guns are very good. I know them from the Civil War.'

'Vannikov,' replied Zhdanov, 'always opposes everything. That's his style of working.'

'You're the main artillery expert we have,' Stalin commissioned Zhdanov to settle the question, 'and the 107mm is a good gun.' Zhdanov called the meeting where Vannikov defied Kulik. Zhdanov accused him of 'sabotage'. 'The dead hold back the living,' he added ominously. Vannikov shouted back:

'You're tolerating disarmament in the face of an approaching war.' Zhdanov stiffly 'declared he was going to complain about me to Stalin'. Stalin accepted Kulik's solution, which had to be reversed when the war began. Vannikov was arrested.* Only in Stalin's realm could the country's greatest armaments expert be imprisoned just weeks before a war. But Kulik's motto, 'Prison or a medal,' had triumphed again. As the poison spread, it reached Kaganovich's brother. In the almost biblical sacrifice of a beloved sibling, Lazar's steeliness was grievously tested.

* * *

Vannikov was cruelly tortured about his recent post as deputy to Mikhail Kaganovich, Lazar's eldest brother and Commissar for Aircraft Production. The air force was always the most accident-prone service. Not only did the planes crash with alarming regularity, reflecting the haste and sloppiness of Soviet manu-facturing, but someone had to pay for these accidents. In one year four Heroes of the Soviet Union were lost in crashes and Stalin himself questioned the air-force generals even down to the

---

* This was far from the only such madness: on other occasions, Stalin commissioned a tank based on a crazy principle that 'in being destroyed, it protects'.

engineers working on each plane. 'What kind of man is he?' Stalin asked about one technician. 'Maybe he's a bastard, a *svoloch*.' The crashes had to be the fault of 'bastards'. Vannikov was forced to implicate Mikhail Kaganovich as the 'bastard' in this case.

Meanwhile, Vasily Stalin, now a pilot avid to win paternal love, usually by denouncing his superiors to his father, played some part in this tragedy. He remained so nervous that, Svetlana recalled, when his father addressed him at dinner, he jumped and often could not even reply, stammering, 'I didn't hear what you said, Father ... What?' In 1940, he fell in love with a pretty trumpet-playing blonde from an NKVD family, Galina Bourdonovskaya, and married her. Yet he was truculent, arrogant, drunken and, while often bighearted, more often, dangerous. In this peculiar world, the 'Crown Prince' became, according to Svetlana, 'a menace'.

'Hello dear Father,' he wrote on 4 March 1941. 'How's your health? Recently I was in Moscow on the orders of Rychagov [the Chief of the Main Directorate of the Air Force], I wanted to see you so much but they said you were busy ... They won't let me fly ... Rychagov called me and abused me very much saying that instead of studying theory, I was starting to visit commanders proving to them I had to fly. He ordered me to inform you of this conversation.' Vasily had to fly in old planes 'that are terrible to see' and even future officers could not train in the new planes: 'Father, write me just a couple of words, if you have time, it's the biggest joy for me because I miss you so much. Your Vasya.'

This subtle denunciation cannot have helped Pavel Rychagov, thirty-nine, a dashing pilot just promoted to the high command. He arrived drunk at a meeting to discuss the planes. When Stalin criticized the air force, Rychagov shouted that the death rate was so high 'because you're making us fly in coffins!' Silence fell but Stalin continued to walk around the room, the only sounds being the puffing of the pipe and the pad of soft boots.

'You shouldn't have said that.' He walked round the deathly quiet table one more time and repeated: 'You shouldn't have said that.' Rychagov was arrested within the week along with several air-force top brass, and General Shtern, Far Eastern commander, all later shot. They, like Vannikov, implicated Mikhail Kaganovich.

'We received testimonies,' Stalin told Kaganovich. 'Your brother's implicated in the conspiracy.' The brother was accused of building the aircraft factories close to the Russian border to help Berlin. Stalin explained that Mikhail, a Jew, had been designated head of Hitler's puppet Government-in-waiting, an idea so preposterous that it was either the moronic solecism of a NKGB simpleton or, more likely, a joke between Stalin and Beria. Did they remember Ordzhonikidze's fury on the arrest of his brother? Ordzhonikidze had been Kaganovich's closest friend.

'It's a lie,' Kaganovich claimed to have replied. 'I know my brother. He's a Bolshevik since 1905, devoted to the Central Committee.'

'How can it be a lie?' retorted Stalin. 'I've got the testimonies.'

'It's a lie. I demand a confrontation.' Decades later, Kaganovich denied that he had betrayed his own brother: 'If my brother had been an Enemy I'd have been against him … I was sure he was right. I protected him. I protected him!' Kaganovich could afford to give an opinion but he also had to make clear that if the Party needed to destroy his brother, his brother must die. 'Well, so what?' he added. 'If necessary, arrest him.'

Stalin ordered Mikoyan and that sinister duo Beria and Malenkov to arrange a confrontation between Mikhail Kaganovich and his accuser, Vannikov, but 'Iron Lazar' was not invited to attend.

'Don't make him anxious, don't bother him,' said Stalin.

Mikoyan held the 'confrontation' in his office in the same building as the Little Corner where Mikhail defended himself 'passionately' against Vannikov.

'Are you insane?' he asked his former deputy who had spent nights at his home during the Terror, afraid of arrest.

'No, you were part of the same organization with me,' replied Vannikov.

Beria and Malenkov told Mikhail to wait in the corridor while they interrogated Vannikov some more. Mikhail went into Mikoyan's private lavatory (one of the perks of power). There was a shot. The three of them found Kaganovich's brother dead. By killing himself before his arrest, he saved his family. Lazar passed the test. A scapegoat for the aircraft blunders had been found.*

* * *

As these commissars travelled from Kremlin to torture chamber and back, the Germans surreptitiously deployed their legions along the Soviet frontier while Stalin channelled much of his

---

* Kaganovich was despised for not saving his brother but he buried him with honour as a Central Committee member in the Novodevichy Cemetery, not far from Nadya Stalin. Vannikov survived but remained in prison.

energy into reasserting Russian influence in the Balkans. But by March, Hitler had managed to lure Bulgaria, Romania and Yugoslavia into his camp. Then, on 26 March, the pro-German Government in Yugoslavia was overthrown, probably with the help of the NKGB and the British secret service. Hitler could not afford such a sore on his flank so the Germans prepared to invade Yugoslavia, which delayed Operation Barbarossa by a month.

On 4 April, Stalin threw himself into negotiations with the new Yugoslav Government, hoping this glitch in Hitler's plan would either drive Hitler back to the negotiating table or, at the very least, delay the invasion until 1942. When he signed a treaty with the Yugoslavs just as the Wehrmacht began to bombard Belgrade, Stalin cheerfully dismissed the threat: 'Let them come. We've strong nerves.' But Yugoslavia was Hitler's most successful *Blitzkrieg* of all: ten days later, Belgrade surrendered. Events were moving faster than the erosion of Stalin's illusions.

That same day, Yosuke Matsuoka, the Japanese Foreign Minister, arrived in Moscow on his way back from Berlin. As the *Wehrmacht* crushed the Yugoslavs, Stalin realized that he required a fresh path back to Hitler. But he was also aware of the priceless benefit of a quiet Far Eastern front if Hitler invaded. Zhukov's victory in the Far East had persuaded Tokyo that their destiny lay southwards in the juicier tidbits of the British Empire. On 14 April 1941, when Matsuoka signed a non-aggression pact with the Soviet Union, Stalin and Molotov reacted with almost febrile excitement, as if they had single-handedly changed the shape of Europe and saved Russia. Stalin exclaimed how rare it was 'to find a diplomat who speaks openly what is on his mind. What Talleyrand told Napoleon was well known, "the tongue was given the diplomat so that he could conceal his thoughts". We Russians and Bolsheviks are different ...' For once, Stalin unwound at the resulting Bacchanal, while Molotov tossed back the champagne until both were as drunk as Matsuoka.

'Stalin and I made him drink a lot,' boasted Molotov later. By 6 a.m., Matsuoka 'almost had to be carried to the train. We could barely stand up.' Stalin, Molotov and Matsuoka burst into song, rendering that Russian favourite, 'Shoumel Kamysh' that went: 'The reeds were rustling, the trees are crackling in the wind, the night was very dark ... And the lovers stayed awake all night', to guffaws. At Yaroslavsky Station, the assembled diplomats were amazed to see an intoxicated Stalin, in his greatcoat, brownvizored cap and boots, accompanied by Matsuoka and Molotov who kept saluting and shouting: 'I'm a Pioneer! I'm ready!' – the Soviet equivalent of the Boy Scout's 'Dib! Dib! Be prepared!' The Bulgarian Ambassador judged Molotov 'the least drunk'. Stalin, who had never before seen any visitor off at the station, hugged the staggering Japanese but since neither could speak the other's language, their new intimacy was expressed in embraces and grunts of 'Ah! Ah!'

Stalin was so excited that he jovially punched the minuscule bald Japanese Ambassador-General on the shoulder so hard that he 'staggered back three or four steps which caused Matsuoka to laugh in glee'. Then Stalin noticed the tall attaché Colonel Hans Krebs and, abandoning the Japanese, tapped him on the chest:

'German?' he asked. Krebs stiffened to attention, towering over Stalin who slapped him on the back, wrung his hand and said loudly, 'We've been friends with you and we'll remain friends with you.'

'I'm sure of that,' replied Krebs, though the Swedish Ambassador thought he 'did not seem so convinced of it'.* Finally lumbering back to the Japanese, Stalin again embraced the much-hugged Matsuoka, exclaiming, 'We'll organize Europe and Asia!' Arm in arm, he led Matsuoka into his carriage and waited until the train departed. Japanese diplomats escorted Stalin to his armoured Packard while their Ambassador, 'standing on a bench, waved his handkerchief and cried in a strident voice, "Thank you thank you!"'

* * *

The celebration was not over for Stalin and Molotov. As he got into the car, Stalin ordered Vlasik to call the dacha at Zubalovo and tell Svetlana, now fifteen, that she was to assemble the family for a party:

'Stalin's arriving any minute.' Svetlana ran to tell her aunt, Anna Redens, who was there with her children and Gulia Djugashvili, aged three, Yakov's daughter:

'Father's coming!' Anna Redens had not seen Stalin since the row about her husband's arrest and certainly not since his execution. All of them gathered on the steps. Minutes later, the tipsy, unusually cheerful Stalin arrived. Throwing open the car door, he hailed the twelve-year-old Leonid Redens:

* Krebs was Chief of Staff of the Wehrmacht during the last hours of the Third Reich in April 1945.

'Get in – let's go for a drive!' The driver sped them round the flower-bed. Then Stalin got out and hugged the apprehensive Anna Redens, who was holding her younger son Vladimir, now six. Stalin admired this angelic nephew: 'For the sake of such a wonderful son, let's make peace. I forgive you.' Little Gulia, Stalin's first grandchild, was brought out to be admired but she waved her arms and screamed and was swiftly taken to her room. Stalin sat at the table where he had once presided with Nadya over their young family. Cakes and chocolates were brought. Stalin took Vladimir on to his lap and started opening the chocolates: the little boy noticed his 'very beautiful long fingers'.

'You're spoiling the children by buying them presents they don't even want,' Stalin reprimanded the staff but, Vladimir says, 'in his gentle way that made him very loved by them'.

After tea, Stalin went upstairs for a catnap. He had not slept the previous night. Then Molotov, Beria and Mikoyan arrived for dinner* at which 'Stalin threw orange peel at everyone's plates. Then he threw a cork right into the ice-cream' which delighted Vladimir Alliluyev. The family could not know that Hitler's imminent invasion, and Stalin's exhaustion and paranoia, would make this the end of an era.

* * *

This was an oasis of exhilaration in a darkening sky. Torn between the wishful thinking of his powerful will – and the mounting evidence – Stalin persisted in believing that a diplomatic breakthrough with Hitler was just round the corner, even though he now knew the date of Operation Barbarossa from his spy-masters. When Stafford Cripps, the British Ambassador delivered a letter from Winston Churchill warning of the invasion, it backfired, convincing Stalin that Britain was trying to entrap Russia: 'We're being threatened with the Germans, and the Germans with the Soviet Union,' Stalin told Zhukov. 'They're playing us off against each other.'

Yet he was not completely oblivious: in the contest that Molotov called 'the great game', Stalin thought Russia might

---

* On 13 March 1941, Svetlana wrote to her father: 'My dear little Secretary! Why have you recently been coming home so late? ... Never mind, I wouldn't make my respected Secretaries miserable with my strictness. Eat as much as you like. You can drink too. I only ask you not to put vegetables or other food on the chairs in the hope that someone will sit on it. It will damage the chairs ...' This was an early hint of the brutish games that characterized Stalin's dinners after the war. 'We obey,' replied Stalin. 'Kisses to my little sparrow. Your little Secretary, Stalin.'

manage to stay out of the war until 1942. 'Only by 1943 could we meet the Germans on an equal footing,' he told Molotov. As ever Stalin was trying to read himself out of the problem, carefully studying a history of the German–French war of 1870. He and Zhdanov repeatedly quoted Bismarck's sensible dictum that Germany should never face war on two fronts: Britain remained undefeated hence Hitler would not attack. 'Hitler's not such a fool,' Stalin said, 'that he's unable to understand the difference between the USSR and Poland or France, or even England, indeed all of them put together.' Yet his entire career was a triumph of will over reality.

He persisted in believing that Hitler, the reckless gambler and world-historical 'sleepwalker', was a rational Bismarckian Great Power statesman, like himself. After the war, talking to a small group that included Dekanozov, his Ambassador to Berlin in 1941, Stalin, thinking aloud about this time, obliquely explained his behaviour: 'When you're trying to make a decision, NEVER put yourself into the mind of the other person because if you do, you can make a terrible mistake.'*

Military measures were agonizingly slow. Zhdanov and Kulik proposed removing the old armaments from the Fortified Areas and putting them in the unfinished new ones. Zhukov objected: there was no time. Stalin backed his cronies, so the fortifications were unfinished when the onslaught came.

On 20 April, Ilya Ehrenburg, the Jewish novelist whom Stalin admired, learned that his anti-German novel, *The Fall of Paris*, had been refused by the censors who were still following Stalin's orders not to offend Hitler. Four days later, Poskrebyshev called, telling him to dial a number: 'Comrade Stalin wants to talk to you.' As soon as he got through, his dogs started barking; his wife had to drive them out of the room. Stalin told him he liked the book: did Ehrenburg intend to denounce Fascism? The novelist replied that it was hard to attack the Fascists since he was not allowed to use the word. 'Just go on writing,' said Stalin jocularly, 'you and I will try to push the third part through.' It was typical of this strangely literary dictator to think this would alarm the Germans: Hitler was beyond literary nuances.

* Dekanozov repeatedly told this story to his young son, Reginald, who recorded it in his Notes before his own recent death. It has never been published. The author is most grateful to Nadya Dekanozova of Tbilisi, Georgia, for making this source available.

Even Stalin's inner circle could smell war now. It was so pervasive that Zhdanov suggested they cancel the May Day Parade in case it was too 'provocative'. Stalin did not cancel it but he placed Dekanozov, the Ambassador to Germany, right next to him on the Mausoleum to signal his warmth towards Berlin.

On 4 May, he sent another signal to Hitler that he was ready to talk: Stalin replaced Molotov as Premier, promoting Zhdanov's protégé, Nikolai Voznesensky, the brash economic maestro, as his deputy on the inner Buro. At thirty-eight, Voznesensky's rise had been meteoric and this angered the others: Mikoyan, who was particularly sore, thought he was 'economically educated but a professor-type without practical experience'. This good-looking, intelligent but arrogant Leningrader was 'naïvely happy with his appointment', but Beria and Malenkov already resented the acerbic technocrat: Stalin's 'promoting a teacher to give us lessons', Malenkov whispered to Beria. Henceforth, Stalin ruled as Premier through his deputies as Lenin had, balancing the rivalry between Beria and Malenkov, on the one hand, and Zhdanov and Voznesensky, on the other. Stalin expressed his emergence on the world stage sartorially, discarding his baggy trousers and boots. He 'started wearing well ironed, untucked ones with lace-up bootkins'.

Finally, Stalin prepared the military for the possibility of war. On 5 May, he saw only one visitor: Zhdanov, just promoted to Stalin's Party Deputy, visited him for twenty-five minutes. At 6 p.m. the two men walked from the Little Corner to the Great Kremlin Palace where two thousand officers awaited them: Stalin entered with Zhdanov, Timoshenko and Zhukov. President Kalinin introduced a 'severe' Stalin who praised the modern mechanization of his 'new army'. Then he eccentrically attributed the French defeat to amorous disappointment: the French were 'so dizzy with self-satisfaction' that they disdained their own warriors to the extent that 'girls wouldn't even marry soldiers'. Was the German army unbeatable? 'There are no invincible armies in the world' but war was coming. 'If VM Molotov … can delay the start of war for 2–3 months, this'll be our good fortune.' At the dinner, he toasted: 'Long live the dynamic offensive policy of the Soviet State,' adding, 'anyone who doesn't recognize this is a Philistine and a fool.' This was a relief to the military: Stalin was not living in cloud cuckoo land. The State was ready to fight, or was it? The State was not sure.*

The magnates tried to steer a path between Stalin's infallibility and Hitler's reality: the absurdity of explaining how the army had to be ready to fight an offensive war which was definitely not going to happen, while claiming this was not a change of policy, was so ridiculous that they tied themselves in knots of Stalinist sophistry and Neroesque folly. 'We need a new type of propaganda,' declared Zhdanov at the Supreme Military Council. 'There is only one step between war and peace. So our propaganda can't be peaceful.'

'We ourselves designed the propaganda this way,' Budyonny exploded, so they had to explain why it was changing.

'We're only altering the slogan,' claimed Zhdanov.

'As if we were going to war tomorrow!' sneered the pusillanimous Malenkov, eighteen days before the invasion.

On 7 May, Schulenburg, secretly opposed to Hitler's invasion, breakfasted with the Soviet Ambassador to Berlin, Dekanozov, whom he ambiguously tried to warn. They met thrice but 'he did not warn,' said Molotov later, 'he hinted and pushed for diplomatic negotiations.' Dekanozov informed Stalin who was becoming ever more bad-tempered and nervous. 'So, disinformation has now reached ambassadorial level,' he growled. Dekanozov disagreed.

'How could you allow yourself to argue with Comrade Stalin! He knows more and can see further than all of us!' Voroshilov threatened Dekanozov during a recess.

On 10 May, Stalin learned of Deputy Führer Hess's quixotic peace flight to Scotland. His magnates, remembered Khrushchev who was in the office that day, were all understandably convinced that Hess's mission was aimed at Moscow. But Stalin was finally willing to prepare for war, admittedly in a manner so timid that it was barely effective. On 12 May, Stalin allowed the generals to

---

* But the speeches have spawned a grand debate about whether Stalin was planning a pre-emptive strike against Hitler: the so-called Suvorov Debate following Victor Suvorov's article in June 1985. Suvorov argued that Stalin was about to attack Hitler because of the partial mobilization and build-up on Western borders, the proximity of airfields, and because General Zhukov produced such a plan of attack. His view is now discredited. It now seems that the real view of the General Staff, including General Vasilevsky, was that they would have to retreat much deeper into their territory – hence Vasilevsky's proposal to move airfields and infrastructure back to the Volga, a proposal attacked as 'defeatist' by Kulik and Mekhlis. However, Stalin always kept an offensive war as a real possibility as well as an ideological necessity. As for the speeches, they were designed purely to raise the morale of the army and display a measure of realism about the Soviet situation.

strengthen the borders, calling up 500,000 reserves, but was terrified of offending the Germans. When Timoshenko reported German reconnaissance flights, Stalin mused, 'I'm not sure Hitler knows about those flights.' On the 24th, he refused to take any further measures.

The paralysis struck again. Stalin never apologized but he very indirectly acknowledged his mistakes when he later thanked the Russian people for their 'patience'. But he blamed most of his blunders on others, admitting that he 'trusted too much in cavalrymen'. Zhukov confessed his own failures: 'Possibly I did not have enough influence.' This was not the real reason for his quiescence. If he had demanded mobilization, Stalin would have asked: 'On what basis? Well, Beria, take him to your dungeons!' Kulik caught the attitude of most soldiers: 'This is high politics. It's not our business.'

The intelligence was now flooding in. Earlier it had been presented in an ambiguous way but now it was surely clear that something ominous was darkening the Western border. Merkulov daily reported to Stalin who was now defying an avalanche of information from all manner of sources. On 9 June, when Timoshenko and Zhukov mentioned the array of intelligence, Stalin tossed their papers at them and snarled, 'And I have different documents.' He mocked Richard Sorge, the masterspy in Tokyo who used his amorous and sybaritic appetites to conceal his peerless intelligence-gathering: 'There's this bastard who's set up factories and brothels in Japan and even deigned to report the date of the German attack as 22 June. Are you suggesting I should believe him too?'

32

The Countdown: 22 June 1941

On 13 June, Timoshenko and Zhukov, themselves depressed and baffled, alerted Stalin to further border activities. 'We'll think it over,' snapped Stalin who next day lost his temper with Zhukov's proposal of mobilization: 'That means war. Do you two understand that or not?' Then he asked how many divisions there were in the border areas:

Zhukov told him there were 149.

'Well, isn't that enough? The Germans don't have so many ...' But the Germans were on a war footing, replied Zhukov. 'You can't believe everything in intelligence reports,' said Stalin.

On the 16th, Merkulov confirmed the final decision to attack, which came from agent 'Starshina' in Luftwaffe headquarters.* 'Tell the "source" in the Staff of the German Air Force to fuck his mother!' he scrawled to Merkulov. 'This is no source but a disinformer. J.St.' Even Molotov struggled to convince himself: 'They'd be fools to attack us,' he told Admiral Kuznetsov.

Two days later, at a three-hour meeting described by Timoshenko, he and Zhukov beseeched Stalin for a full alert, with the *Vozhd* fidgeting and tapping his pipe on the table, and the magnates agreeing with Stalin's maniacal delusions or else brooding in sullen silence, the only way of protesting they possessed. Stalin suddenly leapt to his feet and shouted at Zhukov:

'Have you come to scare us with war, or do you want a war because you're not sufficiently decorated or your rank isn't high enough?'

Zhukov paled and sat down but Timoshenko warned Stalin again, which aroused a frenzy:

'It's all Timoshenko's work, he's preparing everyone for war. He

---

* On 14 June, Hitler held his last military conference before the beginning of Barbarossa, with the generals arriving at the Chancellery at different times so as not to raise suspicion. On the 16th, he summoned Goebbels to brief him.

ought to have been shot, but I've known him as a good soldier since the Civil War.'

Timoshenko replied he was only repeating Stalin's own speech that war was inevitable.

'So you see,' Stalin retorted to the Politburo. 'Timoshenko's a fine man with a big head but apparently a small brain,' and he held up his thumb. 'I said it for the people, we have to raise their alertness, while you have to realize that Germany will never fight Russia on her own. You must understand this.' Stalin stormed out leaving an excruciating silence but then he 'opened the door and stuck his pock-marked face round it and uttered in a loud voice: "If you're going to provoke the Germans on the frontier by moving troops there without our permission, then heads will roll, mark my words" – and he slammed the door.'

Stalin summoned Khrushchev, who should have been monitoring the Ukrainian border, to Moscow and would not let him leave: 'Stalin kept ordering me to postpone my departure: "Wait," he said, "Don't be in such a hurry. There's no need to rush back."' Khrushchev held a special place in Stalin's affections: perhaps his irrepressible optimism, sycophantic devotion and practical cunning made him a useful companion at such a moment. Stalin was in a 'state of confusion, anxiety, demoralization, even paralysis', according to Khrushchev, soothing his anxiety with sleepless nights and heavy drinking at endless Kuntsevo dinners. 'You could feel the static,' said Khrushchev, 'the discharge of tension.' On Friday the 20th, Khrushchev finally said,

'I have to go. The war is about to break out. It may catch me here in Moscow or on the way back to the Ukraine.'

'Right,' said Stalin. 'Just go.'

On the 19th, Zhdanov, who was running the country with Stalin and Molotov, left for one and a half months' holiday. Suffering from asthma, and Stalin's boa-constrictor-like friendship, he was exhausted. 'But I have a bad foreboding the Germans could invade,' Zhdanov told Stalin.

'The Germans have already missed the best moment,' replied Stalin. 'Apparently they'll attack in 1942. Go on holiday.'* Mikoyan thought he was naïve to go but Molotov shrugged:

---

* Perhaps Stalin had encouraged Zhdanov to bolster his own wavering confidence: when Dmitrov passed on an Austrian warning, Stalin replied that there could not be anything to worry about if Zhdanov, who ran the Leningrad Military District and the navy, had gone on holiday.

'A sick man has to rest.' So 'we went on holiday', remembers Zhdanov's son Yury. 'We arrived in Sochi on Saturday 21 June.'

On 20 June, Dekanozov, back in Berlin, warned Beria firmly that the attack was imminent. Beria threatened his protégé while Stalin muttered that 'Slow Kartvelian' 'wasn't clever enough to work it out'. Beria forwarded the 'disinformation' to Stalin with the sycophantic but slightly mocking note:

'My people and I, Joseph Vissarionovich, firmly remember your wise prediction: Hitler will not attack us in 1941!'

At about 7.30 p.m., Mikoyan, the Deputy Premier in charge of the merchant navy, was called by the harbourmaster of Riga: twenty-five German ships were setting sail, even though many had not yet unloaded. He rushed along to Stalin's office where some of the leaders were gathered.

'That'll be a provocation,' Stalin angrily told Mikoyan. 'Let them leave.' The Politburo were alarmed – but of course said nothing. Molotov was deeply worried: 'The situation is unclear, a great game is being played,' he confided to the Bulgarian Communist Dmitrov, on Saturday 21 June. 'Not everything depends on us.' General Golikov brought Stalin further evidence: 'This information,' Stalin wrote on it, 'is an English provocation. Find out who the author is and punish him.' The fire brigade reported that the German Embassy was burning documents. The British Government and even Mao Tse-tung (a surprising source, via the Comintern) sent warnings. Stalin telephoned Khrushchev to warn him the war might begin the next day and asked Tiulenev, the commander of Moscow:

'How do things stand with the anti-aircraft defence of Moscow? Note the situation's tense ... Bring the troops of Moscow's anti-aircraft defence to 75 per cent of combat readiness.'

Saturday the 21st was a warm and uneasy day in Moscow. The schools had broken up for the holidays. Dynamo Moscow, the football team, lost its game. The theatres were showing *Rigoletto*, *La Traviata* and Chekhov's *Three Sisters*. Stalin and the Politburo sat all day, coming and going. By early evening, Stalin was deeply disturbed by the persistently ominous reports that even his Terror could not disperse. Molotov joined him again around 6.30.

Outside the Little Corner, Poskrebyshev sat by the open window, sipping Narzan water: he called Chadaev, the young Sovnarkom assistant. 'Something important?' whispered Chadaev.

'I'd say so,' replied Poskrebyshev. 'The Boss talked to Timoshenko, he was very agitated ... They're waiting for ... you know ... the German attack ...'

At about seven, Stalin ordered Molotov to summon Schulenburg to protest about the German reconnaissance flights – and find out what he could. The Count sped into the Kremlin. Molotov hurried along to his office in the same building. Meanwhile* Timoshenko telephoned to report that a German deserter had revealed the German invasion plan for dawn. Stalin swung between the force of reality and the self-delusion of his infallibility.

In Molotov's office, Schulenburg was relieved to see that the Foreign Commissar was still oblivious to the enormity of his country's plight. The Russian asked him why Germany seemed dissatisfied with their Soviet allies. And why had the women and children of the German Embassy left Moscow?

'Not ALL the women,' said Schulenburg. 'My wife is still in town.' Molotov gave what the Ambassador's aide, Hilger, called a 'resigned shrug of the shoulders' and returned to Stalin's office.

Timoshenko then arrived, along with most of the magnates: Voroshilov, Beria, Malenkov and the powerful young Deputy Premier Voznesensky. At 8.15 p.m., Timoshenko returned to the Defence Commissariat whence he informed Stalin that a second deserter had warned that war would begin at 4 a.m. Stalin called him back. Timoshenko arrived at 8.50 with Zhukov and Budyonny, Deputy Defence Commissar, who knew Stalin much better than they did and was less frightened of the *Vozhd*. Budyonny admitted that he did not know what was happening at the frontier since he was only in command of the home front. The outspoken Budyonny had played an ambiguous role in the Terror but even then he was willing to speak his mind, a rare quality in those circles. Stalin appointed him commander of the Reserve Army. Then Mekhlis, newly restored to his old job – head of the army's Political Department, Stalin's military enforcer, joined this funereal vigil.

---

* This account is based on the memoirs of Molotov, Mikoyan, Zhukov, Timoshenko, Hilger and others but the times are based on the Kremlin Logbook which is clearly incomplete but since the fear, uncertainty and chaos of that night ensured that everyone gave different times for their meetings, it at least provides a framework. Zhukov is not shown as attending the first meeting at 7.05 and Vatutin, who was deputy Chief of Staff and appears in Zhukov's account, is not mentioned at all. Nor is Mikoyan. That does not mean they were not there: in the manic comings and goings, even Poskrebyshev could be forgiven a few mistakes.

'Well what now?' the pacing Stalin asked them. There was silence. The Politburo sat like dummies. Timoshenko raised his voice: 'All troops in frontier districts' must be placed on 'full battle alert!'

'Didn't they send the deserter on purpose to provoke us?' said Stalin but then he ordered Zhukov: 'Read this out.' When Zhukov reached his order of High Alert, Stalin interrupted, 'It would be premature to issue that order now. It might still be possible to settle the situation by peaceful means.' They had to avoid any provocations. Zhukov obeyed his instructions exactly – he knew the alternative: 'Beria's dungeon!'

The magnates now spoke up diffidently, agreeing with the generals that the troops had to be put on alert 'just in case'. Stalin nodded at the generals who hurried next door to Poskrebyshev's office to redraft the order. When they returned, the obsessive editor watered it down even more. The generals rushed back to the Defence Commissariat to transmit the order to the military districts: 'A surprise attack by the Germans is possible during 22–23 June ... The task of our forces is to refrain from any kind of provocative action ...' This was only completed just after midnight on Sunday 22 June.

Stalin told Budyonny that the war would probably start tomorrow. Budyonny left at ten, while Timoshenko, Zhukov and Mekhlis left later. Stalin kept pacing. Beria left, presumably to check the latest intelligence reports, and reported back at ten-forty. At eleven, the leaders moved upstairs to Stalin's apartment where they sat in the dining room. 'Stalin kept reassuring us that Hitler would not begin the war,' claimed Mikoyan.

'I think Hitler's trying to provoke us,' said Stalin, according to Mikoyan. 'He surely hasn't decided to make war?'

Zhukov phoned again at twelve-thirty: a third deserter, a Communist labourer from Berlin named Alfred Liskov, had swum the Pruth to report that the order to invade had been read to his unit. Stalin checked that the High Alert order was being transmitted, then commanded that Liskov should be shot 'for his disinformation'. Even on such a night, it was impossible to break the Stalinist routine of brutality – and entertainment: the Politburo headed out through the Borovitsky Gate to Kuntsevo in a convoy of limousines, speeding through the empty streets with their NKGB escorts. The generals, watched by Mekhlis, remained tensely in the Defence Commissariat. But elsewhere in the city, the weary commissars, guards and typists who waited every night (even Saturdays) until Stalin left the Kremlin, could stagger home to sleep. By Stalin's standards, it was early.

Molotov drove to the Foreign Commissariat to send a final telegram to Dekanozov in Berlin, who was already trying to get through to Ribbentrop, to put the questions Schulenburg had failed to answer. Molotov then joined the others at Kuntsevo: 'we might even have watched a film,' he said. At around 2 a.m., after an hour or so of dining, drinking and talking (the memories of Zhukov, Molotov and Mikoyan are confused about that night), they headed back to their Kremlin apartments.*

Far away, all along the Soviet border, *Luftwaffe* bombers were heading for their targets. On the same day that Napoleon's Grand Army had invaded Russia 129 years earlier, Hitler's over three million soldiers – Germans, Croats, Finns, Romanians, Hungarians, Italians and even Spaniards backed by 3,600 tanks, 600,000 motorized vehicles, 7,000 artillery pieces, 2,500 aircraft and about 625,000 horses, were crossing the border to engage the Soviet forces of almost equal strength, as many as 14,000 tanks (2,000 of them modern), 34,000 guns and over 8,000 planes. The greatest war of all time was about to begin in the duel between those two brutal and reckless egomaniacs. And both were probably still asleep.

---

* At roughly the same time, Hitler decided to snatch an hour's sleep before the invasion started: 'The fortune of war must now decide.' Earlier, an overtired and anxious Hitler had been pacing up and down the office with Goebbels working out the proclamation to be read to the German people the next day. 'This cancerous growth has to be burned out,' Hitler told Goebbels, 'Stalin will fall.' Liskov, the German defector, was still being interrogated two and a half hours later when the invasion began: he was not shot. The events of that night were so dramatic that the participants all recall different times: Molotov thought he had left Stalin at midnight, Mikoyan at 3 a.m. Molotov claimed Zhukov, who is used as a source by most historians, placed events later to amplify his own role. At least some of the confusion is due to the hour difference between German and Russian times: this account is based on Russian time. But it is easier to pace events according to the Teutonic efficiency of the German invasion that started at 3.30 a.m. German summertime (4.30 a.m. Russian time) and the arrival of Schulenberg's instructions from Berlin. It is clear from the three memoirs that the group moved from Stalin's office, to the apartment and then to Kuntsevo in the course of the hours between 9 p.m. and 3 a.m.

33

Optimism and Breakdown

Stalin had retired when Zhukov called Kuntsevo.

'Who's calling?' the sleepy voice of the NKGB general answered.

'Zhukov. Chief of Staff. Please connect me to Comrade Stalin. It's urgent.'

'What, right now? Comrade Stalin's sleeping.'

'Wake him immediately,' Zhukov told the duty officer. 'The Germans are bombing our cities.'

There was a silence. Zhukov waited for what seemed like an eternity. He was not the only one trying to report the invasion to Stalin, but the generals remained as petrified of their own leader as they were of the Germans. At 4.17 a.m. (Russian time) the Black Sea command called Zhukov at the Defence Commissariat to report a swarm of bombers. At 4.30 a.m. the Western Front was on the line, at 4.40, the Baltic was under attack. Around the same time, Admiral Kuznetsov was telephoned by his Sebastopol commander: the German bombing had started. Kuznetsov immediately phoned the Kremlin where he encountered the bureaucratic narrow-mindedness that is so characteristic of tyrannies. It was meant to be a secret that Stalin lived at Kuntsevo, so the officer replied:

'Comrade Stalin is not here and I don't know where he is.'

'I have an exceedingly important message which I must immediately relay to Comrade Stalin personally ...'

'I can't help you in any way,' he replied and hung up, so Kuznetsov called Timoshenko who, deluged with such calls, was afraid to inform Stalin. Kuznetsov tried all the numbers he had for Stalin but to no avail, so he called the Kremlin again:

'I request you to inform Comrade Stalin that German planes are bombing Sebastopol. This is war!'

'I shall report it to the proper person.' A few minutes later the Admiral discovered who 'the proper person' was: flabby, quiet-spoken Malenkov called, asking in 'a dissatisfied, irritated voice':

'Do you understand what you're reporting?' Even as German bombers strafed Kiev and Sebastopol and as their troops crossed the borders, Stalin's courtiers were still trying to bully away reality. Malenkov rang off and called Sebastopol to check the story.

Timoshenko was not alone in his office: Mekhlis, 'the Shark', spent the night with the generals. Like Malenkov, he was determined that there would be no invasion that night. When the head of anti-aircraft artillery, Voronov, hurried in to report, Timoshenko was so nervous that he handed him a notebook and absurdly 'told me to present my report in writing' so that if they were all arrested for treason, he would be responsible for his crimes. Mekhlis sidled up behind him and read over his shoulder to check that he was writing exactly what he had said. Then Mekhlis made him sign it. Timoshenko ordered anti-aircraft forces not to respond: Voronov realized 'he did not believe the war had begun'.

Timoshenko was called by the Deputy Commander of the Western Special Military District, Boldin, who frantically reported that the Germans were advancing. Timoshenko ordered him not to react.

'What do you mean?' shouted Boldin. 'Our troops are retreating, towns are in flames, people are dying ...'

'Joseph Vissarionovich believes this could be a provocation by some German generals.' Timoshenko's instinct was to persuade someone else to break the news to Stalin. He asked Budyonny: 'The Germans are bombing Sebastopol. Should I or shouldn't I tell Stalin?'

'Inform him immediately!'

'You call him,' beseeched Timoshenko. 'I'm afraid.'

'No, you call him,' retorted Budyonny. 'You're Defence Commissar!' Finally, Budyonny agreed and started calling Kuntsevo. Timoshenko, who could not spread this task widely enough, ordered Zhukov to telephone Stalin too.

Zhukov was still waiting on the line to Kuntsevo as Stalin was roused. Three minutes later, he came to the phone. Zhukov reported and asked permission to counter-attack. There was silence. He could just hear Stalin breathing.

'Did you understand me?' asked Zhukov. 'Comrade Stalin?' He could still only hear heavy breathing. Then Stalin spoke: 'Bring Timoshenko to the Kremlin. Tell Poskrebyshev to summon the Politburo.' Mikoyan and the Politburo were already being rung:

'It's war!' Now Budyonny reached Stalin at the dacha and added that Riga was being bombed as well. Stalin called Poskrebyshev, who was sleeping in his study: 'The bombing's started.'*

Stalin sped into town: he had banned the Politburo from staying in their dachas so they were already there. Stalin rode up in the lift to the second floor, hurried along the red-carpeted corridors with their wooden panelling and snapped at Poskrebyshev as he walked into his office: 'Get the others here now.' Zhukov claimed the Politburo assembled at 4.30 a.m. but Molotov thought it was earlier. However, Stalin's office logbook shows the meeting started at 5.45 a.m., just over an hour after the full German attack. Molotov, who lived in the same building, not far from Stalin's flat, arrived first, swiftly joined by Beria, Timoshenko, Zhukov and Mekhlis.

Stalin did not collapse: Mikoyan thought he was 'subdued'. Zhukov noticed he was 'pale' and 'bewildered' sitting at the green baize table, 'a pipe in his hand'. Voronov thought him 'depressed and nervy', but he was in command of his office at least. Outside the fronts were in anarchy. But here, Chadaev, the Sovnarkom assistant, remembered that Stalin 'spoke slowly, choosing his words carefully, occasionally his voice broke down. When he had finished, everybody was silent for some time and so was he.' But amazingly, he still persisted in the idea that the war might be 'a provocation by the German officers', convinced that Hitler might have a Tukhachevsky among the high command of the *Wehrmacht*. 'Hitler simply does not know about it.' Stalin would not order resistance until he had heard from Berlin.

'That scoundrel Ribbentrop tricked us,' he said to Mikoyan several times, still not blaming Hitler. It was now almost five: Stalin ordered Molotov: 'We have to call the German Embassy immediately.' Molotov called from Stalin's desk, laden with telephones, and stammered, 'Tell him to come.' Schulenburg had already contacted Molotov's office, asking to see the Foreign Commissar. 'I started from Stalin's office upstairs to my own office' which took about three minutes. Schulenburg, accompanied by Hilger, arrived in the office overlooking Ivan the Terrible's church for the second time that night – and the last time in his career. The

---

* The telephone was ringing in Zhdanov's dacha in Sochi that morning too: 'My mother came into my room first thing,' recalled Yury Zhdanov, 'and she said, "It's war!" and we headed back to Moscow with my father.'

summery Kremlin was bathed in the first light and fragrant with the acacias and roses of the Alexandrovsky Gardens.*

Schulenburg read out the telegram that had arrived at 3 a.m. Berlin time: the concentrations of Soviet forces had forced the Reich to take military 'counter measures'. He finished. Molotov's face twitched with disbelief and anger. Finally, he stammered:

'Is this supposed to be a declaration of war?' Schulenburg could not speak either: he shrugged sadly. Molotov's anger overcame his shock: 'The message I have just been given couldn't mean anything but a declaration of war since German troops have already crossed the border and Soviet cities like Odessa, Kiev and Minsk have been bombed by German aircraft for an hour and a half.' Molotov was shouting now. This was 'a breach of confidence unprecedented in history'. Now Germany had unleashed a terrible war. 'Surely we haven't deserved that.' There was nothing more to say: Count von der Schulenburg, who would be executed by Hitler for his part in the July 1944 plot, shook hands and departed, passing limousines rolling into the Kremlin bearing generals. Molotov rushed to Stalin's office where he announced: 'Germany's declared war on us.'

Stalin subsided into his chair, 'lost in thought'. The silence was 'long and pregnant'. Stalin 'looked tired, worn out', recalled Chadaev. 'His pock-marked face was drawn and haggard.' This, recalled Zhukov, 'was the only time I saw Stalin depressed'. Then he roused himself with a wildly optimistic slogan: 'The enemy will be beaten all along the line' – and he turned to the generals: 'What do you recommend?'

Zhukov suggested that the frontier districts must 'hold up' the Germans –

'Annihilate,' interrupted Timoshenko, 'not "hold up".'

'Issue a directive,' said Stalin, still under the spell of his grand delusion. 'Do not cross the border.' Timoshenko, not Stalin,

* Simultaneously, in Berlin, Soviet Ambassador Dekanozov was summoned to the Foreign Ministry. As he arrived, he noticed that the German press was present to record the moment. Adopting his most 'freezing manner', Ribbentrop received him in the office of Prince Bismarck, the statesman who had warned Germany against a war on two fronts and who had been quoted to this effect so often by Stalin and Zhdanov. Apparently drunk, 'purple-faced' and 'swaying a little', Ribbentrop read his statement. 'I deeply regret this …' replied Dekanozov. He departed without shaking hands. But as he was leaving, Ribbentrop trotted after him, whispering that he had tried to stop Hitler from launching this war but he would not listen to anyone. 'Tell Moscow I was against the attack,' he hissed. Ribbentrop sensed the Soviet Pact had been the climax of his career.

signed the series of directives that were issued throughout the morning. Chadaev noticed the mood improve: 'on that first day of war, everyone was … quite optimistic.'

Yet despite everything, Stalin persisted in clinging on to shards of his shattered illusion: he said he hoped to settle things diplomatically. No one dared contradict this absurdity except Molotov, his comrade since 1912 who was one of the last who could openly argue with him.

'No!' replied Molotov emphatically. It was war and 'nothing could be done about it'. The scale of the invasion and Molotov's stark insistence managed to shake the reality into Stalin. When Dmitrov, the Comintern leader, arrived, the outer office was a hive of activity with Poskrebyshev, Mekhlis (in uniform again), Marshal Timoshenko, Admiral Kuznetsov at work – and Beria 'giving orders on the phone'. Inside, he noticed Stalin's 'striking calmness, resoluteness, confidence …'

'They fell on us, without making any claims, making a vile attack like bandits,' he told Dmitrov. The 'bandits' had the advantage of total surprise. The Soviet front line had been overwhelmed. Stalin's armies were strongest in the south. However, while the Germans thrust towards Leningrad and the Ukraine, Hitler's strongest army group was meant to take Moscow. Army Group Centre's two pincers shattered the Soviet Western Front, under Colonel-General Pavlov whose counter-attack was tossed aside as the Panzers charged towards Minsk and the road to Moscow.

Stalin reacted with a steady stream of orders that admittedly bore little relation to the disaster at the front: none the less, Beria, Malenkov, Mikoyan, Kaganovich and Voroshilov came, went and returned to the Little Corner throughout the morning so that by midday, all of them had been there at least twice, Beria thrice. Mekhlis was one of the first to arrive, Kulik came later. The *Vozhd* ordered Kaganovich to prepare the trains to remove factories and 20 million people from the front – nothing was to fall into German hands. Mikoyan was to supply the armies.

Stalin retained minute control over everything, from the size and shape of bayonets to the *Pravda* headlines and who wrote the articles, losing neither his jealousy of others' glory nor his flawless instinct for self-preservation. When General Koniev received several mentions in the newspapers during the first week, Stalin found the time to telephone the editor and snap: 'You've printed enough on Koniev.' When the same editor asked if he would publish one writer whom Stalin had savagely denounced before the war, he replied: 'You may print. Comrade Adveenko has atoned.' Meanwhile he himself deliberately disappeared from the public eye. His appearances on the front page of *Pravda* fell dramatically. Amazingly, the USSR possessed no Supreme Command: at nine that morning, Stalin created an early version, the *Stavka*. Naturally, the decree named Stalin as Commander-in-Chief but he crossed it out and put Timoshenko's name instead.

Everyone agreed that the Government had to announce the war. Mikoyan and the others proposed Stalin should do it but he refused: 'Let Molotov speak.' After all, Molotov had signed the treaty with Ribbentrop. The entourage disagreed – surely the people would not understand why they were not hearing from the Premier. Stalin insisted that he would speak another time. 'He didn't want to be first to speak,' said Molotov. 'He needed a clear picture ... He couldn't respond like an automaton to everything ... He was a human being after all.'

Molotov, who still regarded himself as a political journalist, immediately set to work on the announcement but Stalin dominated the drafting for he possessed the gift of distilling complex ideas into the simple and stirring phrases that henceforth characterized his war speeches. At midday, Molotov drove to the Central Telegraph Office on Gorky Street, just up from the Kremlin. He mastered his stammer and delivered the famous speech in his flat but quavering voice:

'Our cause is just. The enemy will be crushed. Victory will be ours.'

When Molotov returned, Stalin walked up to his office to congratulate him: 'Well, you sounded a bit flustered but the speech went well.' Molotov needed praise: he was much vainer than he looked. Just then the *vertushka* rang: it was Timoshenko reporting on the chaos of the frontier where the commanders, especially Pavlov on the vital Western Front that covered Minsk and the road to Moscow, had lost contact with their troops. Stalin fulminated about how 'unexpected attack is very important in war. It gives the initiative to the attackers ... You must strictly prevent ... any panic. Call the commanders, clear the situation and report ... How long will you need? Two hours, well not more ... How is the situation with Pavlov?' But Pavlov, bearing the brunt of the German attack, 'has no connection with the staff of his armies ...'

Attended by Molotov, Malenkov and Beria, the threesome who were to spend most of the war in the Little Corner, Stalin gradually learned of the startling German successes and the Soviet collapse. During that first week, Beria, master of the Special Department, the *Osobyi Otdel*, the secret police in every military unit responsible for hunting down traitors, met Stalin fifteen times while Mekhlis, political boss of the army, virtually resided in the Little Corner: terror was Stalin's solution to defeat. But these two, along with Civil War cronies like Voroshilov and Kulik, were little comfort when Timoshenko reported that almost a thousand planes had been eliminated on the ground by the end of the day.

'Surely the German air force didn't manage to reach every single airfield?' Stalin asked pathetically.

'Unfortunately it did.' But it was the disaster of Pavlov's Western Front that reduced Stalin to wild, if impotent, fury:

'This is a monstrous crime. Those responsible must lose their heads.' Stalin abruptly ordered his most trusted cronies to travel to the fronts and find out what was happening. When they hesitated, Stalin shouted:

'Immediately.' Chief of Staff Zhukov headed for the South-Western Front but asked who would run things in his absence.

'Don't waste time,' scoffed Stalin. 'We'll manage somehow.' Malenkov and Budyonny, a strange coupling, the bloodless bureaucrat and the swashbuckling Cossack, flew to Briansk; Kulik to the Western Front.

The whirlwind almost consumed them: in a series of semi-farcical fiascos, all were lucky to escape with their lives. Meanwhile, in the Little Corner, Stalin's hours were as inconsistent as the performance of his armies. Stalin and Beria were the last two to leave at 4.45 that afternoon, having been up since dawn. They still believed their counter-offensives would throw the battle on to enemy territory. They must have grabbed some sleep but Stalin was back in the office at 3.20 on the morning of 23 June to meet Molotov, Mekhlis and Beria until the early hours. By the 25th, faced with the free fall of the fronts, Stalin was spending the whole night, from 1.00 to 5.50 a.m., in the office in a state of rising outrage as one by one his special envoys disappeared into the cataclysm.

'That good-for-nothing Kulik needs a kick in the arse,' he said. Only Zhukov, brutal, courageous and energetic, managed to counter-attack on the South-Western Front, brandishing the Stalinist ruthlessness that distinguished him throughout the war: 'Arrest immediately', reads one of his typical orders to the Special Departments about retreating officers. 'And bring them to trial urgently as traitors and cowards.'

The boozy buffoon Marshal Kulik, whose war was to be a chronicle of tragicomical blunders, outfitted himself in a pilot's fetching leathers, cap and goggles and arrived on the Western Front like a Stalinist Biggles on the evening of 23 June. Bewildered by the rout of the Tenth Army, he was cut off, surrounded and almost captured. He had to escape in fancy dress. 'The behaviour of Marshal Kulik was incomprehensible,' the regimental Commissar denounced Kulik to Mekhlis. 'He ordered everyone to take off their regalia, throw out documents and then change into peasant garb,' a disguise he was more than capable of carrying off. Burning his marshal's uniform (and his Biggles outfit), 'he proposed to throw away our arms and he told me personally to throw away my medals and documents ... Kulik rode on a horse-drawn cart along the very road just taken by German tanks ...' The Western Front itself was disintegrating. Ailing Marshal Shaposhnikov collapsed from the strain. Headquarters lost him too.

Like a game of hide-and-seek, in which more and more children are sent to find the ones hiding, Stalin sent Voroshilov to find Kulik and Shaposhnikov. On 26 June, the 'First Marshal' arrived in Mogilev on a special train but was unable to find either the Western Front or the two marshals. Eventually his adjutant came upon a pitiful sight that looked more like a 'gypsy encampment' than a headquarters and espied Shaposhnikov on the ground covered by a coat, looking very dead. Then he saw Pavlov, the commander, lying alone beneath a tree eating *kasha* out of a mess-tin in the pouring rain which he did not seem to have noticed. Shaposhnikov stirred. The adjutant realized he was alive and introduced himself. Shaposhnikov, wincing with pain, thanked God that Voroshilov had come and started to shave. Pavlov, who had now finished his *kasha*, was dazed and desperate:

'I'm done for!' Voroshilov descended on the camp with an explosion of threats, while sending his adjutant to hunt for Kulik. Then the two marshals retired to the special train to decide what to do about poor Pavlov. Voroshilov ordered dinner: a cook brought in ham, bread and tea, a repast that evidently disappointed the

Marshal because he became furious, screaming for his cook, Comrade Franz, who emerged and stood to attention. Voroshilov demanded to know how he dared serve such a meal for two marshals.

'Why've you sliced the ham? Do people cut ham this way? In a goddamn inn, they serve better ham!' Voroshilov summoned Pavlov, berating him for his failures. In another of those moments that reveal the importance of personal vendetta, he reminded Pavlov that he had once complained to Stalin about him. Pavlov fell to his knees, begged for forgiveness and kissed the Marshal's boots. Voroshilov returned to Moscow.

At dawn on 4 July, Mekhlis arrested Pavlov for treason:

'We ask you to confirm arrest and prosecution,' Mekhlis reported. Stalin welcomed it 'as one of the true ways to improve the health of the Front'. Under torture, Pavlov implicated General Meretskov who was immediately arrested too. Before Pavlov's 'trial', Poskrebyshev brought Stalin the '[Draft] Sentence'. Seeing that it contained the traditional inventions, Stalin told Poskrebyshev: 'I approve the sentence but tell Ulrikh to get rid of all that rubbish about "conspiratorial activity". The case shouldn't drag out. No appeal. And then inform the fronts so that they know that defeatists will be punished without mercy.' Mikoyan (and presumably the rest of the Politburo) approved of the sentence and still did so thirty years later when he wrote his memoirs: 'It was a pity to lose him but it was justified.' On 22 July, the four commanding officers of the Western Front were shot. So many telegrams flooded in asking permission to shoot traitors, they blocked up the wires in Mekhlis's office. That day, he told them to sentence and shoot their own traitors.

Stalin was absorbing the scale of the catastrophe. The fronts were out of control: the Nazis were approaching Minsk, the air force decimated, thirty divisions shattered. On the 26th Stalin urgently recalled Zhukov from the South-Western Front: the Chief of Staff found Timoshenko and General Vatutin standing to attention before Stalin, their 'eyes red from lack of sleep'. Stalin ordered: 'Put your heads together and tell me what can be done.'* He gave them forty minutes to propose new lines of defence.

* * *

---

* Some time that day, the Politburo secretly ordered Lenin's body to be removed from the Mausoleum and despatched to Tyumen in Siberia.

Yet even in these frantic times, Stalin remembered his own family. On 25 June, Stalin was meeting with Timoshenko to discuss a 'situation that was extremely serious on all fronts' when the Defence Commissar plucked up the courage to ask if Yakov Djugashvili, the leader's oldest son by his first marriage who had always disappointed him and whom he had treated callously, should be sent to the front, as he requested. Stifling his anger, Stalin replied,

'Some, to put it mildly, inordinately zealous officials are always trying too hard to please their superiors. I don't include you in that number but I advise you never to ask me questions like that again.' Stalin said nothing else about it but later, he checked that the elder boys, Yakov and Artyom, both artillerymen, were to be sent to the front line. After Vasily threw a goodbye party, Yakov's wife, Julia, saw off her beloved Yasha in her red dress, which she later believed was cursed.

One night during the first ten days of the war, Stalin called Zhenya Alliluyeva whom he had cut ever since her remarriage. Visiting Kuntsevo, she had 'never seen Joseph so crushed'. He asked her to take Svetlana and the children to the dacha in Sochi and then gave her a stunningly honest précis of the war situation that shocked her since the propaganda was still claiming that the heroic Red Army was about to crush the Fascist invader: 'The war will be long. Lots of blood will be shed ... Please take Svetlana southwards.' It was a mark of Zhenya's force of personality, the very thing that made her so attractive and irritating, that she refused. She must accompany her husband. Stalin was 'upset and angry'. He never saw Zhenya again.

Instead Anna Redens shepherded Svetlana, Alexandra Nakashidze, Vasily's wife Galina, Yakov's daughter Gulia as well as her own sons to the dacha in Sochi where they remained until the front approached there.

* * *

On 28 June, the Germans, who had penetrated three hundred miles into Soviet territory, closed the net on the encirclement of 400,000 troops – and took the capital of Belorussia, Minsk. As scraps of this information reached the Little Corner during a long session from mid-afternoon until 2.40 a.m., Stalin was beside himself. After a few hours' sleep, he visited the Defence Commissariat to find out more, probably accompanied by Molotov, Malenkov and Budyonny. The fall of Minsk would open the road to Smolensk and Moscow, but such was the rout that Timoshenko again lost contact with the armies. This infuriated Stalin who arrived back at the Little Corner at 7.35 p.m. While Timoshenko and Zhukov came and went with worsening news, Beria and Mikoyan arrived to join their comrades in an emergency Politburo. After midnight, Stalin called Timoshenko for some concrete news from Belorussia: there was none. This was the final straw.* Stalin stormed out of the office. Poskrebyshev and Chadaev watched Stalin, Molotov and Beria getting into their Packard outside.

'The Germans have obviously taken Minsk,' said Poskrebyshev.

Minutes later, the 'Five' pulled up at the Defence Commissariat. Stalin led his men into Timoshenko's office and announced that he wanted to acquaint himself personally with the reports from the front. Zhukov was about to leave but Timoshenko gestured for him to stay. The 'Five' gathered around the operations map.

'What's happening at Minsk?' asked Stalin.

'I'm not yet able to report on that,' replied Timoshenko.

'It's your duty to have the facts clearly before you at all times and keep us up to date,' said Stalin. 'At present, you're simply afraid to tell us the truth.' At this, the fearless Zhukov interjected rudely:

'Comrade Stalin, have we permission to get on with our work?'

'Are we perhaps in your way?' sneered Beria, who must have been shocked to see Stalin addressed in such a way. The meeting now degenerated into a row between Zhukov and Beria, with a bristling Stalin standing in the middle.

'You know that the situation on all fronts is critical. The front commanders await instructions and it's better if we do it ourselves,' replied Zhukov.

'We too are capable of giving orders,' shouted Beria.

'If you think you can, do it!' retorted Zhukov.

'If the Party tells us to, we will.'

---

* Now that we have access to so many different sources on this remarkable episode, from Molotov and Mikoyan's memoirs to those of Chadaev, the Sovnarkom assistant, who recorded Deputy Chief of Staff Vatutin's account, we can reconstruct this heretofore obscure story. Mikoyan dates the scene at the Defence Commissariat 29 and Chadaev 27 June, an indication of the chaos of those days. In fact, it was the 28th since we know from his logbook that Stalin was in his office throughout the 28th but did not appear on the 29th or 30th. Zhukov says that Stalin visited the Commissariat twice that day but it is likely that the showdown was in the evening, as Mikoyan recalled it.

'So wait until it tells you to. As things are, we've been told to do the job.' Zhukov appealed to Stalin: 'Excuse my outspokenness, Comrade Stalin, we shall certainly get it worked out. Then we'll come to the Kremlin and report.' Zhukov was implying that the generals might be more competent than the Politburo. Stalin, who had been quiet up to this point, could no longer contain his fury:

'You're making a crass mistake trying to draw a line between yourselves and us ... We must all be thinking how to help the fronts.' Stalin, in Mikoyan's words, now 'erupted': 'What is General Headquarters? What sort of Chief of Staff is it who since the first day of the war has no connection with his troops, represents nobody, and commands nobody?'

The granite-faced Zhukov collapsed under this barrage and burst into tears, 'sobbing like a woman' and 'ran out into another room'. Molotov followed him. One of the harshest Bolsheviks comforted one of the most severe soldiers of that bloody century: did Molotov offer a handkerchief or put a hand on Zhukov's shoulder? Five minutes later, that incongruous duo returned. Zhukov was 'quiet but his eyes were moist'.

'We were all depressed,' admitted Mikoyan. Stalin suggested that Voroshilov or someone else be despatched to make contact with the Belorussian front. 'Stalin was very depressed.' Then he looked at his comrades.

'There we are then,' said Stalin. 'Let them get it sorted out themselves first. Let's go, comrades.' Stalin led the way out of the office. As they climbed into the cars outside, Stalin uttered his first words of truth since the war began: 'Everything's lost. I give up. Lenin founded our state and we've fucked it up.' Stalin cursed all the way to Kuntsevo. 'Lenin left us a great heritage and we his successors have shitted it all up ...' Even when they had arrived at the house, Molotov remembered him swearing, '"We fucked it up!" The "we" was meant to include all of us!' Stalin said he could no longer be the leader. He resigned. At Kuntsevo, Molotov 'tried to cheer him up'. They left the broken Stalin sulking at the dacha.*

* The versions used here are Molotov's: 'We've fucked it up'; Mikoyan's: 'Lenin left us a great heritage and we his successors have shitted it up'; Beria's (via Khrushchev who was himself not in Moscow): 'Everything is lost. I give up. Lenin left us a proletarian state and now we've been caught with our pants down and let the whole thing go to shit'; and Chadaev's: 'Lenin founded our state and we've fucked it up.'

Mikoyan was not impressed with this performance. On the way home, he discussed it with Molotov, whom he disliked but trusted: they knew Stalin as well as anyone. 'We were struck by this statement of Stalin's. What now, is everything irrevocably lost? We thought he said it for effect.' They were right that Stalin was partly performing but 'he was a human being too', in Molotov's words. The fall of Minsk jolted Stalin, who lost face in front of his comrades and generals. This was the gravest crisis of his career.

The next day they discovered it was not merely 'for effect'. At midday, when Stalin usually arrived at the Kremlin, he did not come. He did not appear later in the day. The vacuum of power was palpable: the titan who, in fourteen-hour marathons, decided every tiny detail left a gaping hole. When Stalin's phone rang, Poskrebyshev responded.

'Comrade Stalin's not here and I don't know when he will be.' When Mekhlis tried to ring Stalin at Kuntsevo, there was no reply. 'I don't understand it,' sighed Poskrebyshev. By the end of the day, Stalin's *chef de cabinet* was saying: 'Comrade Stalin is not here and is unlikely to be here.'

'Has he gone to the front?' asked young Chadaev.

'Why do you keep bothering me? I've told you he isn't here and won't be here.'

Stalin 'had shut himself away from everybody, was receiving nobody and was not answering the phone'. Molotov told Mikoyan and the others that 'Stalin had been in such a state of prostration for the last two days that he was not interested in anything, didn't show any initiative and was in a bad way.' Stalin could not sleep. He did not even bother to undress but simply wandered around the dacha. At one point, he opened the door of the guardhouse where Vlasik's deputy, Major-General Rumiantsev, leapt to attention, but Stalin did not say a word and just returned to his room. He later told Poskrebyshev, he had the taste of wormwood in his mouth. Yet Stalin had read his history: he knew that Ivan the Terrible, his 'teacher', had also withdrawn from power to test the loyalty of his *boyars*.

The Soviet *boyars* were alarmed but the experienced ones sensed danger. Molotov was careful not to sign any documents. As the Germans advanced, the Government was paralysed for two long days.

'You've no idea what it's like here,' Malenkov told Khrushchev.

On the evening of the 30th, Chadaev returned to the office to get Stalin's signature as Premier but there was still no sign of him: 'He wasn't here yesterday either.'

'No, he wasn't here yesterday either,' Poskrebyshev replied, without a trace of sarcasm. But something had to be done. The new boy, Voznesensky, appeared at Poskrebyshev's desk like all the others. When Chadaev asked him to sign the documents, he refused and called Stalin himself but 'No reply from the dacha.' So he called upstairs to Molotov who suggested meeting later but gave no clue that he was already closeted with Beria, Malenkov and Voroshilov, arranging what to do. Now the dynamic Beria devised a new super-war cabinet, an ultra-Politburo with a tiny membership and sweeping powers, chaired by Stalin, if he would accept it, and containing Molotov, Voroshilov, Malenkov and himself: three Old Bolsheviks and two ascendant meteors. The exclusion of many of the magnates was a triumph for Beria and Malenkov, who were not even full Politburo members.

Once this was fixed, Molotov called Mikoyan, who was talking to Voznesensky, and the Politburo gathered. The magnates had never been so powerful: these manoeuvres most resembled the intrigues just after Stalin's stroke twelve years later, for this was the only real opportunity they had to overthrow Stalin since the revelation of Lenin's damning Testament almost twenty years earlier. Molotov told them about Stalin's breakdown but Mikoyan replied that, even if the *Vozhd* was incapacitated, 'the very name Stalin was a great force for rousing the morale of the people.' But bumptious Voznesensky made what ultimately proved to be a fatal mistake:

'Vyacheslav!' he hailed Molotov. 'You go ahead and we'll follow you!' Molotov must have blanched at this deadly suggestion and turned to Beria* who proposed his State Defence Committee. They decided to go out to Kuntsevo.

When they arrived, they cautiously stepped into the gloomy, dark-green house, shrouded in pinewoods, and were shown into the little dining room. There, sitting nervously in an armchair, was a 'thinner ... haggard ... gloomy' Stalin. When he saw the

* Beria's son Sergo, whose memoirs are reliable on personal anecdotes and unreliable on political matters, claims it was Alexander Shcherbakov, the Moscow Party leader, who made this mistake and used to ask Beria if he would ever betray him to Stalin. Mikoyan, who was actually there, is much more trustworthy but Shcherbakov may have lost his nerve on another occasion, the threat to Moscow in October.

seven or so Politburo members entering, Stalin 'turned to stone'. In one account, Stalin greeted them with more depressed ramblings: 'great Lenin's no more ... If only he could see us now. See those to whom he entrusted the fate of his country ... I am inundated with letters from Soviet people, rightly rebuking us ... Maybe some among you wouldn't mind putting the blame on me.' Then, he looked at them searchingly and asked: 'Why've you come?'

Stalin 'looked alert, somewhat strange', recalled Mikoyan, 'and his question was no less strange. Actually he should have summoned us himself. I had no doubt: he decided we had arrived to arrest him.' Beria watched Stalin's face carefully. 'It was obvious,' he later told his wife, 'Stalin expected anything could happen, even the worst.'

The magnates were frightened too: Beria later teased Mikoyan for hiding behind the others. Molotov, who was the most senior and therefore the most exposed to Stalin's vengeance, stepped forward:

'Thank you for your frankness,' said Molotov, according to a possibly secondary source, 'but I tell you here and now that if some idiot tried to turn me against you, I'd see him damned. We're asking you to come back to work ...'

'Yes but think about it,' answered Stalin. 'Can I live up to people's hopes any more? Can I lead the country to final victory? There may be more deserving candidates.'

'I believe I shall be voicing the unanimous opinion,' interjected Voroshilov. 'There's none more worthy.'

'*Pravilno!* Right!' repeated the magnates. Molotov told Stalin that Malenkov and Beria proposed to form a State Defence Committee.

'With whom at its head?' Stalin asked.

'You, Comrade Stalin.' Stalin's relief was palpable: 'the tension left his face' – but he did not say anything for a while, then:

'Well ...' Beria stepped forward and said:

'You Comrade Stalin will be the head' and he listed the members.

Stalin noticed Mikoyan and Voznesensky had been excluded but Beria suggested they should run the Government. The pragmatic Mikoyan, knowing that his responsibilities for army supply were relevant, asked to be a special representative. Stalin assigned industries – Malenkov took over aeroplanes; Molotov, tanks; Voznesensky, armaments. Stalin was back in power.

So had Stalin really suffered a nervous breakdown or was this simply a performance? Nothing was ever straightforward with this adept political actor. The breakdown was real enough: he was depressed and exhausted. It was not out of character: he had suffered similar moments on Nadya's death and during the Finnish war. His collapse was an understandable reaction to his failure to read Hitler, a mistake which could not be hidden from his courtiers who had repeatedly heard him insist there would be no invasion in 1941. But that was only the first part of this disaster: the military collapse had revealed the damage that Stalin had done and his ineptitude as commander. The Emperor had no clothes. Only a dictator who had killed any possible challengers could have survived it. In any other system, this would have brought about a change of government but no such change was available here.

Yet Molotov and Mikoyan were right: it was also 'for effect'. The withdrawal from power was a well-tried pose, successfully employed from Achilles and Alexander the Great to Ivan. Stalin's retreat allowed him to be effectively re-elected by the Politburo, with the added benefit of drawing a line under the bungles up to that point. These had been forgiven: 'Stalin enjoyed our support again,' Mikoyan wrote pointedly. So it was both a breakdown and a political restoration.

'We were witnesses to Stalin's moments of weakness,' said Beria afterwards. 'Joseph Vissarionovich will never forgive that move of ours.' Mikoyan had been right to hide.

* * *

Next afternoon, Stalin reappeared in the office, 'a new man' committed to play the role of warlord for which he believed himself specially qualified. On 1 July, the newspapers announced that Stalin was the Chairman of the State Defence Committee, the GKO. Soon afterwards he sent Timoshenko to command the Western Front defending Moscow: on 19 July, Stalin became Commissar of Defence and, on 8 August, Supreme Commander-in-Chief: henceforth, the generals called him *Verkhovnyi*, Supremo. On 16 July, he restored the dual command of political commissars that the army so hated, abolished after Finland: the commissars, led by Mekhlis, were to conduct 'ceaseless struggles against cowards, panic-mongers and deserters' but these overweening amateurs often took actual command, like their master. 'The Defence Commissariat,' said Khrushchev, 'was like a kennel of mad dogs with Kulik and Mekhlis.'* Meanwhile Stalin reunited the security forces, the NKVD and NKGB, under Beria. On 3 July, Stalin spoke to the people in a new voice, as a Russian national leader:

'Comrades, citizens,' he began conventionally, his voice low, his breathing audible across the radio waves of the Imperium, along with his sips of water and the clink of his glass. 'Brothers and sisters! Warriors of the army and the fleet! I call upon you, my friends.' This was a patriotic war but patriotism stiffened by terror: 'Cowards, deserters, panic-mongers' would be crushed in a 'merciless struggle'. A couple of nights later, Stalin and Kalinin walked out of the Kremlin at 2 a.m. under heavy guard, commanded by Vlasik, and entered Lenin's Mausoleum to bid goodbye to the mummy of their late leader before it set off by secret sealed train to Siberia.

Stalin's new resolve hardly improved the plight of the fronts. Within three weeks of war, Russia had lost around 2,000,000 men, 3,500 tanks, and over 6,000 aircraft. On 10 July, the Germans Panzers renewed their advance on the gateway to Moscow, Smolensk, which fell six days later. The Germans broke through to take another 300,000 Red Army prisoners and capture 3,000 guns and 3,000 tanks – but Timoshenko's hard fighting temporarily sapped their momentum. Hitler ordered Army Group Centre to regroup at the end of July. As he pressed his advance, in the south towards Kiev, and in the north towards Leningrad, Hitler had won astounding victories yet none of Barbarossa's objectives – Moscow, Leningrad and the Donets Basin – had fallen. The Soviet army had not been obliterated. While German generals begged him to throw their Panzers against Moscow, Hitler, perhaps recalling Napoleon's empty conquest, wanted to seize the oil and grain of the south. Instead he compromised with a new strategy, 'Moscow and Ukraine'.

The new Stalin even took some lip from the Politburo. Just after the fall of Smolensk, Stalin summoned Zhukov and Timoshenko to the dacha, where they found him wearing an old tunic, pacing, pipe unlit, always a sign of trouble, accompanied by some of the

---

* The see-saw between traditional 'single command' by a general, and 'dual command' by generals and Party Commissars, charted the progress of the Party: the Commissars were introduced three times – in 1918, 1937 and 1941 – and abolished three times when the prestige of the soldiers needed to be raised – in 1925, 1940 and 1942.

Politburo. 'The Politburo has discussed dismissing Timoshenko ... What do you think of that?' Timoshenko said nothing but Zhukov objected.

'I rather think he's right,' said old Kalinin who had barely disagreed with Stalin since 1930. Stalin 'unhurriedly lit the pipe and eyed the Politburo'.

'What if we agree with Comrade Zhukov?' he asked.

'You're right, Comrade Stalin,' they replied in one voice. But Zhukov did not always get his way.

Faced with the threat of more giant encirclements in the south, Stalin devised draconian measures to terrorize his men into fighting. In the first week, he approved NKGB Order No. 246 that stipulated the destruction of the families of men who were captured, and now he made this public in his notorious Order No. 270. He ordered it to be signed by Molotov, Budyonny, Voroshilov and Zhukov, even though some of them were not present, but it was, after all, a traditional method of Bolshevik rule. These measures ruined the lives of millions of innocent soldiers and their families, including Stalin's own.*

* * *

On 16 July, in one of the encirclements, this one at Vitebsk, an artillery lieutenant of 14th Howitzer Regiment of the 14th Armoured Division, found himself overrun by German forces. Feeling himself special, he did not withdraw: 'I am Stalin's son and I won't allow my battery to retreat,' but nor did he honourably commit suicide. On 19 July, Berlin announced that, amongst the teeming mass of Soviet prisoners, was Yakov Djugashvili. Zhdanov sent Stalin a sealed package that contained a photograph of Yakov that his father examined closely, tormented by the thought of his weak son breaking and betraying him. For the second time in Yakov's life, Stalin cursed that his own son could not kill himself:

'The fool – he couldn't even shoot himself!' he muttered to Vasily. Stalin was immediately suspicious of Yakov's wife Julia. 'Don't say anything to Yasha's wife for the time being,' Stalin told

---

* Order No. 270 is written very much in Stalin's personal style: 'I order that (1) anyone who removes his insignia ... and surrenders should be regarded as a malicious deserter whose family is to be arrested as a family of a breaker of the oath and betrayer of the Motherland. Such deserters are to be shot on the spot. (2) Those falling into encirclement are to fight to the last ... those who prefer to surrender are to be destroyed by any available means while their families are to be deprived of all assistance.'

Svetlana. Soon afterwards, under Order No. 270, Julia was arrested. Her three-year-old daughter Gulia did not see her mother for two years. Yet we now know how Stalin fretted about Yakov's fate and how he mulled over it for the rest of his life.

He quickly banned Vasily from flying on active missions: 'One prisoner's more than enough for me!' But he was irritated when the 'Crown Prince' phoned to ask for more pocket money for a new uniform and more food:

'1. As far as I know [wrote Stalin] the rations in the air force are quite sufficient. 2. A special uniform for Stalin's son is not on the agenda.'

Around the time of Yakov's capture, Stalin made his first approach to Hitler. He and Molotov ordered Beria to sound out the Bulgarian Ambassador, Ivan Stamenov. Beria gave the job to the assassination/ intelligence specialist Sudoplatov, who told the story in his semi-reliable memoirs: his instructions were to ask why Germany had violated the Pact, on what conditions Hitler would end the war, and whether he would be satisfied with the Ukraine, Belorussia, Moldova and the Baltics, a second Brest-Litovsk? Beria told Sudoplatov this was to win time. Sudoplatov met Stamenov at Beria's favourite Georgian restaurant, Aragvi, on 25 July but the Bulgarian never passed on the message to Berlin, saying:

'Even if you retreat to the Urals, you'll still win in the end.'

* * *

Meanwhile the German advance in the south was inexorable: the Panzer pincers of Army Group South, under Guderian and Kleist, swung round Kiev to encircle General Kirponos's South-Western Front with hundreds of thousands more men. It was obvious that Kiev would have to be abandoned but on 29 July, Stalin summoned Zhukov to discuss all fronts. Poskrebyshev ominously said the meeting would not begin until Mekhlis had arrived. When 'the gloomy demon' appeared with Beria and Malenkov, the Chief of Staff predicted, under the Medusan glare of this grim trio, that the Germans would crush the South-Western Front before turning back to Moscow. Mekhlis interrupted to ask, threateningly, how Zhukov knew so much about the German plans.

'What about Kiev?' asked Stalin. Zhukov proposed abandoning it.

'Why talk nonsense?' bawled Stalin.

'If you think the Chief of Staff talks nonsense, then I request you relieve me of my post and send me to the front,' Zhukov shouted back.

'Who gave you the right to speak to Comrade Stalin like that?' snarled Mekhlis.

'Don't get heated,' said Stalin to Zhukov, but 'since you mentioned it, we'll get by without you.' Zhukov gathered his maps and left the room, only to be summoned back forty minutes later to be told that he was relieved as Chief of Staff, a blessing in disguise, which allowed this fighting general to return to his natural habitat. Stalin soothed him: 'Calm down, calm down.' Shaposhnikov was recalled as Chief of Staff. Stalin knew he was ailing but 'we'll help him'. Zhukov asked to leave but Stalin invited him for tea: Stalin was drawn to Zhukov. The unfolding disaster around Kiev soon proved the wisdom of his 'nonsense'.

The Panzer claws were closing around the South-Western Axis, commanded by Marshal Budyonny and Khrushchev who begged to be allowed to withdraw. Stalin was informed by the NKVD that Khrushchev was going to surrender Kiev and rang to threaten him: 'You should be ashamed of yourself! ... What's the matter with you? [You have] given up half of Ukraine. You're ready to give up the other half too ... Do whatever it takes. If not ... we'll make short work of you!' In the alternation of roaring panic and becalmed anxiety that are the moods of a rout, Khrushchev found Budyonny drinking brandy with the front's Operations chief, Bagramian, and affectionately telling him he should be shot.

On 11 September, with time running out, Budyonny, who was both braver and more competent than most of the 'cavalrymen', knew he might be dismissed or even arrested but he now insisted to Stalin that 'delay [will] lead to losses in men and a huge quantity of equipment'. Stalin dismissed him next day. Appointing Timoshenko to the front, Stalin gave him a quaint gift of two pipes marked with a deer to symbolize his transfer from north to south, a rare gesture.

'You take command,' Budyonny told Timoshenko at the front. 'But let's call Stalin together and tell him to retreat from Kiev. We're real Marshals and they'll believe us.'

'I don't want to put my head in the noose,' replied Timoshenko. Two days later, Kleist and Guderian's Panzer Groups One and Two linked up at 18.20 hours a hundred miles east of Kiev, sealing five entire Soviet armies in a giant encirclement, the rotten fruit of

Stalin's obstinacy: 452,720 men were captured. By the 18th, Kiev had fallen. Stalin's nerves held: 'Plug the hole,' he ordered Shaposhnikov. 'Quickly!'

Stalin and Beria stepped up both the repression and the redemption. More 'lucky stiffs' were released to help the war effort. 'There aren't any people on whom one can rely,' Stalin murmured during one meeting on air defence at which the aircraft designer Yakovlev spoke up:

'Comrade Stalin, it's already more than a month since Balandin, our Deputy People's Commissar, was arrested. We don't know what he was arrested for but we can't conceive he was an Enemy. He is needed ... We ask you to examine his case.'

'Yes,' replied Stalin, 'he's already been in prison for forty days but he's confessed nothing. Perhaps he's not guilty of anything.' The next day, Balandin, 'with hollow cheeks and shaven head' appeared for work 'as though nothing had happened'. Beria and Mikoyan requested the freeing of Vannikov, arrested for arguing about artillery with Kulik. He was brought straight from his cell to Stalin who apologized, admitting that Vannikov had been right, and then promoted him to high office.

There was a certain awkwardness when the 'lucky stiffs' met their torturers. Broad-faced, fair-haired General Meretskov, arrested during the first weeks of the war, had been horribly tortured by the debonair Merkulov, 'the Theoretician', with whom he had been friends before his arrest. As one of his interrogators later testified: 'Brutal continuous torture was applied to Meretskov by high-ranking officials ... he was beaten with rubber rods' until he was covered in blood. Now he was cleaned up and brought to Merkulov but Meretskov told his torturer that they could no longer be friends, a conversation unique to this strange time:

'Vsevolod Nikolaievich, we used to meet on informal terms but I'm afraid of you now.' Merkulov smiled. Minutes later, in full uniform, General Meretskov reported for his next assignment to Stalin:

'Hello, Comrade Meretskov? How are you feeling?'

Beria also redoubled the Terror. As the NKVD retreated, the prisoners were not all released – even though Stalin had every opportunity to do so. Those 'German spies' who had been so close to Stalin, Maria and Alyosha Svanidze, had been in prison since December 1937. Stalin remembered Alyosha who, as he himself told Mikoyan, 'was sentenced to death. I ordered Merkulov to tell him before execution that if he asks the Central Committee for forgiveness, he will be pardoned.' But Svanidze proudly replied that he was innocent so 'I can't ask for pardon.' He spat in Merkulov's face:

'That's my answer to him,' he cried. On 20 August 1941, he was shot. A few days later, at Kuntsevo, Stalin turned to Mikoyan:

'Want to hear about Alyosha?'

'What?' Mikoyan, who had adored Svanidze, hoped he would be released. But Stalin matter-of-factly announced his death.

'He wouldn't apologize. Such noble pride!' mused Stalin.

'When was this?' asked Mikoyan.

'He was shot just recently.' Maria Svanidze, who had so worshipped Stalin, was, with Aloysha's sister, Mariko, shot the following year.

34

'Ferocious as a Dog': Zhdanov and the
Siege of Leningrad

While Molotov sat beside Stalin in the Little Corner, Zhdanov ruled beleaguered Leningrad like a mini-Stalin. But Stalin now turned his fury on to the commanders of the city of Lenin.* By 21 August 1941, a German north-easterly thrust almost cut off Leningrad's link with the rest of Russia. Voroshilov, now sixty, took command alongside Zhdanov. Both men had much to prove but as Leningrad was gradually enveloped, they struggled to keep Stalin's confidence.

Day by day, the Germans tightened their grip and Stalin smelt defeatism. In a stream of dictated anxiety, he accused them of failing to grasp 'this fatal danger. Stavka cannot agree with the mood of doom, and impossibility of taking strong measures and conversations about how everything possible has been done and it's impossible to do any more ...' Then Stalin heard that Voroshilov, replaying his glory days of Tsaritsyn in 1918, was planning to raise morale by electing officers – but this time the outraged War Commissar was not Trotsky.

'Immediately stop the elections because it will paralyse the army and elect impotent leaders,' ordered Stalin, together with Molotov and Mikoyan. 'We need all-powerful leaders. It will spread like a disease. This isn't Vologda – this is the second city of the country!' He added: 'We ask Voroshilov and Zhdanov to inform us about operations. They have not done so yet. That's a pity.'

'All's clear,' replied Leningrad. 'Goodbye Comrade Stalin. That helps. Great gratitude!'

Zhdanov took control of every facet of Leningrad life, declaring famously: 'the enemy is at the gates.' Now plump, asthmatic and exhausted, always chain smoking his Belomor cigarettes, clad in

---

* The opening of Stalin's and Zhdanov's papers allows us for the first time to listen in on their frantic efforts to save Leningrad.

an olive-green belted tunic, pistol in holster, Zhdanov ran the front from the third floor of the right wing of the Smolny Institute from an office hung with pictures of Stalin, Marx and Engels. His long table was covered in red baize just as Stalin's was in green. His desk was set with Urals stone, a present from some Leningrad factory. He drank tea, like Stalin, from a glass held in a silver holder, chewing sugar lumps and, like him, slept on his office divan. He wrote the newspaper editorials, personally allocated every volt of electricity, threatened 'panic-mongers' with instant death, and shared command of the front.

Voroshilov meanwhile displayed the admirable courage that he had shown at Tsaritsyn. When he appeared at the front at Ivanovskoye, the soldiers watched as the First Marshal pranced around under heavy shellfire:

'That's him! Voroshilov! Klim!' gasped the soldiers. 'Look how he stands as if he grew out of the earth!' A few miles away, the Marshal came upon some troops who had broken under a German attack. He stopped his staff car, pulled out his pistol and led the troops against the Germans to the shout of 'Hurrah!' The old cavalryman could buckle his swash but was unable to stabilize the front.

Stalin was unmoved by the heroic ineptitude of this *beau sabreur*. His warmth towards Zhdanov was cooling fast. When the Leningraders referred respectfully to their boss as 'Andrei Alexandrovich', Stalin answered icily: 'Andrei Alexandrovich? Now which Andrei Alexandrovich do you mean?' The terrified agreement to his own orders did not help matters: 'If you don't agree,' he told Zhdanov, 'say it straight.' But he also showed his sarcastic irritation, scribbling in his red pencil: 'You didn't answer the proposal. You didn't answer? Why not? ... Is it understood? When do you begin the attack? We demand an immediate answer in two words: "Yes" will mean a positive answer and swift implementation and "No" will mean a negative. Answer yes or no. Stalin.' None the less he resisted any attempt to dismiss Zhdanov even though he was staggering under the burden of Leningrad's plight.

On the 21st Stalin, realizing the desperate situation, ordered Molotov and Malenkov, armed with his full authority, to descend on Leningrad and designate a scapegoat, marking Zhdanov's fall from grace. 'To Voroshilov, Malenkov, Zhdanov ... Leningrad Front thinks of only one thing: any way to retreat ... Isn't it time you got rid of these heroes of retreat?' But they also had a bigger unspoken mission: should Leningrad be abandoned?

Their journey itself was an adventure: they flew to Cherepovets where they took a special train westward but suddenly the train could go no further and stopped at the little station of Mga, twenty-five miles east of the city. The magnates could see a German bombing raid up ahead but they did not realize this was the beginning of the German advance that would encircle Leningrad only two days later: Mga had been the last way in. Molotov and Malenkov were unsure what to do. They walked along the tracks towards Leningrad until they found a suburban trolleybus which they boarded like commuters. They were met further up the line by an armoured train.

They found Zhdanov just about holding things together, but comforting himself with drink and struggling against his asthma. Zhdanov was never the strongest of Stalin's men: 'a bit spineless', thought Molotov. Alcohol became the one flaw in this perfect Stalinist. He was now close to collapse, admitting openly to Stalin that he had at one point lost his nerve, panicked during the bombardment and hidden, drinking, in the Smolny bunker. But the very confession helped keep Stalin's favour. He worked like a man possessed but his health never recovered.

Malenkov enjoying spreading the story of Zhdanov's alcoholic cowardice while boasting that he never reported it to Stalin, which is hard to believe. Zhdanov got on well with Molotov but had despised Malenkov since the late thirties. It was he who had coined the nickname for that fat, eunuch-like bureaucrat: 'Malanya.' The mutual hatred of these two noble scions of the provincial intelligentsia would seethe until it ended in a massacre. Malenkov probably proposed Zhdanov's arrest but Beria, knowing Stalin's fondness for 'the Pianist', said this was no time for court-martialling Politburo members. Molotov agreed: 'Zhdanov was a good comrade' but he was 'very dejected'.

Apart from hunting scapegoats, Stalin's plenipotentiaries hardly improved matters: 'I fear,' Stalin wrote hysterically to Molotov and Malenkov, 'Leningrad will be lost through imbecilic folly, and all Leningrad risks encirclement. What are Popov [front commander] and Voroshilov doing? They don't even tell us of the measures they're taking against the danger. They're busy looking for new lines of retreat. As far as I can see, this is their only purpose ... This is pure peasant fatalism ... What people! I can't

understand anything. Don't you think someone's opening the
road to the Germans in this important direction? On purpose?
What's this man Popov? What's Voroshilov doing? How's he
helping Leningrad? I write about this because I'm disturbed by the
lack of activity of Leningrad's commander ... return to Moscow.
Don't be late. Stalin.'

On their return, the emissaries advised Stalin to scrap Voroshilov's
North-Western Axis and sack the First Marshal who spent 'all his
time in the trenches'. Meanwhile Schlüsselberg, the fortress on the
Neva, and Mga, fell. Voroshilov did not tell Moscow, and when
Stalin discovered these prevarications, he was outraged.

'We're so indignant about your conduct,' he told Voroshilov
and Zhdanov. 'You tell us only of losses but no word of measures
to save towns ... and the loss of Schlüsselberg? What'll be the end
of our losses? Have you decided to surrender Leningrad?'

On 8 September, Stalin summoned Zhukov to his flat where he
was dining with his usual companions – Molotov, Malenkov and
the Moscow boss, Alexander Shcherbakov.*

'Where will you be off to now?' Stalin asked casually.

'Back to the front,' replied Zhukov.

'Which front?'

'The one you consider most necessary.'

'Then go to Leningrad at once ... The situation is almost
hopeless there ...' and he handed Zhukov a note to Voroshilov
that read: 'Hand over command to Zhukov and fly to Moscow
immediately.' Stalin scrawled to Zhdanov: 'Today Voroshilov's
recalled!'

Zhukov took command at Leningrad's Smolny headquarters,
combining professionalism with draconian ruthlessness, shouting
at the staff: 'Don't you understand that if Antonov's division
doesn't occupy the line ... the Germans'll break into the city? And
then I'll have you shot in front of the Smolny as a traitor.'
Zhdanov, standing beside his new partner in command, frowned:
he disapproved of swearing.

---

* Shcherbakov was one of those New Men who had risen over the bodies of the dead
of the thirties. 'With his impassive Buddha face, with thick horn-rimmed glasses
resting on the tiny turned-up button of a nose', Shcherbakov, who was Zhdanov's
brother-in-law, another example of the intermarriage of the élite, had made his name
managing cultural questions, then succeeded Khrushchev as Moscow First Secretary,
becoming a candidate member of the Politburo in 1941 with Malenkov and
Voznesensky. A coarse alcoholic anti-Semite, Khrushchev called him: 'a snake ... one
of the worst.'

The crestfallen Voroshilov addressed his staff: 'Goodbye comrades,' he said. 'Stavka's recalled me back.' He paused. 'That's what an old man like me deserves. This isn't the Civil War. Now we have to fight differently ... But don't doubt for a minute that we'll smash the Fascist scum!'

Back in Moscow, Stalin admitted, 'We might have to abandon "Peter".' But Zhukov stiffened resistance to the German attack and then counter-attacked. Zhdanov, working closely with Zhukov, now showed his steel, complaining that his 'tribunals are being inactive against spreaders of false and provocative rumours ... The Special Departments should arrange trials of provocateurs and rumour-mongers. The public should know how we regard these bastards.' Whatever Stalin suggested was put into action.* On 13 November, Stalin told him that the Germans were constructing strongholds in the cellars of ordinary homes: 'People's Commissar of Defence Comrade Stalin gives the following instructions,' wrote Zhdanov. 'When moving forward don't try to capture one or other point but ... burn to ashes these populated areas. So the German staffs and units will be buried ... Toss away any sentiment and destroy all populated areas you meet on your way!'

Zhukov and Zhdanov succeeded in making the storming of Leningrad very costly for the Germans. Hitler hesitated, cancelled the assault and ordered instead that Leningrad be starved into submission and then razed to the ground: the 900-day siege of the city had begun. Zhdanov had not lost the habit of writing Stalin personal letters with a fine ink pen: 'The main cause of our failure was the weak performance of our infantry ... We remembered what you told us during the Finnish War' but 'our people have a bad habit of not finishing things and analysing them – and then running in different directions ... Today we're working strongly to change our style of attack ... The worst is that the hunger is spreading.'

There were 2.2 million people trapped in Leningrad. That December alone, 53,000 died and there would be many more to follow. People dropped dead in the streets, in their beds, whole

* When, on 31 October, Stalin heard that the Nazis were using 'delegations' of Russian men and women as human shields, he ordered Zhdanov: 'It's said that amongst the Leningrad Bolsheviks there are those who thought it impossible to use arms against these "delegates". If there are such people ... they must be liquidated first of all because they are more dangerous than German soldiers. My advice – no sentiment ... Destroy the Germans and their delegates!'

families died one by one. There were too many bodies and everyone was too weak to bury them. Cannibalism flourished: it was not rare to find a body lying in the hall of an apartment block with thighs and breasts carved off. Between now and July 1942, it is estimated that a million people died in Leningrad.

Zhdanov, assisted by his respected Second Secretary, Alexei Kuznetsov, won back Stalin's respect and that of the Leningraders. They gradually became heroes as they shared the plight of their citizens, personally living on a full military ration of a pound of bread a day plus a bowl of meat or fish soup and some *kasha*. While hundreds of thousands were dying in the streets, the leaders worked day and night. Kuznetsov, a tall, gangly young man with a long handsome face, kept Leningrad together during Zhdanov's moments of weakness, touring the trenches accompanied by his little son. Stalin himself praised Kuznetsov: 'The Motherland won't forget you!' he wrote.

In November, they ordered the building of the 'Road of Life' across the ice of Lake Ladoga which became the city's only channel for the supply of food. During the famine, Zhdanov assigned food supplies in such detail that, at one point, he was the only man allowed to replace a lost ration card. He sometimes displayed flashes of human decency: when dysentery broke out in a school, he suspected the staff of stealing the children's food and sent in a general who reported that the children were taking the food in jars to their families – but he did not stop them.

'I'd have done the same thing,' Zhdanov admitted and ordered the evacuation of the children. After the war, Zhdanov was quoted as saying that 'people died like flies' but 'history would have never have forgiven me had I given up Leningrad'.

Still Stalin became furious when Zhdanov showed dangerous independence: 'Do you imagine Leningrad under Zhdanov is not situated in the USSR but is somewhere on an island in the middle of the Pacific?'

'We admit our mistake,' replied Zhdanov, who then reported a problem with the operations on Lake Lagoda which he blamed on the 'cowardice and betrayal' of the commanders of the 80th Division. 'We send a demand to let us ... shoot the chief of 80th Frolov and his commissar Ivanov ... The Council needs to fight panic and cowardice even among officers.'

'Frolov and Ivanov should be shot and tell the media,' replied Stalin.

'Understood. All will be done.'

'Don't waste time,' said Stalin. 'Every moment's dear. The enemy concentrates power against Moscow. All other fronts have the chance to counter-attack. Seize the moment!'

Zhdanov ended his handwritten reply: 'We're waiting the start of the German defeat outside Moscow. Be healthy!' Then he added this: 'PS: I've become as ferocious as a dog!'*

* * *

Hitler switched his Panzers to Operation Typhoon, the grand offensive against Moscow, designed to deliver the knockout blow to Soviet Russia. Guderian's Panzers surprised and then out-flanked the Briansk Front just as Stalin welcomed Lord Beaverbrook, the puckish Canadian press baron and member of the British War Cabinet, and Averell Harriman, the handsome lantern-jawed railway heir and American envoy, who had come to negotiate military aid to keep Russia in the war.

The two plutocrats observed Stalin play the gracious host while facing catastrophe. 'Stalin was very restless, walking about and smoking continuously and appeared to both of us to be under an intense strain,' recalled Beaverbrook. As always, Stalin swung between rudeness and charm, sketching wolves on his notepad one moment, and then tossing aside an unopened letter from Churchill to exclaim:

'The paucity of your offers clearly shows you want to see the Soviet Union defeated.' He was 'sallow, tired, pock-marked … almost emaciated'. By 1 October, the Moscow front was collapsing just as Stalin laid on a lavish banquet in the Great Kremlin Palace. At 7.30 p.m., the hundred guests chattered loudly in the eighteenth-century Catherine Hall, with its chairs and divans covered in the monograms of Catherine the Great, green silk wallpaper, and the old portraits in their golden frames. Just before eight, the Russian guests began to glance anxiously at the high, gilded door and on the hour, silence fell as Stalin, in a tunic that 'seemed to hang off his wasted frame', walked slowly down the line.

At dinner, he placed himself between the tycoons, with Molotov in his accustomed seat opposite him and, down the table, Voroshilov and Mikoyan, who henceforth negotiated the

* Perhaps as a reward for his ferocity, on 11 December, Zhdanov, who had not seen Stalin since 24 June, flew to Moscow and began to climb back to the top.

Western aid.* As the waiters unleashed upon the guests a barrage of hors d'oeuvres, caviar, soup, and fish, suckling pig, chicken and game, ice-cream and cakes, washed down with champagne, vodka, wine and Armenian brandy, Stalin toasted victory before Molotov took up the baton. There were thirty-two toasts before the night was done. When Stalin enjoyed a toast, he would clap his hands before drinking to it but he happily talked on while others were speaking. He 'drank continuously from a small glass (liqueur),' wrote Beaverbrook, who recorded everything with the avidity of one of his *Daily Express* columnists. 'He ate well and even heartily', nibbling caviar off his knife, without bread and butter. Stalin and Beaverbrook, two mercurial rogues, jousted mischievously. Pointing at President Kalinin, Beaverbrook, who had heard about his taste for ballerinas, asked if the old man had a mistress. 'He's too old,' chuckled Stalin. 'Do you?'

Stalin then led the way, with hands behind his back, to the cinema where he intently watched two movies, drinking champagne and laughing. Even though it was already 1.30 a.m., the omnipotent insomniac suggested a third movie but Beaverbrook was too tired. As the Westerners departed, the Germans broke through towards Moscow.

On 3 October, Guderian took Orel, 125 miles behind the supposed Russian front line. Yeremenko's Briansk and Budyonny's Reserve Fronts were smashed: 665,000 Russians surrounded. On the 4th Stalin lost contact with the shattered Western Front under Koniev, leaving a twelve-mile hole in Moscow's defences. Early on the 5th, the Moscow air commander, Sbytov, reported the almost incredible news that a long column of German tanks was heading for Moscow along the Ukhnovo highway, 100 kilometres from the Kremlin. A second reconnaissance plane confirmed the same sight. 'Very well,' Stalin told the Moscow Commissar Telegin. 'Act decisively and energetically ... mobilize every available resource to hold the enemy ...'

Simultaneously, Stalin's entourage tried to crush this news as they had tried to deny the German invasion. 'Look,' Beria threatened Telegin, 'do you take every bit of nonsense as the truth? You've evidently received information from panic-mongers

---

* Even Stalin admitted how this Western assistance decisively aided his war effort. Mikoyan reported to him in detail as the aid arrived, whether trucks via Persia or weapons via Archangel. Such was the urgency that in November 1941, Stalin totted up the number of planes (432) in his red pen on Mikoyan's notes.

and provocateurs!' Minutes later, poor Colonel Sbytov ran into Telegin's office, 'pale and trembling'. Beria had ordered him to report at once to the feared chief of the Special Department, Victor Abakumov who threatened Sbytov and his pilots with arrest for 'cowardice and panic-mongering'. When a third plane confirmed that all three fronts had collapsed, the hyenas were called off.

Stalin telephoned Zhukov in Leningrad: 'I've only got one request. Can you get on a plane and come to Moscow?'

'I request to fly at dawn.'

'We await you in Moscow.'

'I'll be there.'

'All the best,' said Stalin. Meanwhile he sent Voroshilov to find the fronts and learn what he could.

At dusk on 7 October, Vlasik sped Zhukov straight to the Kremlin flat where Stalin, suffering from flu, was chatting to Beria. Probably 'unaware of my arrival', in Zhukov's words, Stalin was ordering Beria to 'use his "Organ" to sound out the possibilities of making a separate peace with Germany, given the critical situation ...' Stalin was probing German resolve but there was no moment when Hitler was less likely to make peace than when Moscow seemed to be falling.* Beria is said to have arranged a second probe, either using a Bulgarian 'banker' or the Ambassador again but with no results.

Without a wisp of small talk, Stalin ordered Zhukov to fly to Koniev's and Budyonny's fronts. Stalin needed a scapegoat, wondering if Koniev was a 'traitor'. Heading into the whirlwind, Zhukov found the dazed commanders of the Western Front, the tough, shaven-headed Koniev and the Commissar, Bulganin, in a desolate room barely lit by candles. Bulganin had just spoken to Stalin but could not tell him anything 'because we ourselves don't know'. At 2.30 a.m. on the 8th, Zhukov called Stalin, who was still ill: 'The main danger now is that the roads into Moscow are virtually undefended.' And the reserves? Stalin asked:

'Encircled.'

'What do you intend to do?'

'I will go to Budyonny ...'

'And do you know where his headquarters are?' Stalin inquired.

---

* In 1966, when Zhukov's memoirs were published in Moscow, this was regarded as too dangerous to be included. It was only in 1990, when the full version was published, that this account appeared.

'No ... I'll look for him ...'

Stalin despatched Molotov and Malenkov into this cauldron to take control – and assign blame. Such was the havoc that Zhukov could not find Budyonny. At Maloyaroslavets, he found a small town completely deserted except for a chauffeur asleep in a jeep who turned out to be Budyonny's driver. The Marshal was inside the district Soviet, trying to find his own armies on his map. The two cavalrymen embraced warmly. Budyonny had saved Zhukov from arrest during the Terror, but now he was confused and exhausted. The next morning, Stalin ordered Zhukov to return to the Western Front headquarters north of Mozhaisk and take command.

There he found Molotov, Malenkov, Voroshilov and Bulganin indulging in an ugly hunt for the scapegoat: a stand-up row broke out between Koniev and Voroshilov about who had ordered what withdrawal. Koniev's life hung in the balance when Voroshilov shrieked that he was 'a traitor'. He was supported by Nikolai Bulganin, that blond and goatee-bearded ex-Chekist who had been Mayor of Moscow and boss of the State Bank. This apparently affable womanizer, who cultivated an aristocratic elegance but was nicknamed 'the Plumber' by Beria because of his work on the Moscow sewers, was deftly ambitious and suavely ruthless: he wanted Koniev shot, perhaps to save his own skin.

Stalin phoned to order Koniev's arrest but Zhukov persuaded the Supremo that he needed Koniev as his deputy: 'If Moscow falls,' Stalin threatened, 'both your heads'll roll ... Organize the Western Front quickly and act!' Two days later, Molotov telephoned and threatened to shoot Zhukov if he did not stop the retreat. If Molotov could do any better, he was welcome to try, retorted Zhukov. Molotov hung up.

Zhukov stiffened the resistance though he possessed only 90,000 men to defend Moscow. He fought for time, with the fray reaching unprecedented frenzies of savagery. By the 18th, Kalinin had fallen to the north and Kaluga to the south and there were Panzers on the battlefield of Borodino. Snow fell, then thawed, stirring up a boggy quagmire which temporarily halted the Germans. Both sides fought heroically, tank helm to tank helm, like two giants wrestling in a sea of mud.

35

'Can You Hold Moscow?'

Stalin controlled every aspect of the battle, keeping a list of men and tanks in his little leather notebook. 'Are they hiding guns from me again?' he asked Voronov. As early as 3 August, he had secretly ordered the creation of a special tank reserve for Moscow: these tanks were 'to be given to nobody', he specified. But visitors were amazed 'by Zhukov's tone': he spoke to Stalin 'in sharp commanding tones as if he was the superior officer and Stalin accepted this'.

Again and again, he raised the intensity of cruelty. It was perhaps now that he marked the passage in d'Abernon that claimed that the Germans were more afraid of their officers than of the enemy. First he unleashed his 'scorched earth' policy 'to destroy and burn to ashes all populated areas in the German rear to a depth of 40–60 kms from the front line'. Beria, Mekhlis and the rising head of the Special Departments, Abakumov, reported every week on the arrests and shootings of Soviet troops: for example, Beria wrote to Mekhlis during the Battle of Moscow to report that 638,112 men had been detained in the rear since the start of the war, with 82,865 arrested, while Abakumov reported to Stalin that in one week, his Special Departments arrested 1,189 and shot 505 deserters. Now on the front near Moscow, Bulganin's 'interceptor battalions', set up to terrorize cowards, arrested 23,064 'deserters' in just three days. There is a myth that the only time Stalin ceased the war against his own people was during 1941 and 1942; but during that period, 994,000 servicemen were condemned, and 157,000 shot, more than fifteen divisions.

Beria was also liquidating old prisoners: on 13 October, Poskrebyshev's wife, the once effervescent Bronka was shot, an event, like the murder of the Svanidzes, that could only have happened on Stalin's order. As they moved back, the NKVD tossed grenades into their own prisons or transferred prisoners to the interior. On 3 October, Beria liquidated 157 'celebrity' prisoners

such as Kameneva, Trotsky's sister and Kamenev's widow, in
Medvedev Forest near Orel. On the 28th, Beria ordered the shooting of another twenty-five, including the ex-Air Force commander,
Rychagov, who had answered back to Stalin about the 'flying
coffins'. The 4,905 unfortunates on death row were despatched
within eight days.

On the streets of Moscow, the chains of Stalinist control were
snapped by the fear of the German armies. Law broke down. By
14 October, food shops were being looted; empty apartments
burgled. Refugees clogged the streets, harassed by gangs of
desperadoes. The smoke of bonfires hung over the city as officials
burned papers. At Kursk Station, 'a crush of women, children and
old people filled the square. The cold was piercing. Children were
weeping' but the masses waited 'patiently and submissively'. A
hundred soldiers joined arms to hold back the mob. Some
commissariats and the families of most officials were evacuated to
Kuibyshev. AA guns illuminated the sky while the half-deserted
Kremlin was blacked out and weirdly camouflaged: a huge canvas
painted with the façades of a row of houses, a veritable Potemkin
village, had been hoisted up over the walls facing the river.

Beria, Malenkov and Kaganovich, according to Stalin's bodyguards, 'lost their self-control', encouraging the popular flight.
'We shall be shot down like partridges,' Beria told one meeting,
advocating the swift abandonment of Moscow. These magnates
advised Stalin to evacuate to Kuibyshev. Beria summoned
Sudoplatov, his expert on 'Special Tasks', to his Lubianka office
where he was sitting with Malenkov, and ordered him to
dynamite all the main buildings, from the Kaganovich Metro to
the football stadium. On the night of the 15th, Beria made things
worse, calling a meeting of the local Party leaders in his office
in the bomb-proof basement at 2 Dzerzhinsky Street, and
announcing: 'The connection with the front is broken.' He
ordered them to 'evacuate everyone who's unable to defend
Moscow. Distribute food to the inhabitants.' There were riots at
factories because the workers could not get in since the buildings
were mined. Molotov told ambassadors that they would be
immediately evacuated.

Stalin himself presented an air of solitary inscrutability,
revealing his plans to no one, while the magnates prepared for
evacuation. As the air raids on Moscow intensified, Stalin climbed
up on to the sunroof at Kuntsevo and watched the dogfights.

Once some shrapnel fell near him as he watched from his garden and Vlasik handed him the warm fragments. Vasily Stalin arrived one night to visit his father. When a German plane passed over the house, the guards did not open fire since they did not want to draw attention to Stalin's residence.

'Cowards!' shouted Vasily, firing the guns himself.

Stalin came out: 'Did he hit anything?' he asked.

'No, he didn't.'

'Winner of the Voroshilov Marksman Prize,' he said drily. But the stress was telling on him: no one could believe how much he had aged. Stalin was now a 'short man with a tired haggard face ... his eyes had lost their old steadiness, his voice lacked assurance.' Khrushchev was appalled to see this 'bag of bones'. When Andreyev and his daughter Natasha walked around the freezing Kremlin, they saw Stalin strolling up and down beside the battlements, quite alone and, as usual, under-dressed, with no gloves on and his face blue with the chill. In his spare moments, he kept reading history: it was now that he scribbled on a new biography of Ivan the Terrible: 'teacher teacher' and then: 'We shall overcome!' His moods swung between Spartan grit and hysterical rantings. Koniev was amazed to receive a call in which Stalin cried:

'Comrade Stalin's not a traitor. Comrade Stalin's an honourable man; his only mistake was that he trusted too much in cavalrymen.' He was harassed by constant 'sightings' of Nazi parachutists landing in the middle of Moscow: 'Parachutist? How many? A company?' Stalin was barking into the phone when one general arrived to report. 'And who saw them? Did you see them? And where did they land? You're insane ... I tell you I don't believe it. The next thing you'll be telling me is that they have already landed on your office!' He slammed down the phone. 'For several hours now they've been tormenting me with wails about German parachutists. They won't let me work. Blabbermouths!'

Stalin's staff prepared for his departure, without actually checking with him. The dachas were dynamited. A special train was prepared, standing in a hidden siding, packed with belongings from his houses such as his beloved library. Four American Douglas DC-3 aeroplanes stood ready.

At the end of 15 October, Stalin ordered his guards to drive him out to Kuntsevo, which had been closed down and mined. The commandant told him he could not go in but Stalin ordered:

'Clear the mines in two or three hours, stoke the stove in the little house and I'll work there.'

The next morning he headed into the Kremlin earlier than usual. On the way, this worshipper of order was amazed to see mobs looting the shops along his route. His guards claimed that he ordered the car to stop on Smolensk Square, where he was surrounded by a crowd who asked rather pertinent questions such as: 'When will the Soviet Army stop the enemy?'

'That day's near,' he replied before driving on to the Kremlin.

At 8 a.m., Mikoyan, who had been working as usual until six in the morning, was woken up and summoned. At nine, the magnates gathered in Stalin's flat to debate the great decision of the war. Stalin proposed to evacuate the whole Government to Kuibyshev, to order the army to defend the capital and keep the Germans fighting until he could throw in his reserves. Molotov and Mikoyan were ordered to manage the evacuation, with Kaganovich providing the trains. Stalin proposed that all the Politburo leave that day and, he added sensationally, 'I will leave tomorrow morning.'

'Why do we have to leave today if you're leaving tomorrow?' Mikoyan indignantly asked Stalin. 'We can also go tomorrow. Shcherbakov and Beria shouldn't leave until they've organized the underground resistance. I'm staying and I'll go tomorrow with you.' Stalin agreed. Molotov and Mikoyan began to brief the commissars: the Foreign Commissariat was called at 11 a.m. and ordered to report to Kazan Station at once. In the lift from Stalin's office, Kaganovich said to Mikoyan:

'Listen, when you leave, please tell me so I don't get left behind.' As the leaders rushed in and out of Stalin's office, their families were given just an hour's notice to evacuate the city.* At 7 p.m. the next day, Ashken Mikoyan and the three younger Mikoyanchiks, along with President Kalinin and other top

---

* In distant Kuibyshev, the ancient city of Samara on the Volga that had been chosen as the new capital should Moscow have to be abandoned, several buildings, including the local Party headquarters and a mansion in a narrow gully beside the steep banks of the Volga, surrounded by paved walks overlooking the river, were prepared for Stalin. A special air-raid shelter, reached by a lift, was constructed whence he could rule what was left of Russia. Svetlana Stalin was set up in a small town house with a courtyard along with her housekeeper Alexandra Nakashidze, and Galina, Vasily's pregnant wife and Yakov's daughter, Gulia (without her arrested mother), Kalinin and his mistress shared a small house with the Mikoyans, the Khrushchevs shared with the Malenkovs. The Poskrebyshevs, Litvinovs and others lived in the local sanatorium.

families, boarded the CC train. In the heavily guarded station, women in fur coats stood chatting with their well-dressed children amidst the steam of the trains while soldiers carefully loaded crates marked 'handle with care – crystal'. Poskrebyshev sobbed as he put three-year-old Natasha on the train with her nanny, unaware that her mother, Bronka, had been executed three days earlier. He promised to visit his daughter as soon as possible – and hurried back to Stalin. As he waited, Valentin Berezhkov, Molotov's interpreter, noticed that the puddles of melted snow were freezing. The German Panzers could advance again.

Zhukov resolved to hold the line. But he could sense the panic at the top. He was convinced he could save Moscow, he told a visiting editor, 'but are THEY, there?' he asked, meaning Stalin in the Kremlin.

That evening, the leaders arrived in an eerily deserted Kremlin. As one commissar entered his apartment, Stalin appeared from his bedroom, smoking and pacing, in his old tunic and baggy, booted trousers. They noticed that the bookcases were empty, books all loaded on to the train. No one sat down. Then Stalin stopped pacing:

'What's the situation like in Moscow?' The magnates remained silent but a junior commissar spoke up: the Metro was not running, the bakeries were closed. The factories thought the Government had fled. Half of them had not been paid. Workers believed the boss of the State Bank had run off with the money.

'Well, it's not so bad. I thought it would be worse.' Stalin ordered the money be flown back from Gorky. Shcherbakov and Pronin, Moscow's Party chief and Mayor, must restore order and broadcast the fact that Moscow would be held to the last drop of blood: Stalin remained in the Kremlin. The leaders headed out into the town: Mikoyan appeared before five thousand restless, unpaid workers at the Stalin Automobile Works. But the panic continued: stragglers and thieves patrolled the streets. Even the British Embassy across the Moskva from the Kremlin was looted, its guards having fled. Demolition units mined Moscow's sixteen bridges.

* * *

Stalin hesitated for two long days. No one knows his exact movements but he no longer appeared in his office. At the height of the legendary struggle for Moscow the Supremo actually dossed down in his greatcoat on a mattress in the subterranean halls of the Metro, not unlike an omnipotent tramp. Stalin's working arrangements reveal the dire lack of preparation for war. There were frequent air raids but there were no bunkers at either the Kremlin or Kuntsevo. While Kaganovich supervised the urgent construction of bunkers precisely modelled on Stalin's study, the Supremo moved to work in the only proper command post available, the air defence HQ in the town house at 33 Kirov Street (Myasnitskaya Street), where he had a bedroom. During air raids, he descended by elevator to work in the Kirov Metro Station (now Chistye Prudy) until, on 28 October, a bomb fell in the courtyard of the house. Then Stalin started to work permanently in the station, where he also slept.

In the Metro, he bunked in a specially constructed compartment that was sealed off from the running trains by plywood panels. Many of his staff slept on ordinary subway trains parked in the station, while the General Staff worked in the Belorusski Metro Station. Offices, desks and sleeping compartments divided up this subterranean headquarters deep under Kirov Street. Passing trains caused pages to fly so they were pinned to desks. After working all day in his subterranean offices, Stalin would finally stagger over to his sleeping compartment in the early hours. Vlasik and his bodyguards stood on guard around this flimsy refuge and probably slept across the doors like squires guarding a medieval king. A staff colonel, Sergei Shtemenko, an efficient, charismatic Cossack of thirty-four, with a lush black moustache, worked closely with Stalin and sometimes they simply 'bunked together', sleeping in their greatcoats on mattresses in the office. It is hard to imagine any of the other warlords living in such a way but Stalin was accustomed to dossing down like the young revolutionary he once was.

* * *

On 17 October Shcherbakov made his radio broadcast to restore morale in Moscow. It had little effect as the streets were clogged with gangs of deserters and refugees piling their belongings on to carts. Stalin was still debating whether to leave Moscow but the moment finally arrived, probably late on the evening of the 18th, when he had to make this decision. Air Force General Golovanov remembered seeing Stalin depressed and undecided. 'What shall we do?' he kept repeating. 'What shall we do?'

At the most world-shattering moment of his career, Stalin

discussed the decision with generals and commissars, bodyguards and servants, and of course he read his history. He was reading the biography, published in 1941, of Kutuzov – who had abandoned Moscow. 'Until the last minute,' he underlined heavily, 'no one knew what Kutuzov intended to do.' Back in his apartment, Valechka in her white apron was cheerfully serving Stalin and the magnates their dinner. When some of them seemed to lean towards evacuation, Stalin's eyes fell on his 'ever-smiling' mistress.

'Valentina Vasilevna,' Stalin asked her suddenly. 'Are you preparing to leave Moscow?'

'Comrade Stalin,' she replied in peasant idiom, 'Moscow is our Mother, our home. It should be defended.'

'That's how how Muscovites talk!' Stalin told the Politburo.

Svetlana also seemed to discourage the abandonment of Moscow when she wrote from Kuibyshev: 'Dear Papa, my precious joy, hello ... Papa, why do the Germans keep creeping nearer all the time? When are they going to get it in the neck as they deserve? After all, we can't go on surrendering all our industrial towns to them.'

Stalin called Zhukov and asked him: 'Are we certain we can hold Moscow? I ask you this with pain in my heart. Speak the truth, like a Bolshevik?'* Zhukov replied that it could be held. 'It's encouraging you're so certain.'

Stalin ordered the guards to take him out to his 'faraway' dacha at Semyonovskoe, which was further from the fighting than Kuntsevo. Beria replied in Georgian that this too was dynamited. But Stalin angrily insisted on going. Once he was there, he found the commandant packing up the last belongings.

'What sort of removals are going on here?' he asked gruffly.

'We're preparing, Comrade Stalin, for the evacuation to Kuibyshev.' Stalin may also have ordered his driver to take him to the special train that was parked under close guard at the Abelmanovsky junction, normally used for storing wooden sleepers. One source in Stalin's office recounted how he walked alongside the train. Mikoyan and Molotov do not mention it, and even a hint of Stalin near a train would have caused panic, but it was the sort of melodramatic scene that Stalin would have

---

* Zhukov recalled him asking this again in mid-November but V. P. Pronin, Chairman of the Moscow Soviet (Mayor), remembered the question being asked on '16 or 17 October'. He surely asked it several times.

relished. If it happened, the image of this tiny, thin figure 'with his tired haggard face' in its tattered army greatcoat and boots, strolling along the almost deserted but heavily guarded siding through the steam of the ever-ready locomotive is as emotionally potent as it was to be historically decisive. For Stalin ordered the commandants of his dacha to stop loading: 'No evacuation. We'll stay here until victory,' he ordered 'calmly but firmly.'

When he got back to the Kremlin, he gathered his guards and told them: 'I'm not leaving Moscow. You'll stay here with me.' He ordered Kaganovich to cancel the special train. The Stalinist system allowed the magnates, who swung between defeatism and defiance, to pursue their own policies until Stalin himself spoke. Then his word was law. On the 'damp dank' evening of the 18 October, the team in charge of defending the city were gathered at Beria's office where the Georgian 'tried to convince us that Moscow must be abandoned. He considered,' wrote one of those present, 'that we have to withdraw behind the Volga. With what are we going to defend Moscow? We have nothing ... They'll smother us all here.' Malenkov agreed with him. Molotov, to his credit, 'muttered objections'. The others 'remained silent'. Beria was said to be the main advocate of withdrawal though he became the scapegoat for everything unsavoury that happened under Stalin. The alcoholic Moscow boss Shcherbakov wanted to withdraw too and it seems that he lost his composure: afterwards, 'in a state of terror', he asked Beria what would happen if Stalin found out.

On the 19th at 3.40 in the afternoon, Stalin summoned his magnates and generals to the the Little Corner. Stalin 'stepped up to the table and said:

"The situation is known to all of you. Should we defend Moscow?"' No one answered. The silence was 'gloomy'. Stalin waited, then said: 'If you don't want to speak, I shall ask each of you to give his opinion.' He started with Molotov, who stuck to his opinion:

'We must defend Moscow.' Everyone, including Beria and Malenkov, gave the same answer. Beria had converted to Stalin's view, as his son admitted: 'My father would never have acted as he did if he had not known ... [and] anticipated [Stalin's] reactions.'

'If you go, Moscow will be lost,' Beria declared. Shcherbakov was one of those who sounded doubtful.

'Your attitude can be explained in two ways,' said Stalin. 'Either you're good-for-nothings and traitors or idiots. I prefer to regard you as idiots.' Then he expressed his opinion and asked Poskrebyshev to bring in the generals. When Telegin and the commander of Moscow, NKVD General Artemev, arrived, Stalin was pacing tensely up and down the narrow carpet, smoking his pipe. 'The faces of those present,' recalled Commissar Telegin, 'revealed that a stormy discussion had just taken place and that feeling was still running high. Turning to us without a greeting, Stalin asked:

'What's the situation in Moscow?'

'Alarming,' reported Artemev.

'What do you suggest?' snapped Stalin.

'A state of siege' should be declared in Moscow, answered Artemev.

'Correct!' and Stalin ordered his 'best clerk', Malenkov, to draft it. When Malenkov read out his verbose decree, Stalin became so irritated that he rushed up and 'literally snatched the sheets of paper from him'. Then he briskly dictated his decree to Shcherbakov, ordering 'the shooting on the spot' of suspected offenders.

Stalin brought up the divisions to defend Moscow, naming many of them from memory, then calling their commanders directly. The NKVD was unleashed on to the streets, executing deserters and even concierges who had tried to leave. The decision to stay and fight had been made. The presence of Stalin in Moscow, said the Comintern leader Dmitrov, was 'worth a good-sized army'. Stalin was refreshed by the end of the uncertainty: when a commissar phoned in from the front to discuss evacuation eastwards, Stalin interrupted him:

'Find out, do your comrades have spades?'

'What, Comrade Stalin?'

'Do they have spades?' The Commissar asked in the background if they had spades.

'What kind of spades, Comrade Stalin – ordinary ones or digging tools?'

'It doesn't matter.'

'Yes, we've got spades! What shall we do with them?'

'Tell your comrades,' replied Stalin calmly, 'to take their spades and dig their own graves. We won't leave Moscow. They won't leave either ...'

Even now Stalin's courtiers bickered among themselves: Stalin ordered Molotov to travel down to Kuibyshev to check on Voznesensky, who was running the Government there.

'Let Mikoyan come with me,' said Molotov.

'I'm not your tail,' Mikoyan shouted, 'am I?'

'Why don't you go too?' suggested Stalin. Five days later Stalin recalled them.

The Panzers were still advancing on the frozen snow and threatening to encircle Moscow. Zhukov had no reserves left. Having lost three million of his soldiers since June, Stalin's notebook was virtually empty. Like a despotic shopkeeper, assisted by his fat accountant son, Stalin jealously guarded his secret reserves while Malenkov sat beside him, keeping tally. When Stalin asked one general what would save the capital, he replied, 'Reserves.'

'Any idiot,' snapped Stalin, 'could defend the city with reserves.' Stalin generously gave him fifteen tanks, at which Malenkov observed that this was all they had left. Amazingly, in just a few months, the vast military resources of this endless empire had been reduced to fifteen tanks in a notebook. In Berlin, the Reich Press Office declared that 'Russia was finished' but Stalin's iron husbandry of his reserves, coupled with Zhukov's brilliant and brutal fighting, was telling on the Germans whose machines were beginning to suffer from the mud and ice while their men were freezing and exhausted. They again halted to prepare for a final push, convinced that Stalin's resources were exhausted. But there was a page in the notebook that they had forgotten.

Stalin's Far Eastern Army, 700,000 strong, guarded against Japan but in late September, Richard Sorge, the spy Stalin called a brothel-keeper, reported that Japan would not attack Russia. On 12 October, Stalin discussed this with his Far Eastern satraps who then confirmed Tokyo's lack of hostile intentions from local intelligence. Kaganovich arranged non-stop trains that, within days and hours, rushed 400,000 fresh troops, 1,000 tanks and 1,000 planes across the Eurasian wastes, in one of most decisive logistical miracles of the war. The last train left on the 17th and these secret legions began to mass behind Moscow.

* * *

Stalin moved into his new Kremlin bunker, an exact replica of the Little Corner, even down to the wood panelling, though its long corridors resembled nothing so much as a 'railway sleeping car. To the right was a row of doors' with 'a heavy security guard'. The officers waited in 'one of the sleeping compartments to the left' until Poskrebyshev appeared and led them into a 'spacious brightly lit room with a big desk in the corner' where they came upon the pacing Stalin, usually accompanied by his Chief of Staff, the ailing gentleman officer, Marshal Shaposhnikov.

Just younger than Stalin, with his thinning hair centre-parted and a tired, yellow face with Tartar cheekbones, Shaposhnikov seemed 'propelled by some special act of Voodooism as he looked quite dead (at least 3 months gone) and must, even when alive, have been very very old', according to a British diplomat. Shaposhnikov called everyone *golubchik*, dear fellow, and Stalin was charmed by the gentility of this Tsarist colonel. When some generals had not reported one day, Stalin angrily asked Shaposhnikov if he had punished them. Oh yes, retorted Shaposhnikov: he had given them a 'severe reprimand'. This did not impress Stalin:

'For a soldier that's no punishment!' But Shaposhnikov patiently explained 'the old military tradition that if the Chief of Staff reprimands [an officer], the guilty party must offer his resignation'. Stalin could only chuckle at this old-worldliness. But Shaposhnikov was a survivor: he had attacked Tukhachevsky in the twenties, served as his judge in 1937 and even denounced a cook saboteur for over-salting the meat. He never signed anything without checking first. In Stalin's presence, he was 'without an opinion'. While he never renounced his views, he never objected to being overruled. He was the only general Stalin called by his name and patronymic, the only one allowed to smoke* in his office.

The war had truly reached the Kremlin, which was now peppered by bomb craters. Mikoyan was knocked down by a bomb. On 28 October, Malenkov was working at Old Square when Stalin called him to the Kremlin: he had no sooner left than a German bomb destroyed the building. 'I saved your life,' Stalin told him.

One day, Stalin insisted that he wanted to witness an artillery barrage against German positions. Beria, in attendance, was very

---

* No one else was ever invited to join Stalin in his constant smoking. This honour to Shaposhnikov resembles Queen Victoria graciously permitting the old Disraeli to sit during their audiences, the only Prime Minister to receive such a privilege.

anxious that he would be blamed if something went wrong. Stalin's car and bodyguards set off down the Volokolamsk highway towards the front but as they were approaching the fighting, Vlasik refused to let them proceed any further. Stalin had to watch the explosions from a distance. Then a tank splashed his limousine, which sent his bodyguards into palpitations. Beria forced Stalin to change cars and go home. Yet Stalin had regained some spirit: he even let Svetlana visit him for a couple of days but then gruffly ignored her in the bunker, cursing the privileges of the 'damned caste' of the élite in Kuibyshev. More importantly, the great actor-manager now devised a scene of reckless but inspired showmanship.

* * *

On 30 October, Stalin suddenly asked General Artemev: 'How are we going to have the military parade?'

There could be no parade, answered Artemev. The Germans were less than fifty miles away. Molotov and Beria thought he was joking. But Stalin calmly ignored them:

'A parade will be held on 7th November ... I'll see to it personally. If there's an air raid during the parade and there are dead and wounded, they must be quickly removed and the parade allowed to go on. A newsreel should be made and distributed throughout the country. I'll make a speech ... What do you think?'

'But what about the risk?' mused Molotov. 'Though I admit the political response ... would be enormous.'

'So it's decided!'

Artemev asked when the parade should begin. 'See to it that no one knows, not even I,' said Stalin, 'until the last hour.' A week later, German spies might have glimpsed the odd sight of Muscovites, supervised by Chekists, collecting chairs from the Bolshoi Theatre and carrying them down the stairs to the Mayakovsky Metro. That evening, the magnates caught the elevator down into Mayakovsky Station where they found a train parked on one side, with its doors open. There were tables inside with sandwiches and soft drinks. After these refreshments, they took their seats on those theatrical chairs. Then, in a slightly vaudeville touch, Stalin, accompanied by Molotov, Mikoyan, Beria, Kaganovich and Malenkov, assembled at the next station, and caught the subway to Mayakovsky. They took their places on the Politburo rostrum to wild applause. Levitan the newsreader broadcast the programme from a radio-station-carriage. The

NKVD Ensemble played the songs of Dunaevsky and Alexandrov. Kozlovsky sang. Stalin spoke for half an hour in a tone of inspiring calm, warning:

'If they want a war of extermination, they shall have one.'

Afterwards, General Artemev approached Stalin: the parade was set for 8 a.m. Even the officers involved were not to know the full details until 2 a.m.

Just before eight o'clock, in a snowstorm and with biting winds that preserved them from German air attack, Stalin led the Politburo up the steps to the Mausoleum, just like old times – except it was earlier and everyone was extremely nervous. Beria and Malenkov ordered their wizard of Special Tasks, Sudoplatov, to report to them on the Mausoleum if the Germans attacked. The public favourite at parades, Budyonny, sabre drawn on a white stallion, rode out from the Spassky Gates, saluted and then mounted to review the parade. The tanks, including the T34s, the outstanding machine of the war, and troops paraded in columns, U-turned at St Basil's, then headed up Gorky Street to the front.

There was a tense moment when a heavy Kliment Voroshilov tank stopped abruptly and turned in the wrong direction, followed by another. Since they were all fully armed, and since Stalin was watching this blunder carefully, Artemev ordered his subordinates to investigate at once. Having caught up with the tanks, their crews were interrogated and innocently revealed that the first tank had simply received a message that another tank was in trouble; following their training the other tanks had gone to its aid. When Artemev reported this on the Mausoleum, the potentates were so relieved that they laughed: no one was punished. Stalin spoke shortly about the patriotic struggle of the Russia of Suvorov, Kutuzov and Alexander Nevsky. The Motherland was in peril but defiant. Appropriately, that very night, the Russian freeze really set in.

On 13 November, Stalin called Zhukov to plan the counter-attacks to put the German attacks off balance. Zhukov and Commissar Bulganin felt that their resources were so low they could not attack but Stalin insisted. 'What forces are we to use?' asked Zhukov.

'Consider it settled!' Stalin rang off but immediately telephoned Bulganin:

'You and Zhukov're giving yourselves airs. But we'll put a stop to that.'

Afterwards Bulganin ran into Zhukov's office: 'Well, I got it really hard this time!' he said.

The counter-attacks were subsumed in the grinding German offensive of 15 November, the last push to take Moscow. The Germans broke through. Again Stalin asked Zhukov: could he hold Moscow?

'We'll hold Moscow without doubt. But we've got to have at least two more armies and no fewer than two hundred tanks.' Stalin delivered the armies 'but for the time being, we don't have any tanks'. Zhukov fought the Germans to a standstill on 5 December, having lost 155,000 men in twenty days. Effectively, Hitler's *Blitzkrieg* had failed. On 6 December, Stalin delivered three new armies to Zhukov and ordered a grand counter-offensive on the four nearest fronts. The next day, Japan attacked America at Pearl Harbor.

Zhukov drove the Germans back two hundred miles. Yet even in such a desperate battle, the generals never forgot Stalin's imperial vanity: just as Mekhlis had tried to win victory on Stalin's birthday in Finland, so now Zhukov and Bulganin ordered Golubev, commander of the Tenth Army: 'Tomorrow will be the birthday of Stalin. Try to mark this day by the capture of Balabanovo. To include this message in our report to Stalin, inform us of its fulfilment not later than 7 p.m. 21 December.' The Battle of Moscow was Stalin's first victory, but a limited one. However, he was immediately dangerously over-optimistic, telling the visiting British Foreign Secretary, Anthony Eden: 'The Russians have already been in Berlin twice and will be a third time.'* It would take millions more dead and almost four years to reach Berlin. Zhukov was so exhausted that, even when Stalin telephoned, his adjutants had to tell him:

'Zhukov is asleep and we can't wake him.'

'Don't wake him up until he wakes himself,' answered the Supremo benevolently. 'Let him sleep.'

* * *

On 5 January, the over-confident Supremo gathered Zhukov and the generals to hear the plan for a massive offensive from Leningrad to the Black Sea to capitalize on the German defeat before Moscow.

---

* In 1760, during the Seven Years War, Empress Elizabeth's General Todtleben took Berlin. Alexander I took the Prussian capital in 1813.

'Who wishes to speak?' asked Stalin. Zhukov criticized the offensive, saying the army needed more men and tanks. Voznesensky was against it too, saying he could not supply the necessary tanks. Stalin insisted on the offensive, at which Malenkov and Beria attacked Voznesensky for 'always finding insuperable and unforeseen' objections. 'On that,' said Stalin, 'we'll conclude the meeting.' In Stalin's anteroom, old Shaposhnikov tried to console Zhukov:

'You argued in vain. These issues had been decided beforehand by the Supremo ...'

'Then why was our opinion solicited?'

'I don't know, dear fellow.'

The intelligent and indefatigable Beria, now forty-three, proved a voracious empire-builder in running the war, but he delivered the tanks and guns Stalin needed. Beria was keen to win points off Voznesensky, whom he loathed, and he soon outstripped Molotov and the older generation. No industry was too complex or too vast for Beria to master: he was in many ways not only the Himmler of Stalin's entourage but also the Speer, another architect. He used the most colourful threats he could muster, asking his subordinates: 'Do you care about seeing the sun rise and fall every day? Be careful!'

In early January 1942, at his flat, Stalin consulted this top industrial *troika*, Beria, Malenkov and Mikoyan, about the armaments shortage.

'What's the problem?' exclaimed Stalin. Beria produced a diagram that showed how Voznesensky was failing to produce enough guns. 'And what should be done?'

'I don't know, Comrade Stalin,' replied Beria artfully. Stalin immediately gave him control of this vital industry.

'Comrade Stalin, I don't know whether I can manage it ... I'm inexperienced in this sort of thing ...'

'It's not experience that's needed here but a strong organizer ... Use prisoners for labour.'

The railways remained impossible to run, even by the energetic and bellowing Kaganovich. When one commissar, Baibakov, reported to Kaganovich, 'the Locomotive' jumped up and shook him by the lapels. Beria reported Kaganovich's table-thumping tempers to Stalin:

'The railways deteriorate because [Kaganovich] won't listen to advice ... he just answers with hysterics.' Kaganovich was criticized for mismanaging the evacuations of industry and, twice, sacked 'for being unable to cope with work under wartime conditions' but he was soon back. Molotov fared no better at running tank production:

'How's [Molotov] managing?' Stalin asked Beria, again accompanied by Malenkov and Mikoyan.

'He has no communication with the factories, doesn't manage them properly ... and holds endless meetings ...' replied Beria, who added tanks to his empire. Molotov lost the tanks but gained the world.

36

Molotov in London, Mekhlis in the
Crimea, Khrushchev in Collapse

On 8 May, the Foreign Commissar took off in a four-engine bomber for London. Stalin instructed him to win a promise of a Second Front – and to clinch recognition of the Soviet borders of 1941, including the Baltics.

He personally charged his favourite air-force general, Golovanov, to plan the route. 'Stalin was a great conspirator,' recalled Golovanov. 'The journey was planned in total secrecy. I had to hide a map of the route in my desk even when my assistant entered my office. Stalin ... told me "Only the three of us know about this – you, Molotov and me." '

'Mr Brown', Molotov's codename, landed in Scotland and was greeted by Eden with whom he took a train from Glasgow to London. When he learned the Second Front was out of the question, Molotov refused to discuss Eden's proposal of a treaty that did not mention the Soviet borders. Molotov immediately reported this to Stalin: 'We consider the treaty unacceptable ... an empty declaration,' but the Supremo changed his mind:

'1. We don't consider it an empty declaration but regard it as important ... Not bad perhaps. It gives us a free hand. The question of borders will be decided by force. 2. It is desirable to sign the treaty as soon as possible and fly to America.'

Meanwhile Molotov also got a taste of English country-house life: he had requested to be lodged outside London, perhaps for security reasons, so Churchill handed over Chequers, his official country mansion. 'Mr Brown' was unimpressed by its Tudor elegance. 'Not a fancy old building,' he mused. 'Some sort of small garden. Apparently some nobleman* had given it to the Government.' Stalin and Molotov were infinitely snobbish about the superiority of Russian grandeur: after all, they lived and

---

* This description certainly complimented Arthur Lee, the colourful adventurer and Conservative MP who bought the house with the fortune of his American heiress wife. He was ennobled as Baron (later Viscount) Lee of Fareham by Lloyd George.

worked in Catherine the Great's palaces. However Molotov had an eye for bathrooms: he remembered the lavatories long after he had forgotten the negotiations. 'There was a bathroom,' he complained, 'but no shower.' As soon as he arrived, his guards asked 'for the keys to all the bedrooms' and he locked himself in every night. 'When the staff at Chequers succeeded in getting in to make the beds,' wrote Churchill, 'they were disturbed to find pistols under the pillows. At night, a revolver was laid out beside his dressing-gown and his despatch cases.' When Molotov was out, his 'maids' guarded his bedroom like Cerberus.

After signing the treaty on 26 May, Molotov flew to Washington to meet President Roosevelt who presented him with a signed photograph, framed in green silk, that read: 'To my friend Vyacheslav Molotov from Franklin Roosevelt 30 May 1942.' Finding FDR 'sociable and pleasant', he was more impressed by the White House than Chequers, especially in the bathroom department: 'Everything there was as it should be,' he said. 'It had a bathroom with a shower too.'

On 9 June, he stopped in London on his way home. Before he left on his dangerous return journey, there was a moment of sentiment when Churchill stood talking with the iron-arsed Russian at the garden gate of 10 Downing Street: 'I gripped his arm,' wrote Churchill, 'and we looked each other in the face. Suddenly he appeared deeply moved. Inside the image, there appeared the man. He responded with equal pressure. Silently we wrung each other's hands ... We were all together and it was life or death for the lot.' Molotov admitted to getting on well with Churchill:

'Yes, we drank a glass or two,' he reminisced. 'We talked the whole night long.' But he could never forget that Churchill was 'an Imperialist, the strongest, the cleverest among them ... 100% Imperialist. So I came to be friends with the bourgeoisie.' He returned with the vague promise of a Second Front, an invaluable Lend-Lease treaty with America, and an alliance with Britain: 'My journey and its results were a great victory for us.' On the flight back to Moscow, Molotov's plane was attacked by enemy fighters and then by Russian ones.

* * *

As Molotov set off for the West, Stalin was launching a wave of counter-attacks along the entire front. He quite reasonably presumed that Hitler would again attack Moscow but the *Führer* actually planned a powerful summer offensive to seize the grain of the Ukraine and, more importantly, the oil of the Caucasus. But Stalin's real fault lay in his raging over-confidence: he lacked the resources for this vast enterprise which, instead of capitalizing on his Moscow victory, handed Hitler the constellation of stunning victories that led to the ultimate crisis of Stalingrad.

He certainly did not help matters by granting draconian powers to his crew of military amateurs. Apart from Stalin himself, no one contributed more to these defeats than the brave, indefatigable and blood-thirsty Mekhlis, now at the height of his power. 'The Shark' could never resist showing off his privileged access: 'When he arrived in the anteroom to Stalin's office,' remembered one commissar, Mekhlis 'didn't even wait for an invitation to go in, he crossed the waiting-room and went straight in.' But 'he never hid anything from Stalin ... who knew this and trusted him.' This gave him the power to get things done: 'If Mekhlis wrote to the Supremo, the measures were very quick.' Yet his antics were always uneasily suspended between the farcical and the diabolical: once when Stalin asked which front needed supplies, the generals were silent except for Mekhlis who piped up to criticize the quartermaster Khrulev. Stalin angrily looked up and asked who was complaining.

'Mekhlis most likely,' replied Khrulev to peals of laughter. Stalin asked Mekhlis to list his needs. 'We lack vinegar, pepper and mustard,' retorted Mekhlis. Even Stalin laughed.

When Mekhlis learned that an arsenal of German pornography had been captured, he immediately launched a new front against Nazi erotica, writing a leaflet called 'How Hitler Corrupts His Army'. His advisers suggested that pornography was natural in a bourgeois army and their nocturnal reading habits were not dictated by Hitler personally, but Mekhlis ignored them and printed eleven million copies of this much mocked document.

He started the year with a visit to the Volkhov Front which had been ordered to relieve the Siege of Leningrad. It was in no shape to launch an offensive which predictably ended in disaster. Mekhlis arrived to investigate, arrest and shoot the culprits. Stalin then offered the front to Voroshilov who courageously, having finally realized his limits, refused it. This outraged Stalin who dictated a sarcastic denunciation of Klim's 'bankruptcy of leadership'. The conclusion was humiliating but not fatal: 'That

Comrade Voroshilov be posted ... to the rear.'* By the end of June, none of these murderous amateurs could save the Volkhov Front: the army was lost along with its talented young General Vlasov. Exhausted and sickened by Stalin's blunders, he turned traitor. Stalin raged about the betrayal to Beria and Molotov, who asked revealingly:

'How did we miss him before the war?' Stalin tried to blame Khrushchev for Vlasov but the Ukrainian boss argued back 'that Stalin had put him in charge of the Moscow counter-offensive'. Stalin, who reacted well to courageous defiance, let the matter drop.

Voroshilov had finally been discredited but Mekhlis and Kulik, despite the latter's string of disasters, still rode high. In October 1941, Kulik had failed to relieve Leningrad; in November at the opposite end of the front, he had been sent to save the city of Kerch in the Crimea. Kulik arrived late and Kerch was temporarily lost to Manstein, one of Hitler's finest captains. Now Stalin considered shooting Kulik and scribbled a note: 'Today. Kulik to Siberia?' but finally settled for demoting him to Major-General and sending Mekhlis to investigate Kulik's late arrival in his DC-3 plane.

'The Gloomy Demon' exposed Kulik's hedonistic junket involving barrels of wine and vodka, a missing 85,898 roubles and the Marshal's new teenage wife. Kulik had soon recovered from the disappearance of his last wife and swiftly romanced this friend of his daughter, a misalliance that Stalin mocked as cradle-snatching. He sacked Kulik as Deputy Commissar yet Zhukov interceded for him. This primitive but popular martinet was reprieved again and, amazingly, promoted. However, his old friendship with Stalin would not end well.

That March, Stalin ordered an assault from Kerch towards the centre of the Crimea to relieve the besieged Sebastopol. Mekhlis, who like his amateur Supremo believed himself a true soldier, gleefully took over the command of these 250,000 men, terrorizing their general, Kozlov, and ignoring the front commander, Budyonny. In this sensitive and complicated battle, Stalin had exchanged an inept and corrupt drunkard for an inept and incorruptible maniac. As Stalin pressured Mekhlis to launch the

---

* Stalin's nephew, Leonid Redens, met the crestfallen Marshal bathing affably with children in the Volga at Kuibyshev.

offensive on time, 'the Shark' replied that his ammunition was low but 'I'll arrest [the officer] if he doesn't straighten out the situation in two days ... We're organizing the big music for the Germans!'

On 2 March, Mekhlis launched his 'big music' in a fiasco that proved to be the insane apogee of terror applied to military science. He banned the digging of trenches 'so that the offensive spirit of the soldiers would not be undermined' and insisted that anyone who took 'elementary security measures' was a 'panic-monger'. All were 'mashed into a bloody porridge'. He bombarded Stalin with demands for more terror: 'Comrade Beria,' Stalin wrote on one of Mekhlis's notes. 'Right! In Novorossisk, make sure that not one scum, not one scoundrel is breathing.'

Mekhlis himself, speeding around the front in his jeep waving a pistol trying to stop the retreat, displayed 'irreproachable personal courage and did nothing for his own glory' yet the 'stupid tyranny and wildly arbitrary ways of this military illiterate', in the words of the poet Konstantin Simonov, a witness, proved disastrous.

On 7 May, Manstein's counter-attack drove Mekhlis off the Crimea altogether, capturing an awesome bag of 176,000 men, 400 planes and 347 tanks. Mekhlis lashed about him, blaming Kozlov and begging Stalin for a great general, a Hindenburg. Stalin was beside himself:

'You take the strange attitude of an outside observer not responsible for the Crimean Front,' he castigated Mekhlis. 'It's a very comfortable position – but it absolutely stinks! You're not an outsider but the representative of Stavka ... You demand the replacement of Kozlov by someone like Hindenburg. But ... we don't have any Hindenburgs ... If you had used aviation against tanks and enemy soldiers and not for sideshows, the enemy would not have broken the front ... You don't have to be Hindenburg to understand this simple thing ...' It was a mark of the obsolete standards of Stalin's court that Hindenburg, the German hero of 1914, was still their paragon in 1942: they needed Guderians not Hindenburgs.

On 28 May, a haggard Mekhlis was waiting in Stalin's anteroom where one could always see the Supremo reflected in the attitudes of his assistants. Poskrebyshev ignored him, then said: 'The Boss's very busy today. Dammit, there are many troubles.'

'Probably something's gone wrong at the front?' asked Mekhlis disingenuously.

'You'd know,' replied Poskrebyshev.

'Yes, I want to report our unfortunate business to Comrade Stalin.'

'Apparently,' said Poskrebyshev, 'the running of the operation wasn't equal to the task. Comrade Stalin's very unhappy ...'

Mekhlis blushed. Young Chadaev joined in:

'I suppose you think the defeat was caused by circumstances?'

'What did you say?' Mekhlis turned on the whippersnapper. 'You're not a soldier! I'm a real soldier. How dare you ...' Then Stalin emerged from his office.

'Hello Comrade Stalin, may I report ...' said Mekhlis.

'Go to hell!' snarled Stalin, slamming his door. Mekhlis, according to Poskrebyshev, later 'almost threw himself at Stalin's feet'. He was courtmartialled, demoted, sacked as Deputy Defence Commissar.

'It's all over!' sobbed Mekhlis but Stalin remained amazingly loyal: twenty-four days later, he was appointed a Front Commissar and later promoted to Colonel-General.

* * *

As if Stalin, Kulik and Mekhlis had not wrought enough defeat, the worst was befalling the South-Western Front where Timoshenko and Khrushchev were launching their offensive from a Soviet salient to retake Kharkov, oblivious of Hitler's imminent attack. Zhukov and Shaposhnikov wisely warned against it but Timoshenko, Stalin's favourite fighting general, insisted on proceeding and the Supremo agreed.

On 12 May, Timoshenko and Khrushchev, both uneducated, crude and energetic, successfully attacked and pushed back the Germans. If Stalin was delighted, Hitler could not believe his luck. Five days later, his Panzers smashed through Timoshenko's flanks, enveloping Soviet forces in steel pincers so that the Russians were no longer advancing but simply burrowing deeper into a trap. The Staff begged Stalin to call off the operation and he warned Timoshenko of the German forces on his flank, but the Marshal jovially reassured him that all was well. By the 18th, 250,000 men were almost encircled when Timoshenko and Khrushchev finally realized their plight.

Around midnight, Timoshenko, the 'brave peasant' terrified of Stalin, persuaded Khrushchev to beg the Supremo to cancel their offensive. At Kuntsevo, Stalin asked Malenkov to answer the phone. Khrushchev asked to speak to Stalin.

'Tell ME!' said Malenkov.

'Who's calling?' Stalin called out.

'Khrushchev,' replied Malenkov.

'Ask him what he wants!'

'Comrade Stalin repeats that you should tell me,' said Malenkov. Then, 'He says the advance on Kharkov should be called off ...'

'Put down the receiver,' yelled Stalin. 'As if he knows what he's talking about! Military orders must be obeyed ... Khrushchev's poking his nose into other people's business ... My military advisers know better.' Mikoyan was shocked that Khrushchev 'was calling him from the front line in battle with people dying around him' and Stalin 'would not walk ten steps across the room'.

The trap snapped shut on a quarter of a million men and 1,200 tanks. The next day, Stalin called off the offensive but it was too late. The exhilarated Germans pushed on towards the Volga and the Caucasus: the road to Stalingrad was open.

* * *

Timoshenko and Khrushchev feared they would be shot. The two friends soon fell out in the scramble to save their careers and lives. There is a story that Khrushchev suffered a nervous breakdown after the encirclement, flying to Baku where he stayed with Bagirov, Beria's ally, who naturally reported Khrushchev's arrival. An unstable Khrushchev started vehemently denouncing Timoshenko, who repaid him in kind:

'Comrade Stalin,' wrote Timoshenko by hand, 'I must add something to our report. The increasingly nervous state of Comrade Khrushchev influences our work. Comrade Khrushchev has no faith in anything – one can't make decisions in doubt ... The whole Council think this is the reason for our fall!' He seems to confirm that Khrushchev did have a mental breakdown: 'It's difficult to discuss – Comrade Khrushchev is very ill ... We gave our report without saying who was guilty. Comrade Khrushchev wants to blame only me.'

Stalin played with the idea of appointing Bulganin to investigate the situation. Bulganin, sensing Stalin's reluctance and, perhaps, guilt, begged to be excused for the un-Bolshevik reason that he and Khrushchev were such friends. Stalin did not insist but reflected mildly on Khrushchev's simplicity: 'He doesn't understand statistics,' said Stalin, 'but we have to put up with him' since only he, Kalinin and Andreyev were 'real proletarians'.

Instead Stalin summoned Khrushchev for a threatening history lesson: 'You know in World War One, after our army fell into German encirclement, the general was court-martialled by the Tsar – hanged.' But Stalin forgave him and sent him back to the front. Khrushchev was still terrified since 'I knew of many cases when Stalin reassured people by letting them leave his office with good news and then had them picked up.'

Stalin was also astonishingly tolerant when Timoshenko asked for more men, having squandered so many: 'Maybe the time has come for you to wage war by losing less blood, as the Germans are doing? Wage war not by quantity but by skill. If you won't learn how to fight better, all the armaments produced in our whole country won't be enough for you ...' This was highly ironic from the most wasteful Supremo in history. Even as they retreated, Stalin remained sarcastically mild to Timoshenko: 'Don't be afraid of Germans – Hitler's not as bad as they say.'

Khrushchev thought they were spared because Mikoyan and Malenkov had witnessed his call to Kuntsevo but it was perhaps simpler: life and death was Stalin's prerogative, and he liked* Khrushchev and Timoshenko. Either way, this was Khrushchev's greatest crisis until, as Stalin's successor, he blundered into the Cuban Missile Crisis twenty years later. Later, Stalin humiliatingly emptied his pipe on Khrushchev's head: 'That's in accordance with Roman tradition,' he said. 'When a Roman commander lost a battle, he poured ashes on his own head ... the greatest disgrace a commander could endure.'

* * *

On 19 June, a *Luftwaffe* aircraft crashed beyond German lines, containing a briefcase bearing the plans for Hitler's summer offensive to exploit the Kharkov disaster and push towards Stalingrad and the North Caucasus. But Stalin decided that the information was either incomplete or a plant. A week later, the Germans attacked exactly as the plans warned, smashing a hole between the Briansk and South-Western Fronts, heading towards Voronezh and then Stalingrad. But it was the oilfields that Hitler really coveted. When he flew in to headquarters at Poltava, he told Field Marshal von Bock: 'If we don't take Maikop and Grozny, then I must put an end to the war.'

---

* Timoshenko's letters to Stalin, scribbled on pages torn out of a notebook, which are in the newly opened Stalin archive, shed light on the Kharkov offensive and Khrushchev's near breakdown.

Timoshenko and Khrushchev fell back towards Stalingrad. When Timoshenko asked for more divisions, Stalin replied sharply:

'If they sold divisions in the market, I'd buy you one or two but unfortunately they don't.' Once again, Timoshenko's front was in free fall. On 4 July, Stalin sarcastically quizzed the Marshal: 'So is it a fact that the 301st and 227th Divisions are now encircled and you're surrendering to the enemy?'

'The 227th is retreating,' replied Timoshenko pathetically, 'but the 301st – we can't find it ...'

'Your guesses sound like lies. If you continue to lose divisions like this, you'll soon be commander of nothing. Divisions aren't needles and it's a very complicated matter to lose them.'

Dizzy with over-confidence, Hitler divided his forces into two: one to push across the Don to Stalingrad while the other headed southwards towards those Caucasian oilfields. When Rostov-on-Don fell, Stalin drafted another savage order: 'Not One Step Backwards', decreeing that 'panic-mongers and cowards must be liquidated on the spot' and 'blocking units' must be formed behind the lines to kill waverers. None the less, Hitler's southern Army Group A broke into the Caucasus. On 4 and 5 August, Stalin, Beria and Molotov spent most of the nights in the office as the Germans took Voroshilovsk (Stravropol), racing towards Grozny and Ordzhonikidze (Vladikavkaz), in the Caucasus and, on the Volga, approached Stalingrad. Von Paulus's Sixth Army was poised to take the city and split Russia in two.

* * *

On 12 August, amidst the calamitous stirrings of the decisive battle of the entire war, Winston Churchill arrived in Moscow to tell Stalin that there would be no Second Front soon, a mission he compared to 'carrying a lump of ice to the North Pole'. Molotov met him at the airport and then escorted him to the residence he had been assigned. On the way, Churchill noticed that the Packard's windows were over two inches thick:

'It's more prudent,' said Molotov. Stalin and Beria took Churchill's visit very seriously, assigning him a bodyguard of 120. The defences around the Kremlin were redoubled. Stalin gave up his own house, Kuntsevo, dacha No. 7. It is a mark of Soviet obscurity that the British were never told and it has taken sixty years to emerge. Perhaps Stalin was repaying Churchill in kind for lending *his* dacha, Chequers, to Molotov.

37

Churchill Visits Stalin:
Marlborough vs Wellington

A strapping aide-de-camp of a princely family, according to Churchill, acted as his host at Kuntsevo. Churchill was shown into Stalin's dining room, where the long table was laden with 'every delicacy and stimulant that supreme power can command'. The British curiously explored.* Without realizing it, Churchill described Stalin's home: surrounded by a stockade, fifteen feet high, guarded on both sides, it was a 'fine large house standing in its own extensive lawns and gardens in a fir wood of about twenty acres. There were agreeable walks ... fountains ... and a large glass tank with ... goldfish. I was conducted through a spacious reception room to a bedroom and bathroom† of almost equal size. Blazing almost dazzling electric lights displayed the spotless cleanliness.'

Within three hours, Churchill, Harriman, and the British Ambassador Sir Archibald Clark Kerr, were driven into the Kremlin to meet with Stalin, Molotov and Voroshilov who, banned from front-line commands, now became the *Vozhd*'s diplomatic gimp, a comedic sideshow to Stalin's diplomatic double act with Molotov. Churchill decided to declare the bad news first: no Second Front that year. Stalin, faced with a fight for his life on the Volga, reacted sarcastically:

'You can't win wars without taking risks,' he said and later: 'You mustn't be so afraid of the Germans.' Churchill growled that

---

* Kuntsevo's furniture was 'stylish "Utility", sumptuous and brightly coloured', thought a young British diplomat, John Reed, 'vulgarly furnished and possessed of every convenience a Soviet commissar's heart could desire. Even the lavatories were modern and ... clean.' A hundred yards from the house was Stalin's new air-raid shelter of the 'latest and most luxurious type', with lifts descending ninety feet into the ground where there were eight or ten rooms inside a concrete box of massive thickness, divided by sliding doors. 'The whole airconditioned and execrably furnished ... like some monstrous ... Lyons Corner House,' wrote Reed.
† The bathrooms in all Stalin's dachas were capacious with the baths specially constructed to fit his precise height.

Britain had fought alone in 1940. Having got the worst bit out of the way, Churchill revealed that the British and Americans were about to launch Operation Torch to seize North Africa, which he illustrated with the drawing of a soft-bellied crocodile and the big globe that stood in the room adjacent to Stalin's office. In an impressive demonstration of his geopolitical instincts, Stalin immediately rattled off the reasons that this operation made sense. This, wrote Churchill, 'showed the Russian Dictator's swift and complete mastery' of military strategy. Then Stalin surprised them more: 'Let God help the success of this enterprise!'

The next morning, Churchill met that 'urbane, rigid diplomatist' Molotov alone to warn him: 'Stalin will make a great mistake to treat us roughly when we have come so far.'

'Stalin's a very wise man,' Molotov replied. 'You may be sure that, however he argues, he understands all.'

At eleven, Stalin and Molotov, accompanied by the usual inter-preter Pavlov, received Churchill in the Little Corner where the *Vozhd* handed his guest a memorandum attacking the West for not launching a Second Front, and again mocked British cowardice.

'I pardon that remark only on account of the bravery of Russian troops,' replied the Prime Minister, who then launched into a magnificent Churchillian soliloquy on the Western commitment to the war. When Churchill poked his unsatisfactory interpreter Dunlop: 'Did you tell him this? Did you tell him that?', Stalin finally smiled:

'Your words are of no importance. What's important is your spirit.' But the conviviality was ice-thin: Stalin's insults infuriated Churchill, who afterwards stalked Kuntsevo, no stranger to gloom and malice, threatening to go home.

Still angry and sullen, Churchill had to appear at the Catherine Hall for the Bacchanalian banquet Stalin held in his honour. Stalin sat in the centre with Churchill on his right, Harriman on his left, then an interpreter followed by General Alan Brooke, Chief of Imperial General Staff, and Voroshilov. Molotov kept the toasts coming for over three hours as nineteen courses were piled on to the table, which was 'groaning with every description of hors d'oeuvre and fish etc.,' wrote Brooke, 'a complete orgy ... Among the many fish dishes was a small suckling pig ... He was never eaten and, as the evening slipped by, his black eye remained fixed on me, and the orange peel mouth developed a sardonic smile!'

Stalin was at his most charming, making it clear that 'he wanted to make amends', thought Clark Kerr, 'but the PM ... cold-shouldered him'. Stalin tried backhanded flattery:

'Some years ago, we had a visit from Lady Astor,' Stalin recounted mischievously. When she suggested inviting Lloyd George to Russia, Stalin had replied: 'Why should we invite ... the head of the Intervention?' Lady Astor corrected him: 'That's not true ... It was Churchill.' Stalin told Astor: 'If a great crisis comes, the English ... might turn to the old warhorse.' Besides, he added, 'we like a downright enemy better than a false friend.'

'Have you forgiven me?' asked Churchill.

'All that is in the past,' replied the ex-seminarian, 'and the past belongs to God. History will judge us.' There was then a crash as Churchill's bodyguard, Commander Thompson, slumped backwards knocking the ice-cream out of a waiter's hand, which then narrowly missed Stalin himself.

'Then,' recorded the Soviet interpeter Pavlov portentously in his notes, 'Stalin spoke.' During the Supremo's toasts, Voroshilov, whom Brooke thought 'a fine hearty old soul, willing to talk about anything with great vivacity' though with the military expertise of a 'child', spotted the Ulsterman was drinking water instead of vodka. Voroshilov ordered yellow pepper vodka, with an ominous chilli floating in it, with which he filled both their glasses:

'No heel taps,' he said – but Brooke managed to sip his glass. Voroshilov then downed two glasses of this firewater: 'The result did not take long to show itself. His forehead broke out in beads of perspiration which soon started to flow down his face. He became sullen and quiet sitting with a fixed stare straight to his front and I wondered whether the moment had arrived for him to slip under the table. No, he retained his seat ...' But just as this cherubic inebriate subsided into peppery oblivion, Stalin, who noticed everything, 'descended straight on him' with a toast the irony of which was missed by the Westerners.

'One of the main organizers of the Red Army was Marshal Voroshilov and he, Stalin, would like to raise a toast to Marshal Voroshilov.' Stalin grinned roguishly like a wicked old satyr because, as Molotov and the others knew well, it was only three months since he had denounced Voroshilov's 'bankruptcy'. Voroshilov struggled to his feet, holding on tightly to the table with both hands, 'swaying gently backwards and forwards with a distant and vacant look in his eyes'. When Stalin raised his toast, Voroshilov tried to focus and then lurched forward, just managing to clink glasses. As Stalin swaggered off to toast Shaposhnikov, 'Voroshilov, with a deep sigh, sank back on to his chair.'

After dinner, Stalin invited Churchill to watch a film – *The German Rout before Moscow* – but Churchill was too angry and tired. He said goodbye and was halfway across the crowded room before Stalin hurried after him and accompanied him to his car.

Churchill awoke as sulky as 'a spoilt child' according to Clark Kerr who arrived at the dacha to discover that 'the PM had decided to pack up and go'. Sporting 'a preposterous ten-gallon hat', surely the most bizarre headgear ever seen at Kuntsevo, Churchill stomped into the garden and turned his back on Clark Kerr who found himself addressing 'a pink and swollen neck'. The Ambassador explained that Churchill 'was an aristocrat and a man of the world and he expected these people to be like him. They weren't. They were straight from the plough or the lathe.'

'This man has insulted me,' retorted Churchill. 'From now on, he can fight his battles alone.' Finally he stopped: 'Well, and what do you want me to do?'

Within the hour, Churchill's entourage was calling the Kremlin to ask for a tête-à-tête with Stalin. The only response was that 'Stalin was out walking', surely a diplomatic promenade since Churchill's tantrum coincided with momentous events that would lead directly to the Battle of Stalingrad: at 4.30 that morning, the German Sixth Army had attacked and smashed the Fourth Tank Army in the loop of the Don River, a more immediate crisis than a pinguid Englishman fulminating in a 'ten-gallon hat'.

At 6 p.m., Stalin agreed to meet. Churchill bade Stalin goodbye in the Little Corner. When he was about to leave, Stalin 'seemed embarrassed' and then asked when they would meet again: 'Why don't you come to my house and have a little drink?'

'I replied,' wrote Churchill, 'that I was in principle always in favour of such a policy.' So Stalin led Churchill and his interpreter, Major Birse, 'through many passages and rooms till we came out into a still roadway within the Kremlin and in a couple of hundred yards gained the apartment where he lived.' Stalin showed the Englishman round his 'simple, dignified' four-room apartment with its empty bookshelves: the library was in Kuibyshev. A housekeeper, not Valechka, since Churchill described her as 'ancient', started to lay up dinner in the dining room. Stalin had planned this dinner: that afternoon, Alexandra Nakashidze called Zubalovo and announced that Stalin had ordered Svetlana to be ready that evening 'to be shown off to Churchill'. Stalin brought the conversation round to daughters. Churchill said his daughter Sarah was a redhead. So is mine, said Stalin who had his cue: he asked the housekeeper to get Svetlana.

A 'handsome red-haired girl' arrived and kissed her father, who rather ostentatiously presented her with a little present. He patted her on the head: 'She's a redhead,' he smiled. Churchill said he had been a redhead as a young man.

'My father,' wrote Svetlana, 'was in one of those amiable and hospitable moods when he could charm anyone.' She helped lay the table while Stalin uncorked the wine. Svetlana hoped to stay for dinner but when the conversation returned to 'guns and howitzers', Stalin kissed her and 'told me to go about my business'. She was disappointed but dutifully disappeared.

'Why shouldn't we have Molotov?' Stalin asked. 'He's worrying about the communiqué. We could settle it here. There's one thing about Molotov – he can drink.' When Molotov joined them, followed by a parade of heavy dishes, culminating in the inevitable suckling pig, Stalin started to tease his Foreign Commissar 'unmercifully'. Churchill joined in:

'Was Mr Stalin aware that his Foreign Secretary on his recent visit to Washington had said he was determined to pay a visit to New York entirely by himself and that the delay in his return was not due to any defect in the aeroplane but because he was off on his own?'

Molotov frowned, Churchill noticed, not realizing he may have been sowing the seeds of mistrust that almost cost Molotov his life. But Stalin's face lit with merriment: 'It was not to New York he went. He went to Chicago where the other gangsters live.'

'Have the stresses of this war been as bad to you personally as carrying through the policy of collective farms,' Churchill asked.

'Oh no,' replied Stalin revealingly. That had been 'a terrible struggle'.

Churchill invited Stalin to London and the *Vozhd* recalled his visit in 1907 with Lenin, Gorky and Trotsky. On the subject of great historical figures, Churchill praised his ancestor the Duke of Marlborough as an inspiration for he, 'in his time, put an end to the danger to European freedom during the War of Spanish

Succession'. Churchill got 'carried away' praising Marlborough's military brilliance. But a roguish 'smile loomed on Stalin's face':

'I think Britain had a more talented military leader,' teased Stalin, 'in the person of Wellington who crushed Napoleon who presented the greatest danger in History.' By 1.30 a.m., they had not yet started eating but Stalin popped out, probably to hear the latest dire news from the Caucasus. When Sir Alexander Cadogan, Permanent Under-Secretary at the Foreign Office, arrived with a draft of the press release, Stalin offered him the suckling pig. 'When my friend excused himself,' wrote Churchill, 'our host fell upon the victim single-handedly.' The dinner finally ended around 3 a.m. Churchill begged Molotov not to see him off at dawn for he 'was clearly tired out'.

'Do you really think I would fail to be there?' replied Molotov urbanely.

Back at Kuntsevo, Churchill lay full length on Stalin's sofa, 'started to chuckle and to stick a pair of gay legs in the air: Stalin had been splendid ... What a pleasure it was to work with "that great man".' As before Churchill, undressed to reveal a 'skimpy crumpled vest' whence 'a pair of wrinkled creamy buttocks protruded', he continued to rave as he finally climbed into a bath, 'Stalin this, Stalin that.' It was already dawn; the alliance was saved; Molotov arrived to take him to the airport.

38

Stalingrad and the Caucasus:
Beria and Kaganovich at War

Stalin recuperated from his Churchillian carousal at home but at 11.30 p.m., he arrived at the office to face the deteriorating crisis in the North Caucasus where the Germans were approaching Ordzhonikidze and Grozny. Budyonny, commander of the North Caucasus Front, had just been joined by Kaganovich who had demanded the right to redeem himself at the front after being sacked as railway boss. Stalin agreed, saying he 'knows the North Caucasus well and got on well with Budyonny in the Civil War'. The bow-legged Cossack and the Jewish Iron Commissar struggled to stop the Germans. Budyonny lost none of 'his dash and sense of irony', refusing to go into his shelter during raids: 'Never mind: let them bomb!' but 'the Locomotive' at war was not a pretty sight.

Surrounded by a 'suite of officers from his personal bodyguard and consultants from Moscow ... toadies, wranglers and intriguers', working all night in a permanent state of bellowing hysteria, always playing with his trademark worry-beads or a key chain, Kaganovich fancied himself 'a great strategist ... issuing orders all on his own' and insisted on interfering in every military plan, setting impossible deadlines, shouting, 'Report personally ... on the fulfilment of the order – or else!' When some trucks blocked the path of his limousine, 'Lazarus,' as his officers nicknamed him, went berserk, bellowing: 'Demote! Arrest! Court martial! Shoot!' But these bawlings did not stop the Germans:

'What's the good of a defence ridge if it isn't defended?' Stalin reprimanded Kaganovich. 'And it seems you have not managed to turn the situation around even where there is no panic and the troops fight quite well.'

Kaganovich however came closer to war than many others. He was hit by shrapnel in the hand, a badge of honour of which he was deeply proud. He was the only Politburo member to be wounded.* When Kaganovich flew back to Moscow for meetings, Stalin, whom he regarded as 'our father', tenderly inquired about his health and then toasted his wound. However, he was also incensed that one of his closest comrades had risked his life in this way.

As the Germans pushed southwards, Stalin feared the Transcaucasus Front would collapse, yielding the oilfields, possibly bringing Turkey into the war, and tempting the restless Caucasian peoples to rebel. Four days after Churchill's departure, Stalin turned to Beria:

'Lavrenti Pavlovich,' he respectfully addressed him. 'Take with you whoever you like and all the armaments you think necessary, but please stop the Germans.' As the Germans took Mount Elbrus, Beria and Merkulov recruited Stalin's staff officer, Shtemenko, ordered Sudoplatov to bring 150 Georgian Alpinists, assembled his flashy entourage, as well as his son Sergo, aged eighteen – and all flew down in a fleet of American C-47s stopping in Tiflis on the way. The generals were contemplating a strategic abandonment of Ordzhonikidze but on the 22nd, Beria, accompanied by his posse, arrived there to terrorize the Transcaucasus commanders. Charkviani, the Georgian boss, was in the room when Beria 'peered coldly round the table with a piercing stare' and told them:

'I'll break your back if you mention a word of this retreat again. You will defend the town!' When one general suggested placing 20,000 NKVD troops in the front line, Beria exploded into 'foul abuse and threatened to break my back if I ever mentioned it again'. Though Charkviani (no great admirer of Beria) thought the NKVD chief saved the day, the generals, all writing after his downfall, complained that his progress along the front was simply 'showiness and noise' which seriously disrupted their work.

Beria also had to destroy any oil that might fall into Nazi hands. Back in Moscow, Stalin summoned Nikolai Baibakov, thirty, Deputy Commissar of Oil Production, to his office. He was alone:

'Comrade Baibakov, you know Hitler wants the oil of the Caucasus. That's why I'm sending you there – you're responsible on the pain of losing your head for ensuring no oil is left behind.' But he would also 'lose his head' if he DID destroy the oil too early.

---

* He received an engraved clock from the Front to show its gratitude: it is now in the Kaganovich archive at RGASPI. Interestingly, both Leonid Brezhnev and Mikhail Suslov, who together ruled the Soviet Union for almost two decades after 1964, got to know Kaganovich on this front.

As he left, with his head spinning, Stalin added: 'Do you know that Hitler has declared that without oil, he'll lose the war?'

Beria added more gruesome threats. 'I was just weighed down by the great responsibility,' says Baibakov who was not afraid but perhaps should have been. 'I underestimated the danger of my personal position.' The correct oilfields were dynamited with minutes to spare. Baibakov kept his head.*

Beria's other mission was to stamp out the embers of treason among the ethnic groups in the North Caucasus. Hence he set up his own NKVD command. As a Georgian Mingrel brought up among non-Georgian Abkhazians, Beria possessed all the prejudices of one tiny Caucasian people for another. The Georgians had always been particularly suspicious of Moslem peoples like the Chechens: in Grozny, Beria investigated the reports that some Chechens had greeted the Germans with open arms. Sergo Beria, who accompanied his father, wrote that they sent delegations to show their support for Moscow, promising to fight like their national hero, Shamyl. Since Shamyl had defied Russia for thirty years, this analogy did their cause no good at all. Beria's cheerfulness with the Chechens concealed his distrust.

Beria descended on Kaganovich and Budyonny in Novorossisk but was not impressed by their demeanour: 'These two idiots disorganized everything,' wrote Sergo Beria, exaggerating somewhat. They found Budyonny 'dead drunk' and in 'a deep torpor' while Kaganovich was 'sober' but 'trembled like a leaf and crawled on his knees before my father'.

'Don't make such an exhibition of yourself,' Beria told Kaganovich.

The German advance ebbed outside Ordzhonikidze and Grozny, undermined by the Soviet resistance at Stalingrad. Beria returned triumphant to Moscow where Stalin, who was viciously jealous of anyone else's military glory, overheard him boasting to Malenkov of his exploits.

---

* Baibakov's interview for this book has been invaluable as he is one of the last of Stalin's Ministers still living. Baibakov became a perennial member of the Soviet Government: Stalin appointed him Commissar for Oil in 1944 and later he ran Gosplan, the main economic agency, except for a short interval, until being sacked by Gorbachev in the eighties. It is a mark of the obsolescence of Soviet economics that the young men Stalin appointed were still running it forty years later. At the time of writing, this tireless nonagenerian is working in the oil industry, taking conference calls with Stalinist dynamism while wearing his medals, beneath a portrait of Lenin.

'Now Beria's going to imagine he's a military leader,' Stalin growled to Shaposhnikov. Beria recommended the sacking of Budyonny, who returned to Moscow from his last active command to be placed in charge of the cavalry. But he appealed to Stalin:

'My soul longs to be in battle. Let me go to Stalingrad!' Stalingrad was indeed about to become the battle of battles, the focus of the world.

* * *

The Germans attacked by land and devastated Stalin's city from the sky, destroying that industrial leviathan in an infernal bombardment that converted its stark Stalinist factories into a primeval landscape of caves and canyons. Stalin, in the office in the early hours, was beside himself, berating his envoys to Stalingrad, Malenkov and Chief of Staff Vasilevsky: 'The enemy broke through ... with small forces. You have enough forces to annihilate the enemy ... Mobilize armoured trains ... Use smoke-screens ... Fight day and night ... The most important thing now is – don't panic, don't fear the impudent enemy and keep up your confidence in our success.'

The gravity of Stalingrad finally concentrated Stalin's mind and brought about a revolution in his conduct of the war. Now he realized that the road to survival and glory lay with professional generals instead of his own impatient amateurism and his bungling cavalrymen. On 27 August, he ordered Zhukov to rush to Stalingrad and promoted him to Deputy Supreme Commander. Zhukov refused the promotion:

'My character wouldn't let us work together.'

'Disaster threatens the country,' replied Stalin. 'We must save the Motherland by every possible means, no matter the sacrifice. What of our characters? Let's subordinate them to the interests of the Motherland. When will you leave?'

'I need a day.'

'Well, that's fine. But aren't you hungry? It wouldn't hurt to have a little refreshment.' Tea and cakes were brought in to celebrate the beginning of the war's most successful partnership.

Zhukov met up with Vasilevsky in Stalingrad where he found the Germans creeping into the city. Stalin demanded counter-attacks but his forces were not yet up to it. Stalin was so anxious that he now slept on a couch in his office with Poskrebyshev waking him every two hours. He was so pale, tired and skinny that Poskrebyshev let him sleep an extra half-hour because he had not the heart to wake him: 'A philanthropist all of a sudden. Get Vasilevsky on the line. Quick! The bald philanthropist!'

Stalin yelled at Vasilevsky: 'What's the matter with them? Don't they understand if we surrender Stalingrad, the south of the country'll be cut off from the centre and we'll probably not be able to defend it? Don't they realize that this isn't only a catastrophe for Stalingrad? We'd lose our main waterway and soon our oil too!' But its importance was no longer merely strategic: Stalingrad bore his name because it had played a formative part in his life. There, at Tsaritsyn in 1918, he had gained his confidence as a man of action, learned how to govern by terror, won Lenin's trust and Trotsky's hatred. At the 'Red Verdun', he had met his cronies, from Voroshilov to Budyonny, and embarked on his marriage with Nadya.

'I think there's still a chance we won't lose the city,' replied Vasilevsky carefully. Stalin rang Zhukov and ordered the attack:

'Delay's equivalent to a crime.' When Zhukov reported that there would be a delay, Stalin sneered: 'Do you think the enemy's going to wait until you bestir yourselves?'

At dawn the Russians attacked again – but made limited gains. The Germans had almost taken the city but one force stood in their way: the 62nd Army under General Vasily Chuikov, spiky-haired, snub-nosed, gold-fanged, clung on to the Volga's west bank, commanding from dugouts and fighting in the skeletal ruins of an apocalyptic industrial landscape, supplied only by ferryboats that crossed the burning Volga in which the destiny of Russia was reflected. The valour, nobility, despair and brutality is best described in Vasily Grossman's epic *Life and Fate*. They fought with modern weapons and ancient ones, sniper rifles and grenades, spades, pipes and fingers, dying to win time:

'Blood,' said Chuikov, 'is time.'

The attention of virtually every minute of Stalin's day was concentrated on one of the most intense battles ever fought: Chuikov's direct commanders were General Andrei Yeremenko and Commissar Khrushchev, now back in favour, but it was much too important to be left to them. Stalin himself supervised the front with Zhukov and Vasilevsky in active command while Malenkov acted as his personal spy. They would appear in Yeremenko's dugout. 'I'd notice Vasilevsky and Malenkov whispering,' said Khrushchev, 'preparing to denounce someone.'

Stalin was shocked and bewildered by Hitler's attack, but after a crisis Stalin assumed the role he believed was made for him: supreme warlord. Initially, Stalin worked with his magnates and generals in an almost collegiate atmosphere before success allowed him to play the military genius. Here, Stalin runs the war assisted by (standing, from left): Bulganin (in uniform), Mikoyan, Khrushchev, Andreyev, Voznesensky, Voroshilov (in uniform) and Kaganovich; (seated, from left): Shvernik, Molotov, Beria and Malenkov.

The outstanding military partnership of the war: in late 1942, after his bungles had caused a series of unnecessary disasters, Stalin appointed Georgi Zhukov his deputy. He admired his military gifts, energy and brutal drive. Zhukov played a decisive role in the victories of Moscow, Leningrad, Stalingrad and Berlin. At the victory parade, Stalin allowed Zhukov to take the salute, but afterwards jealousy and paranoia led him to demote and humiliate his greatest general. Here in 1945, Stalin places Zhukov on his right, but is flanked on the other side by his 'political' Marshals, Voroshilov, who proved brave but inept, and Bulganin, who rose ruthlessly but without trace to become heir apparent.

Stalin as the arbiter of the Grand Alliance, playing Roosevelt against Churchill: here at Teheran in 1943, a grinning Voroshilov stands behind his master while General Alan Brooke (behind Churchill and Roosevelt) glances sardonically at their unsavoury ally.

Churchill and Stalin at Yalta, followed by General Vlasik.

At the Potsdam Conference, Stalin, resplendent in his white Generalissimo's uniform, poses with Churchill, who was about to be thrown out by the British electorate, and the new US President Harry Truman who informed him that America had the Bomb. Stalin despised Truman, missed Roosevelt, and thought Churchill the strongest of the capitalists.

WORDS EXCHANGED BETWEEN THE PRIME MINISTER OF GREAT
BRITAIN THE RT.HON.WINSTON CHURCHILL M.P. AND MARSHAL
OF THE SOVIET UNION K.E.VOROSHILOV AT THE CONCLUSION
OF THE THIRD PLENARY CONFERENCE OF THE THREE POWER
CONFERENCES (GREAT BRITAIN, U.S.S.R. and U.S.A) HELD
AT TEHRAN, IRAN, 28th.NOVEMBER TO 1st.DECEMBER 1943.
        (Interpreted by Captain H.A.Lunghi,R.A.).
        ----

29 Nov. 1943

Marshal Voroshilov: I congratulate you heartily.

The Prime Minister: Thank you.

Marshal Voroshilov: I wish you a hundred more
                    years of life displaying the same
                    fine spirit and vigour as
                    now.

The Prime Minister: Thank you very much.

30 Nov. 1943
The Prime Minister's
Birthday.

Winston S. Churchill

At Teheran, Churchill presented the Sword of Stalingrad to an emotional Stalin who passed it to Voroshilov who dropped it. Stalin sent Voroshilov to apologise to Churchill. A blushing Voroshilov grabbed Hugh Lunghi, a young English diplomat, to interpret. Voroshilov apologised, then wished Churchill a happy birthday. The British Prime Minister thought the Marshal was angling for a party invitation.

At Potsdam, Stalin placed Beria in charge of the race to get the Bomb, the greatest challenge of his career – he could not afford to fail. Here, Beria and Molotov visit the sights in the ruins of Hitler's Berlin, flanked by secret policemen Kruglov (left) and Serov, the expert on deportations.

Beria and family around 1946. Beria was a rapist and sadist – but a delightful father-in-law and grandfather. His blonde, clever and long-suffering wife, Nina (second from left) was the most beautiful of all the grandees' spouses – Stalin treated her like a daughter. Svetlana Stalin was in love with his handsome, dashing son Sergo (far left) whom Stalin also liked. But Sergo married Gorky's lissom granddaughter Martha Peshkova (far right), much to Svetlana's ire.

In 1938, when he promoted him to NKVD boss and brought him to Moscow, Stalin chose Beria's house himself. Only Beria was allowed this sumptuous nobleman's mansion (now the Tunisian Embassy). His wife and son lived in one wing; his own rooms and offices were in another: here many of his female victims were raped. When one refused him and was presented by a guard with the usual bouquet, Beria allegedly snarled: 'It's not a bouquet, it's a wreath.'

Just across from the Kremlin, the hideous colossus, the House on the Embankment, with its own cinema, built for the government in the early 1930s, was decimated during the 1937 Terror when many of its inhabitants were shot. In the morning the doorman told the survivors who had been arrested overnight. Here Natalya Rykova saw off her father for the last time. Stalin's family, such as Pavel and Zhenya Alliluyev, lived here; after the war Svetlana and Vasily had flats here.

In 1949, death stalked the elegant, pink Granovsky apartment block close to the Kremlin where the younger magnates lived in palatial apartments: Khrushchev and Bulganin on the fifth floor, Malenkov on the fourth. Beria was often to be seen waiting at the gates in a black limousine for his friends Khrushchev and Malenkov.

STALIN'S RESIDENCES.
Left His main Moscow house, Kuntsevo, from 1932, the place where he died. Like most of his residences, it was painted a gloomy khaki green.

Middle His favourite holiday house before the war: Sochi (viewed from outside the security gate), and (inset) inside the courtyard.

Bottom The centre of all his houses was always the vaulted dining room where he enjoyed long Georgian feasts with his henchmen, this one at Sochi. On the left his specially built paddling pool since he did not like swimming.

Opposite page STALIN'S FAVOURITE SOUTHERN HOUSES. From top: his post-war holiday headquarters, Coldstream; the millionaire's mansion in Sukhumi; and Museri.

Over-promoted, alcoholic, unstable, cruel and terrified, General Vasily Stalin abandoned two wives whom he treated abysmally and tried to win his father's favour by denouncing air force officers, often with fatal results. Stalin, ashamed of his wartime debauchery and hi-jinks, demoted him. Vasily feared that after his father's death, Bulganin and Khrushchev would kill him: he preferred the bottle or suicide. Girls flocked to the 'Crown Prince'.

After the war, General Vasily Stalin persuaded General Vlasik to give him his exquisite townhouse not far from the Kremlin.

Power and family: the heir apparent Zhdanov. At the end of the war, a tired but cheerful Stalin sits between the two rivals: the flabby, vicious and pusillanimous 'clerk', Malenkov – who was nicknamed 'Melanie' for his broad hips – and (right) smiling, alcoholic Zhdanov. Kaganovich sits on the left. (Back row, left to right): unknown, Vasily Stalin, Svetlana, Poskrebyshev. Stalin pushed Svetlana to marry Zhdanov's son. But the struggle between Zhdanov and Malenkov ended in a massacre.

Malenkov summoned officers to be dressed down. They arrived in the dugout to find a 'short man with a soft puffy face in a tunic' alongside ruffians like Zhukov and Yeremenko. During one dressing-down, Malenkov found himself addressing Vasily Stalin who, though banned from flying active missions himself, was commanding a division:

'Colonel Stalin!' Malenkov said. 'The combat performance of your flyers is revolting ...' Then he turned to another officer: 'And you, the general in the skull-cap? Did you intend to fight or simply play around?' After Malenkov had gone, Khrushchev and Yeremenko would be left alone again in their dugout 'in an eerie silence ... like a forest after a storm'. It was Khrushchev's finest hour,* living in his dugout building the friendships with generals that were to be so useful after Stalin's death.

On 12 September, the rival commanders of Stalingrad flew simultaneously to see their respective Supremos with a neat dictatorial symmetry. As von Paulus met the *Führer* at his *Werwolf* headquarters, a stockade of wooden cabins and bunkers at Vinnitsa, Zhukov and Vasilevsky were on their way to see their *Vozhd*. As Hitler ordered von Paulus to 'capture as quickly as possible the whole of Stalingrad', Zhukov and Malenkov, the rough-hewn soldier and the silky-palmed courtier, presented a report for Stalin proposing further offensives 'to grind down the enemy ... and simultaneously to prepare ... a more powerful blow'. But what? Stalin looked at his own map and studied it quietly, ignoring the soldiers for a long moment, lost in his thoughts.

Zhukov and Vasilevsky retreated from the green baize table, talking to one another in low voices. There might be 'some other solution'.

'And what does "another solution" mean?' asked Stalin, suddenly raising his head. 'I never thought he had such a keen ear,' noted Zhukov. Before the generals could answer, Stalin added: 'Go over to the General Staff and think over carefully what must be done . . We'll meet here at nine tomorrow night.' Victory has many fathers and many claimed paternity for Stalingrad but it was really the child of the unique collaboration between Stalin, Vasilevsky and Zhukov, all gifted in their own ways.

---

* When Khrushchev was in power, he ordered his cronies like Yeremenko to inflate his heroic role at Stalingrad, just like Stalin himself.

At 10 p.m. on 13 September, Stalin welcomed Zhukov and Vasilevsky to his study with an unusual gesture – a handshake: 'Well, what are your views? What have you come up with? Who's making the report?'

'Either of us,' Vasilevsky replied. They handed over their map which showed their basic plan to launch a massive offensive against the German flanks, held by the weaker Romanian forces, smashing into their rear and linking up to encircle them: Operation Uranus. Just at this moment, the German attack, ordered by Hitler at Vinnitsa earlier that day, descended on the embattled 62nd Army. Poskrebyshev entered the room – Yeremenko was on the line from Stalingrad. Chuikov was just maintaining his bare-knuckle grip on the west bank of the Volga while Stavka prepared the operation. Sending both generals straight back to Stalingrad to reconnoitre Uranus, Stalin said portentously:

'No one else knows what we three have discussed here. No one beyond the three of us is to know about it for the time being.'

On 9 October, Stalin restored the unitary command of the armies to the generals. He again celebrated by shaking hands with Zhukov and Vasilevsky, whom he used as special representatives at the fronts: he did not like them 'sitting around' in Moscow. Chief of Staff since May, Alexander Vasilevsky, aged forty-seven, was the third of the extraordinary Stalingrad team. In many ways, he was closer to Stalin even than Zhukov.

* * *

Broad-shouldered and barrel-chested but with a sensitive expression and a gentle, courtly charm, Vasilevsky had been groomed by Shaposhnikov. This outstanding staff officer was his successor not only professionally but also as the sole gentleman among cut-throats, and as Stalin's special confidant. His decency puzzled, impressed and amused Stalin who so lacked it himself:

'You command so many armies,' he reflected, 'yet you wouldn't hurt a fly.' Vasilevsky also hailed from a vanished world that fascinated Stalin: his father had been a prosperous village priest on the Volga and he was educated for the priesthood but became a captain in the Tsar's army. When he joined the Red Army, he had had to forsake his priest-father and cut off relations. After meetings, Stalin frequently asked Vasilevsky to stay behind to discuss whether he was tempted by the priesthood: 'Well, well, I didn't want you to be,' laughed Stalin. 'That's clear. But Mikoyan and I wanted to be priests but were rejected. Until now, I can't understand why!' Then: 'Did your religious education do anything for you?'

'No knowledge is entirely wasted,' Vasilevsky replied cautiously: 'Some of it turned out to be useful in military life.'

'The thing priests teach best, is how to understand people,' mused Stalin, who once said his father was a priest. Perhaps he sometimes thought about his own paternity for around this time, he told Vasilevsky: 'One shouldn't forget one's parents.' On a later occasion he asked him: 'When did you last see your parents?'

'I've forsaken them,' replied the General, worried that this was a test. 'My father's a priest, Comrade Stalin.'

'But is he a counter-revolutionary?'

'No, Comrade Stalin, he believes in God as a priest but he's not a counter-revolutionary.'

'When the war's quieter, I think you should take a plane, visit your parents and ask for their forgiveness.' Stalin did not forget Vasilevsky's father:

'Did you ever fly and see your parents and ask their blessing?' he asked later.

'Yes, Comrade Stalin,' replied Vasilevsky.

'It'll be a long time before you pay off your debt to me.' Stalin then opened his safe and showed him some papers. They were money orders in Stalin's own name that had been sent to Vasilevsky's father throughout the war. The son, amazed and somewhat moved, thanked Stalin profusely. Now, Vasilevsky's special responsibility was Stalingrad.

* * *

The two messianic tyrants almost simultaneously prepared their peoples for victory. 'There will be a holiday on our street too,' Stalin hinted in his 7 November speech. The next day, Hitler boasted to his people:

'I wanted to reach the Volga ... at a particular city. By chance it bore the name of Stalin himself ... I wanted to capture it and ... we have as good as got it!'

The Little Corner was now a-quiver with tension. Stalin agonized that the Germans would guess what was afoot. On the 11th he was worrying that he did not have enough aircraft. On the 13th, as von Paulus launched a last attempt to dislodge Chuikov, now holding a ruined splinter of territory only fifty yards deep, Zhukov and Vasilevsky flew into Moscow for a final briefing. 'By the way Stalin smoked his pipe, smoothed his moustache and never interrupted once, we could see he was pleased,' wrote Zhukov. Afterwards, Vasilevsky returned to Stalingrad.

On the 18th, Stalin, accompanied by Beria, Molotov, Malenkov, and Zhukov, who remained to command Operation Mars* before Moscow, worked in the Little Corner until 11.50 p.m. Three hours before the attack, the three fronts facing Stalingrad, under Generals Yeremenko, Rokossovsky and Vatutin, were informed they were to attack imminently. Presumably Stalin and his comrades then went to dinner or watched a movie to pass the time. Stalin rarely slept before 4 a.m. – 'the need just passed', he later told Churchill – so he surely stayed up to hear that the troops had gone in. At 7.20 on the misty morning of 19 November, the 3,500 guns on the northern sector opened up. When this Jupiterian thunderclap was unleashed, the earth shook thirty miles away. A million men, 13,541 guns, 1,400 tanks and 1,115 planes, smashed into Hitler's forces.

---

* Simultaneously with Stalingrad's Operation Uranus, Zhukov launched the forgotten Operation Mars against the Rzhev salient facing Moscow, probably his greatest defeat: hundreds of thousands of men were lost in just two days of an operation that illustrated his bold but crude style.

Part Eight

War: The Triumphant Genius,
1942–1945

39

The Supremo of Stalingrad

During Stalingrad, the Supremo usually fell asleep wearing all his clothes on the metal campbed that stood under the stairs that led to the second floor at Kuntsevo. If there was an emergency, the 'bald philanthropist' Poskrebyshev, who slept in his office, would call. He awoke around eleven when Shtemenko called from the Operations Department to give him his first report of the day. The Politburo and Staff had already been working for hours since they not only had to share Stalin's insomnia but also had their own onerous empires to run: Mikoyan worked from 10 a.m. until almost 5 a.m., napping in his office.

At noon, Stalin ate a light breakfast, served by Valechka, often remaining at home, whether at Kuntsevo or the Kremlin, to work in the early afternoon. But wherever he was, the Supremo, now sixty-three, would spend the next sixteen hours running the war. He now received bulletins from all his roving Stavka plenipotentiaries, who had to report twice a day, noon and 9 p.m.: Vasilevsky in Stalingrad was the most eagerly awaited that day. Stalin turned very nasty if his envoys neglected to report. When Vasilevsky once failed to do so, Stalin wrote:

> It's already 3.30 ... and you have not yet deigned to report ... You cannot use the excuse that you have no time as Zhukov is doing just as much at the front as you yet he sends his report every day. The difference between you and Zhukov is that he is disciplined ... whereas you lack discipline ... I am warning you for the last time that if you allow yourself to forget your duty ... once more, you will be removed as Chief of General Staff and sent to the front.

Malenkov was always punctilious in his reports but even the meticulous Zhdanov was sometimes distracted by battle, provoking another reprimand: 'It's extremely strange that Comrade Zhdanov feels no need to come to the phone or to ask us for mutual advice at this dangerous time for Leningrad.' Independence was dangerous in Stalin's eyes.

At 4 p.m., General Alexei Antonov, 'young, very handsome, dark and lithe', who became his trusted Chief of Operations, after Vasilevsky's promotion, and after trying a series of officers all of whom were swiftly sacked, arrived with the next report. Antonov was a 'peerlessly able general and a man of great culture and charm', wrote Zhukov. Stalin was a stickler for accurate reporting and would, recalled Shtemenko, 'not tolerate the slightest ... embellishment'. Antonov handled him deftly: always calm, 'a master at assessing the situation', he graded the urgency of his files by colour and 'knew when to say, "Give me the green folder".' Then Stalin smilingly replied: 'Well now, let's look at your "green file".'

In the early evening, Stalin arrived in the Kremlin in his convoy of speeding Packards or else walked downstairs from his flat to the Little Corner where the 'cosy' anteroom, with its comfortable armchairs, strictly policed by Poskrebyshev, was already full. Visitors found themselves in a world of control, sparseness and cleanliness. There was nothing unnecessary anywhere. Everyone had shown their papers repeatedly and been searched for weapons. Even Zhukov had to surrender his pistol. 'The inspection was repeated over and over again.' Poskrebyshev, now in NKVD General's uniform, greeted them at his desk. They waited in silence though regulars greeted one another before falling quiet. It was tense. Those who had never met Stalin before were full of anticipation but as one colonel recalled, 'I noticed that those ... *not* here for the first time, were considerably more perturbed than those ... here for the first time.'

At around 8 p.m., when Stalin arrived, a murmur passed through the room. He said nothing, but nodded at some. The colonel noticed 'my neighbour wiped drops of sweat from his brow and dried his hands on a handkerchief'. A small room, a cubbyhole, contained the last bodyguards at a desk before the office. Stalin entered that 'bright spacious room', with its long green table. At the other end of the room was his desk, on which there was always a heap of documents in their *papki*, a broad-frequency telephone, a line of different-coloured telephones, a pile of sharpened pencils. Behind the desk, there was a door that led to Stalin's own lavatory and the signal room which contained easy chairs, all the Baudot and telegraph equipment to connect

Stalin to the fronts, and the famous globe at which he had discussed Operation Torch with Churchill.

* * *

That night, Molotov, Beria and Malenkov, the perennial three-some, were waiting with Voroshilov and Kaganovich. Stalin nodded and opened the GKO with no chit-chat; its sessions continued until he left many hours later. Stalin sat at his desk and then paced up and down, returning to get his Herzogovina Flor cigarettes which he broke into pieces to fill his pipe. The civilians, as always, sat with their backs against the wall, looking up at the new portraits of Suvorov and Kutuzov while the generals sat on the other side of the table, looking up at Marx and Lenin, a deployment that reflected the constant war between them. The generals immediately spread their maps on the table and Stalin continued his pacing, waddling somewhat. 'He would stop in front of the person he was addressing and look straight into his face' with what Zhukov called a 'clear tenacious gaze that seemed to envelop and pierce through the visitor'.

Poskrebyshev began calling in the experts from the anteroom: 'soon my neighbour also rose ... the receptionist called him by name, he went livid, wiped his trembling hands on his handkerchief, picked up his file ... and went with hesitant steps.' As he showed them in, Poskrebyshev advised:

'Don't get excited. Don't think about disagreeing with anything. Comrade Stalin knows everything.' The visitor must report quickly, no small talk, then leave. Inside the room, the grim *troika* of Molotov, Beria and Malenkov swivelled to peer coolly at the newcomer.

Stalin exuded power and energy. 'One felt oppressed by Stalin's power,' wrote his new Railways Commissar who reported to him hundreds of times, 'but also by his phenomenal memory and the fact he knew so much. He made one feel even less important than one was.' Stalin drove the pace, restless, fidgeting, never far from an eruption. Most of the time he was laconic, tireless and icily cold. If he was displeased, wrote Zhukov, 'he lost his temper and objectivity failed him'.

The visitors could always sense the danger, yet they were also surprised by the genuinely collegiate argument at these sessions. Mikoyan looked back on the 'wonderfully friendly atmosphere' among the magnates during the first three years of the war. The country was run in the form of the GKO through Stalin's meetings

with key leaders in the presence of whoever was in his office –
usually the GKO with Mikoyan, and, later, Zhdanov, Kaganovich
and Voznesensky.

'Sharp arguments arose,' recalled Zhukov, with 'views expressed
in definite and sharp terms' as Stalin paced up and down. Stalin
would ask the generals' opinions: 'Stalin listened more' when
'they disagreed. I suspect', thought Admiral Kuznetsov, 'he even
liked people who had their own point of view and weren't afraid
to stand up for it.' Having created an environment of boot-licking
idolatry, Stalin was irritated by it.

'What's the point of talking to you?' he would shout. 'Whatever
I say, you reply, "Yes Comrade Stalin; of course, Comrade Stalin ...
wise decision, Comrade Stalin."' The generals noticed how 'his
associates always agreed with him', while the generals could
argue, though they had to be very careful. But Molotov and the
brash newcomer Voznesensky did argue with him: 'The
discussions were frank,' recalled Mikoyan. When Stalin, reading
one of Churchill's letters, said the Englishman thought 'he had
saddled the horse and now he can enjoy a free ride ... Am I right,
Vyacheslav?', Molotov replied:

'I don't think so.' Zhukov 'witnessed arguments and ...
stubborn resistance ... especially from Molotov when the
situation got to the point where Stalin had to raise his voice and
was even beside himself, while Molotov merely stood up with a
smile and stuck to his point of view.' When Stalin asked Khrulev
to take over the railways, he tolerated his refusal: 'I don't think
you respect me, refusing my proposal,' he said, indulging the
quartermaster, one of his favourites. Amidst rows, Stalin insisted
'Come to the point' or 'Make yourself clear!'

Once Stalin had formed his opinion and argument had ceased,
he appointed a man to do the job with the usual death threat as
an added incentive. 'This very severe man controlled the
fulfilment of every order,' recalls Baibakov, the oil engineer,
'When he gave the command, he always helped you to carry it
out so you received every possible means necessary to do it. Hence
I wasn't scared of Stalin – we were direct with one another. I
fulfilled my tasks.' But Stalin had a 'knack for detecting weak
spots in reports'. Woe betide anyone who appeared before him
without mastery of their front. 'He would at once drop his voice
ominously and say, "Don't you know? What are you doing
then?"'

Operation Uranus seemed to refresh Stalin who, observed Khrushchev, started to act 'like a real soldier', considering himself 'a great military strategist'. He was never a general let alone a military genius but, according to Zhukov, who knew better than anyone, this 'outstanding organizer ... displayed his ability as Supremo starting with Stalingrad'. He 'mastered the technique of organizing front operations ... and guided them with skill, thoroughly understanding complicated strategic questions', always displaying his 'natural intelligence ... professional intuition' and a 'tenacious memory'. He was 'many-sided and gifted' but had 'no knowledge of all the details'. Mikoyan was probably right when he summed up in his practical way that Stalin 'knew as much about military matters as a statesman should – but no more'.

* * *

At about 10 p.m., Antonov made his second report. There were limits to the friendly spirit that Mikoyan described. War was the natural state of the Bolsheviks and they were good at it. Terror and struggle, the ruling Bolshevik passions, pervaded these meetings. Stalin liberally used fear but he himself lived on his nerves: when the new Railways Commissar arrived, Stalin simply said, 'Transport is a matter of life and death ... Remember, failure to carry out ... orders means the Military Tribunal', at which the young man felt 'a chill run down my spine'. When a train was lost in the spaghetti of fronts and railways, Stalin threatened, 'If you don't find it as general, you'll be going to the front as a private.' Seconds later the Commissar, 'white as a sheet', was being shown out by Poskrebyshev who added,

'See you don't slip up. The Boss's at the end of his tether.' Stalin was always pacing up and down. There were various warning signals of a black temper: if the pipe was unlit, it was a bad omen. If Stalin put it down, an explosion was imminent. Yet if he stroked his moustache with the mouthpiece of the pipe, this meant he was pleased. The pipe was both a prop and a weather vane.* His tempers were terrifying: 'he virtually changed before one's eyes,' wrote Zhukov, 'turning pale, a bitter expression in his eyes, his

---

* As the war went on, it became a symbol of his avuncular image in the West – Uncle Joe – and statesmen tended to send him pipes as presents. Maisky, Ambassador to London, for example, wrote to Stalin: 'After Mr Kerr [British Ambassador] gave you a pipe and it was reported in the press, I was presented with pipes for you from two firms ... and I send herewith an example for you ...'

gaze heavy and spiteful.' When some armies complained that they had not received their supplies, Stalin berated Khrulev:

'You're worse than the Enemy: you work for Hitler.'

The three guard dogs of the Little Corner, Molotov, Malenkov and Beria, 'never asked questions, just sat there and listened, sometimes jotting a note ... and looking at either Stalin or whoever came in. It was as if Stalin needed them either to deal with anything that came up or as witnesses to history.' Their purpose was to preserve the illusion of collective rule and terrorize the generals. Stalin and the magnates all regarded themselves as amateur commanders and shared their Civil War suspicion of 'military experts'.

'Look at an old coachman,' Mekhlis explained. 'They love and pity the animals but the whip is always ready. The horse sees it and draws its own conclusions.' There in a nutshell, from one of Stalin's mini-dictators, was the essence of the Supremo's style of command. 'We could all remember 1937,' said Zhukov. If anything went wrong, they knew 'you'd end up in Beria's hands and Beria was always present during my meetings with Stalin'. The generals' sins were recorded: Mekhlis had accused Koniev of having kulak parents in 1938. Rokossovsky and Meretskov were naturally keen not to return to Beria's torture chambers. Stalin received information, complaints and denunciations from the secret police and from his generals.

When they wrote their memoirs in the sixties, the generals presented themselves as Beria's innocent victims. They were certainly under the constant threat of arrest but were themselves avid denouncers. Timoshenko had denounced Budyonny and Khrushchev. Even now Operation Uranus was launched in a fever of denunciations: Golikov (the hapless pre-war spymaster), denounced the commander Yeremenko. Stalin simultaneously used Malenkov to watch Khrushchev and Yeremenko. When Stalin accused Khrushchev of wanting to surrender Stalingrad, the Commissar started to distrust his own staff. But Khrushchev himself was no slouch at denouncing generals, having blamed Kharkov on Timoshenko. Simultaneously at Stalingrad, a member of the rising General Malinovsky's staff had committed suicide, leaving a note emblazoned 'Long Live Lenin' but not mentioning Stalin: perhaps Malinovsky, who had served in the Russian Legion in France during WW1, was an Enemy?

'You'd better keep an eye on Malinovsky,' Stalin ordered Khrushchev, who protected the general.

The magnates fought ferociously for power and resources with one another and with the generals. When Beria requested 50,000 extra rifles for the NKVD, General Voronov showed the request to Stalin.

'Who made this request?' he snapped.

'Comrade Beria.'

'Send for Beria.' Beria arrived and started trying to persuade Stalin, speaking in Georgian. Stalin interrupted him angrily and told him to speak Russian.

'Half'll be enough,' ruled Stalin but Beria argued back. Stalin, 'irritated to his limit', reduced the numbers again. Afterwards, Beria caught up with Voronov outside.

'Just you wait,' he hissed, 'we'll fix your guts.' Voronov hoped this was an 'Oriental joke'. It was not.

Stalin frequently acted as a conciliator in rows over resources: when he ordered that the artillery be given 900 trucks, Beria and Malenkov, who worked as a gruesome duo, caught up with Voronov. 'Take 400 trucks.'

'I'll go back and report to the Supremo,' threatened the general. Malenkov delivered the full quota of trucks.

Living in this environment of fear and competition, the magnates themselves were tormented by mutual jealousies: 'Molotov was always with Stalin,' wrote Mikoyan disdainfully, 'just sitting in the office, looking important, but really discharged from actual business.' Stalin only needed him 'as the second man, being a Russian' but kept him 'isolated'. Molotov assisted on foreign policy but lacked the responsibilities of the others. Mikoyan was one of the chief workhorses, overseeing the rear, rations, medical supplies, ammunition, the merchant navy, food, fuel, clothing for the people and armies, while also as Commissar of Foreign Trade negotiating Lend-Lease with the Allies, a stupendous portfolio. 'Only Molotov saw Stalin as often as I did,' he boasted, forgetting the tireless, omnipresent Beria.

The 'terror of the Party', Beria, who behaved like a villain in a *film noir*, blossomed in wartime,* using the Gulag's 1.7 million slave labourers to build Stalin's weapons and railways. It is

---

* His commissars included Boris Vannikov and I. F. Tevosian, both arrested and released, and D. F. Ustinov who was just thirty-three and would rise to be the ultimate master of the Soviet military-industrial complex, becoming a CC Secretary, Marshal – and the Defence Minister who would order the Soviet invasion of Afghanistan in 1979.

estimated that around 930,000 of these labourers perished during the war. But his NKVD was the pillar of Stalin's regime, representing the supremacy of the Party over the military. After General Voronov had twice defied him in front of Stalin, Beria was finally allowed to arrest him. When Voronov did not appear at a meeting, Stalin casually asked Beria:

'Is Voronov at your place?' Beria replied that he would be back in two days. The generals are said to have coined a euphemism for these terrifying interludes: 'Going to have coffee with Beria.' His minions watched the soldiers on every front, their reports pouring in to Beria and often to Stalin himself. In 1942, Stalin raised the surveillance another step by ordering Kobulov to bug Voroshilov, Budyonny – and Zhukov himself whose officers were harassed and arrested.

Yet Stalin was wary of Beria's empire-building. When Beria got Kaganovich dismissed from the railways, he tried to nominate his successor.

'Do you think I'd agree to the candidate ... Beria imposes on me? I'll never agree to it ...' But the railways were a constant headache and only Kaganovich, that 'real man of iron' in Stalin's admiring words, could perform the necessary miracles.

* * *

For sixteen hours, Stalin never ceased 'issuing instructions, talking on the phone, signing papers, calling in Poskrebyshev and giving him orders'. When he heard from Mikoyan and Khrulev that the soldiers were short of cigarettes, he made time during the battle of Stalingrad to telephone Akaki Mgeladze, Party boss of Abkhazia, where the tobacco was grown: 'Our soldiers have nothing to smoke! Tobacco's absolutely necessary at the front!' He personally drafted every press release, a master of succinct yet rousing phrases such as 'Blood for blood!', inserting quotations from Suvorov. Yet while jealously checking the kudos of his generals, he was punctilious in giving them credit for their victories.

Stalin's hours of pressure and work were awesome but his commissars and generals had invariably been up since dawn, a life that demanded 'enormous physical and moral resources' with 'nervous exhaustion' a real danger. Stalin legislated the lives of his generals, personally decreeing their rota of work and rest. Vasilevsky had to sleep from 4 a.m to 10 a.m. without fail. Stalin sometimes rang Vasilevsky like a strict nanny to check he was asleep. If he answered the phone, Stalin cursed him. Yet Vasilevsky found it impossible to attend Stalin's nocturnal dinners and films and then do all his work, so he had to break the rules, stationing his adjutant at the telephone to reply: 'Comrade Vasilevsky's resting until ten.' Stalin's other workhorses, Beria and Mikoyan, were expected to spend most nights with him while achieving a Herculean workload, yet they managed it, running sprawling and sleepless administrative empires on the adrenalin of war and patriotism, Bolshevik threats and the talent to survive.

Stalin drank little and expected others to be sober. Artillery general Yakovlev once arrived to report, fortified with cognac. Without raising his head from his desk, Stalin said: 'Come closer, Comrade Yakovlev.' Yakovlev stepped forward. 'Come closer.' Then: 'You're a little drunk, aren't you?'

'Yes slightly, Comrade Stalin.' Stalin said no more about it.

* * *

At midnight, Vasilevsky reported jubilantly from Stalingrad: Hitler's Romanian allies were crumbling. As he listened, Stalin called Poskrebyshev and ordered tea. When the tea arrived in a glass in a silver ornamental holder, the commissar or general, usually Antonov, fell silent. All watched Stalin's ritual as he squeezed his lemon into the tea, then slowly got up, opened the door behind his desk into the restroom, opened the cupboard, built into the wall and took out a bottle of Armenian brandy. Then he returned, poured a half a teaspoon of this into the tea, replaced the brandy, sat, stirred it and said: 'Carry on.'

In high spirits at this instant success, Stalin and his companions left the Little Corner and probably headed over to Kuntsevo for dinner and then a film, but these dinners were not the drunken carousals of later years. When the exhausted Berias and Molotovs staggered home with only a few hours until they had to start work again, Stalin read his history books on his divan until he fell asleep in the early hours.

* * *

Within four days of the launch of Operation Uranus, the German Sixth Army, 330,000 men, was encircled in what Stalin called the 'decisive moment of the war'. As the Russians tightened their grip, von Manstein's counter-attack failed to break through. The *Luftwaffe* proved incapable of supplying from the air. The encircled Germans suffered a cruel slow death from starvation, ice and dynamite. On 16 December, the Russians counter-attacked into Manstein's rear, threatening to cut off Army Group Don and break through towards Rostov. In the Little Corner, the impatient Stalin chose General Rokossovsky, not the Stalingrad commander Yeremenko, to oversee Operation Ring, the liquidation of the Sixth Army.

'Why don't you say anything?' he asked Zhukov, who had frowned.

'Yeremenko will be very hurt,' replied Zhukov.

'It's no time for feeling hurt,' said Stalin. 'We're not schoolgirls. We're Bolsheviks!'

On 10 January, Rokossovsky attacked the benighted Germans, slicing their pocket in half. The Sixth Army diminished daily. The military defeat became a human struggle for survival, as the Germans ate horsemeat, cats, rats, each other, and finally nothing. On 31 January, Field Marshal Paulus surrendered and 92,000 starving, frostbitten scarecrows, barely recognizable as men let alone soldiers, became prisoners. Stalin himself wrote out this newsflash: 'Today our armies trapped the commander of the Sixth Army near Stalingrad with all his staff ...'

* * *

Now a confident, preening Stalin and a gold-braided, bemedalled, imperial Bolshevik Russia emerged, blood-spattered but swaggering with pride, from behind the iron mask of Soviet austerity, to fight their way into Europe.*

On 6 January 1943 Stalin, having consulted two old comrades Kalinin and Budyonny, overturned the Bolshevik slogan 'Down with the golden shoulderboards!' and restored the auric epaulettes and braid of Tsarist officers. He teased Khrulev 'for suggesting we restore the old regime' but personally instructed the media how to spin it: the gold braid was not 'just decoration but also about order and discipline: tell about this.'

Two weeks later, he promoted Zhukov to Marshal. On 23 February, the omniscient military amateur himself joined the Marshalate: during the next two years, Stalin rarely appeared out of its uniform.

---

* This confidence was immediately reflected in Stalin's ungrateful treatment of his Western allies despite their gallantry in risking their lives to deliver aid to Russia: Mikoyan reported that the British had brought radio equipment on their Naval Mission in Murmansk 'without documentation. Either we should ask them to take it back or give it to us. I ask directions.' Molotov simply wrote 'Agreed.' But Stalin grumpily scribbled in his blue crayon: 'Comrade Molotov agreed – while Mikoyan suggested nothing!' As for the Royal Navy's radio: 'I propose confiscate the equipment as contraband!'

Simultaneously, he slightly clipped Beria's powerful wings: in April,* he brought military counter-intelligence, with its dreaded Special Departments, under his own aegis as Defence Commissar. He renamed it *Smersh*, an acronym for 'Death to Spies' that he coined himself, but kept Abakumov in charge. This slick but vicious secret policeman of thirty-five had worked closely with Beria but Stalin, the ultimate patron, now took him under his wing.

Yet Stalin's world-historical triumphs were always embittered by private disappointments. Soon after Stalingrad, Stalin received two disturbing messages: a letter that denounced the debauchery of his son Vasily and revealed the seduction of his adored Svetlana, and a German offer to exchange his prisoner son, Yakov.

---

* On 16 April 1943, Stalin once again split the huge NKVD into two separate agencies – the NKGB under Merkulov, containing the State Security police, and the NKVD under Beria that controlled the normal police and the huge slave labour camps. However, Beria remained *curator* or overlord of both 'Organs'.

40

Sons and Daughters: Stalin and the
Politburo's Children at War

The unprecedented surrender of a German Field Marshal humiliated Hitler just as acutely as Yakov's capture exposed Stalin: both
dictators expected these embarrassments to fall on their swords.
Now Count Bernadotte of the Red Cross approached Molotov
with an offer to swap Yakov for von Paulus. Molotov mentioned
the offer but Stalin refused to swap a marshal for a soldier:

'All of them are my sons,' Stalin replied like a good Tsar, telling
Svetlana, 'War is war!'

The refusal to swap Yakov has been treated as evidence of
Stalin's loveless cruelty but this is unfair. Stalin was a mass
murderer but in this case, it is hard to imagine that either
Churchill or Roosevelt could have swapped their sons if they had
been captured – when thousands of ordinary men were being
killed or captured.* After the war, a Georgian confidant plucked
up the courage to ask Stalin if the Paulus offer was a myth. He
'hung his head', answering 'in a sad, piercing voice':

'Not a myth ... Just think how many sons ended in camps! Who
would swap them for Paulus? Were they worse than Yakov? I had
to refuse ... What would they have said of me, our millions of
Party fathers, if having forgotten about them, I had agreed to
swapping Yakov? No, I had no right ...' Then he again showed the
struggle between the nervy, angry, tormented man within and the
persona he had become: 'Otherwise, I'd no longer be "Stalin".' He
added: 'I so pitied Yasha!'

---

* Yakov's daughter Gulia believes Stalin 'did the right thing'. Svetlana Stalin
compares his behaviour to Margaret Thatcher's refusal to negotiate with the terrorists
holding Terry Waite: 'We don't talk to those people.' Yakov was not the only one of
Stalin's family in encirclements: Artyom Sergeev was caught too – but he broke out
and made it back to Moscow where he told his story to Mikoyan. He was sent to a
Deputy Defence Commissar who told him: 'You're a Lieutenant and I'm Deputy
Commissar. You mustn't repeat this to anyone more senior. Forget it all There are
those who might not understand and this could ruin your life so write and sign here:
"I was not there and I saw nothing."'

A few weeks later, on 14 April in a POW camp near Lübeck, Yakov, who courageously refused to co-operate with the Germans, committed suicide by throwing himself on to the camp wire. At the Little Corner that night, oblivious to Yasha's heroism, Stalin worked with Molotov and Beria before heading off to dinner at about 1 a.m. He did not find out the truth for some time but when he did, he regarded his son with pride. Once at Kuntsevo, he left his own dinner and was found looking at Yasha's photograph.

'Did you ever see Yasha?' he asked the Georgian after the war, drawing out the photograph. 'Look! He's a real man eh! A noble man right to the end! Fate treated him unjustly ...' He ordered the release of Yakov's wife Julia (though she returned damaged by the trauma). Like Nadya, Yakov for ever troubled him.

* * *

Stalin now received a letter from the leading documentary film-maker Roman Karmen that denounced Colonel Vasily Stalin for the seduction of his wife and flaunting his debauchery. This letter opened a can of worms that ruined Stalin's relationships with both drunken Vasily and treasured Svetlana. Stalin started to look into their lives and what he found, shocked him profoundly.

By the climax of Stalingrad, Vasily was back in Moscow, living a life that was a caricature of the decadent wassails of aristocratic swells in Pushkin's *Onegin*. Spoiled by the sycophancy of his own Tsarevich's court, scarred by a mother's loss and a father's irritation, over-promoted and arrogant yet also terrified of his eminence and wildly generous to friends, Vasily took over Zubalovo, once the home of his ascetic mother and severe father, and turned this mansion (rebuilt after its dynamiting) into a pleasure dome of drinking, dancing and womanizing. The Tsarevich's set were glamorous film stars, screenwriters, pilots, ballerinas and free-loaders, a sort of Stalinist 'Ratpack': Karmen and his beautiful actress wife, Nina, were the centre of it along with the dashing poet Konstantin Simonov and his film-star wife, Valentina Serova. Stalin knew them all personally and liked Simonov's best-selling collection of love poems *With You and Without You*.

'How many copies are you printing?' Stalin asked Merkulov.

'Two hundred thousand,' replied the secret policeman.

'I read it,' joked Stalin, 'and I think it would have been enough to print just two: one for her and one for him.' Stalin was so pleased with this joke that he repeated it throughout the war.

The fun at Vasily's orgies was often rather desperate. He was 'permanently drunk' and often hit his wife Galina who had recently given birth to their son, Alexander. He was always drawing his revolver and firing at the chandeliers with his daredevil friends. Frustrated by Stalin's ban on his active missions, reckless of his own safety and that of his companions, Vasily enjoyed flying planes drunk, an aerodynamic version of Russian roulette. When he wanted to show off to his sister's pretty friend Martha Peshkova, he arrived drunk in Tashkent and insisted on flying her to see Svetlana in Kuibyshev. 'He flew me, legless, and with a drunk crew,' she recalls. 'Even though there was ice on the wings, they drank the spirit instead of using it for de-icing so the plane would not keep its height. Finally we had to crash-land and glided into a haystack in a clearing.' Martha was terrified. Vasily hiked to the nearest collective farm from where he despatched a rescue mission and was fêted in the local Party Chairman's house. He was so drunk that the Chairman's wife locked Martha in her room to protect her. Even his friend Vladimir Mikoyan, killed at Stalingrad, complained of Vasily's 'drinking, wilfulness and outbursts of rudeness: what a cretin!'

Yet for the young heroes and artistic stars during the war, Zubalovo was 'like Heaven', says Vasily's cousin Leonid Redens, 'because it was piled high with all that food and drink and far away from the fighting!' The Crown Prince had his pick of the girls at Zubalovo but when he began an affair with Nina Karmen, he fell in love with her and moved her into the mansion. Even though his wife Galina and baby had long since returned from Kuibyshev, along with Svetlana, and were meant to be living at Zubalovo, he flaunted the affair which, says Redens, 'went beyond all bounds'. No one could stop the Tsarevich except the Tsar himself, so the aggrieved husband wrote to Stalin who was outraged. When he ordered the NKGB to investigate Vasily's set, he discovered something that was enough to provoke any Georgian father to reach for his shotgun.

* * *

Svetlana, sixteen, living between the sterile austerity of the Kremlin apartment and the vapid degeneracy of Zubalovo, felt 'lonely' and unappreciated both by her busy father and her 'unpleasant' brother but this freckled redhead had matured early into a curvaceous, intelligent and sensitive girl who resembled Stalin's mother and possessed much of her father's obstinacy and toughness. Indeed her Redens cousins thought Vasily, for all his faults, was 'much softer and gentler'. A voracious reader and with fluent English, Svetlana found a copy of the *Illustrated London News*, perhaps at Beria's house, which she often visited, with the revelation about her mother's suicide: 'Something in me was destroyed,' she wrote. 'I was no longer able to obey the word and will of my father ... without question.'

At one of Vasily's parties during Stalingrad, a handsome, worldly and famous screenwriter named Alexei Kapler arrived at Zubalovo. Kapler, nicknamed Lyusia, was a suave and mesmerizing raconteur and Casanova, though married: 'Oh he could talk and had the gift of communication with any age group, he was like a child himself,' wrote Svetlana. Stalin himself was his patron, supervising his own portrayal in Kapler's scripts for the films *Lenin in October* and *Lenin in 1918*. Kapler brought a reel of film of Greta Garbo in *Queen Christina*. He was immediately charmed by Svetlana, imagining their situation resembled the movie. 'She was the great lady and I was poor Don Alphonso. She was bold and unpretentious. I was forty and someone of importance in cinema' yet 'she was surrounded and oppressed in an atmosphere worthy of a god'. To the clever but brooding Svetlana, he was like a character out of one of her Dumas novels.

'Can you do the foxtrot?' he asked. Svetlana felt awkward in her flat shoes – but 'Kapler assured me I was a good dancer ... I was wearing my first good dress from a dressmaker' with 'an old garnet brooch of my mother's'. She trusted him.

'Why are you so unhappy today?' he asked. Svetlana explained that 'it was ten years to the day since my mother's death yet no one seemed to remember'. The two were 'irresistibly drawn to one another' – it was wartime 'and we reached out to each other'. He lent her 'adult' books and poetry about love which helped overcome her fear of the vulgarity of sex about which Vasily constantly told her: 'I was afraid of this part of life presented to me in an ugly way by Vasily's dirty talk.'

Their relationship was passionate but never fully sexual: 'A kiss, that's all,' remembered Kapler. Yet it was thrilling for Svetlana: 'Romantic and pure. I was brought up that sex was only for marriage,' she revealed later. 'Father would not think to permit me anything outside of marriage.' But the war had changed everything: at any other time, Kapler might have thought the better of seducing Stalin's only daughter but 'I thought she really needed me.'

'To me,' said Svetlana, 'Kapler was the cleverest, kindest, most wonderful person on earth. He radiated knowledge and all its fascination,' introducing the schoolgirl to the exciting wartime freedoms: he took her to the theatre, lent her an illegal translation of Hemingway's *For Whom the Bell Tolls*. Vasily held wild parties at the Aragvi restaurant where they foxtrotted to a jazz orchestra. Svetlana breathlessly recounted her romance to Martha Peshkova at school every day: Kapler gave her an expensive brooch – a leaf with an insect on it.

This charismatic womanizer was moved by Svetlana's plight but he also revelled in his new adventure, boasting to movie director Mikhail Romm that he was now close to Stalin. He was despatched to cover Stalingrad for *Pravda*, filing his 'Letters of Lieutenant L from Stalingrad' in which he daringly paraded his affair with the words: 'It's probably snowing in Moscow. You can see the crenellated wall of the Kremlin from your window.' The *cognoscenti* were amazed at the folly of taunting a vindictive Georgian father on the front page of *Pravda* but to Svetlana, this was 'staggering in its chivalry and recklessness. The moment I saw it, I froze' but 'I sensed the whole thing might come to a terrible end.' At school, Svetlana showed Martha the article under the desk.

When Kapler returned, Svetlana begged him not to see her but, as he said, 'I don't remember who suggested the risk of that heart-rending farewell.' They met in an empty apartment near Kursk Station where Vasily's pals had assignations. Her bodyguard Klimov sat anxiously next door.

Beria had already informed Stalin, who warned Svetlana 'in a tone of extreme displeasure that I was behaving in a manner that could not be tolerated' but he blamed Vasily for corrupting her. Seething about Vasily's debauchery, Stalin dismissed his son as Air-force Inspector for conduct unbecoming, and ordered him to be locked up in the guardhouse for ten days, then posted to the North-West Front. Vlasik, Stalin's domestic panjandrum, suggested Kapler leave Moscow. Kapler told him to 'go to hell' but arranged an assignment away from the city.

Meanwhile Merkulov handed Stalin the phone intercepts of Svetlana and Kapler's conversations, a tool not usually available to the irate fathers of errant daughters. Stalin was enraged. On 2 March, Kapler was bundled into a car which was followed by a sinister black Packard 'in which General Vlasik sat, looking very important'. At the Lubianka, Vlasik and Kobulov supervised his sentencing for 'anti-Soviet opinions' to five years in Vorkuta.

The next day, already under pressure as Manstein's counter-offensive retook Kharkov and threatened the success of Stalingrad, Stalin was so angry he got up hours earlier than usual. Svetlana was getting dressed for school with her nanny when Stalin 'strode briskly into my bedroom, something he had never done before'. The look in his eyes was 'enough to rivet my nurse to the floor'. Svetlana had 'never seen my father look that way before'. Stalin, in a blazing Georgian temper, was 'choking with anger and nearly speechless'.

'Where, where are they all?' he spluttered. 'Where are all these letters from your "writer"? I know the whole story! I've got all your telephone conversations right here!' He tapped his tunic pocket. 'All right! Hand them over! Your Kapler's a British spy. He's under arrest!' Svetlana surrendered Kapler's letters and screenplays, but shouted: 'But I love him!'

'Love!' shrieked Stalin 'with hatred of the very word', and, 'for the first time in my life', slapped her twice across the face. Then he turned to the nanny: 'Just think, nurse, how low she's sunk. Such a war going on and she's busy fucking!'

'No, no, no,' the nanny tried to explain, fat hands flapping.

'What do you mean "no",' Stalin asked more calmly, 'when I know the whole story?' Then to Svetlana: 'Take a look at yourself! Who'd want you? You fool! He's got women all around him!' Stalin gathered up the letters and took them into the dining room where he sat at the table where Churchill had dined – and, ignoring the war altogether, started to read them. He did not appear at the Little Corner that day.

That afternoon, when Svetlana returned from school, Stalin was waiting for her in the dining room, tearing up Kapler's letters and photographs. 'Writer!' he sneered. 'He can't even write decent Russian! She couldn't even find herself a Russian!' Kapler's Jewishness especially riled him. She left the room and they did not speak again for many months: their loving relationship was shattered for ever.

This is often presented as the height of Stalin's brutality yet, even today, no parents would be delighted by the seduction (as he thought) of their schoolgirl daughters, especially by a married middle-aged playboy. Yet Stalin was a traditional Georgian steeped in nineteenth-century prudery and to this day, Georgian fathers are liable to resort to their shotguns at the least provocation. 'Being a Georgian, he SHOULD have shot that ladies' man,' says Vladimir Redens. Long after she wrote her memoirs, Svetlana understood that 'my father over-reacted': he thought he was 'protecting his daughter from a dirty older man'.*

Days later, Vasily and his retinue flew up to the North-Western Front where he finally flew one or two combat missions, but his outrages continued. In May, he set off on a drunken fishing expedition in which the pilots caught fish by tossing aircraft rockets into a pond with delayed fuses. One of the rockets exploded, killing a Hero of the Soviet Union.

On 26 May, Stalin ordered Air-force Commander Novikov to '1. dismiss Colonel VJ Stalin immediately from ... command of air regiment; 2. announce to the regimental officers and VJ Stalin that Colonel Stalin is dismissed for hard drinking, debauchery and corrupting the regiment.' But it was impossible to keep a dictator's son down: by the end of the year, the scapegrace had once again been promoted and he was soon driving his Rolls-Royce along the front, borrowing official planes whenever it suited him. One of his boon companions was alarmed when he insisted on trying to overtake an army lorry on the crowded roads of the Baltic front. When the lorry refused to give way, Vasily simply shot out the tyres.

As for Svetlana, she was soon in love with someone whose name was so dreaded that, in two published memoirs and many interviews over fifty years, she has still never revealed his identity.

* * *

Not until March 1943, shortly after the Kapler affair, did Stalin finally contain Manstein's counter-attack, leaving a swollen Soviet salient bulging into the German lines around Kursk. Hitler approved Operation Citadel to cut off the bulge while Stalin and his generals debated what to do. His instincts were always to attack, but Zhukov and Vasilevsky managed to persuade him to wait and break the Germans in a defensive position. This made Stalin even more agitated and nervous, but he had learned the great lesson of Stalingrad: he took their advice on what would become the world's greatest tank battle, Kursk.

* Their age difference was twenty-four years, not much more than that between Stalin and Nadya in 1918 but this was a parallel that may have intensified his anger. The two slaps are not Stalin's greatest crimes. Kapler's five years were cruel but he was fortunate not to be quietly shot. On his release in 1948, he returned against his parole to Moscow, was rearrested and sentenced to another five years in the mines. He returned after Stalin's death, remarried and was then reunited with Svetlana with whom he finally enjoyed a passionate affair. He died in 1979.

After a dinner with Stalin that lasted from 3 to 7 a.m., Zhukov and Vasilevsky rushed to the front to plan the battle. Malenkov supervised the generals, Mikoyan amassed the reserves, Beria provided 300,000 slave labourers to dig an unbreachable 3,000 miles of trenches. Over a million men and, including reserves, around 6,000 tanks waited.

The waiting was agony for the jittery Supremo who let off steam in a volcanic tantrum with his aircraft designer. Yakovlev arrived in the study to find Stalin and Vasilevsky examining fragments of the wing of his Yak-9 fighter. Stalin pointed to the pieces ... and asked:

'Do you know anything about this?' He then exploded in a frenzied rant: 'I had never seen Stalin in such a rage,' remembered Yakovlev. Stalin demanded to know when this fault had been discovered. When he heard that it had only been noticed 'in the face of the enemy', he 'lost his composure even more'.

'Do you know that only the most cunning enemy could do such a thing – turn out planes in such a way that they would seem good at the plant and no good at the front. This is working for Hitler! Do you know what a service you've rendered Hitler? You Hitlerites!'

'It was difficult to imagine our condition at that moment ... I was shivering,' admitted Yakovlev. The silence was 'tomb-like' as Stalin paced the room until he asked:

'What are we going to do?'

At dawn on 5 July, the Germans threw 900,000 men and 2,700 tanks into this colossal battle of machines in which fleets of metallic giants clashed, helm to helm, barrel to barrel. By the 9th, the Germans had reached their limit. On the 12th, Zhukov unleashed the costly but highly successful counter-attack. The Battle of Kursk was the climax of the Panzer era, the 'mechanized equivalent of hand-to-hand combat', which left a graveyard of 700 tanks and burnt flesh. Agreeing to cancel Citadel, Hitler had lost his last chance to win the war.

On the afternoon of 24 July, Stalin welcomed Antonov and Shtemenko to the Little Corner in a 'joyously jubilant mood'. Stalin did not even want to hear their report – just tinkered cheerfully with the victory communiqué, adding the words: 'Eternal glory to the heroes who fell on the battlefield in the struggle for the liberty and honour of our Motherland!'

* * *

Stalin was not alone in finding it difficult to control his own
children during wartime: Khrushchev and Mikoyan played stellar
roles in the Kursk triumph, the former as Front Commissar, the
latter as Supply maestro, but simultaneously they both found
their children embroiled in dangerous crises. Stalin was both
sympathetic and heartless in dealing with the tragedies of the
Politburo families.

Leonid Khrushchev, Nikita's eldest son from his first marriage,
was already notorious as a ne'er-do-well. Now he became a Stalinist
William Tell. Reprimanded by Komsomol for 'drunkenness', he had
settled down, married Lyubov Kutuzova, with whom he had a little
girl, Julia, and shown courage as a bomber pilot, though he
remained a drunken brawler.* Leonid boasted boozily of his
marksmanship and was challenged to balance a bottle on a pilot's
head. He shot off the neck of the bottle. This did not satisfy these
daredevils. Leonid shot again, fatally wounding the officer in the
forehead. He was court-martialled.

Khrushchev may have appealed to Stalin for clemency, citing
the boy's bravery. But Stalin, who would not save Yakov, 'did not
want to pardon Khrushchev's son', as Molotov recalled. However,
he was not sentenced but allowed to retrain as a fighter pilot. On
11 March 1943, he was shot down during a dogfight with two
FockeWulf 190s near Smolensk. He was never found. Rumours
spread that he had turned traitor – which, in Stalin's system, cast
doubt on his widow, Lyubov, who had visited the theatre in
Kuibyshev with an 'amazingly attractive' French military attaché.
Lyubov was probably denounced by Khrushchev's chief bodyguard. She was arrested and interrogated by Abakumov himself,
and condemned.

In another of those tragedies of Stalinist family life, little Julia
was told her mother was dead. The memory of her parents was
obliterated and she was adopted by her grandfather, Khrushchev
himself, whom she called 'Papa'.† The Khrushchevs were cold
parents. Nikita himself seemed to believe the charges against
Lyubov. 'Stalin played this game,' recalls Julia, 'and Khrushchev

* In 1941, Leonid had shouted that Stalin was far from being 'the greatest one and
father of peoples' – he was a 'damned scoundrel' and Kirov's murderer!
† Her mother served five years in a Mordovia labour camp, followed by five years in
exile. When she returned in 1954, Khrushchev refused to meet her. Julia only met
her mother again in 1956. They were strangers – and remain so: the mother is still
alive, living in Kiev. In 1995, a plane was discovered near Smolensk containing the
skeleton of a pilot still in his goggles and helmet: it was probably Leonid.

was playing for his life' but 'Nikita never spoke about it and even as a pensioner, he spoke only in general terms. This was very humiliating and painful for him.' Perhaps, says Julia Khrushcheva, it contributed to his later decision to denounce Stalin.

* * *

That summer, it was Mikoyan's turn. Two of his sons were pilots. Stepan was wounded, then during Stalingrad, 18-year-old Vladimir was killed. So Stalin 'expressly ordered' his son Vasily to take Stepan into his own division and 'make sure not to lose any more Mikoyans'. On Vasily's orders, Stepan's engineer claimed the plane was not ready for him to fly whenever possible. This indulgence did not last.

Among all the other children in Kuibyshev, Mikoyan's younger boys Vano, fifteen, and Sergo, fourteen, were friends with the unhinged son of Shakhurin, the Aircraft Production Commissar. Volodya Shakhurin played a silly but risky game in which he pretended to 'appoint' a mock government with the teenage Mikoyans as ministers, all recorded in his exercise book. When they returned to Moscow, this Volodya Shakhurin fell in love with Nina, daughter of Ambassador Umansky who was just leaving for his next posting.

'I won't let you go,' young Shakhurin told Nina. The schoolchildren were walking across the Kamennyi Most, close to the Kremlin, when Shakhurin borrowed Vano Mikoyan's pistol which he had been lent by his father's bodyguards. The boy ran ahead with Nina then, on the bridge, shot her dead and killed himself. A horrified Vano Mikoyan ran back to the Kremlin to tell his mother. The NKGB discovered the gun belonged to the young Mikoyans who were also 'ministers' in the schoolboy 'government', which was obviously a conspiracy. Vano was arrested.

'Vano just disappeared,' remembers Sergo. 'My mother was frantic and they called the police stations.' Mikoyan, working down the corridor from Stalin himself, rang Beria, then called his wife Ashken:

'Don't worry. Vano's in the Lubianka.' Mikoyan knew that this could only happen with Stalin's permission. The shrewd Armenian decided not to appeal to Stalin 'so as not to make things worse'. Ten days later, Sergo was also arrested at Zubalovo and taken to the Lubianka in his pyjamas:

'I must tell mama.'

'It'll only take an hour,' they replied. Twenty-six schoolboys were arrested and imprisoned, including Stalin's nephew, Leonid Redens, whose father had been shot in 1940. The secret police reported the children's innocence but Stalin replied:

'They must be punished.' This was so vague that no one was quite sure what to do with the young prisoners. The boys were interrogated by Lieut.-Gen. Vlodzirmirsky, one of Beria's cruellest torturers, 'tall and handsome in his uniform', who was, says Sergo, 'very nasty. He shouted at us.' Sergo was placed in solitary for a week. In December, after six months in the Lubianka, the interrogations ceased and the children became really frightened. Sergo's interrogator showed him a confession that he had been 'a participant in an organization ... to overthrow the existing government'.

'Just sign and you can see your mother again!'

'I won't sign, it's not true,' said Sergo.

'It doesn't make any difference,' bellowed the general. 'Sign – you go home. If not, back to your cell. Listen!' He could hear his mother's voice in the next room. All the children signed their confessions. 'Of course this could have been used against my father.' Sergo and Vano were driven with their mother back to the Kremlin. 'I was very glad my father wasn't there – I was afraid of his anger,' says Sergo.

Mikoyan told the elder boy:

'If you're guilty, I'd strangle you with my own hands. Go and rest.' He never mentioned it to the youngest. But the matter was not closed: after three days at home, the children had to go into exile. The Mikoyans spent a year in Stalinabad, cared for by their housemaid. Stalin never forgot the case and later considered using it against Mikoyan.

41

Stalin's Song Contest

At about 11 p.m. on 1 August 1943, Stalin and Beria arrived at Kuntsevo Station and boarded a special train, camouflaged with birch branches, armed with howitzers and packed with specially tested provisions. The train, which, with its theatrical shrubbery poking out of its guns, must have resembled a locomotive Birnam Wood, puffed westwards. The Kursk counter-attacks, Operations Rumiantsev, to the north, and Kutuzov, to the south, both named after Tsarist heroes, were so successful that Stalin felt safe to embark on this preposterously staged visit to the front.

Stalin slept at Gzhatsk, then headed towards Rzhev on the Kalinin Front. Transferring into his Packard, he set up his headquarters in a self-consciously humble wooden cottage with a picturesque veranda (still a museum today) in the hamlet of Khoroshevo where he received his generals. Knowing from Zhukov that Orel and Belgorod would fall imminently, Stalin ate 'a cheerful supper' with his entourage.

The old lady who lived there was on hand to provide a touch of folksy authenticity until Stalin, who prided himself on his popular touch, unexpectedly insisted that he must pay her for his stay. He was unable to work out a sensible sum because he had not handled money since 1917 but, in any case, he had no cash on him. Stalin asked his flunkies for the money. Here was a classic moment in the farce of the workers' State when, with much tapping of tunic pockets, jiggling of medals and rustling of gold braid, not one of the boozy, paunchy commissars could find a single kopeck to pay her. Stalin cursed the 'spongers'. Since he could not pay in cash, he compensated the crone with his own provisions.

Then Stalin peered grumpily out at the village which he immediately noticed was teeming with ill-concealed Chekists: he asked how many there were, but the NKVD tried to conceal the real number. When Stalin exploded, they admitted there was an

entire division. Indeed, the generals noticed that the village itself
had been completely emptied: there was no one except the NKVD
for miles around.

He slept on the old lady's bed in his greatcoat. Yeremenko
briefed him. Voronov was summoned, covering miles to make it
to the mysterious meeting. 'Finally we came to a beautiful grove
where small wooden structures nestled among the trees.' Led into
the cottage, Stalin stood in front of a 'wretched wooden table that
had been hastily dashed together' and two crude benches. A
special telephone had been fixed to link Stalin to the fronts, with
the wires going out of the window. Waiting to report to the
Supremo, the generals were unimpressed with this *mise-en-scène*.

'Well, this is some situation!' whispered one general to Voronov
who suddenly realized: 'It's intentional – to resemble the front.'
Stalin cut off the briefing, contenting himself with giving some
orders, then dismissed the generals who had to slog back to the
real fray. Stalin asked if he could go further towards the fighting
but Beria forbade him. He visited the hospital at Yukono,
according to his bodyguards, and was depressed by so many
amputees. Afterwards, he felt ill and his arthritis played up.*
Stalin returned by road in his armoured Packard and a convoy of
security cars.

Suddenly the cars stopped. 'He needed to defecate,' wrote
Mikoyan, who heard the story from someone who was there.
Stalin got out of the car and asked 'whether the bushes along the
roadside were mined. Of course no one could give such a
guarantee ... Then the Supreme Commander-in-Chief pulled
down his trousers in everyone's presence.' In a metaphorical
commentary on his treatment of the Soviet people, and his
performance as military commander, he 'shamed himself in front
of his generals and officers ... and did his business right there on
the road.'

On his return, Stalin was immediately able to deploy his heroic
journey in a letter to President Franklin D. Roosevelt, with whom
he was discussing the venue for the first meeting of the three
leaders of the Grand Alliance: 'Having just returned from the
front, I am only now able to reply to your letter ...' He could not
meet FDR and Churchill at Scapa Flow in Orkney – 'I have to

---

* This scene resembles the moment when Hitler, in his train, found himself looking
into a hospital train on its way back from the Eastern Front: he and the wounded
stared at each other for a second before he ordered the blinds to be closed.

make personal visits to ... the front more and more often.' He proposed they meet in a more convenient place – Teheran, the capital of Iran, occupied by British-Soviet forces.

Stalin's courtiers knew the significance of this visit to the front. A month later, Yeremenko, his host, prodded by Beria and Malenkov, proposed that Stalin receive the Order of Suvorov First Class for Stalingrad, and for giving 'such valuable orders that guaranteed victory on the Kalinin Front, ... inspired by the visit to the front of the Supreme Commander-in-Chief...'

On 5 August, when Orel and Belgorod fell, Stalin jovially asked Antonov and Shtemenko: 'Do you read military history?' Shtemenko admitted he was 'confused, not knowing how to answer'. Stalin, who had been rereading Vipper's *History of Ancient Greece*, went on: 'In ancient times, when troops won victories, all the bells would be rung in honour of the commanders and their troops. It wouldn't be a bad idea for us to signify victories more impressively ... We' – and he nodded at his comrades, 'we're thinking of giving artillery salutes and arranging some kind of fireworks ...' That day, the guns of the Kremlin fired the first victory salvo. Henceforth, Stalin punctiliously worked out the salutes to be given for each victory and the staff had to get every detail correct. Just before 11 p.m. the messages were rushed to the stentorian newsreader Levitan who telephoned Poskrebyshev for Stalin's approval. Then the salvoes resounded across the Motherland.

'Let's listen to it,' Stalin often suggested in the Little Corner. The generals now competed to be the first to give Stalin good news. On the 28th, Koniev phoned to announce he had taken Kharkov but was told that Stalin always slept in in the mornings. Koniev daringly phoned Kuntsevo directly. A delighted Stalin answered it himself. But when there was a mistake in the victory announcements, Stalin yelled: 'Why did Levitan omit Koniev's name? Let me see the message!' Shtemenko had left it out. Stalin was 'dreadfully furious'. 'What kind of anonymous message is this? What have you got on your shoulders? Stop that broadcast and read everything over again. You may go!'

The next time, he asked Shtemenko to bring the communiqué on his own, asking, 'You didn't leave out the name?' Shtemenko was forgiven.

As he massed fifty-eight armies, from Finland to the Black Sea, to embark on a colossal wave of offensives, an elated Stalin,

having closed down the Comintern and enlisted the support of
the Church by appointing a Patriarch, decided to create a new
national anthem to replace the *Internationale*. It was to catch
Russia's new euphoric confidence. Stalin decided the quickest way
to find the tune and words was to hold a competition that
resembled a dictatorial Eurovision Song Contest, with Molotov
and Voroshilov contributing to the lyrics, and Shostakovich and
Prokofiev to the music.

* * *

In one week in late October, while the Allied Foreign Ministers
were in Moscow preparing for the Big Three meeting, the anthem
was forged in the white-hot frenzy of musical Stakhanovitism to
be ready for the 7 November celebrations. In late September,
Stalin invited composers from all over the Soviet Union to put
forward their offerings. In mid-October, fifty-four composers,
including Uzbeks, Georgians and some singing Jews, in traditional
costume, arrived in Moscow to perform round one in the Stalin
song contest. Before the music was even decided, Stalin appointed
the lyricists, Sergei Mikhalkov and El-Registan, whose notes in the
archives tell this story. They handed in their first draft. At
lunchtime on the 23rd, the lyricists were summoned from the
Moskva Hotel, that colossal Stalinist pile, across to the Kremlin
where Molotov and Voroshilov received them. 'Come in,' they
said. 'He is reading the lyrics.' They did not need to ask who 'he'
was. Two minutes later, Stalin called. Voroshilov, who was
'cheerful and smiling', took El-Registan's hands: 'Comrade Stalin,'
he announced, 'has made some corrections.' These were words
they would hear often during the next two weeks. Meanwhile the
dour Molotov was suggesting changes of his own.

'You must add some thoughts about peace, I don't know where,
but it must be done.'

'We'll give you a room,' said Voroshilov. 'It has to be warm.
Give 'em tea or they'll start drinking! And don't let them out until
they've finished.' They worked for four hours.

'We need to think about this overnight,' said Mikhalkov.

'Think all you like,' snapped Molotov, 'but we can't wait.' As
they left, they heard him order: 'Send it to Stalin!'

At a quarter to midnight, Stalin tinkered with the new draft in
his red pencil, changing the words of the verses, sending it to
Molotov and Voroshilov: 'Look at this. Do you agree?' On 26
October, Voroshilov, the Marshal demoted to song judge, was

diligently listening to another thirty anthems in the Bolshoi's Beethoven Hall, when suddenly 'Stalin arrived and all was done very fast.' It was now a remarkable gathering, with Stalin, Voroshilov and Beria sitting down with Shostakovich and Prokofiev to discuss the composition. When the lyricists arrived, they found Stalin, 'very grey and very energetic' in his new Marshal's uniform. Walking around as he listened to the melodies, Stalin asked Shostakovich and Prokofiev which orchestra was best – should it be an ecclesiastical one? It was hard to choose without an orchestra. Stalin gave them five days to prepare some more anthems, said goodbye and left the hall.

At three the following morning, Poskrebyshev called the lyricists, putting through the Supreme Songwriter who said that he now liked the text, but it was too 'thin' and short. They must add one verse, one rousing verse about the Red Army, power, 'the defeat of the Fascist hordes'.*

Stalin celebrated the Allied conference with a banquet on 30 October and then returned to music. At 9 a.m. on 1 November, flanked by Molotov, Beria and Voroshilov, he arrived at the Beethoven Hall and listened to forty anthems in four hours. Over dinner afterwards, the magnates finally came to a decision: Voroshilov telephoned the two lyricists in the middle of the night to announce that they liked the anthem of A. V. Alexandrov. He then handed the phone to Stalin who was still tinkering:

'You can leave the verses,' he said, 'but rewrite the refrains. "Country of Soviets" – if it's not a problem, change it to "country of socialism". Status: secret!' The lyricists worked all night, now with Alexandrov's music. Voroshilov sent it to Stalin and invited the composers to his dacha where he presided like 'a very funny and cheerful uncle' over a sumptuous feast.

At nine the next evening, Stalin was ready. The composers

---

* When they sang 'the Fascist hordes were beaten, are beaten and will be beaten', they started laughing because the words 'are beaten' in Russian sounded like 'are fucking us' when sung. Laughing, they quickly changed the words to 'We'll beat them to death and we'll beat them.' Marshal Voroshilov returned from his meetings and 'liked it very very much' so they told him about the problem with the 'fucking' and the 'defeating'. This of course greatly appealed to Voroshilov's earthy cavalryman's humour: 'Wonderful for a village song but not so good for a national anthem!' he laughed and then they started remembering all the hilarities of the song contest. What about those four Jewish singers in traditional dress who sang their Jewish song looking right into the eyes of Voroshilov! The Marshal guffawed heartily: 'Bring me some vodka! We must drink. From us in your honour! I present it to you!' In the late afternoon, they left the Kremlin exhausted.

arrived. Beria, Voroshilov and Malenkov sat round the table. Stalin formally shook their hands, that special sign of battles won and songs written:

'How's everything?' he asked warmly, but had not yet finished his tinkering. He wanted to emphasize the role of 'the Motherland! Motherland's good!' The writers rushed off to type in the changes. Stalin wanted Shostakovich involved in the orchestration.

'All right. Done!' snapped Beria. Then Malenkov sensibly piped up that they should listen once to the entire anthem. Stalin assigned this to Voroshilov who, demonstrating his rambunctious disrespect that belonged in another era, retorted:

'Let someone else do it – I've heard it a hundred times until I'm foaming at the mouth!' The new Soviet national anthem, Stalin raved, 'parts the sky and heaven like a boundless wave'. At its first playing at the Bolshoi Theatre, Stalin arrived to toast the composers who were invited up to the box and then to a dinner in the *avant-loge*. When Mikhalkov* and El-Registan downed their vodkas, Stalin bantered:

'Why drain your glasses? You won't be interesting to chat to!'

* * *

The elation spread from the top down. As the national anthem was unveiled, Molotov presided over a 7 November party that few would ever forget. The élite emerged that night from the grimness of the thirties and the austerity of years of defeat. 'The whole party,' noted the journalist Alexander Werth, 'sparkled with jewels, furs, gold braid and celebrities ... The party had something of that wild and irresponsible extravagance which one usually associates with pre-Revolution Moscow.' The dress was white tie and tails, which made Shostakovich look 'like a college boy who had put it on for the first time'. Henceforth, Stalin's court began to behave more like the rulers of an empire than dour Bolsheviks. Molotov sported the new diplomatic uniform that, like the gold braid, marked the new imperial era: it was 'black, trimmed in

---

* Sergei Mikhalkov remained a favoured Stalinist wordsmith: the archives contain his note to Stalin, 'At the Bolshoi Theatre on 30 December 1943, I promised you and Comrade Molotov to write a poem for children. I'm sending you "A Fable for Children".' Stalin liked it: 'It's a very good poem,' he scrawled to Molotov. 'It must be published today in *Pravda* and some other edition for children ...' Mikhalkov's son Nikita is today Russia's greatest film director, *auteur* of *Burnt by the Sun* and *Barber of Siberia*.

gold, with a small dagger at the belt ... much like Hitler's élite SS', thought the US diplomat Chip Bohlen.

Molotov, Vyshinsky and Stalin's old friend Sergo 'Tojo' Kavtaradze greeted the guests in a receiving line. Kavtaradze's companion was his beautiful daughter Maya, now eighteen and wearing the long flowing ball gown of the era. She caught the eye of Vyshinsky who 'oiled his way across the floor' to ask her to open the dancing with him.

A 'jovial' Molotov proceeded to become uproariously drunk, tottering up to Averell Harriman's daughter Kathleen and slurringly asking why she alone had failed to compliment him on his gorgeous uniform. Didn't she like it? She thought the Russians were as excited about their regalia 'as a little boy all dressed up in his new Christmas-present fireman's suit'. When he spotted the Swedish Ambassador, Molotov staggered up to him and declared that he did not like neutrals.

The Politburo members then each hit on a Western ambassador whom they tried to get as drunk as they were: Mikoyan, 'famous for his ability to put any guy under the table' according to Kathleen Harriman, worked on her father along with Shcherbakov, himself in the later stages of alcoholism. Molotov, who 'carried his liquor better than others', managed to remain on his feet while Clark Kerr, the British Ambassador 'fell flat on his face on to a table covered with bottles and wineglasses', cutting his face. Maya Kavtaradze saw an American general arrive accompanied by two prostitutes. Later in the evening, she noticed that all the potentates had disappeared and went to look for her father. She found him in a red hall, the Bolshevik equivalent of the 'VIP room', with the dashing and exuberant Mikoyan who was serenading the hussies on one knee.

The next day, Roosevelt finally agreed to meet at Teheran twenty days later: 'The whole world is watching for this meeting of the three of us ...'

42

Teheran: Roosevelt and Stalin

On 26 November 1943, Colonel-General Golovanov, the bomber commander who was to be Stalin's pilot, drove out to Kuntsevo to begin their long voyage to Persia. When he arrived, he heard shouting and found Stalin 'giving Beria a good dressing-down' while Molotov watched, perched on the window-sill. Beria sat in a chair 'with his ears all red' as Stalin sneered at him:

'Look at him Comrade Golovanov! He's got snake's eyes!' Molotov had jokingly complained that he could not read Beria's spidery handwriting. 'Our Vyacheslav Mikhailovich can't see very well. Beria keeps sending him messages and he insists on wearing his pince-nez with blank glasses!' This marked Stalin's growing disdain for the dynamic Georgian.

Afterwards, they boarded their train that arrived in Baku at 8 a.m., driving straight to the aerodrome where four SI-47s were gathered under the command of Air Marshal Novikov. Stalin had never flown before – and did not like the sound of it. But there was no other way from Baku. As he approached his plane with Golovanov, he glanced at Beria's plane standing next door with his pilot, Colonel Grachev, and decided to switch planes.

'Colonel-Generals don't often pilot aircraft,' he said, 'we'd better go with the Colonel,' reassuring Golovanov: 'Don't take it badly' – and he climbed into Beria's own plane. Guarded by twenty-seven fighters, Stalin was terrified when the plane hit an air pocket.

A few hours later, Stalin arrived in warm, dusty Teheran ('very dirty place, great poverty,' wrote Roosevelt) where he was speeded the five miles to the Soviet Embassy which was separated from the British Legation by two walls and a narrow road. Only the American Legation was out of town.

Teheran was the cosiest of the Big Three meetings: Stalin himself travelled with a tiny delegation. There were only Molotov and Voroshilov, his official deputies in the negotiations, Beria as security overlord, Vlasik as head of personal security and his physician Professor Vinogradov. Stalin's bodyguard of twelve Georgians was led by Tsereteli, whom Westerners found 'good-looking, highly intelligent and courteous'. None the less there was something appropriate about the master of this Eastern Empire being protected by a guard of his fellow countrymen led by a cut-throat Prince. Perhaps Churchill thought the same way for his bodyguard there was made up of turbaned Sikhs with tommy-guns.

The Soviet Embassy was an elegant estate, built for some Persian magnate, surrounded by a high wall. There were several cottages and villas in the grounds: Stalin lived in one house while Molotov and Voroshilov shared the two-storey Ambassador's residence. The advance guard of the NKVD had been frantically preparing the Embassy for two weeks. 'No one dared disobey' Beria, wrote Zoya Zarubina, a young NKGB officer in Teheran.*

As soon as Roosevelt arrived, Stalin invited him to move into the Soviet compound. The drive from the Soviet complex to the US Legation along narrow Oriental streets was impossible to guard – and no doubt Beria was more concerned about Stalin's security than Roosevelt's. Soviet intelligence had allegedly uncovered a Nazi plot to assassinate the leaders. Stalin was also determined to separate the Westerners, whom he expected to gang up on him. It happened that this also suited Roosevelt's strategy to engage Stalin directly, without the British, to prove his suspicions groundless. Harriman hurried over. Molotov explained their security worries. Molotov later ordered Zarubina to call and find out when FDR would be moving in. Admiral William Leahy, White House Chief of Staff, replied: 'We'll come tomorrow.'

When Zarubina reported this back to Molotov, he exploded: 'What do you think you're doing? Who the hell are you anyway? Who commanded you to do this job? Are you sure? What am I going to say to Stalin?'

Meanwhile, in one of those forgotten meetings between

* Beria personally ordered one of the Chekists, the young Zoya Zarubina, the step-daughter of NKGB General Leonid Eitingon (who had arranged Trotsky's assassination), to choose the furniture for the conference. There was no round table so it had to be made. Since the conference was a closely guarded secret, Beria told Zarubina to go into Teheran city and pretend to order a table to seat twenty-two 'for a wedding'.

potentates who seem to belong to different epochs, Stalin called
on the proud Mohammed Pahlavi, the 21-year-old Shah of an
occupied Iran, whose father Reza Shah, a former Cossack officer
and founder of the dynasty, had been deposed for pro-German
leanings in 1941. Stalin believed he could charm this imperial
boy, whose Empire had once embraced Georgia, into granting
him an Iranian foothold. Molotov, already a master of the
diplomatically possible, was sceptical. Beria advised against
this excursion for security reasons. Stalin insisted. The King of
Kings was pleasantly 'surprised' by the feline Stalin who was
'particularly polite and well-mannered and he seemed intent on
making a good impression on me'. His offer of 'a regiment of T-34
tanks and one of our fighter planes' impressed the Shah too. 'I was
most tempted,' he later wrote, but he sensed danger in this
Georgian bearing gifts. Molotov grumbled that Stalin 'did not
understand the Shah and got into a bit of an awkward situation.
Stalin thought he could impress him but it didn't work.' The gifts
were to come with Soviet officers. 'I declined with thanks,' wrote
the Shah.

Next morning, Beria personally patrolled the gates, waiting
for Roosevelt who finally arrived at the Soviet Embassy with
the Secret Service riding on the running-boards and brandishing tommy-guns in a gangsterish manner that the NKVD
thought unprofessional. A jeep-load of Roosevelt's Filipino
mess-boys confused the NKVD but they finally admitted them
too.

Stalin sent word that he would call on the President, a meeting
he had prepared for carefully. Naturally Beria bugged the
presidential suite. Beria's handsome scientist son, Sergo, whom
Stalin knew well, was among the Soviet eavesdroppers. Stalin
summoned him: 'How's your mother?' he asked, Nina Beria being
a favourite. Small talk out of the way, he ordered Sergo to
undertake the 'morally reprehensible and delicate' mission of
briefing him every morning at 8 a.m. Stalin always quizzed him,
even on Roosevelt's tone: 'Did he say that with conviction or
without enthusiasm? How did Roosevelt react?' He was surprised
at the naïvety of the Americans: 'Do they know we are listening
to them?'* Stalin rehearsed strategies with Molotov and Beria,

---

* Roosevelt presumed he was being bugged but hoped the results might fortify
Stalin's confidence in his honesty. Sergo Beria's account suggests this worked.

even down to where he would sit.* He did the same for his meetings with Churchill, according to Beria's son, saying, 'You can expect absolutely anything from him.'

Just before three, on this 'beautiful Iranian Sunday afternoon, gold and blue, mild and sunny', Stalin, accompanied by Vlasik and Pavlov, his interpreter, and surrounded by his Georgian bodyguards, who walked ten metres ahead and behind, as they did in the Kremlin, strode 'clumsily like a small bear' out of his residence in his Marshal's mustard-coloured summer tunic, with the Order of Lenin on his chest, and across the compound, to call on Roosevelt in the mansion. A young US officer met Stalin with a salute and led him into the President's room but then found himself inside the meeting-room with just the two leaders and their interpreters. He was about to panic until Bohlen, acting as interpreter, whispered that he should leave.

'Hello Marshal Stalin,' said Roosevelt as the men shook hands. His 'round tubby figure', with swarthy pock-marked face, grey hair, broken stained teeth and yellow Oriental eyes, was worlds away from the aristocratic blue-suited President sitting erect in his wheelchair: 'If he'd dressed in Chinese robes,' wrote Bohlen, 'he would be the perfect subject for a Chinese ancestor portrait.'

Stalin stressed his need for the Second Front before Roosevelt established a rapport by undermining the British Empire. India was ripe for a revolution 'from the bottom', like Russia, said FDR, who was as ill-informed about Leninism as he was about the untouchables. Stalin showed that he knew more about India, replying that the question of castes was more complicated. This short *tour d'horizon* established the unlikely partnership between the crippled New York Brahmin and the Georgian Bolshevik. Both of legendary charm when they wished to be, Stalin's fondness for Roosevelt was as genuine a diplomatic friendship as he ever managed with any imperialist. Stalin left Roosevelt to rest.

At 4 p.m., the Big Three gathered around the specially constructed 'wedding feast table' in a big hall decorated in heavy

* In a piece of interpreter mountebankism, the second Soviet interpreter Valentin Berezhkov described how Stalin rehearsed the meeting and how Roosevelt came to Stalin's residence without an interpreter. In fact, Stalin went to Roosevelt's rooms where Chip Bohlen interpreted for the Americans and Pavlov for the Soviets. Pavlov was Stalin and Molotov's interpreter in English and German; Berezhkov occasionally worked for Molotov. The only part of this incident that holds together is Stalin rehearsing positions, which was typical of him. Perhaps Berezhkov did witness this scene.

imperial style with striped silk armchairs and armrests: Stalin sat next to Molotov and Pavlov. Voroshilov often sat in a chair in the second row. Stalin and Churchill agreed that Roosevelt was to chair the meeting: 'As the youngest!' joked the President.

'In our hands,' declaimed Churchill, 'we have the future of mankind.' Stalin completed this declamatory triumvirate:

'History has spoiled us,' he said. 'She's given us very great power and very great opportunities … Let's begin our work.' When they turned to the question of Operation Overlord, the invasion of France, Stalin complained that he had not expected to discuss military issues so he had no military staff. 'But I've only got Marshal Voroshilov,' he said rudely. 'I hope he'll do.' He then ignored Voroshilov and handled all military matters himself. A young British interpreter, Hugh Lunghi,* was shocked to see that Stalin treated Voroshilov 'like a dog'. Stalin insisted on the earliest preference for Overlord, the cross-Channel invasion – and then quietly filled his pipe. Churchill was still unconvinced, preferring a preliminary Mediterranean operation, using troops already in the area. However FDR was already committed to the Channel. As a flustered Churchill realized he was outvoted, Roosevelt winked at Stalin, the start of his gauche flirtation that greatly enhanced the Marshal's position as arbiter of the Grand Alliance. Churchill handled Stalin much better by being himself.

Stalin was expansively charming to the foreigners but grumpy with his own delegates. When Bohlen approached him from behind, mid-session, Stalin snapped without turning, 'For God's sake, allow us to finish this work.' He was embarrassed when he found it was the young American. That night, Roosevelt held a dinner at his residence. His mess-boys prepared steaks and baked potatoes while the President shook up his cocktails of vermouth, gin and ice. Stalin sipped and winced: 'Well, it's all right but cold on the stomach.' Roosevelt suddenly turned 'green and great drops of sweat began to bead off his face'. He was wheeled to his room. When Churchill said God was on the side of the Allies, Stalin chaffed, 'And the Devil's on my side. The Devil's a Communist and God's a good Conservative!'

On the 29th, Stalin and Roosevelt met again: the Supremo knew from his briefing from Sergo Beria that his charm had worked.

* Major Hugh Lunghi, whose interview has greatly helped with this account, is probably the last man living to attend all the Plenary Big Three meetings at Teheran, Yalta and Potsdam.

'Roosevelt always expressed a high opinion of Stalin', recalled Sergo, which allowed him to put pressure on Churchill. That morning, the President proposed the creation of an international organization that became the United Nations. Meanwhile the generals were meeting with Voroshilov who, according to Lunghi, absolutely refused to understand the amphibious challenge of an invasion of France, thinking it was like crossing a Russian river on a raft.

Before the next session, Churchill, the only British Prime Minister to sport military uniforms in office, arrived in a blue RAF uniform with pilot's wings, to open a solemn ceremony to celebrate Stalingrad. At 3.30 p.m., all the delegations assembled in the hall of the Embassy. Then the Big Three arrived. A guard of honour formed up of British infantry with bayonets and NKVD troops in blue uniforms, red tabs and slung tommy-guns. An orchestra played their national anthems, in the Soviet case, the old one. The music stopped. There was silence. Then the officer of the British guard approached the large black box on the table and opened it. A gleaming sword lay on a bed of 'claret-coloured velvet'. He handed it to Churchill, who, laying the sword across his hands, turned to Stalin:

'I've been commanded by His Majesty King George VI to present to you ... this sword of honour ... The blade of the sword bears the inscription: "To the steel-hearted citizens of Stalingrad, a gift from King George VI as a token of the homage of the British People."' Churchill stepped forward and presented the sword to Stalin who held it reverently in his hands for a long moment and then, with tears in his eyes, raised it to his lips and kissed it. Stalin was moved.

'On behalf of the citizens of Stalingrad,' he answered in 'a low husky voice', 'I wish to express my appreciation ...' He walked round to Roosevelt to show him the sword. The American read out the inscription: 'Truly they had hearts of steel.' Stalin handed the sword to Voroshilov. There was a crash as Voroshilov let the scabbard slip off the sword and on to his toes. The bungling cavalryman, who had charged waving his sabre many a time, had managed to introduce comedy in the most solemn moment of Stalin's international career. His cherubic cheeks blushing a bright scarlet, Klim remastered the sword. The Supremo, noticed Lunghi, frowned with irritation then gave 'a frosty, grim, forced-looking smile'. The NKVD lieutenant held the sword aloft and carried it away. Stalin must have snarled that Voroshilov should apologize because when he returned, he chased after Churchill, recruiting Lunghi to interpret. Flushed, he 'stammered his apologies' but then suddenly wished Churchill 'a happy birthday' for the following day. A special birthday banquet was being planned at the British Legation. 'I wish you a hundred more years of life,' said the Marshal, 'with the same spirit and vigour'. Churchill thanked him but whispered to Lunghi:

'Isn't he a bit premature? Must be angling for an invitation.'* Then the Big Three went outside for the famous photograph of the conference.

After a short interval, the delegations moved back to the round table for the next session. As ever, Stalin made sure that he always arrived last. When everyone was ready the Chekist Zoya Zarubina, on duty outside, was sent on an errand. She ran headlong down the steps and 'hit someone on the shoulder'. To her horror, it was Stalin. 'I stood frozen, stiff at attention ...' she wrote. 'I thought they'd surely shoot me on the spot.' Stalin did not react and walked on, followed by Molotov. But Voroshilov, always kind to the young and with more reason than most to indulge bunglers, 'patted me on the hand and said, "It's all right, kid, it's all right."'

Stalin, 'always smoking and doodling wolf-heads on a pad with his red pencil', was never agitated, rarely gestured and seldom consulted Molotov and Voroshilov. But he kept up the pressure on Churchill for the Second Front:

'Do the British really believe in Overlord or are you only saying so to reassure the Russians?' When he heard that the Allies had not yet agreed on a commander, he growled: 'Then nothing will come of these operations.' The Soviet Union had tried committee rule and found it had not worked. One man had to make the decisions. Finally, when Churchill would not give a date, Stalin suddenly got to his feet and turning to Molotov and Voroshilov, said,

'Let's not waste our time here. We've got plenty to do at the front.' Roosevelt managed to pour unction on troubled waters.

That night, it was Stalin's turn to host a banquet in the usual Soviet style with an 'unbelievable quantity of food'. A huge Russian 'waiter' in a white coat stood behind the Supremo's chair

---

* Hugh Lunghi typed up this farcical exchange and asked Churchill to sign it for him the next day. As interpreter for the British Chiefs of Staff, he also deputized for Churchill's principal interpreter, Major Arthur Birse.

throughout the meal.* Stalin 'drank little' but got his kicks by needling Churchill, exchanges in which Roosevelt seemed to take an undignified pleasure. Stalin sneered that he was glad Churchill was not a 'liberal', that most loathsome of creatures in the Bolshevik lexicon, but he then tested his severity by joking that 50,000 or perhaps 100,000 German officers should be executed. Churchill was furious: pushing his glass forward, knocking it over so brandy spread across the table, he growled:

'Such an attitude is contrary to the British sense of justice. The British Parliament and public would never support the execution of honest men who had fought for their country.' Roosevelt quipped that he would like to compromise: only 49,000 should be shot. Elliott Roosevelt, the President's ne'er-do-well son who was also present, jumped tipsily to his feet to josh: wouldn't the 50,000 fall in battle anyway?

'To your health, Elliott!' Stalin clinked glasses with him. But Churchill snarled at Roosevelt *fils*:

'Are you interested in damaging relations between the Allies ... How dare you!'† He headed for the door but as he reached it, 'hands were clapped on my shoulders from behind, and there was Stalin, with Molotov at his side, both grinning broadly and eagerly declaring that they were only playing ... Stalin has a very captivating manner when he chooses to use it.' Roosevelt's deference to Stalin and shabbiness to Churchill were both unseemly and counterproductive but the heartiness was restored by Stalin tormenting Molotov:

'Come here, Molotov, and tell us about your pact with Hitler.'

The finale was Churchill's sixty-ninth birthday held in the dining-hall of the British Legation which, Alan Brooke wrote in his diary, resembled 'a Persian temple', with the walls 'covered in a mosaic of small pieces of looking glass' and 'heavy deep red curtains. The Persian waiters were in blue and red livery' with

---

* The Americans thought he was the *maitre d'* and at the end of the conference were going to present him with some cigarettes when they found him resplendent in the uniform of an NKVD Major-General.

† Stalin had specially invited Elliott to the dinner. Perhaps he sensed the similarity with his own scapegrace son, Vasily. Both were pilots, inadequate yet arrogant drunks who were intimidated and dominated by brilliant fathers. Both exploited the family name and embarrassed their fathers. Both failed in multiple marriages and abandoned their wives. Perhaps there is no sadder curse than the gift of a titanic father.

oversized 'white cotton gloves, the tips of the fingers of which hung limply and flapped about'. Sikhs guarded the doorways.

Beria, who was there *incognito*, insisted that the NKVD search the British Legation, which was supervised by him personally with that glossy ruffian Tsereteli. 'There simply cannot be any doubt,' wrote a British security officer, Beria 'was an extremely intelligent and shrewd man with tremendous willpower and ability to impress, command and lead other men.' He disdained anyone else's opinion, becoming 'very angry if anyone ... opposed his proposals'. The other Russians 'behaved like slaves in his presence'.

Once Beria had signed off, Stalin arrived, but when a valet tried to take his coat, a bodyguard overreacted by reaching for his pistol. Calm was quickly restored. A cake with sixty-nine candles stood on the main table. Stalin toasted 'Churchill my fighting friend, if it is possible to consider Mr Churchill my friend' and then walked round to clink glasses with the Englishman, putting his arm around his shoulders. Churchill answered: 'To Stalin the Great!' When Churchill joked that Britain was 'becoming pinker', Stalin joked: 'A sign of good health.'

At the climax, the chef of the Legation cuisine produced a creation that came closer to assassinating Stalin than all the German agents in all the *souks* of Persia. Stalin was making a toast when two mountainous ice-cream pyramids were wheeled in with 'a base of ice one foot square and four inches deep', a religious nightlight inside it and a tube rising ten inches out of the middle on which a plate supporting a 'a vast ice-cream' had been secured with icing sugar. But as these creations approached Stalin, Brooke noticed that the lamp was melting the ice and 'now looked more like the Tower of Pisa'. Suddenly the tilt assumed a more dangerous angle and the British Chief of Staff shouted to his neighbours to duck. 'With the noise of an avalanche the whole wonderful construction slid over our heads and exploded in a clatter of plates.' Lunghi saw the nervous Persian waiter 'stagger sideways at the last moment'. Pavlov in his new diplomatic uniform 'came in for the full blast! ... splashed from head to foot' but Brooke guessed 'it was more than his life was worth to stop interpreting'. Stalin was unblemished.

'Missed the target,' whispered Air Marshal Sir Charles Portal.

At the final meetings next day, Roosevelt explained privately to Stalin that, since he had a Presidential election coming up, he could not discuss Poland at this meeting. The subordination of the fate of the country for which the war was fought to American machine politics can only have encouraged Stalin's plans for a tame Poland. At the last plenary meeting, it was a sign of the amateurism and immediacy of this intimate conference that Churchill and Stalin discussed Polish borders using a map torn out of *The Times*. The dangers of these meetings for Stalin's entourage were underestimated by the Westerners until Churchill's interpreter Birse presented his opposite number Pavlov with a set of Charles Dickens. Pavlov uneasily accepted the present.

'You're getting VERY close to our Western friends,' smiled Stalin to Pavlov's anxious discomfort.

On 2 December, Stalin, 'satisfied' that the Allies had finally promised to launch Overlord in the spring, flew out of Teheran and changed out of his Marshal's togs at Baku aerodrome, re-emerging in his old greatcoat, cap and boots. His train conveyed him to Stalingrad, his only post-battle visit to the city that had played such a decisive role in his life. He visited Paulus's headquarters but his limousine drove too fast down the narrow streets strewn with heaps of German equipment. It collided with a woman driver who almost expired when she realized with whom she had crashed. She started crying:

'It's my fault.' Stalin got out and calmed her:

'Don't cry. It's not your fault. Blame the war. Our car's armoured and didn't suffer. You can repair yours.' Afterwards he headed back to Moscow.

* * *

Stalingrad, Kursk and Teheran restored Stalin's zealous faith in his own infallible greatness. 'When victory became obvious,' wrote Mikoyan, 'Stalin got too big for his boots and became capricious.' The long boozy dinners started again: Stalin began to drink again, playing the ringmaster of a circus of uncouth hijinks, but in the mass of information he received from Beria, there was always much to worry him.

Beria arrested 931,544 persons in the liberated territory in 1943. As many as 250,000 people in Moscow attended Easter church services. He delivered the phone intercepts and informer reports to Stalin who read them carefully. Here the Supremo learned how Eisenstein was cutting his new movie, *Ivan the Terrible, Part Two*, because the Tsar's murders reminded him of Yezhov's Terror 'which he couldn't recall without shuddering ...' The message was clear: liberalism and ill-discipline threatened the State. The cost of Stalin's victories were vast: almost 26 million were dead, another 26 million homeless. There was a raging famine, treason among the Caucasian peoples, a Ukrainian nationalist civil war, and dangerous liberalism among the Russians themselves. All these had to be solved with the traditional Bolshevik solution, Terror.

Before they turned to terrorizing Russia proper, Beria and the local boss, Khrushchev, were running a new war in the Ukraine where three nationalist armies were fighting Soviet forces. Then there was the the dubious loyalty of the Caucasus and Crimea.

In February 1944, Beria proposed the deportation of the Moslem Chechen and Ingush. There had been cases of treason but most had been loyal. None the less Stalin and the GKO agreed – though Mikoyan claimed that he objected to it. On 20 February, Beria, Kobulov and the deportations expert, Serov, arrived in Grozny along with 19,000 Chekists and 100,000 NKVD troops. On 23 February, the locals were ordered to gather in their squares, then suddenly arrested and piled into trains bound for the East. By 7 March, Beria reported to Stalin that 500,000 innocents were on their way.

Other peoples, the Karachai and Kalmyks, joined the Volga Germans who had been deported in 1941. Beria constantly expanded the net: 'The Balkars are bandits and ... attacked the Red Army,' he wrote to Stalin on 25 February. 'If you agree, before my return to Moscow, I can take necessary measures to resettle the Balkars. I ask your orders.' Over 300,000 of these people were deported, but where to dump them all? Like the Nazis with their Jews, Stalin's men had to distribute this unwanted human flotsam throughout their Empire. Molotov suggested 40,000 in Kazakhstan, 14,000 somewhere else. Kaganovich found the trains. Andreyev, now running Agriculture, dealt with their farming equipment. Everyone was involved. When an official noticed that there were 1,300 Kalmyks still living in Rostov, Molotov replied that they must be deported at once. Mikoyan may have disapproved but the capital of the Karachais, Karachaevsk, was now renamed after him. In the dry language of these bureaucratic notes, we can only glimpse the tragedy and suffering of this monumental crime.

Then Beria reported the treason of Tatars in the Crimea and soon 160,000 were on their way eastwards in forty-five trains: he listed their food allowance to Stalin but given the thousands who died, it is unlikely that they received most of it. Throughout the year, Beria kept finding more pockets of these poor people: on 20 May, there were 'still German supporters in the Kabardin republic after resettlement of Balkars' and he asked if he could 'remove' another 2,467 people: 'Agreed. J. Stalin' is written at the bottom. By the time he had finished, a triumphant Beria had removed 1.5 million people. Stalin approved 413 medals for Beria's Chekists. More than a quarter of the deportees died, according to the NKVD, but as many as 530,000 perished en route or on arrival at the camps. For each of these peoples, this was an apocalypse that approached the Holocaust.

While these cattle cars of human cargo trundled eastwards, famine was raging in Russia, Central Asia and the Ukraine. In a replay of collectivization, Stalin sensed weakness in his Politburo. There are hints of disturbing things in the archives: in November 1943, Andreyev reported to Malenkov from Saratov that 'things are very bad here ... Yesterday driving from Stalingrad ... I saw terrible sights ...' On 22 November 1944, Beria reported to Stalin another case of cannibalism in the Urals when two women kidnapped and ate four children. Mikoyan and Andreyev suggested giving the peasants seeds:

'To Molotov and Mikoyan,' Stalin scrawled on their note, 'I vote against. Mikoyan's behaviour is anti-state ... he has absolutely corrupted Andreyev. Patronage over Narkomzag [Commissariat of Supply] should be taken away from Mikoyan and given to Malenkov ...' This was the beginning of a growing iciness between Stalin and Mikoyan that was to become increasingly dangerous.

* * *

On 20 May 1944, Stalin met his generals to co-ordinate the vast summer offensive that would finally toss the Germans off Soviet territory. Much of the Ukraine was already liberated and the Leningrad siege finally lifted. Stalin proposed a single thrust towards Bobruisk to Rokossovsky, who knew two thrusts were required to avoid senseless casualties. But Stalin was set on just one. Rokossovsky, the tall and graceful half-Polish general who was favoured by Stalin yet had been tortured just before the war, was brave enough to insist on his own view.

'Go out and think it over again,' said Stalin, who later summoned him back: 'Have you thought it through, General?' asked Stalin again.

'Yes sir, Comrade Stalin.'

'Well then ... a single thrust?' – and Stalin marked it on the map. There was silence until Rokossovsky replied:

'Two thrusts are more advisable, Comrade Stalin.' Again silence fell.

'Go out and think it over again. Don't be stubborn, Rokossovsky.' The general again sat next door until he realized he was not alone: Molotov and Malenkov loomed over him. Rokossovsky stood up.

'Don't forget where you are and with whom you're talking, General,' Malenkov threatened him. 'You're disagreeing with Comrade Stalin.'

'You'll have to agree, Rokossovsky,' added Molotov. 'Agree – that's all there is to it!' The general was summoned back into the study:

'So which is better?' asked Stalin.

'Two,' answered Rokossovsky. Silence descended until Stalin asked:

'Can it be that two blows are really better?' Stalin accepted Rokossovsky's plan. On 23 June, the offensive shattered the German forces. Minsk and then Lvov were recaptured. On 8 July, Zhukov found Stalin at Kuntsevo in 'great gaiety'. As he ordered the advance on the Vistula, Stalin was determined to impose his own government on Poland so that it would never again threaten Russia: on 22 July, he established a Polish Committee under Boleslaw Bierut to form the new government.

'Hitler's like a gambler staking his last coin!' exulted Stalin.

'Germany will try to make peace with Churchill and Roosevelt,' said Molotov.

'Right,' said Stalin, 'but Roosevelt and Churchill won't agree.' Then the Poles threw a spanner into the works of the Grand Alliance.

* * *

The Red Army offensive ground to an exhausted halt on the Vistula just east of Warsaw when, on 1 August, General Tadeusz Bor-Komorowski and the 20,000 patriots of the Polish Home Army rose against the Germans in the Warsaw Rising. But the patriots, in the words of one distinguished historian, aimed 'not to help the Soviet advance but to forestall it'. Hitler ordered that Warsaw be razed, deploying a ghoulish crew of SS fanatics, convicts and Russian renegades to slaughter 225,000 civilians in one merciless inferno.

The extermination of the Home Army completed the 'black work' of Katyn Forest for Stalin who had no interest in coming to their rescue. Yet the rising and, more particularly, the Western sympathy for it, sent Stalin into a spin. If its success threatened his Polish plans, then Anglo-American fury about its failure threatened the Grand Alliance.

On 1 August, Zhukov and Rokossovsky arrived to find Stalin 'agitated', pacing up to the maps and then striding off again, even putting down his unlit pipe, always a storm petrel. Stalin pressured the generals – could their armies advance? Zhukov and Rokossovsky said they must rest. Stalin seemed angry. Beria and Molotov threatened them. Stalin sent the generals into the library next door where they nervously discussed their plight. Rokossovsky thought Beria was inciting Stalin. Things could end badly: 'I know very well what Beria is capable of,' whispered Rokossovsky, ultra-cautious as the son of a Polish officer. 'I've been in his prisons.' Twenty minutes later, Malenkov appeared and claimed he was supporting the generals. There would be no rescue of Warsaw.

Zhukov suspected the Supremo had set up this charade as an alibi. But Soviet forces were exhausted: as Rokossovsky told a Western journalist, 'The rising would have made sense only if we were on the point of taking Warsaw. That point had not been reached at any stage ... We were pushed back.' Meanwhile, as Churchill and Roosevelt exerted intense pressure on their ally to aid the Poles, Stalin coolly claimed that their account of the rising was 'greatly exaggerated'. By the time his armies pushed into Poland, Hungary and Romania, it was much too late for the patriots of Warsaw.

* * *

Seven days after the surrender of the Home Army, Churchill arrived in Moscow to divide up the spoils of Eastern Europe. Stalin had stated his real view to Molotov in 1942: 'The question of borders will be decided by force.' At Stalin's Kremlin flat, Churchill, who was this time staying in a town house, proposed a 'naughty document' to list their interests in the small countries by percentage. The Soviet record in Stalin's own archives showed that, just as Roosevelt had undermined Churchill at Teheran, so now the Englishman opened this conversation by saying that the 'Americans including the President would be shocked by the division of Europe into spheres of influence'. In Romania, Russia had 90 per cent, Britain 10 per cent; in Greece, Britain had 90 per cent, Russia 10 per cent. Stalin ticked it.

'Might it not be thought cynical if it seemed we'd disposed of these issues, so fateful to millions of people, in such an offhand manner?' said Churchill, half guilty at, and half-revelling in, the arrogance of the Great Powers.

'No, you keep it,' replied Stalin. The document was taken seriously enough for Eden and Molotov to negotiate for two more days about the percentage of Soviet influence in Bulgaria and Hungary, both raised to 80 per cent, and Stalin did stick to his part of the deal on Greece but that was because it suited him. The percentages agreement was, from Stalin's point of view, surely a bemusing attempt to negotiate what was already a *fait accompli*.

The climax of the visit was Stalin's first public appearance at the Bolshoi since the war began, accompanied by Churchill, Molotov, Harriman and his daughter Kathleen. When they arrived at the theatre, the lights were already dimmed – Stalin usually slipped in after the play had started. When the lights went up and the audience saw Stalin and Churchill, there were 'thunderous cheers and clapping'. Stalin withdrew modestly but Churchill sent Vyshinsky to bring him back. The two stood there together, beaming amidst cheering so loud it was 'like a cloudburst on a tin roof'. Stalin and Molotov then shepherded their guests into the *avant-loge* where a dinner for twelve was laid out. Quaffing champagne, Stalin performed like a roguish old satyr, charming and chilling his guests in equal parts. When Molotov raised his glass to the 'great leader', Stalin quipped:

'I thought he was going to say something new about me.' Someone joked that the Big Three were like the Trinity.

'If that's so,' said Stalin, 'Churchill must be the Holy Ghost. He flies about so much.'* When Churchill finally left on 19 October, having made little progress over Poland, Stalin personally came to the airport to see him off, waving his handkerchief.

Stalin was now enjoying the power of victory – and the bullying showman who emerged was not a pretty sight. His respectful

* Stalin made one joke about Maisky, the ex-embassador to London, who was present, that was not translated. The Russians though laughed uproariously at it so Brooke asked him what was so funny. Maisky glumly explained, 'The Marshal has referred to me as the Poet-Diplomat because I have written a few verses at times but our last poet-diplomat was liquidated – that is the joke.' The original Poet-Diplomat was the Russian Ambassador to Persia, Griboyedov, who was torn to pieces by the Teheran mob in 1829. Maisky was later arrested and tortured.

gaiety with Churchill metamorphosed into threatening drunkenness with the less powerful such as Charles de Gaulle. In December, the Frenchman visited Moscow to sign a treaty of alliance and mutual assistance. In return, Stalin wanted French recognition of Bierut's Polish Government which de Gaulle refused to give. By the time of the banquet, the negotiations were stuck. This did not stop Stalin getting swaggeringly drunk, to the horror of the gloomy de Gaulle. Stalin complained to Harriman that de Gaulle was 'an awkward and clumsy man', but that did not matter because they 'must drink more wine and then everything will straighten out'.

Stalin, swigging champagne, took over the toasts from Molotov. After praising Roosevelt and Churchill, while pointedly ignoring de Gaulle, Stalin embarked on a terrifying gallows tour of his entourage: he toasted Kaganovich, 'a brave man. He knows that if the trains do not arrive on time' – he paused – 'we shall shoot him!' Then: 'Come here!' Kaganovich rose and they clinked glasses jovially. Then Stalin lauded Air Force Commander Novikov, this 'good Marshal, let's drink to him. And if he doesn't do his job properly, we'll hang him.' (Novikov would soon be arrested and tortured.) Then he spotted Khrulev: 'He'd better do his best, or he'll be hanged for it, that's the custom in our country!' Again: 'Come here!' Noticing the distaste on de Gaulle's face, Stalin chuckled: 'People call me a monster, but as you see, I make a joke of it. Maybe I'm not horrible after all.'

Molotov collared his French opposite number, Bidault, with whom he began arguing over the treaty. Stalin gestured at them, calling out to Bulganin: 'Bring the machine guns. Let's liquidate the diplomats.' Leading his guests out for coffee and movies, Stalin 'kept hugging the French and lurching around', noticed Khrushchev who was also present but had avoided a threatening toast. He was 'completely drunk'. While the diplomats negotiated, Stalin drank more champagne. Finally in the early hours, when de Gaulle had gone to bed, the Russians suddenly agreed to sign the treaty without recognition of Bierut. De Gaulle was rushed back into the Kremlin where Stalin first asked him to sign the original treaty. When de Gaulle angrily retorted: 'France has been insulted', Stalin cheerfully called for the new draft which was then signed at 6.30 a.m.

As the fastidious Frenchman left, Stalin called for his interpreter and laughed: 'You know too much. I'd better send you to Siberia!'

De Gaulle looked back one last time: 'I saw Stalin sitting alone at a table. He had started eating again.'

The same exuberant victor presided over a series of dinners and banquets for the visiting Yugoslavs that winter. Stalin was outraged that the Yugoslav Politburo member Milovan Djilas had complained about the rape and pillage of the Red Army. Stalin regarded any criticism of the army as an attack on himself. He drunkenly lectured the Yugoslavs about his army 'which pushed its way across thousands of miles' only to be attacked 'by none other than Djilas! Djilas whcm I received so well!' In the absence of the man himself, Djilas's wife, Mitra Mitrovic, one of the delegates, caught his eye and he 'proposed toasts, joked, teased, wept' before kissing her repeatedly, jesting salaciously: 'I'll kiss you even if the Yugoslavs and Djilas accuse me of having raped you!'

When Stalin invited some American officials to the Kremlin cinema, he moved to sit between the leading Westerners but then he turned round to Kavtaradze:

'Come on, boy, sit next to me!'

'How can I?' answered Kavtaradze. 'You've guests.' Stalin waved his hand, adding in Georgian:

'Fuck them!'

That New Year's Eve, Stalin and his magnates, along with General Khrulev, saw in 1945 with an all-night, singing and dancing Bacchanal.

43

The Swaggering Conqueror:
Yalta and Berlin

When Stalin eyed the great prize of Berlin, he decided to change the way he ran the war: there would be no more Stavka representatives in charge of fronts. Henceforth, the Supremo would command directly.

Zhukov was to command the First Belorussian Front that was to fight the five hundred miles to Berlin. Six million Soviet soldiers were massed for the Vistula–Oder offensive. Two weeks later, Koniev was plunging into the 'gold' of industrial Silesia, Zhukov had expelled the Germans from central Poland, and Malinovsky was fighting frenziedly for Budapest. The Second and Third Belorussian Fronts broke into East Prussia, Germany itself, in a fiesta of vengeance: two million German women were to be raped in the coming months. Russian soldiers even raped Russian women newly liberated from Nazi camps. Stalin cared little about this, telling Djilas: 'You have of course read Dostoevsky? Do you see what a complicated thing is man's soul ...? Well then, imagine a man who has fought from Stalingrad to Belgrade – over thousands of kilometres of his own devastated land, across the dead bodies of his comrades and dearest ones? How can such a man react normally? And what is so awful about his having fun with a woman after such horrors?'

Roosevelt and Churchill had been discussing the next Big Three meeting ever since July 1944. Stalin was reluctant: when, in September, Harriman suggested a meeting in the Mediterranean, Stalin retorted that his doctors had told him 'any change of climate would have a bad effect', this from a man who distrusted doctors intensely. Molotov could go instead. Molotov politely insisted that he could never replace Marshal Stalin.

'You're too modest,' said Stalin drily. They agreed on Yalta. By 29 January, Zhukov was on the Oder. As German forces counter-attacked the Soviet bridgeheads, Roosevelt and Churchill were being greeted on 3 February at Saki airforce base in the Crimea by

Molotov, in stiff white collar, black coat and fur hat, and Vyshinsky, resplendent in his diplomatic uniform, who hosted a 'magnificent luncheon' on their way to Yalta.

* * *

Stalin himself had not yet left Moscow but he had approved Beria's arrangements in a memorandum so secret that key names were left out and only filled in by hand. The conference would be guarded by four NKVD regiments and defended by arrays of AA guns and 160 fighter planes. Stalin's security was described thus: 'For the guarding of the chief of the Soviet delegation, besides the bodyguards under Comrade Vlasik, there are additionally 100 operative workers and a special detachment of 500 from NKVD regiments.' In other words, Stalin himself had a bodyguard of about 620 men but in addition, there were two circles of guards by day, three circles by night, and guard dogs. Five districts spanning twenty kilometres had been 'purged of suspicious elements' – 74,000 people had been checked and 835 arrested. With its towns deserted and ruined after the depredations of the Nazis and the deportation of the Tartars, it was no wonder Churchill dubbed Yalta 'The Riviera of Hades'.

On Sunday morning, 4 February, Stalin boarded his green railway car, accompanied by Poskrebyshev and Vlasik, travelling south via Kharkov. His residence, the Yusupov Palace, once the home of the Croesian transvestite prince who had assassinated Rasputin, was ready for the Soviet delegation with its twenty rooms and its 77-square-foot hall. Everything had been brought down from Moscow including plates, cutlery and the trusty waiters of the Metropol and National hotels. Special bakeries made bread and special fisherman delivered fresh fish. 'A special "*Vch*" high frequency telephone and Baudot telegraph as well as an automatic telephone station of 20 numbers ... possible to increase to 50' had been set up so that Stalin could 'call Moscow, the fronts, and all towns'. He could avail himself of a bomb shelter that could withstand 500kg bombs.

Stalin immediately received his delegates in the study, Beria's room being almost next door, while the younger diplomats stayed in the adjoining wing. Sudoplatov delivered psychological portraits of the Western leaders, Molotov evaluated intelligence and again, Sergo Beria claimed he was on bugging duty. This time, they even used positional directional microphones to listen to FDR as he was wheeled outside.

At 3 p.m., Stalin* called on Churchill at his residence, the fantastical palace of Prince Michael Vorontsov, an Anglophile who had created a unique architectural pot-pourri of Scottish baronial, neo-Gothic and Moorish Arabesque. He then drove to Roosevelt's white granite Livadia Palace, built in 1911 as the summer home of the last Tsar.† At dinner that night, Roosevelt misjudged Stalin's prickly self-image when he confided that his nickname was 'Uncle Joe'. Stalin was offended, muttering,

'When can I leave this table?' He was assured it was a joke. At 4 p.m. next day, the conference opened in the Livadia's ballroom. Sitting between Molotov and Maisky, chain-smoking cigarettes, Stalin greatly impressed the young Andrei Gromyko, his Ambassador to America who later became Brezhnev's perennial Foreign Minister: he 'missed nothing' and worked 'with no papers, no notes', using a 'memory like a computer'. It was during these plenary meetings that Stalin delivered his most famous one-liner. As always with his jokes, he repeated it frequently and it entered the political vernacular as an expression of force over sentiment. They were discussing the Pope:

'Let's make him our ally,' proposed Churchill.

'All right,' smiled Stalin, 'but as you know, gentlemen, war is waged with soldiers, guns, tanks. How many divisions has the Pope? If he tells us … let him become our ally.'‡

In the evenings, Stalin held little parties to meet his entourage, where Gromyko noticed how he 'exchanged a few words with each member', and moved from group to group, making jokes, remembering all fifty-three delegates by name. There were meetings every morning and evening: he was often crushing to his advisers if they did not do their job. Hugh Lunghi, once again

---

*A month later, the editor of *Izvestiya* prepared a special photographic album which he sent to Poskrebyshev: 'Esteemed Alexander Nikolaievich, I send you the photographs of the Crimean conference for JV Stalin.' Its front was embossed in big letters to him. Stalin was a shabby sight next to the dapper Molotov: his Yalta photo album shows the poorly darned pockets of his beloved but rumpled old greatcoat. The porcine Vlasik was always just a step behind him, beaming affably, but Stalin's security was as tight as ever. Once when Bohlen noticed Stalin visit the lavatory, two Soviet bodyguards ran around, yelling, 'Where's Stalin! Where's he gone?' Bohlen pointed to the W.C.

† The President was exhausted and ailing. His suite had a living room, a dining room (the Tsar's billiard room), bedroom and bathroom. His closest adviser Harry Hopkins was so ill that he spent most of the time in bed. According to Alan Brooke, General Marshall 'is in the Tsarina's bedroom' and Admiral King 'in her boudoir with the special staircase for Rasputin to visit her!'

‡ Stalin told his version to Enver Hoxha, the Albanian leader.

interpreting at the conference, heard him saying, 'I don't trust Vyshinsky but with him all things are possible. He'll jump whichever way we tell him.' Vyshinsky reacted to Stalin 'like a frightened hound'.

When Roosevelt was ill, Stalin, Molotov and Gromyko visited him for twenty minutes. Afterwards, coming down the stairs, 'Stalin suddenly stopped, took the pipe out of his pocket, filled it unhurriedly and as if to himself said quietly, "Why did nature have to punish him so? Is he any worse than other people?"' He had always distrusted Churchill but Roosevelt seemed to fascinate him:

'Tell me,' he asked Gromyko, 'what do you think of Roosevelt? Is he clever?' Stalin did not hide his fondness for FDR from Gromyko which amazed the young diplomat because his character was so harsh that he 'rarely bestowed his sympathy on anyone from another social system'. Only occasionally did he 'give way to positive human emotions'.

The next day, 6 February, they met to discuss the painful subject of Poland and the world organization that would become the UN. Russia would take eastern slices of Poland in exchange for grants of German territory in the west. Stalin assented only to include a few Polish nationalists in his Communist-dominated government. When FDR said the Polish elections had to be 'beyond question like Caesar's wife', Stalin quipped,

'They said that about her but she had her sins.' Stalin explained the Russian obsession with Poland: 'Throughout history, Poland has served as a corridor for enemies coming to attack Russia' – hence he wanted a strong Poland. If Beria's son can be believed, his father came into his room that day saying, 'Joseph Vissarionovich has not moved an inch on Poland.' They approved the three zones of occupation in a demilitarized and de-Nazified Germany. The Americans were pleased by Stalin's repeated promise to intervene against Japan, agreeing to his demands for Sakhalin and the Kurile Islands.

On the 8th, after another meeting, they dined with Stalin at the Yusupov Palace where their opening speeches became more and more emotional as the Big Three, all aged by the war, contemplated their victory. Stalin rose to the occasion, toasting Churchill, 'a man who is born once in a hundred years, and who bravely held up the banner of Great Britain. I've said what I feel, what I have in my heart, and of what I'm conscious.' Stalin was 'in the very best of form', wrote Brooke, 'and was full of fun and good humour.' Stalin, who fooled no one when he described himself as a 'naïve ... garrulous old man', ominously toasted the generals 'who are recognized only during a war and whose services after the war are quickly forgotten. After the war, their prestige goes down and the ladies turn their back on them.' The generals did not yet realize he meant to forget them himself.

This epic dinner boasted one unusual guest: Stalin invited a delighted Beria, who was beginning to find his secret role constricting. Roosevelt noticed him and asked Stalin:

'Who's that in the pince-nez opposite Ambassador Gromyko?'

'Ah, that one. That's our Himmler,' replied Stalin with deliberate malice. 'That's Beria.' The secret policeman 'said nothing, just smiled, showing his yellow teeth' but 'it must have cut him to the quick', wrote his son, who knew how he longed to step on to the world stage. Roosevelt was upset by this, observed Gromyko, especially since Beria heard it too. The Americans examined this mysterious figure with fascination: 'He's little and fat with thick lenses which give him a sinister look but quite genial,' said Kathleen Harriman while Bohlen thought him 'plump, pale with pince-nez like a schoolmaster'. The sex-obsessed Beria was soon discussing the sex-life of fishes with the boozy, womanizing Sir Archibald Clark Kerr. When he was thoroughly drunk, Sir Archibald stood up and toasted Beria – 'the man who looks after our bodies', a compliment that was not only inappropriate but bungled. Churchill considered Beria the wrong sort of friend for HM Ambassador:

'No, Archie, none of that. Be careful,' he waved his finger.

On 10 February, at Churchill's dinner, Stalin proposed George VI's health with a proviso that he had always been against kings because he was on the side of the people. Churchill, somewhat irritated, suggested to Molotov that in future he should just propose a toast to the 'three Heads of State'. With only twelve or so at dinner, they discussed the upcoming British elections, which Stalin was sure Churchill would win:

'Who could be a better leader than he who won the victory?' Churchill explained there were two parties.

'One party is much better,' Stalin said. When they talked about Germany, Stalin regaled them with a story about the country's 'unreasonable sense of discipline' which he had told repeatedly to his own circle. When he arrived in Leipzig for a Communist conference, the Germans had arrived at the station but found no ticket collector so they waited for two hours on the platform until he arrived.

After a final dinner in the Tsar's billiard room at Livadia, Molotov escorted Roosevelt back to Saki, getting on to the presidential plane, the *Sacred Cow*, to say goodbye.

Churchill spent the night on the *Franconia* in Sebastopol harbour, flying out next day. Stalin was already on his train to Moscow. Budapest fell two days later.*

Stalin had won virtually all he wanted from the Allies and this is usually blamed on Roosevelt's illness and susceptibility to Stalinist charm. Both Westerners stand accused of 'selling out Eastern Europe to Stalin'.† Roosevelt's courtship of Stalin and discourtesy to Churchill were misguided. FDR was certainly ill and exhausted. But Stalin always believed that force would decide who ruled Eastern Europe which was occupied by 10 million Soviet soldiers. He himself told an anecdote after the war which reveals his view of Yalta. 'Churchill, Roosevelt and Stalin went hunting,' Stalin said. 'They finally killed their bear. Churchill said, "I'll take the bearskin. Let Roosevelt and Stalin divide the meat." Roosevelt said, "No, I'll take the skin. Let Churchill and Stalin divide the meat." Stalin remained silent so Churchill and Roosevelt ask him: "Mister Stalin, what do you say?" Stalin simply replied, "The bear belongs to me – after all, I killed it."' The bear is Hitler, the bearskin is Eastern Europe.

On 8 March, amidst operations to clean up Pomerania, Stalin summoned Zhukov to Kuntsevo for a strange meeting that marked the apotheosis of their close, touchy partnership. The Supremo was ill and 'greatly over-exhausted'. He seemed depressed. 'He had worked too much and slept too little,' thought Zhukov. The Battle for Berlin was his last great effort. Afterwards,

* There is an intriguing note in the archives concerning Churchill: a General Gorbatov reports to Beria on 5 May that orders had been sent to the NKVD with Marshal Malinovsky's army in Hungary to find a relative of Winston Churchill named Betsy Pongrantz and she had been found. The meaning is not precisely clear but none of the Churchills have heard of this 'relative'. Sir Winston's surviving daughter Lady Soames is unaware of the existence of this possibly Hungarian kinswoman: 'Perhaps Mr Beria and the NKVD had just got it wrong!' she suggests.
† If there was a sell-out, it had probably occurred much earlier at the Moscow Foreign Minister's Conference in October 1943. None the less, Stalin was surely delighted to leave Yalta with Foreign Secretary Eden's signature on the agreement to return all 'Soviet' ex-POWs, many of them White Cossack émigrés from the Civil War who had fought for the Nazis. Many were either shot or perished in Stalin's Gulags.

he could no longer sustain that tempo of work. He was not alone: Roosevelt was dying; Hitler almost senile; Churchill often ill. Total war took a total toll on its warlords. The Stalin who emerged from the war was both more sentimental and also more deadly.

'Let's stretch our legs a little, I feel sort of limp,' said Stalin. As they walked, Stalin talked about his childhood for an hour. 'Let's get back and have tea. I want to talk something over with you.' Encouraged by this surprising intimacy, Zhukov asked about Yakov:

'Have you heard about his fate?'

Stalin did not answer. His son Yakov tormented him. After about a hundred steps in silence, he answered in a 'subdued voice':

'Yakov won't be able to get out of captivity. They'll shoot him, the killers. From what we know, they're keeping him separately … and persuading him to betray his country.' Stalin was silent again, then he said, 'No, Yakov would prefer any kind of death to betraying the Motherland.' He was proud of his son at last but did not know he had been dead for almost two years. Stalin did not eat but sat at table: 'What a terrible war. How many lives of our people borne away. There'll probably be few families who haven't lost someone dear to them.' He talked about how he liked Roosevelt. Yalta had been a success. Just then Poskrebyshev arrived with his bag of papers and Stalin turned to Berlin:

'Go to Stavka and look at the calculations for the Berlin operation …' Three weeks later, on the morning of 1 April, Stalin held a conference with his two most aggressive marshals, Zhukov of the 1st Belorussian Front and Koniev of the 1st Ukrainian, at the Little Corner. 'Well. Who's going to take Berlin: we or the Allies?'

'It's we who'll take Berlin!' barked Koniev before Zhukov could even answer.

'So that's the sort of man you are,' Stalin grinned approvingly. Zhukov was to assault Berlin from the Oder bridgeheads over the Seelow Heights; Koniev to push towards Leipzig and Dresden, with his northern flank thrusting towards southern Berlin parallel to Zhukov. The Supremo of ambiguity allowed them both to believe that they could take Berlin: 'without saying a word', Stalin drew the demarcation line between the fronts into Berlin – then stopped and erased the line to the south of Berlin. Koniev understood this allowed him to join in the storming of

Berlin – if he could. 'Whoever breaks in first,' Stalin teased them, 'let him take Berlin.' That very day, in what one historian has described as 'the greatest April Fool in modern history', Stalin reassured Eisenhower that 'Berlin has lost its former strategic importance.' Two days later, the two marshals actually raced to the airport, their planes taking off within two minutes of each other. Such, Koniev admitted, was 'their passionate desire' to take the prize.

As they were marshalling their forces, Roosevelt died, the end of an era for Stalin. Their *entente* had won his paltry trust and roused his meagre human sympathy. Molotov 'seemed deeply moved and disturbed'. Harriman had 'never heard Molotov talk so earnestly'. Stalin, 'deeply distressed', received Harriman, holding his hand for thirty seconds. Years later, Stalin, on holiday at his New Athos dacha, judged 'Roosevelt was a great statesman, a clever, educated, far-sighted and liberal leader who prolonged the life of capitalism ...'

At 5 a.m. on 16 April, Zhukov unleashed a barrage of 14,600 guns against the Seelow Heights. The two marshals wielded 2.5 million men, 41,600 guns, 6,250 tanks and 7,500 aircraft, 'the largest concentration of firepower ever assembled'. But the Heights were a well-defended obstacle. Zhukov's losses were punishing. At midnight, he telephoned Stalin who taunted him:

'So you've underestimated the enemy on the Berlin axis? Things have started more successfully for Koniev.' The Supremo then phoned Koniev: 'Things are pretty hard with Zhukov. He's still hammering at the defences.' Stalin stopped. Koniev, who understood the workings of the Supremo, kept silent until Stalin asked: 'Is it possible to transfer Zhukov's tank forces and send them to Berlin through the gap on your front?' Koniev replied excitedly that his own tank forces could turn on Berlin. Stalin checked the map. 'I agree. Turn your tank armies on Berlin.' Zhukov was determined to take Berlin himself: ignoring tank lore, he stormed the Heights with tanks which became stuck in a churning swamp of pulverized earth and corpses. He lost 30,000 men. Stalin did not call him for three days.

On 20 April, Zhukov reached Berlin's eastern suburbs. Both marshals fought, house by house, street by street, towards Hitler's Chancellery. On the 25th, Koniev ordered an assault towards the Reichstag. Three hundred yards from the Reichstag building, Chuikov, who was leading Zhukov's thrust, encountered Russian forces – Koniev's tanks. Zhukov himself sped up and shouted at Rybalko, Koniev's tank commander:

'Why have you appeared here?' Koniev, disappointed, swerved west, leaving the Reichstag to Zhukov, but Stalin offered another prize:

'Who's going to take Prague?'

Stalin waited at Kuntsevo, only appearing in the office for a couple of hours around midnight each day. On 28 April, in the *Führerbunker*, Hitler married Eva Braun, dictated his testament, and they drank champagne.* Two days later, as Zhukov pushed closer, Hitler tested cyanide ampoules on his Alsatian, Blondi. Around 3.15 p.m., to the distant buzz of partying upstairs, Hitler committed suicide, shooting himself in the head. Eva took poison. Goebbels and Bormann made a final Hitler salute before the pyre of Hitler's body in the Chancellery garden. At 7.30 p.m., an unknowing Stalin arrived at the office to meet Malenkov and Vyshinsky for forty-five minutes before returning to Kuntsevo.

In the early hours of May Day, the German Chief of Staff visited Chuikov, announcing Hitler's death and requesting a ceasefire. Ironically, this was Hans Krebs, the tall German officer whom Stalin, seeing off the Japanese in April 1941, had told: 'We shall remain friends.' Chuikov refused a ceasefire. Krebs left and committed suicide. In a reverse of 22 June 1941, Zhukov, eager to break this world-historical news, telephoned Kuntsevo. Once again, the security refused to help.

'Comrade Stalin's just gone to bed,' replied General Vlasik.

'Please wake him,' retorted Zhukov. 'The matter's urgent and cannot wait until morning.'

Stalin picked up the phone and heard that Hitler was dead.

'So that's the end of the bastard.'

---

* In the higher levels of the Bunker, Hitler's secretary discovered 'an erotic fever seemed to take possession of everybody. Everywhere even on the dentist's chair, I saw bodies interlocked in lascivious embraces. The women had discarded all modesty and were freely exposing their private parts.'

Part Nine

The Dangerous Game of Succession, 1945–1949

44

The Bomb

'Too bad we couldn't take him alive,' Stalin told Zhukov. 'Where's Hitler's body?'

'According to General Krebs, his body was burned.' Stalin banned negotiations, except for unconditional surrender. 'And don't ring me until the morning if there's nothing urgent. I want some rest before tomorrow's parade.'

At 10.15 a.m., Zhukov's artillery bombarded the city centre. By dawn on the 2nd, Berlin was his. On 4 May, a Smersh colonel discovered the wizened, charred remains of Hitler and Eva. The bodies were spirited away. Zhukov was not told. Indeed, Stalin enjoyed humiliating the Marshal by asking if he had heard anything about Hitler's body.* Meanwhile Stalin was fascinated by the Nazi leadership: 'I'm sending you ... the correspondence of the top Germans ... found in Berlin,' Beria wrote to him, listing Himmler's letters to Ribbentrop.

After the war, during a late dinner on the Black Sea coast, Stalin was asked whether Hitler was a lunatic or an adventurer:

'I agree that he was an adventurer but I can't agree he was mad. Hitler was a gifted man. Only a gifted man could unite the German people. Like it or not ... the Soviet Army fought their way into the German land ... and reached Berlin without the German working-class ever striking against ... the Fascist regime. Could a madman so unite his nation?'

On 9 May, Moscow celebrated Victory Day but the curmudgeonly conqueror was wearily impatient with the jubilation. Stalin was furious when a junior general signed the German surrender at Reims and, pacing the floor, ordered Zhukov to sign a proper surrender in Berlin, 'whence German aggression sprang'. But the

---

* The jawbone and a portion of skull were kept in Moscow; the rest of his cadaver was tested by Smersh and then buried beside a garage at a Soviet army base in Magdeburg where it remained until KGB Chairman Yury Andropov ordered it cremated and the ashes scattered in April 1970.

glory days of the generals were over: Vyshinsky arrived to 'handle political matters' and spent the entire ceremony, 'bobbing up to whisper instructions in Zhukov's ear'. Stalin closely watched Zhukov and his supposed delusions of grandeur. Later in the year, he summoned him to the Kremlin to warn him that Beria and Abakumov were gathering evidence against him:

'I don't believe all this nonsense but stay out of Moscow.' That was not a problem since Zhukov was Stalin's proconsul in Berlin. Stalin despatched his satraps to rule his new Empire. Mikoyan flew in to feed the Germans. Malenkov and Voznesensky arrived to fight about whether to loot German industry or preserve it to build a Soviet satellite regime. Zhdanov held court in Finland, Voroshilov in Hungary, Bulganin in Poland, Vyshinsky in Romania. When Khrushchev called to congratulate him, Stalin cut him off for 'wasting his time'.

A call from Svetlana cheered Stalin:

'Congratulations on victory, papa!'

'Yes we've won,' he laughed. 'Congratulations to you too!'

At 8 p.m. on 24 May, Stalin hosted a banquet for the Politburo and marshals, singers, actors and even Polish miners, in the Georgevsky Hall. There was a traffic jam of limousines all the way to the Borovitsky Gate. The guests found their seats and waited eagerly. When Stalin appeared, 'ovations and shouts of "Hurrah" shook the vaulted halls ... with a deafening roar.' Molotov toasted the marshals who clinked glasses with the Politburo. When Admiral Isakov, who had lost his leg in 1942, was toasted, Stalin, still a master of the personal touch, walked all the way over to his distant table to clink glasses. Then Stalin praised the Russian people and referred to his own mistakes: 'Another people could have said to the government: you have not justified our expectations, go away and we will install another government which will conclude peace with Germany and guarantee us a quiet life.'

Later, Stalin asked Zhukov and the marshals:

'Don't you think we should celebrate the defeat of Fascist Germany with a victory parade?' Stalin decided to take the review on horseback. He could not ride but his hunger for glory still burned and he started secretly training to ride a white Arabian stallion, chosen by Budyonny. Around 15 June, a week before the parade, a spurred and booted Stalin in jodhpurs, apparently accompanied by his son Vasily, mounted the steed. He jerked his spurs. The horse reared. Stalin grabbed the mane and tried to stay in the saddle but was thrown, bruising his shoulder. Pulling himself to his feet, he spat:

'Let Zhukov take the parade. He's a cavalryman.' At Kuntsevo, he asked Zhukov if he had forgotten how to ride.

'I haven't,' replied Zhukov. 'I still ride sometimes.'

'Good ... You take the parade.'

'Thanks for the honour. But ... you're the Supremo and by right you should take it.'

'I'm too old ... You do it. You're younger.' Zhukov would ride a white Arabian stallion which Budyonny would show him. The next day, Zhukov was reviewing the rehearsals at the central airfield when Vasily Stalin buttonholed him:

'I'm telling you this as a big secret. Father had himself been preparing to take the parade but ... three days ago, the horse bolted ...'

'And which horse was your father riding?'

'A white Arab stallion, the one on which you're taking the parade. But I beg you not to mention a word of this.' Zhukov mastered the Arabian.

At 9.57 a.m. on 24 June, Zhukov mounted the stallion at the Spassky Gate. It was pouring with rain. The clocks struck ten: 'Parade-shun!'

'My heart beat faster,' wrote Zhukov. Simultaneously, Marshal Rokossovsky was waiting on Budyonny's own black charger, appropriately named Polus – the Pole – at the Nikolsky Gate. Stalin, in his greatcoat, showing no expression, walked clumsily, slowly, out on his own then lightly bounded up the steps to the Mausoleum, with Beria and Malenkov sweating breathlessly in their efforts to keep up. When the crowds saw him, hurrahs resounded across the Square. The rain poured, the water running down his vizor. He never wiped his face. As the chimes rang out, Zhukov and Rokossovsky rode out, both soaked, the bands played Glinka's *'Slavsya!'* – Glory to You – and tanks and Katyushas rumbled over the cobblestones. Silence fell on Red Square. 'Then a menacing staccato beat of hundreds of drums could be heard,' wrote Yakovlev. 'Marching in precise formation and beating out an iron cadence, a column of Soviet soldiers drew nigh.' Two hundred veterans each held a Nazi banner. At the Mausoleum they did a right turn and flung the banners, emblazoned with black and scarlet swastikas, at Stalin's feet where the downpour soaked them. Here was the climax of Stalin's life.

As soon as it was over, Stalin and the top brass poured into the room behind the Mausoleum for a buffet and drinks. It was here, according to Admiral Kuznetsov, that one of the marshals, probably Koniev, first proposed promoting Stalin to Generalissimo. He waved this away but then declared that he was now sixty-seven and weary:

'I'll work another two or three years, then I'll have to retire.' The Politburo and the marshals cried out on cue that he would live to rule the country for a long time yet. During the hard-drinking festivities, Stalin laughed as Poskrebyshev slipped the ceremonial dagger out of Vyshinsky's diplomatic uniform and replaced it with a pickle. Much to Stalin's amusement, the pompous ex-Procurator strutted around for the rest of the day oblivious of the vegetable in his scabbard, and smirks of the magnates.

That night, at a banquet for 2,500 officers, Stalin, who was already thinking about how to tighten discipline and bind the Union together, toasted the 'Russian people ...' and the 'screws', the ordinary people, 'without whom all of us, marshals and commanders of fronts and armies ... would not be worth a damn.'

In these carefully phrased toasts, Stalin set down a marker for his courtiers. The marshals were 'not worth a damn' compared to the Russian people whom only the Party (Stalin) could represent. His talk of retirement unleashed a brutal struggle among ruthless men to succeed a twentieth-century emperor who had no inten-tion of ever retiring. Within five years, three of the contenders would be dead.

Koniev's proposal to Molotov and Malenkov that they promote Stalin to Generalissimo to differentiate him from the marshals was not completely Ruritanian – Suvorov had been Generalissimo – but there was now something of the South American *junta* about it. Stalin was against the idea. He was endowed with all the prestige of a world conqueror, a 'deity ... an ungainly dwarf of a man who passed through gilded and marble Imperial halls', but the magnates were determined to honour him with Hero of the Soviet Union, another Order of Victory, and the rank of Generalissimo.

'Comrade Stalin doesn't need it,' he replied to Koniev. 'Comrade Stalin has the authority without it. Some title you've thought up! Chiang Kai-shek's a Generalissimo. Franco's a Generalissimo – fine company I find myself in!' Kaganovich, proud inventor of 'Stalinism', also suggested renaming Moscow as Stalinodar, an idea that had first been suggested by Yezhov in 1938. Beria seconded him. This simply 'outraged' Stalin: 'What do I need this for?'

The wise courtier senses when his master secretly wants him to disobey. Malenkov and Beria had Kalinin sign the decree. Three days after the parade, *Pravda* announced Stalin's new rank and the Hero of the Soviet Union gold star. He was furious and summoned Molotov, Malenkov, Beria, Zhdanov and old Kalinin, who was already extremely ill with stomach cancer. 'I haven't led regiments in the field ... I'm refusing the star as undeserved.' They argued but he insisted. 'Say what you like. I won't accept the decorations.' But they noticed that he had taken care to accept the Generalissimo.

Since the marshals now resembled Christmas trees of braid and clanking medals, the Generalissimo's uniform had to be completely over-the-top: the tailor of the élite, Lerner, created a gilded Ruritanian extravaganza with a golden cape. Khrulev dressed three strapping officers in these Göringesque outfits. When Stalin wandered out of his office to see Poskrebyshev, he snarled:

'Who are they? What's this peacock doing here?'

'Three samples of the Generalissimo's uniform.'

'They're not right for me. I need something more modest ... Do you want me to look like a doorman?' Stalin finally accepted a white gilded high-collared tunic with black and red-striped trousers which made him look like a bandmaster, if not a Park Avenue doorman. When he put it on, he regretted it, muttering to Molotov: 'Why did I agree?'

Malenkov and Beria were left with the star of Hero of the Soviet Union: how to get him to accept it? Here Stalin's court dissolves into an *opéra bouffe* farce in which the cantankerous Generalissimo was virtually pursued around Moscow by courtiers trying to pin the medal on him. First Malenkov agreed to try but Stalin would not listen. Next he recruited Poskrebyshev who accepted the mission but gave up when Stalin resisted energetically. Beria and Malenkov tried Vlasik but he too failed. They decided it was best to ambush Stalin when he was gardening because he loved his roses and lemon-trees so they persuaded

Orlov, the Kuntsevo commandant, to present it. When Stalin asked for the secateurs to prune his beloved roses, Orlov brought the secateurs but kept the star behind his back, wondering what to do with it.

'What are you hiding?' asked Stalin. 'Let me see.' Orlov gingerly brought out the star. Stalin cursed him:

'Give it back to those who thought up this nonsense!' Finally, he accepted the medal: 'You're indulging an old man. Won't do anything for my health!' Stalin did not just accept the rank of Generalissimo in order to join Franco. Vanity merged with politics: it helped diminish the dangerously prestigious marshalate. On 9 July, he further watered down their honours by promoting Beria, their scourge, to Marshal, equal to Zhukov or Vasilevsky.

The victor's good humour, though, could be chilling. Whenever he saw the Shipbuilding Commissar Nosenko, he joked 'Haven't they arrested you yet?' The next time he saw him, he chuckled: 'Nosenko, have you still not been shot?' Nosenko each time smiled anxiously. Finally at a celebratory Sovnarkom meeting, Stalin declared, 'We believed in victory and ... never lost our sense of humour. Isn't that true, Comrade Nosenko?'

* * *

A week later, Stalin, who, according to Gromyko, now 'always looked tired', mounted his eleven-coach armoured train for the journey to Potsdam: he travelled in four green carriages that had been taken from the Tsar's train in some museum, along a route of exactly 1,923 kilometres, according to Beria, who organized perhaps the tightest security ever for a travelling potentate. 'To provide proper security,' he wrote to Stalin on 2 July, '1,515 NKVD/GB men of operative staff and 17,409 NKVD forces are placed in the following order: on USSR territories, 6 men per kilometre; on territory of Poland, 10 men per kilometre; on German territory, 15 men per kilometre. Besides this on the route of the special train, 8 armoured trains will patrol – 2 in USSR, 2 in Poland and 4 in Germany.' 'To provide security for the chief of the Soviet delegation', there were seven NKVD regiments and 900 bodyguards. The inner security 'will be carried out by the operative staff of the 6th Department of the NKGB' arranged 'in three concentric circles of security, totalling 2,041 NKVD men'. Sixteen companies of NKVD forces alone were responsible for guarding his phone-lines while eleven aeroplanes provided quick links to Moscow. In case of urgent need, Stalin's own three planes, including a Dakota, stood ready. The secret police were 'to guarantee proper order and purges of anti-Soviet elements' at all stations and airports.*

The night before he arrived in Potsdam, Stalin called Zhukov:

'Don't get it into your head to meet us with an honour guard and band. Come to the station yourself and bring anyone you consider necessary.'

At 5.30 a.m. on 16 July, the day of Stalin's arrival, the United States tested a nuclear bomb in New Mexico that would change everything and, in many ways, spoil Stalin's triumph. The news was telegraphed to Harry S. Truman, who had succeeded Roosevelt as President, with the understatement of the century:

'Babies satisfactorily born.'

Stalin and Molotov, attended by Poskrebyshev, Vlasik and Valechka, found the platform virtually empty except for Zhukov, Vyshinsky and a table bearing three telephones connected to the Kremlin and the armies. 'In good spirits', Stalin raised his hat and climbed into the waiting ZiS 101 armoured limousine but then he opened the door and invited Zhukov to ride with him to his Babelsberg residence, 'a stone villa of two floors' with 'fifteen rooms and an open veranda', Beria informed him, 'supplied with all necessary electricity, heating and organized telephone stations with *VCh* for 100 numbers'. It had been Ludendorff's home. Stalin hated the extravagant furniture and ordered much of it to be removed – as he once had done in his Kremlin flat.

Stalin was late for the conference but it mattered little: the great decisions had been made at Yalta. The other leaders had arrived on the 15th and gone sightseeing to Hitler's Chancellery. Beria, who was already in Berlin to oversee the arrangements, accompanied by his son Sergo, longed to visit the ruins but obediently waited to ask Stalin's permission. Stalin refused to go himself, no tourist he. So Beria, in a baggy suit and open-necked shirt, went with the immaculate Molotov.

At midday on Tuesday the 17th, Stalin, resplendent in a fawn Generalissimo's uniform, arrived at Truman's 'Little White House'

---

* The NKVD had mended all the electrical systems of Babelsberg and, as at Yalta, they even brought their own fire brigade. More than that, Stalin had his own 'organized store of economic supplies with 20 refrigerators ... and 3 farms – a cattle farm, a poultry farm and a vegetable farm' plus '2 special bakeries, manned by trusted staff and able to produce 850 kg of bread a day'.

for their first meeting. The new President said nothing about the topic that dominated the conference. Sergo Beria wrote that his father, informed by spies in the American nuclear project, gave Stalin the news during this week: 'I didn't know then, at least not from the Americans,' was how Stalin put it. Beria had first informed him of the Manhattan Project in March 1942: 'We need to get started,' said Stalin, placing Molotov in charge. But, under Iron Arse, it advanced with excruciating, ponderous slowness. Finally in September 1944, the leading Russian nuclear scientist, Professor Igor Kurchatov, wrote to Stalin to denounce plodding Molotov and begged Beria to take it over. Stalin had little conception of nuclear fission's world-shattering importance nor of the vast resources it would require. He and Beria distrusted their own scientists and spies. None the less, they were aware of the urgency in procuring uranium, and twice during the Conference, Stalin and Beria debated how to react to the Americans.* They had agreed that Stalin should 'pretend not to understand', when the subject was mentioned. But so far, Truman said nothing. They discussed Russia's entry into the war against Japan. Truman asked Stalin to stay for lunch but he refused:

'You could if you wanted,' said Truman. Stalin stayed, unimpressed by the Missouri haberdasher who was no substitute for FDR: 'They couldn't be compared,' he said later. 'Truman's neither educated nor clever.' (Truman was none the less charmed: 'I like Stalin!' but, revealingly, he reminded the President of his patron, T. J. Pendergast, the machine politician boss of Kansas City.)

Stalin, ever more sartorially aware, changed into his white, gilded Generalissimo's magnificence with the single Hero of the Soviet Union gold star, and arrived last for the first session at the Cecilienhof Palace, built in 1917 for the last Crown Prince, mocking its Kaiserine grandeur: 'Hmm. Nothing much,' he told Gromyko. 'Modest. The Russian Tsars built themselves something much more solid.' At the Conference, Stalin sat between Molotov and his interpreter Pavlov, flanked by Vyshinsky and Gromyko. Champagne glasses were brought to toast the Conference.

---

* Beria had also secured as much uranium as possible in a special operation in the ruins of Berlin: he and Malenkov reported to Stalin they had found '250 kgs of metallic uranium, 2 tons of uranium oxide and 20 litres of heavy water' at the Kaiser Wilhelm Institute, rounded up key German physicists, and spirited all this treasure back to the USSR. Roy Medvedev in his *Neizvestnyi Stalin* claims Beria did not tell Stalin about the American test until 20 or 21 August but we do not know the precise date.

Churchill, puffing at a cigar, approached Stalin who was himself smoking a Churchillian cigar. If anyone were to photograph the Generalissimo with a cigar, it would 'create an immense sensation', Churchill beamed, 'everyone will say it is my influence'. Actually British influence was greatly diminished in the new world order of the superpowers in which they could agree on the deNazification of Germany but not on reparations or Poland. Now Hitler was gone, the differences were mountainous.

When Stalin decided he wanted a stroll in the gardens after a session, a British delegate was amazed to see 'a platoon of Russian tommy-gunners in skirmishing order, then a number of guards and units of the NKVD army. Finally appeared Uncle Joe on foot with his usual thugs surrounding him, followed by another screen of skirmishers. The enormous officer who always sits behind Uncle at meetings was apparently in charge of operations and was running around directing tommy-gunners to cover all the alleys.' After a few hundred yards, Stalin was picked up by his car.

At 8.30 p.m. on the 18th, Churchill dined at Ludendorff's villa, noticing that Stalin was ill, 'physically oppressed'. Smoking cigars together, they discussed power and death. Stalin admitted that the monarchy held together the British Empire, perhaps considering how to hold together his own.* No psephologist, he predicted that Churchill would win the election by eighty seats. Then he reflected that people in the West wondered what would happen when he died but it had 'all been arranged'. He had promoted 'good people, ready to step' into his shoes.

Finally, on 24 July, two monumental moments symbolized the imminent end of the Grand Alliance. First Churchill attacked Stalin for closing off Eastern Europe, citing the problems of the British mission in Bucharest:

'An iron fence has come down around them,' he said, trying out the phrase that would become 'the iron curtain'.

'Fairy tales!' snapped Stalin. The meeting ended at 7.30 p.m. Stalin headed out of the room but Truman seemed to hurry after him. Interpreter Pavlov deftly appeared beside Stalin. Churchill, who had discussed this moment with the President, watched in

---

* Stalin was a regicide who constantly compared himself to monarchs: he even joked with his Yugoslav visitors, 'Maybe Molotov and I should marry princesses,' a prospect that no doubt sent a shiver through the Almanac de Gotha. He was happy to use monarchies when necessary, urging Tito to restore the young Yugoslav King: 'You can always stick a knife in his back when no one's looking.'

fascination as Truman approached the Generalissimo 'as if by chance', in Stalin's words:

'The USA,' said Truman, 'tested a new bomb of extraordinary destructive power.' Pavlov watched Stalin closely: 'no muscle moved in his face.' He simply said he was glad to hear it:

'A new bomb! Of extraordinary power! Probably decisive on the Japanese! What a bit of luck!' Stalin followed the plan he had agreed with Beria to give the Americans no satisfaction but he still thought the Americans were playing games: 'An A-bomb is a completely new weapon and Truman didn't exactly say that.' He noticed Churchill's glee too: Truman spoke 'not without Churchill's knowledge'.

Back at Ludendorff's villa, Stalin, accompanied by Zhukov and Gromyko, immediately told Molotov about the conversation. But Stalin knew that, as yet, the Americans only possessed one or two Bombs – there was just time to catch up.

'They're raising their price,' said Molotov, who was in charge of the nuclear project.

'Let them,' said Stalin. 'We'll have to talk it over with Kurchatov and get him to speed things up.' Professor Kurchatov told Stalin that he lacked electrical power and had not enough tractors. Stalin immediately ordered power to be switched off in several populated areas and gave him two tank divisions to act as tractors. The Bomb's revolutionary importance was still percolating when the first device was dropped on Hiroshima. The scale of resources needed was just dawning on Stalin.

He then convened a meeting with Molotov and Gromyko at which he announced:

'Our Allies have told us that the USA has a new weapon. I spoke with our physicist Kurchatov as soon as Truman told me. The real question is should countries which have the Bomb simply compete with one another or ... should they seek a solution that would mean prohibition of its production and use?' He realized that America and Britain 'are hoping we won't be able to develop the Bomb ourselves for some time ...' and 'want to force us to accept their plans. Well that's not going to happen.' He cursed them in what Gromyko called 'ripe language', then asked the diplomat if the Allies were satisfied with all the agreements.

'Churchill's so riveted by our women traffic police in their marvellous uniforms that he dropped his cigar ash all over his suit,' replied Gromyko. Stalin smiled.

Next morning, Churchill and the Labour leader Clement Attlee flew back to London where they discovered that the warlord had been roundly defeated in the general election, thereby ending the triumvirate of Teheran and Yalta. Stalin preferred Roosevelt but he most admired Churchill: 'A powerful and cunning politician,' he remembered him in 1950. 'In the war years, he behaved as a gentleman and achieved a lot. He was the strongest personality in the capitalist world.'

During this interval, Stalin met up with his son Vasily, now stationed in Germany, who reported that Soviet aeroplanes were still inferior to the Americans', and dangerous to boot. Vasily's denunciations may have been well-meaning but Stalin always found a deadly use for them. At lunchtime on the 25th, Stalin met Queen Victoria's great-grandson, a cousin of Nicholas II, and Allied Supreme Commander, Southeast Asia, the ebullient Admiral Lord Louis Mountbatten who flattered him that he had diverted his trip from India to Britain 'specially to meet the Generalissimo', having long been 'an admirer of the Generalissimo's achievements not only in war but in peace as well'.

Stalin replied that he had done his best. 'Not everything' had been 'done well' but it was the Russian people 'who achieved these things'. Mountbatten's real motive was to wangle an invitation to visit Russia where he was convinced his Romanov connections would be appreciated, explaining that he had frequently visited the Tsar as a child for 'three or four weeks at a time'.

Stalin inquired drily, with a patronizing smile, whether 'it was some time ago that he had been there'. Mountbatten 'would find things had changed very considerably'. Mountbatten repeatedly asked for an invitation and returned to his imperial connections which he expected to impress Stalin. 'On the contrary,' says Lunghi, Mountbatten's interpreter, 'the meeting was embarrassing because Stalin was so unimpressed. He offered no invitation. Mountbatten left with his tail between his legs.'*

Potsdam ended with an affable but increasingly chilly impasse: Stalin possessed Eastern Europe but Truman had the Bomb. Before he left on 2 August, he realized the Bomb would require a colossal

---

* This may be the reason this story appears in none of Mountbatten's biographies and is told here for the first time. I am grateful to Hugh Lunghi for both his interview on the episode and his generous gift of his unpublished official minutes.

effort and his most dynamic manager. He removed Molotov and commissioned Beria to create the Soviet Bomb. Sergo Beria noticed his father 'making notes on a sheet of paper ... organizing the future commission and selecting its members.' Beria included Malenkov and others in the list.

'What need have you to include these people?' Sergo asked Beria.

'I prefer that they should belong. If they stay outside they'll put spokes in the wheels.' It was the climax of Beria's career.

45

Beria: Potentate, Husband,
Father, Lover, Killer, Rapist

On 6 August 1945, America dropped its bomb on Hiroshima. Stalin did not wish to miss out on the spoils, sending his armies against Japan, but the destruction of Hiroshima made a far greater impact than Truman's warning. Svetlana visited Kuntsevo that day: 'Everyone was busy and paid no attention to me,' she grumbled. 'War is barbaric,' reflected Stalin, 'but using the A-bomb is a superbarbarity. And there was no need to use it. Japan was already doomed!' He had no doubt that Hiroshima was aimed at himself: 'A-bomb blackmail is American policy.'

Next day, Stalin held a series of meetings at Kuntsevo with Beria and the scientists:

'Hiroshima has shaken the whole world. The balance has been destroyed,' he told them. 'That cannot be.' Now Stalin understood that the project was the most important in his world; codenamed 'Task Number One', it was to be run 'on a Russian-scale' by Beria's 'Special Committee' that functioned like an 'Atomic Politburo'. The scientists had to be coaxed and threatened. Prizes and luxuries were vital: 'Surely it's possible to ensure that several thousand people can live very well ... and better than well.' Stalin was 'bored' by the science but treated Kurchatov kindly: 'If a child doesn't cry, the mother does not know what she needs. Ask for whatever you like. You won't be refused.'

Beria threw himself into Task Number One as if his life depended on it – which it did. The project was on a truly Soviet scale, with Beria managing between 330,000 and 460,000 people and 10,000 technicians. Beria was the pre-eminent Terror entrepreneur, telling one of his managers, 'You're a good worker but if you'd served six years in the camps, you'd work even better.' He controlled his scientists in the *sharashki*, special prisons for technical experts, described by Solzhenitsyn in *The First Circle*: when one expert suggested he might work better if he was free,

Beria scoffed, 'Certainly. But it would be risky. The traffic in the streets is crazy and you might get run over.'

Yet he could also be 'ingratiating', asking the physicist Andrei Sakharov charmingly, 'Is there anything you want to ask me?' His handshake, 'plump, moist and deathly cold,' reminded Sakharov of death itself: 'Don't forget we've plenty of room in our prisons!' His name was enough to terrify most people: 'Just one remark like "Beria has ordered" worked absolutely without fail,' remembered Mikoyan. When he called Vyshinsky, he 'leapt out of his chair respectfully' and 'cringed like a servant before a master'.

Task Number One, like all Beria's projects, functioned 'as smoothly and reliably as a Swiss clock'. Kurchatov thought Beria himself 'unusually energetic'. But he also won the scientists' loyalty by protecting them, appealing to Stalin who agreed: 'Leave them in peace. We can always shoot them later.' Mephistophelian brutality, Swiss precision and indefatigable energy were the hallmarks of Beria who was 'incredibly clever ... an unusual man and also a great criminal.'

Beria was one of the few Stalinists who instinctively understood American dynamism: when Sakharov asked why their projects so 'lag behind the USA', only Beria would have answered like an IBM manager: 'we lack R and D.' But the scientific complexities completely foxed Beria himself and his chief manager, Vannikov, the ex-Armaments boss. 'They're speaking while I blink,' admitted Vannikov. 'The words sound Russian but I'm hearing them for the first time.' As for Beria, one scientist joked to Sakharov: 'Even Lavrenti Pavlovich knows what mesons are.' His solution was high-handed arrogance and the threat: 'If this is misinformation, I'll put you in the dungeon!'

This fusion of Beria's bludgeon and Kurchatov's mesons led to some bombastic rows. In November 1945, Pyotr Kapitsa, one of the most brilliant Soviet scientists, complained to Stalin that Beria and the others behaved 'like supermen'. Kapitsa reported his argument with Beria: 'I told him straight, "You don't understand physics."' Beria 'replied that I knew nothing about people'. Beria had 'the conductor's baton' but the conductor 'ought not only to wave the baton but also understand the score'. Beria did not understand the science. Kapitsa suggested that he should study physics and shrewdly ended his letter: 'I wish Comrade Beria to be acquainted with this letter for it is not a denunciation but useful criticism. I would have told him all this myself but it's a great deal of trouble to get to see him.' Stalin told Beria that he had to get on with the scientists. Beria summoned Kapitsa who amazingly refused him:

'If you want to speak to me, then come to the Institute.' Beria ate humble pie and took a hunting rifle as a peace offering. But Kapitsa refused to help any more. Stalin meanwhile wrote him a note:

'I have received all your letters ... There is much that is instructive and I'm thinking of meeting you some time ...' But he never did.

* * *

Beria was at the centre not only of Stalin's political world but also of his private one. Now their families almost merged in a Georgian dynastic alliance. Svetlana, still suffering from the end of her first love affair with Kapler, spent much time at Beria's houses with his wife, Nina, blonde, beautiful (though with stocky legs), and a qualified scientist from an aristocratic family who also managed to be a traditional Georgian housewife. Stalin still treated her paternally even as he began to loathe Beria himself. 'Stalin asked Nina to look after Svetlana because she had no mother,' said Beria's daughter-in-law.

Beria always craved athletic women, haunting the locker-rooms of Soviet swimmers and basketball players. Nina herself was something of an Amazon, always exercising, playing tennis with bodyguards, cycling on a tandem. Beria was, like many a womanizer, a very jealous husband and the bodyguards were the only men allowed close to her. Beria lived in some style: he divided his grand town mansion into offices and private rooms on one side, and apartments for his wife and family on the other. His wife and son mainly lived at his 'sumptuous, immense' white dacha at Sosnovka near Barvikha, which 'was in Jugend style, lots of glass and stone, like art deco with a terrace and lots of guards around,' as well as pet bear cubs and foxes.* Yet Nina kept it 'cosy' and it was always littered with English and German magazines and books. On holidays in the south, Beria, who was a trained architect, designed his own dacha at Gagra close to Stalin's. The Master often invited over the Berias who brought along their son Sergo.

---

* Many of the Soviet leaders had their own zoos or menageries: Bukharin had collected bear cubs and foxes. Khrushchev had foxcubs and deer; Budyonny, Mikoyan and Kaganovich kept horses.

By the end of the war, the balding broad-faced Beria with his swollen, moist lips and the cloudy brown eyes, was 'ugly, flabby and unhealthy-looking with a greyish-yellow complexion'. The life of a Stalinist magnate was not a healthy one. No one worked harder than the 'inhumanly energetic' Beria, but he still played volleyball every weekend with Nina and his team of bodyguards: 'Even though he was so unfit, he was amazingly fast on his feet.' In common with other human predators, Beria became a vegetarian, eating 'grass' and Georgian dishes but only rarely meat. He came home at weekends, practised shooting his pistol in the garden, watched a movie in his cinema and then drove off again.

Dressing like a southern winegrower, Beria hated uniforms, only sporting his Marshal's uniform during 1945: usually he wore a polo-neck sweater, a light jacket, baggy trousers and a floppy hat. Beria was cleverer, brasher and more ambitious than the other magnates and he could not resist letting them know it. He teased Khrushchev about his looks and his womanizing, saying, 'Look at Nikita, he's nothing much to look at but what a ladykiller!', tormented Andreyev about his illnesses, Voroshilov about his stupidity, Malenkov about his flabbiness and he told Kobulov that he dressed like Göring. No one ever forgot any of Beria's wisecracks. Nina begged him to be more circumspect: 'she hated his way of wounding people,' wrote their son. His own courtiers, who 'idealized him,' met like modern corporate directors at his box at the Dynamo football stadium. The major organizations had their own football teams – Beria's MVD had Dynamo, the trade unions had Spartak. The competition was so vicious in 1942 that Beria had the successful manager of the Spartak team, Nikolai Starostin, arrested and sent into exile. An invitation to watch a game in Beria's box for a young Chekist meant entering his circle.

An inventory of his desk after his later arrest revealed his interests: power, terror and sex. In his office, Beria kept blackjack clubs for torturing people and the array of female underwear, sex toys and pornography that seemed to be obligatory for secret-police chiefs. He was found to be keeping eleven pairs of silk stockings, eleven silk corsets, seven silk nighties, female sports outfits, the equivalent of Soviet cheerleaders' costumes, blouses, silk scarves, countless obscene love letters and a 'large quantity of items of male debauchery'.

Despite his mountainous workload, Beria found time for a Draculean sex-life that combined love, rape and perversity in almost equal measure. The war had given him the opportunity to engage in a life of sexual brigandage even more intense and reckless than that enjoyed by his predecessors in the job. The secret-police chiefs always had the greatest sexual licence: only Smersh watched Beria; otherwise he could do whatever he wanted. It was once thought Beria's seductions and rapes were exaggerated but the opening of the archives of his own interrogation, as well as the evidence of witnesses and even those who were raped by him, reveals a sexual predator who used his power to indulge himself in obsessive depravity. It is often impossible to differentiate between women he seduced who went to him to plead for loved ones – and those women he simply kidnapped and raped. Yet mothers often pimped their daughters in return for limousines and privileges. Beria himself could also be a gentleman, treating some mistresses so kindly that they never criticized him even when he had been exposed as a Soviet Bluebeard.* He combined seduction with espionage: he seduced a willing female friend of Kira Alliluyeva's by saying 'What lovely cherry lips you have! A figure like Venus!' Afterwards, he quizzed her on her circle, recruiting her to spy on the Alliluyevs.

He was a familiar sight in Moscow as he cruised the streets in his armoured Packard and sent his Caucasian bodyguards Colonels Sarkisov and Nadaraia to procure women for him. The colonels were not always happy with their role – indeed, Sarkisov kept a record of Beria's perversions with which to denounce him to Stalin. The girls were usually taken to the town house where a Georgian feast and wine awaited them in a caricature of Caucasian chivalry. One of the colonels always proffered a bouquet of flowers on the way home. If they resisted, they were likely to get arrested. The film star Zoya Fyodorovna was picked up by these Chekists at a time when she was still breastfeeding her baby. Taken to a party where there were no other guests, she was

---

* In December 2003, the fiftieth anniversary of Beria's death, the Tunisian Ambassador to Moscow revealed that human remains had been discovered in the cellars of his embassy, Beria's home: presumably Beria's victims. We may never know whether they were rape victims or executed Enemies. On 17 January 2003, the Russian Prosecutor confirmed the existence of forty-seven volumes of files on Beria's criminal activities which were gathered on his arrest after Stalin's death. Even though the case against him was entirely political, with trumped-up charges, the files confirm the dozens of women who accused him of raping them. The State television network RTR was allowed to film the handwritten list of their names and telephone numbers. The files will not be opened for another twenty-five years.

joined by Beria whom she begged to let her go as her breasts were painful. 'Beria was furious.' The officer who was taking her home mistakenly handed her a bouquet at the door. When Beria saw, he shouted: 'It's a wreath not a bouquet. May they rot on your grave!' She was arrested afterwards.

The film actress Tatiana Okunevskaya was even less lucky: at the end of the war, Beria invited her to perform for the Politburo. Instead they went to a dacha. Beria plied her with drink, 'virtually pouring the wine into my lap. He ate greedily, tearing at the food with his hands, chattering away.' Then 'he undresses, rolls around, eyes ogling, an ugly, shapeless toad. "Scream or not, doesn't matter," he said. "Think and behave accordingly." ' Beria softened her up by promising to release her beloved father and grandfather from prison and then raped her. He knew very well both had already been executed. She too was arrested soon afterwards and sentenced to solitary confinement. Felling trees in the Siberian *taiga*, she was saved, like so many others, by the kindness of ordinary people.

These women were just the tip of a degenerate iceberg. Beria's priapic energy was as frenzied and indefatigable as his bureaucratic drive. 'I caught syphilis during the war, in 1943 I think, and I had treatment,' he later confessed. After the war, it was Vlasik and Poskrebyshev, who, remembering Bronka, told Stalin about the syphilis. Lists were already a Stalinist obsession so this sex addict felt compelled to keep a record of his conquests. His colonels kept the score; some say the list numbered thirty-nine, others seventy-nine: 'Most of those women were my mistresses,' he admitted. Beria ordered Sarkisov to destroy the list which he did but being a Chekist, the bodyguard kept a copy, later used against his master ...

Some mistresses, like 'Sophia' and 'Maya', a student at the Institute of Foreign Relations, inconveniently became pregnant. Once again, Colonels Sarkisov and Nadaraia were called upon to arrange abortions at the MVD's Medical Department – and when a child was born, the colonels placed it in an orphanage.*

---

* To this day, Beria's illegitimate children are well known among Moscow and Tbilisi society: they include a highly respected Georgian Member of Parliament and a Soviet matron who married the son of a member of Brezhnev's Politburo. After the war, Stalin changed the People's Commissariats to Ministries so that the NKVD and NKGB became the MVD and MGB. The State Defence Committee, the GKO, was abolished on 4 September 1945. The Politburo once again became the highest Party body though Stalin ruled as Premier, leaving the Party Secretariat to Malenkov.

Beria was also notorious among the magnates themselves: Stalin himself tolerated the peccadilloes of his potentates as long as they were politically reliable. During the war, when Beria was running half the economy and he was informed of his priapism, Stalin answered indulgently, 'Comrade Beria is tired and over-worked.' But the less he trusted Beria, the less tolerant he became. Once, hearing that Svetlana was at Beria's house, Stalin panicked, rang and told her to leave at once. 'I don't trust Beria.' Whether this referred to his sexuality or to his politics is not clear. When Beria told Poskrebyshev that his daughter was as pretty as her mother, the *chef de cabinet* told her, 'Never accept a lift from Beria.' Voroshilov's daughter-in-law was followed by Beria's car all the way back to the Kremlin. Voroshilov's wife was terrified:

'It's Beria! Say nothing! Don't tell a soul!' The leaders' wives hated Beria:

'How can you work with such a man?' Ashken Mikoyan asked her husband.

'Be quiet,' Mikoyan would reply, but Ashken would not go to functions if Beria was likely to be present:

'Say I've a headache!'

Beria's wife Nina told Svetlana and other friends that she 'was terribly unhappy. Lavrenti's never home. I'm always alone.' But her daughter-in-law remembers that 'she never stopped loving Beria'. She knew that he had other women 'but she took a tolerant Georgian view of this'. When he came home for the weekend, 'she spent hours having manicures and putting on makeup. She lived downstairs in her own room but when he came home, she moved upstairs to share his bed.' They 'sat cosily by the fire, watching Western films, usually about cowboys and Mexican banditos. His favourite was *Viva Villa!* about Pancho Villa. They chatted lovingly in Mingrelian.' Nina never believed the scale of his exploits: 'When would Lavrenti have found time to make these hordes of women his mistresses? He spent all day and night at work' so she presumed these women must have been his 'secret agents'.

* * *

Sergo Beria, now twenty-one, named after Ordzhonikidze, had been at School No. 175 with Svetlana Stalin, Martha Peshkova and most of the élite children. As a father, Beria was absent much of the time but he was enormously proud of Sergo. Theirs was a typically formal relationship between a Bolshevik and his son. 'If Sergo wanted to talk to his father,' recalled his wife, 'Lavrenti would say, "Come and see me in the office."' Like Malenkov and most of the other leaders, Beria was determined that his son should not go into politics.

Like all Politburo parents, he encouraged him to become a scientist: Colonel Beria rose to prominence in military technology as head of the sprawling missile Design Bureau Number One. Sergo had grown up around Stalin, and Beria therefore could not prevent the Generalissimo inviting him to the wartime conferences.

Sergo was intelligent, cultured and, according to Martha Peshkova, Svetlana Stalin's best friend, 'so beautifully handsome that he was like a dream – all the girls were in love with him'. In 1944, Svetlana fell for him too, a fact that she leaves out of both her memoirs and her interviews. When Sergo wrote his own memoirs and claimed this was so, many historians disbelieved it. Yet Svetlana wanted to marry him, an ambition she never gave up even when he himself married someone else. When he was in Sverdlovsk during the war, Svetlana got her brother to fly her there. After the Kapler affair, this crush worried the Berias:

'Don't you realize what you're doing?' Nina Beria told Svetlana. 'If your father finds out about this, he'll skin Sergo alive.'

Stalin wanted her to marry one of his potentate's sons, specifying to Svetlana that she should marry either Yury Zhdanov, Sergo Beria or Stepan Mikoyan. But this honour appalled Beria.

'That would be terrible,' he said to Mikoyan. Even though Stalin had shown interest in the idea, both knew that he would actually 'interpret this as an attempt to worm your way into his family', as Beria told Sergo. Svetlana was determined to marry Sergo but the Berias put a firm stop to it. As she obliquely admitted:

'I wanted to marry someone when I was a young girl ... But his parents would not accept me because of who I am. It was a very painful blow.'

Worse was to follow: Martha Peshkova was now 'as pretty and plump as a quail' and seemed to exist in a 'warm scented cloud of strange attraction': it was, recalled Gulia Djugashvili, 'difficult to have Martha as a friend.' Martha's boyfriend was Rem Merkulov, the son of the NKGB boss. Perhaps, having grown up around Yagoda, she had a taste for Cheka princelings because she now fell in love with Sergo Beria whom she married soon afterwards. The Berias did not have a big wedding: 'it was not the style of the time,' says Martha. Beria told Sergo that Stalin would not approve of 'your getting connected with that family' – the Gorkys. Sure enough, Stalin invited Sergo to Kuntsevo:

'Gorky himself wasn't bad but what a lot of anti-Soviet people he had around him. Don't fall under your wife's influence,' warned Stalin, always suspicious of wives.

'But she's quite non-political,' answered Sergo.

'I know. But I regard this marriage as a disloyal act on your part ... not to me, but to the Soviet State. Was it ... forced on you by your father?' He accused Beria of making connections with the 'oppositionist intelligentsia'. Instead Sergo blamed Svetlana for introducing him to Martha.

'You never breathed a word of it to Svetlana,' Stalin replied. 'She told me herself.' Then he smiled at Sergo: 'Don't take any notice, old people are always peevish ... As for Marfochka, I saw her grow up.'

Martha moved into the Berias' dacha where she got to know, and love, the most infamous man of his time.* Beria could not have been kinder to her: 'I was very fond of him. He was very cheerful and very funny, always singing the Mexican song, "La Paloma", and telling comical anecdotes of his life' such as how he lost his virginity in Romania, getting entangled in the woman's voluminous pantaloons. He claimed that as a Herculean baby, he was found crawling in the garden holding a snake in his hands. On Sundays, his only rest day, he and Nina slept late and then played Martha and Sergo at volleyball, each assisted by the bodyguards. When Martha gave Beria his first grandchild, 'he couldn't have been sweeter, spending hours sitting by the cradle just looking at her. In the morning, he'd have the baby brought into his and Nina's room where he'd sit her between them and just smile at her.' He was so indulgent of the child that 'he let her put her whole hands into her birthday cakes'.

Martha was less keen on Nina. Her mother-in-law turned out to be as despotic in the house as her father-in-law was out. Nina was lonely and Martha soon found she was seeing more of her mother-in-law than her husband. She wanted them to set up their

---

* I am fortunate that Martha Peshkova, Gorky's granddaughter, Svetlana's best friend and Beria's daughter-in-law, helped with her unique memories and introduced me to the Gorky/Beria family including Beria's granddaughters (see Postscript). As a wedding present, Stalin gave Sergo and Martha a copy of Rustaveli's *The Knight in the Panther Skin*, which he had edited himself with Professor Nutsibidze, inscribing it teasingly: 'You'd do better to form bonds with the Georgian intelligentsia!'

own home but Nina told her, 'If you mention that again, you'll find yourself very far from your children.'

Beria, says Martha, was 'the cleverest person around Stalin. In a way, I'm sorry for him because it was his fate to be there at that time. In another era, he would have been so different. If he'd been born in America, he would have risen to something like Chairman of General Motors.' She was sure he was never a real Communist: he once amazed her when he was playing with his granddaughter. 'This girl,' he said, 'will be tutored at home and then she's going to Oxford University!' No other Politburo member would have said such a thing.

* * *

Svetlana Stalin rebounded from Sergo into an unsuitable marriage. At Vasily's apartment in the House on the Embankment, Svetlana met Grisha Morozov, who served in the war in the traffic police. 'A friendship developed,' recalls Svetlana, but 'I wasn't in love with him.' However he was in love with her. Stalin was dubious about Morozov, another Jew: after Kapler, he began to feel these Jews were worming their way into his family. But Svetlana was attracted to their warmth and culture, so Stalin said,

'It's spring ... You want to get married. To hell with you. Do what you like.'

'I just wanted to get over the rejection,' explained Svetlana years later, 'so we married but under other circumstances, it wasn't my choice. My first husband was a very good person who always loved me.' There was no ceremony: they just went to the register office where the official looked at her passport and asked:

'Does your papa know?' Marrying into Stalin's family, Morozov 'instantly became rather grand', says Leonid Redens. They quickly had their first baby – a son named Joseph, of course. Svetlana found herself unprepared for marriage: 'I had a son when I was nineteen ... My young husband was a student too. We had people to look after the baby. I had three abortions and then a very bad miscarriage.' Meanwhile Stalin refused to meet Morozov.

Svetlana was still in love with Sergo Beria. 'She never forgave me for marrying him,' says Martha. Svetlana reminded Sergo that Stalin 'was furious' about the marriage. She still visited Nina, her surrogate mother. Once Svetlana suggested that they remove Martha, who could take the elder daughter and then she would move in with Sergo and raise the younger one. 'She's just like her father,' Mikoyan said. 'She always gets what she wants!'

However, she could also be very kind. When Yakov's heroism in German captivity had been proven, his widow Julia was released but found that her seven-year-old daughter, Gulia, hardly knew her. Svetlana agreed to look after Gulia and one day she announced, 'Today we're going to meet Mama.' But the child was afraid of the stranger, so daily, with the most touching sensitivity, Svetlana took her to see her mother until gradually the two bonded. This had to be done surreptitiously because, while Gulia was brought up by nannies, her mother remained outside the family. Finally, she wrote to Stalin: 'Joseph Vissarionovich, I ask you very much not to refuse my request because it's hard to see Gulia. We live in the hope of seeing you and talking about things not put in this letter. We would like you to meet Gulia ...' Later, thanks to Svetlana, Stalin did meet his first granddaughter.

46

A Night in the Nocturnal Life of
Joseph Vissarionovich: Tyranny by
Movies and Dinners

The true victor of the war, Stalin enjoyed the prestige of a world conqueror yet the disparity between his political power and his personal exhaustion made him feel vulnerable.

The Generalissimo and Molotov were satisfied, though never satiated, by their prizes. At a southern dinner, Stalin sent Poskrebyshev to bring the new map. They spread it on the table. Using his pipe as a baton, Stalin reviewed his Empire: 'Let's see what we've got then: in the north, everything's all right, Finland greatly wronged us, so we've moved the frontier farther from Leningrad. The Baltic States, which were Russian territory from ancient times, are ours again, all the Belorussians are ours now, Ukrainians too, and the Moldavians are back with us. So to the west everything's okay.' But he turned to the east: 'What have we got here? The Kurile Islands are ours and all of Sakhalin ... China, Mongolia, all as it should be.' The Dunhill pipe trailed round to the south: 'Now this frontier I don't like at all. The Dardanelles ... We also have claims to Turkish territory and to Libya.' This could have been the speech of a Russian Tsar – it was hardly that of a Georgian Bolshevik. Molotov shared this mission: 'My task as Foreign Minister was to expand the borders of our Motherland. And it seems Stalin and I coped ... quite well. Yes I wouldn't mind getting Alaska back,' he joked. But Molotov understood that there was no contradiction between Bolshevism and empire-building: 'It's good the Russian Tsars took so much land for us in war. This makes our struggle with capitalism easier.'

But Stalin's courtiers noticed that his triumph had turned his head. 'He became conceited,' said Molotov, 'not a good feature in a statesman.' His prestige was so great that he was absolute in all matters: his mere words were taken as 'Party orders and instantly obeyed'. Yet he now ruled in a very different way: he 'stepped aside from direct ruling', said one of his officials, and assumed the Olympian mantle of a paramount leader, like the old Chairman

Mao, who liked to guide his men with anecdotes, signs and hints. He used secrecy, caprice and obscurity to maintain his mastery over his younger, stronger, ambitious magnates. He dominated his entourage by mystery.

'He never gave direct orders,' wrote his Georgian boss, Charkviani, 'so you had to make your own conclusions.' Stalin understood that 'it doesn't matter what part of the pool you throw a stone, the ripples will spread'. He once showed his Abkhazian leader, Mgeladze, his beloved lemon trees again and again until the *apparatchik* finally understood and declared that Abkhazia would produce lemons for the whole USSR.

'Now you've got it!' smiled Stalin. Unless he was in a temper, he usually ended his orders: 'Do as you wish' but no one mistook his meaning. If, on the other hand, he gave a direct order, writing 'I don't think my reasons need to be discussed, they are perfectly clear,' or simply shouted his wishes, he was instantly obeyed. In the MGB, the mere mention of the *Instantsiya* justified any act of barbarism.

However, the Generalissimo was also weaker and older than before. Shortly before the victory parade, Stalin had experienced some sort of heart attack or what Svetlana called 'a minor stroke', hardly surprising given the strain of warlordism on his remarkably durable metabolism. 'Certainly overexhausted,' observed Molotov, Stalin already suffered from arthritris but it was the hardening of his arteries, arteriosclerosis, that reduced the flow of blood to the brain and could only impair his mental faculties. After returning from Potsdam, he fell ill again, making him feel weaker at the very moment when his position was strongest. They brought him under the power of doctors, a profession he despised and which he had corrupted (making his own physician Vinogradov testify at the show trials during the thirties). Poskrebyshev, the ex-nurse, became his secret doctor, prescribing pills and remedies.

These contradictions gave Stalin a deadly unpredictability, lashing out at those around him. The hopes and freedoms of the war made no difference to his belief that the problems of the USSR were best solved by the elimination of individuals. The poverty of his Empire compared to the surging wealth of America dovetailed with his own feeling that his powers were failing, and the inferiority complexes of a lifetime.

Usually 'calm, reserved and patient', he often 'exploded instantly and made irrelevant and wrong decisions'. Khrushchev said, 'after the war, he wasn't quite right in the head'. He remained a supreme manipulator though it is likely that the arteriosclerosis exacerbated his existing tempers, depression and paranoia. He was never mad: indeed, his strangest obsessions always had a basis in real politics. Yet mortality made him realize the sterility he had created inside himself: 'I'm a most unfortunate person,' he told Zhukov, 'I'm afraid of my own shadow.' But it was this super-sensitivity that made him such a frightening but masterful politician. His fear of losing control of his Empire was based on reality: even in his own Politburo, Mikoyan felt the war was a 'great school of freedom' with no need to 'return to terror'.

Stalin despised this laxity. He even joked about it when he sent some writers to tour conquered Japan and asked Molotov if they had departed. It turned out they had put off the trip: 'Why didn't they go?' he asked. 'It was a Politburo decision. Maybe they didn't approve of it and wanted to appeal to the Party Congress?' The writers left quickly. But he sensed this lax attitude all around him.

'He was very jittery,' said Molotov. 'His last years were the most dangerous. He swung to extremes.' He was jealous of Molotov and Zhukov's prestige, suspicious of Beria's power, and disgusted by the soft smugness of his magnates: even when he was ill and old, he was never happier than when he was orchestrating a struggle. It was his gift, his natural state. Some backs would have to be broken. Stalin ruled 'through a small group close to him at all times' and formal 'government ceased to function'. Even on long holidays away from Moscow, he maintained his paramount power by directing each portfolio through his direct relationship with the official in question, and no one else. His interventions were almost deliberately capricious and out of the blue.

More than ever, his courtiers had to know how to handle him but first, they had to survive his nocturnal routine. It is no exaggeration to say that henceforth Stalin ruled, from Berlin to the Kurile Islands, from the dinner-table and the cinema. The defiance of time itself is the ultimate measure of tyranny: the lights in his capitals – from Warsaw to Ulan Bator, from Budapest to Sofia – shone throughout the night.

* * *

The magnates met at the Little Corner after which the Generalissimo always proposed a movie. He led his guests along the red-and-blue-carpeted corridors to the cinema which had been luxuriously built in the old winter garden on the second floor of the Great Kremlin Palace. Beria, Molotov, Mikoyan and Malenkov remained his constant companions but his proconsuls in Finland and Ukraine, Zhdanov and Khrushchev, often visited too.

Then there was the whole new court of European vassals: his favourites were the Polish leader Boleslaw Bierut, 'polite, well-dressed, well-mannered', a 'perfect gentleman with women' but a ruthless Stalinist with 'a fanatical faith in the dogma', his deputy Jakob Berman, the Czech President Clement Gottwald, Hungary's Matyas Rakosi. The prouder Yugoslavs, Marshal Tito and Milovan Djilas, were less liked. Each of them was honoured to come to Moscow to pay homage and receive Stalin's sacerdotal wisdom and imperial commands. They too had to learn how to behave in the cinema and at dinner.

The sight of the Generalissimo and his guards approaching was a terrifying one for any young official who happened to be walking along these corridors. The plain-clothed guards walked twenty-five steps in front and two metres behind Stalin, while the uniformed guards followed him with their eyes. Amidst this phalanx of myrmidons, walking noiselessly but quickly and jauntily, with a heavy, pigeon-toed step, came the potbellied emperor with his fine mountain man's head, his sloping shoulders, the tigerish creases of his roguish smile. Anyone who saw him approaching had to stand back against the wall and show their hands. Anatoly Dobrynin, a young diplomat, once found himself in this dilemma: 'I pressed my back against the wall.' Stalin 'did not fail to notice my confusion' and asked 'who I was and where I worked'. Then 'stressing his words by a slow moving of the finger of his right hand' before Dobrynin's face, he declared,

'Youth must not fear Comrade Stalin. He is its friend.' Dobyrnin shuddered.

The walk to the cinema took a few minutes. Decorated in blue, there were rows of soft upholstered armchairs set in pairs, with tables between each seat with mineral water, wine, cigarettes, boxes of chocolates. The carpet was grey with rugs on it. Before Stalin arrived, the Politburo took their seats, leaving the front row empty. They were met by the Minister of Cinema, Ivan Bolshakov, who had run the film industry since 1939 and became a vital but comical presence in the entourage. Bolshakov was terrified of Stalin since his two cinematic predecessors had been shot. As Stalin got older, the cinema became an obsessive ritual, as well as an aid, and venue, for governing.

Bolshakov's big decision was which film to show. This he judged by trying to guess Stalin's mood. He observed the leader's gait, intonation of voice and sometimes, if he was lucky, Vlasik or Poskrebyshev gave him a clue. If Stalin was in a bad mood, Bolshakov knew it was not a good idea to show a new movie. Stalin was a creature of habit: he loved his old favourites from the thirties like *Volga! Volga!* or foreign films such as *In Old Chicago*, *Mission to Moscow*, the comedy *It Happened One Night*, or any Charlie Chaplin.

Stalin now possessed a new library of American, English and German films that had until recently been the property of Goebbels. If Stalin was in a bad mood, one of the Goebbels films would please him. He liked detective films, Westerns, gangster films – and he enjoyed fights. He banned any hint of sexuality. When Bolshakov once showed him a slightly risqué scene involving a naked girl, he banged the table and said:

'Are you making a brothel here, Bolshakov?' Then he walked out, followed by the Politburo, leaving poor Bolshakov awaiting arrest. From then on, he cut even the slightest glimpse of nudity.

Stalin ordered Bolshakov to interpret the foreign films. Yet Bolshakov spoke only pidgin English. He therefore spent much of his time preparing for these midnight sessions by having interpreters go over the film for him and then learning the script. This was a challenge because at any time, he had hundreds of films to show Stalin. Thus his interpretation was usually absurdly obvious and very late, long after it was clear what the character had already said. The Politburo laughed and teased the flustered Bolshakov on his translations. Beria pointed at the screen and called out:

'Look he's started running ...' All laughed – but Stalin, who evidently enjoyed this farce, never demanded a proper interpreter. In 1951, Bolshakov asked Stalin to approve the *Tarzan* film: one imagines his translation of Tarzan's jungle-swinging shriek and courting grunts with Jane thoroughly entertained his audience. If Bolshakov showed the old favourite, *Volga! Volga!*, Stalin liked to show off how well he knew it and would perform every part just before the actor.

If Stalin was in a good mood, Bolshakov had the chance to choose a new Soviet movie. Stalin remained the censor of the entire industry: no movie could be shown without his personal approval. When he was in the south for months, no decision could be made so he had to see all the new films when he returned.

As Stalin approached, Bolshakov took up position outside the cinema. He once frightened Stalin by lurking in the shadows: 'Who are you? What are you doing?' Stalin barked. 'Why are you hiding?' Stalin scowled at Bolshakov for weeks afterwards. Taking his seat in the front row with his guests around him, usually mixing a spritzer of Georgian wine and mineral water, he always asked:

'What will Comrade Bolshakov show us today?' Bolshakov announced the movie, sat down at the back and ordered the projectionists to begin. Once, one of them dropped and broke part of the projector, which spread mercury on the floor. They were accused of attempting to assassinate the Generalissimo.*

Stalin talked throughout the film. He enjoyed cowboy films, especially those directed by John Ford and admired Spencer Tracy and Clark Gable but he also 'cursed them, giving them an ideological evaluation', recalled Khrushchev, 'and then ordering new ones'.†

Stalin admired the actors, frequently asking 'Where've we seen this actor before?' After the war, actors and directors often joined Stalin's dinners, particularly the Georgian director of films featuring the heroic leader, Mikhail Chiaureli, and the actors who often played him, Mikhail Gelovani (who did Stalin with a Georgian accent) and Alexei Diky (increasingly after the war, with a Russian accent). 'You're observing me thoroughly,' Stalin told Gelovani. 'You don't waste time do you?' He once asked Diky how he would 'play Stalin'.

'As the people see him,' replied the actor.

'The right answer,' said Stalin, giving him a bottle of brandy.

When the film was over, Stalin always asked his fellow intellectual:

'What will Comrade Zhdanov tell us?' Zhdanov gave his

---

* Mercury poisoning had a special pedigree at Stalin's court: Yezhov had sprayed his own office with mercury and claimed that Yagoda was trying to poison him.

† A recent biography of John Wayne claims the film star's symbolism as an American hero and enemy of Communism infuriated Stalin who suggested that 'Duke' should be assassinated. When Khrushchev visited Holywood in 1958, he is said to have explained to Wayne: 'That was the decision of Stalin in his last mad years. When Stalin died, I rescinded the order.' The story is based on rumour; it sounds like the sort of grim joke Stalin favoured in his cups. If true, it is hard to image why Wayne survived – and why Khrushchev did not use the tale against Stalin in his memoirs.

pompous verdict followed by Molotov's laconic judgement and
Beria's sarcastic jokes. Stalin enjoyed joking about the *auteurs*:

'If Comrade [director or screenwriter]'s no good, Comrade
Ulrikh'll sign his death sentence.' Bolshakov once called Beria and
Molotov to ask if *Zhukovsky*, a film about the aviator, could be
launched on Air-force Day, but Stalin, on holiday, had still not
seen it. It was his decision not theirs, they replied, so Bolshakov
launched the film. When Stalin returned, he watched *Zhukovsky*
and then said:

'We know you decided to put it on the screens of the USSR!
They want to trick me but it's impossible.' Bolshakov froze. On
whose authority, asked Stalin? Bolshakov replied that he had
'consulted and decided'.

'You consulted and decided,' repeated Stalin quietly. He got up
and walked to the door, opened it and repeated: 'You decided.' He
went out, leaving a doom-laden silence. Then he opened the door
again, smiling: 'You decided correctly.' If Stalin hated the film, he
would simply walk out but not before teasing Bolshakov.

Bolshakov made notes of all these august critiques. In the
morning, he called the directors or scriptwriters and passed on the
comments without specifying their source but no doubt his
quivering voice and breathless awe made it obvious.*

Stalin imposed politics on film but also film on reality. Djilas
noticed how he seemed to mix up what was going on 'in the
manner of an uneducated man who mistakes artistic reality for
actuality'. He revelled in films about murdering friends and
associates. Khrushchev and Mikoyan repeatedly sat through a
British film, no doubt one of the Goebbels collection, about a
pirate who stole some gold and then, 'one by one', killed his
accomplices to keep the swag.

'What a fellow, look how he did it!' exclaimed Stalin. This was
'depressing' for his comrades who could not forget that, as
Khrushchev put it, 'we were temporary people'. Stalin's isolated
position made these films increasingly powerful. After the war,
Stalin wanted to impose taxes on the peasants even though the
countryside was stricken with famine. The whole Politburo
sensibly opposed this, which angered Stalin. He was convinced
the peasants could afford it: he pointed to the plenty shown in his

---

* Bolshakov survived Stalin to serve Khrushchev as Deputy Trade Minister. He died
in 1980.

propaganda movies, allowing him to ignore the starvation. After seeing the movie on Catherine the Great's admiral, *Ushakov*, Stalin became obsessed with building a powerful fleet, quoting a character in the film who says: 'Land forces are a sword in one hand, sea forces a sword in the other.'

He often insisted on seeing two movies in a row and afterwards, around 2 a.m., would say:

'Let's go and get something to eat,' adding 'if you have time' as if there was any choice in the matter.

'If that's an invitation,' replied Molotov, 'with the greatest satisfaction.' Then Stalin turned to his guests, often Tito or Bierut:

'What are your plans for tonight?' as if they would have any at that hour. Stalin laughed. 'Hmm, a government without a state plan. We'll take a bite.' The average 'bite' lasted the interminable six hours until dawn.

* * *

Stalin ordered the omnipresent Poskrebyshev to summon the cars but when they were delayed, he trembled 'with rage, shouted, his features distorted, sharply motioned and poured invective into the face of his secretary who was … paling as if he had heart failure.' Poskrebyshev rounded up other guests. The guests had to prepare for the dinners, resting in the afternoon because 'those sleeping at Stalin's table came to a bad end', said Khrushchev.* Sometimes he invited his Georgian film directors and actors to liven up the party: 'Do you know if Chiaureli and Gelovani are in Moscow now?'

Foreign guests rode with Stalin who always sat in the fold-up seat right behind the driver and sometimes turned on a light above him to read. Molotov usually took the other folding seat with the favourite, Zhdanov, and any other guests in the back seats. Beria and Malenkov, 'that pair of scoundrels' as Stalin called them, always shared a car.† As the cars sped out of the city at the speed that Stalin relished, he planned the route, taking 'strange detours' to confuse terrorists.

---

* The magnates' families recognized their tense waiting for the call to the cinema or dacha from Stalin's secretaries. At weekends, the only chance they got to see their families, the leaders were especially tense whenever the phone rang. They did not eat during the day to leave room for the endless procession of dishes. But when the call came, Sergei Khrushchev noticed how hastily his father departed.

† The chauffeurs of the leaders were very pleased when their bosses were invited to Stalin's place. Voroshilov was now invited less often than before the war. 'My old man ain't invited there very much any more,' his veteran chauffeur would complain.

After driving ten miles up the Government Highway, they reached a barrier, turned left and approached a clump of young fir trees. After another checkpoint, they entered the gates of Kuntsevo. Once inside, they passed a big map in the hall where Stalin, Zhdanov and Molotov stopped to make grand geopolitical statements and capricious decisions. Zhdanov, his rival Malenkov and Voznesensky always had their notebooks ready to record Stalin's orders while Molotov and Mikoyan, Old Bolsheviks, regarded themselves as above such sycophancy.

The lavatories were in the basement and when the guests washed before dinner, Molotov joked at the urinals: 'We call this unloading before loading!' This lavatory was one of the only rooms in Moscow where the magnates could indulge in honest discussion: Beria and the others whispered to each other about the tedium of Stalin's tales of his Siberian exile. When he claimed to have skied twelve kilometres to shoot twelve partridges, Beria, already coming to loathe Stalin, insisted, 'He's just lying!'

They entered the roomy dining room with a long table with about fourteen covered chairs along each side; there were comfortable chairs alongside it, high windows with long drapes, and two chandeliers and lights set in the walls. As in all Stalin's houses, the walls, floors and ceilings were made of light Karelian pine panelling. It was so clean, so 'dead quiet' and so 'isolated from the other world', that visitors imagined they were 'in a hospital'.

Stalin always sat to the left of the head of the table with Beria at the end, often as *tamada*, and the guest of honour on Stalin's left. As soon as they sat down, the drinking started. At first it was civilized, with a few bottles of wine, sometimes weak Georgian 'juice' and some champagne, which Stalin greatly enjoyed. Mikoyan and Beria used to bring wine.

'Being Caucasian, you understand wine better than the others, try it ...' Stalin would say: it was soon clear that he was testing the wines for poison so they stopped bringing it. Stalin provided his own wine and genially opened the bottles himself. As the evening went on, the toasts of vodka, pepper vodka and brandy became more insistent until even these iron-bellied drinkers were blind drunk. Stalin liked to blame Beria for the excessive drinking. At Georgian dinners, hosts customarily play at forcing their guests to drink, and then taking umbrage if they resist. But by now, this hospitality was grossly distorted and represented nothing but power and fear. After Stalin's binges in 1944–5, Professor Vinogradov warned him to cut down on the drinking and he started to water down his drinks to wine with mineral water. None the less he occasionally over-imbibed and Svetlana saw him singing a duet with the legless but proud Health Minister. Forcing his tough comrades to lose control of themselves became his sport and a measure of dominance.

The drinking started with Stalin not Beria: he 'forced us to drink to loosen our tongues,' wrote Mikoyan. Stalin liked the old drinking game of guessing the temperature. When Djilas was there, Beria was three degrees out and had to drink three vodkas. Beria, whom Svetlana called 'a magnificent modern specimen of the artful courtier', played up to Stalin's longing to see his courtiers humiliate themselves, and policed the drinking, ensuring that no one missed a bumper.

'Come on, drink like everyone else does,' Beria tormented Molotov because he 'always wanted to make a show in front of Stalin – he would never lag behind if Stalin said something'. Sometimes Stalin defended foreign visitors and he spared Kaganovich because 'Jews weren't great drinkers.' Even during these sessions, Beria's mind throbbed with sexual imagery: after forcing Djilas to down a pepper vodka, he sneered that it was 'bad for the sexual glands'. Stalin gazed at his guest to see if he was shocked, 'ready to burst out laughing'.

Secretly, Beria hated these drinking sessions – he complained bitterly about them to Nina, Khrushchev and Molotov. Nina asked why he did it: 'You have to put yourself on the same level as the people you're with,' he replied, but there was more to it than that. Beria relished his power: in this, as in many other things, 'I couldn't resist it.' Khrushchev agreed that the dinners were 'frightful'.

Sometimes the drinking at these Bacchanals was so intense that the potentates, like ageing, bloated students, staggered out to vomit, soiled themselves or simply had to be borne home by their guards. Stalin praised Molotov's capacity but sometimes even he became drunk. Poskrebyshev was the most prolific vomiter. Khrushchev was a prodigious drinker, as eager to please Stalin as Beria. He sometimes became so inebriated that Beria took him home and put him to bed, which he promptly wet. Zhdanov and Shcherbakov could not control their drinking and became alcoholics: the latter died of the disease in May 1945 but Zhdanov tried to fight it. Bulganin was 'practically an alcoholic'. Malenkov just became more bloated.

Beria, Malenkov and Mikoyan managed to suborn a waitress to serve them 'coloured water' but they were betrayed to Stalin by Shcherbakov. After swallowing some colossal brandies, Mikoyan staggered out of the dining-room and found a little room next door with a sofa and a basin. He splashed his face with water, lay down and managed to sleep for a few minutes, which became a secret habit. But Beria sneaked to Stalin who was already turning against the Armenian: 'Want to be smarter than the rest, don't you!' Stalin said slowly. 'See you don't regret it later!' This was always the threat *chez* Stalin.

Stalin's *Mitteleuropean* vassals coped no better. Gottwald was so inebriated that he requested that Czechoslovakia join the USSR. His wife, who came with him, heroically volunteered: 'Allow me, Comrade Stalin, to drink in my husband's place. I'll drink for us both.' Rakosi foolishly told Beria that the Soviets were 'drunkards'.

'We'll see about that!' scoffed Stalin who joined Beria in 'pumping' the Hungarian with drink.

* * *

In summertime, the guests staggered outside on to the verandas. Stalin asked Beria or Khrushchev's advice on his roses (which he lovingly clipped), lemons and kitchen garden. Stalin supervised the planting of a vegetable garden where he devised new varieties such as crossing pumpkins with water melons. He fed the birds every day. Once Beria built a greenhouse as a present to Stalin:

'What fool ordered this?' Stalin asked. 'How much electricity do you spend on floodlights?' He had it destroyed.

The standard of drunken horseplay was not much better than a university fraternity house. Khrushchev and Poskrebyshev drunkenly pushed Kulik into the pond – they knew Stalin had lost respect for the buffoon. Kulik, famously strong, jumped out soaking and chased Poskrebyshev who hid in the bushes. Beria warned: 'If anyone tried something like that on me, I'd make mincemeat of them.' Poskrebyshev was regularly pushed in until the guards became so worried that a drunken magnate would drown, that they discreetly drained the pond. The infantilism delighted Stalin: 'You're like little children!'

One evening, Beria suggested that they do some shooting in the garden. There were quails in a cage. 'If we don't shoot them,' said

Beria, 'the guards'll eat them!' The leader, who was probably already drunk, staggered out and called for guns. Stalin, old, weak and tipsy, not to mention his frail left arm, first felt 'giddy' and fired his gun at the ground, only just missing Mikoyan. He then fired it in the air and managed to pepper his bodyguards, Colonels Tukov and Khrustalev, with shot. Afterwards Stalin apologized to them but blamed Beria.*

* * *

In the dining room, the maids, plump peasant women wearing white pinafores, like Victorian nurses, emerged with an array of Georgian dishes which they laid on the sideboard or the other end of the long table, then disappeared. When one of them was serving tea to Stalin and the Poles, she stopped and hesitated. Stalin noticed immediately: 'What's she listening to?' If there were no foreign eminences, dinner was served by one of the housekeepers, usually Valechka, and a bodyguard. The guests helped themselves, then joined Stalin at the table.

'Gradually Stalin began to take a great interest in his food,' recalled Mikoyan. The weary Generalissimo was fuelling his failing energy with 'enormous quantities of food suitable for a much larger man'. 'He ate at least twice as much as I did,' wrote Mikoyan. 'He took a deep plate, mixed two soups in it, then in a country custom that I knew from my own village, crumbled bread into the hot soup and covered it all by another plate – and then ate it all up to the end. Then there would be entrees, the main course and lots of meat.' He liked fish, especially herring, but 'he also liked game – guinea-fowl, ducks, chickens' and boiled quails. He even invented a new dish which he called *Aragvi*, made of mutton with aubergines, tomatoes, potatoes and black pepper, all in a spicy sauce, which he ordered frequently. Yet he was so suspicious that he usually tried to persuade Khrushchev, the greediest of the magnates, to try his lamb or herring before he did.

The dinners were a sort of culinary imperialism, designed to impress with their simplicity yet awe with their power – and they worked. While the independent Yugoslavs were appalled by the coarseness of the company, the pliant Poles were impressed by the 'delicious roast bear' and regarded their host as 'a charming man' who treated them with paternal warmth, always asking if their

* This resembles the blinding in one eye of Marshal Masséna by the Emperor Napoleon on a shooting expedition. The incident convinced Beria and Khrushchev even more that Stalin's shooting tales were lies and that he could not shoot at all.

families enjoyed their Crimean holidays. With outsiders, Stalin retained his earlier gift of being a masterful practitioner of 'the human touch'. This charm had its limits. Bierut persisted in asking Stalin what had happened to the Polish Communists who had disappeared in 1937.

'Lavrenti, where are they?' Stalin asked Beria. 'I told you to look for them, why haven't you found them?' Stalin and Beria shared a relish for these sinister games. Beria promised to look for the vanished Poles but when Stalin was not listening, he turned on Bierut:

'Why fuck around with Joseph Vissarionovich? Fuck off and leave him alone. Or you'll regret it.' Bierut did not mention his lost friends again.

Stalin suffered from bad teeth which affected his court since he would only eat the softest lamb or the ripest fruit. His dentures, when they were fitted, unleashed yet another vicious competition. This gourmand also insisted on Bolshevik austerity, two instincts that were hard to match as his courtiers competed to procure the choicest cuts for him. Once he enjoyed a delicious lamb but asked a bodyguard:

'Where did you get the lamb?'

'The Caucasus,' replied the guard.

'How did you fuel the plane? With water? This is one of Vlasik's pranks!'* Stalin ordered a farm to be built at Kuntsevo where cows, sheep and chickens could be kept and the lake stocked with fish, and this was managed by a special staff of three agricultural experts. When Beria delivered thirty turbots, Stalin teased his guards: 'You couldn't find turbot but Beria could.' The guards sent them for laboratory analysis and revealed that Beria's fish were rotten.

'That trickster can't be trusted,' said Stalin. Despite his swelling paunch, Stalin criticized the spreading flab of 'Malanya'

---

* Vlasik and Lieut.-Gen. Sasha Egnatashvili, the trusted son of the Gori innkeeper and Keke's protector, were probably responsible for Stalin's food which was prepared at an MGB laboratory named 'The Base' and then marked 'No poisonous elements found'. A recent book claims that Egnatashvili was Stalin's food taster, which is apparently a myth. Stalin however often did get his entourage to try food and wine before he did. When he arrived at a party, he brought his own box of wine and his own cigarettes which he opened himself. He would only eat or drink if he had broken the seal himself, leaving the food, unfinished wine and cigarettes to be divided up by Vlasik. The waste was vast; the temptation for venality irresistible but dangerous. Vlasik could never resist such goodies.

Malenkov, ordering him to take exercise in order to 'recover the look of a human being'. Beria joined in teasing his ally:

'So, that human-being look, where is it? Have you lost any weight?' But Khrushchev's gluttony entertained Stalin who whispered to the guards: 'He needed more than two fish and some pheasants, the glutton!' Yet he encouraged the spherical Khrushchev to eat more: 'Look! The giblets, Nikita. Have you tried them yet?' The potentates tried to control their diets by living on fruit and juices one day a week to 'unload', but it did not seem to work. Beria insisted on eating vegetables as his diet, for he was already as fat as Malenkov.

'Well Comrade Beria, here's your grass,' announced Stalin's housekeeper.

* * *

Stalin believed his dinners resembled a 'political dining society' but his 'fellow intellectual' Zhdanov persuaded him their wide-ranging discussions were the equivalent of the *symposia* of the ancient Greeks. None the less these vomit-flecked routs were the closest he came to cabinet government. The Imperium was truly being 'governed from the dining table', Molotov said. The leadership was like 'a patriarchal family with a crotchety head whose foibles caused the home folks to be apprehensive' but 'unofficially and in actual fact,' wrote Djilas, 'a significant part of Soviet policy was shaped at these dinners. It was here that the destiny of the vast Russian land, of the newly acquired territories and ... the human race was decided.' The conversation meandered from jokes and literature on to 'the most serious political subjects'. The Politburo exchanged news from their fiefdoms but the informality was illusory: 'The uninstructed visitor might hardly have detected any difference between Stalin and the others but it existed.'

At dinner, Zhdanov, 'the Pianist', was the most loquacious, showing off about his latest cultural campaign or grumbling that Molotov should have let him annex Finland, while his chief rival, the obese super-clerk, Malenkov, was usually silent – 'extreme caution with Stalin' was his policy. Beria, the most sycophantic yet the most irreverent, was artful at provoking and manipulating Stalin or, as his wife put it, 'playing with the tiger': he could shoot down anyone else's proposal if they had not first checked it with him. Beria was 'very powerful' because he could 'pick the exact moment to ... turn Stalin's goodwill or ill will to his advantage'.

When foreigners were absent, the fate of men was often decided. Yet Stalin talked about their acquaintances murdered during the thirties 'with the calm detachment of a historian, showing neither sorrow nor rage, just a light humour'. Once he wandered up to one of his marshals who had been arrested and released: 'I heard you were recently in confinement?'

'Yes, Comrade Stalin, I was, but they figured out my case and released me. But how many good and remarkable people perished there.'

'Yes,' mused Stalin thoughtfully, 'we've lost a lot of good and remarkable people.' Then he walked out of the room into the garden. The courtiers turned on the Marshal:

'What did you say to Comrade Stalin?' demanded Malenkov who always behaved like the school prefect. 'Why?' Then Stalin reappeared holding a bouquet of roses which he presented to the Marshal as a weird sort of apology.

* * *

Supreme power is often the supreme power to bore: nothing beats the obligatory tedium and inebriated verbosity of the absolute monarch in decline. The old Generalissimo had become repetitive, irritable and forgetful. Beria and Khrushchev knew by heart Stalin's exaggerated exploits in exile, his trips to London and Vienna, his childhood beatings at the hands of his father. Stalin dwelt more and more on the curious happiness of his exile, perhaps the only true happiness he had known. He now received an appeal for help from a friend from his Turukhansk exile during the First World War: 'I am daring to trouble you from the village of Kureika,' wrote an old teacher named Vasily Solomin who lived on a pension of 150 roubles. 'I remember when ... you caught a sturgeon. How much happiness it gave me!'

'I got your letter,' replied Stalin. 'I haven't forgotten you and my friends from Turukhansk and be sure I'll never forget you. I send you 6,000 roubles from my deputy's salary. The sum isn't very large but it'll be useful. Good health, Stalin.'

Each magnate policed the others, constantly vigilant to protect their interests and avoid provoking the old tiger. It became increasingly difficult to discuss real politics. When Mikoyan told Stalin there was a food shortage, Stalin became anxious and, while feasting on the myriad dishes, kept asking 'Why's there no food?'

'Ask Malenkov, he's in charge of Agriculture,' replied Mikoyan.

At that moment, the heels of both Beria and Malenkov landed hard on Mikoyan's foot under the table.

'What's the use of it?' Beria and Malenkov attacked Mikoyan afterwards. 'It just irritates Stalin. He begins to attack one or other of us. He should be told only what he likes to hear to create a nice atmosphere, not to spoil the dinner!'

* * *

They studied Stalin like zoologists to read his moods, win his favour and survive. The key was to understand Stalin's unique blend of supersensitive discomfiture and world-historical arrogance, his longing to be liked and his heartless cruelty: it was vital not to make him anxious. When Mikoyan's aircraft designer brother was in trouble, he 'advised Artyom how to handle Stalin'. Khrushchev noticed how the Pole, Bierut, 'managed to avoid disaster because he knew how to handle Stalin'.

There were certain key rules which resemble the advice given to a tourist on how to behave if he is unlucky enough to encounter a wild animal on his camping holiday. The first rule was to look him straight in the eyes. Otherwise he asked: 'Why don't you look me in the eye today?' But it was dangerous to look into his eyes too much: Gomulka, one of the Polish leaders, took notes and showed respect but his intensity made Stalin nervous: 'What kind of fellow's Gomulka? He sits there all the time looking into my eyes as though searching for something.' Perhaps he was an agent?

The visitor had to maintain calm at all times: panic alarmed Stalin. Bierut 'never made Stalin nervous and self-conscious'. Visitors must show respect by taking notes, like Malenkov, but not too frantically like Gomulka: 'Why does he bring a notepad with him?' Stalin wondered. If the guards were over-formal in clicking their heels, Stalin became flighty: 'Who are you? Soldier Svejk?' he snapped. Yet firmness and humour with Stalin usually worked well: he admired and protected Zhukov and appreciated Khrushchev for their strong views.

He knew Beria and Malenkov tried to prefix decisions so he appreciated Voznesensky's honesty. But he no longer appreciated the bluntness of old comrades. Voroshilov, 'the most illustrious of the Soviet grandees' whom he now distrusted for his taste for splendour and Bohemian circle, tried to remind him of their long friendship: 'I don't remember,' Stalin replied. Mikoyan was one of the frankest and often contradicted Stalin, which had been acceptable during the war, but no longer: once when they were discussing the Kharkov offensive, Mikoyan courageously blurted out that the disaster was Stalin's fault. The military genius was furious, becoming ever more suspicious of Molotov and Mikoyan.

The potentates could never meet in private: 'Danger lurked in friends and friendship,' wrote Sergei Khrushchev. 'An innocent meeting could end tragically.' Although Khrushchev, Malenkov, Mekhlis, Budyonny and others lived on Granovsky Street, they virtually never visited their neighbours. Stalin relished their mutual hatreds: Beria and Malenkov loathed Zhdanov and Voznesensky; Mikoyan hated Beria; Bulganin hated Malenkov. Their homes were all now bugged. ('I've been bugged all my life,' Molotov admitted when his bodyguard confided that his own house was wired.) But Beria claimed that he deliberately criticized policy at home because otherwise Stalin would become suspicious. Their importance depended, not on seniority, but purely on their relationships with Stalin. Thus Poskrebyshev, a factotum, if CC member, openly insulted Mikoyan, a Politburo member, when the latter was under a cloud.

Stalin had to be consulted about everything, however small, yet he did not want to be harassed for decisions because this too made him nervous. Beria boasted that while Yezhov rushed to Stalin with every detail, he himself only consulted him on major questions. If Stalin was on holiday, the safest option was to make no decisions at all, a strategy perfected by Bulganin who rose without trace as a result. If in doubt, appeal to Stalin's sagacity: 'Without you no one will solve this question,' read one such note. Stalin liked to hear everyone else's opinion before giving his own but Mikoyan preferred 'waiting to hear what Stalin would say'.

Beria said the only way to survive was 'always to strike first'. It was sensible to denounce your fellow bosses at all times or, as Vyshinsky put it, 'keep people on edge'. When Molotov made a mistake, Vyshinsky revelled in it. But the denouncers were on edge too: Manuilsky wrote a ten-page denunciation of Vyshinsky: 'Dear Comrade Stalin, I'm turning to you about the case of Vyshinsky … Abroad without the control of the CC, he is a person of petit bourgeois and boundless self-importance, for whom his own interests take precedence.' Stalin decided to do nothing with this but, as always, he informed the victim: later that day, Vyshinsky was found staring into oblivion: 'I'm only theoretically alive. I just got through the day. Well at least that's something, thank God!'

The overriding rule was to conceal nothing from Stalin: Zhdanov neutralized his crisis in Leningrad, Khrushchev, his youthful Trotskyism, by submissive confession to Stalin. Stalin's eye for any weakness was aquiline: when Vyshinsky felt ill and walked out of a diplomatic meeting, Stalin heard about it instantly and phoned his subordinate, Gromyko: 'What happened to Vyshinsky? Was he drunk?' Gromyko denied it. 'But the doctors say he's an alcoholic ... Oh well all right!'

* * *

After dinner, Stalin solemnly toasted Lenin whose illuminated bust flickered on the wall: 'To Vladimir Illich, our leader, our teacher, our all!' But this sacerdotal blessing ended any remaining decorum. When foreigners were not present, Stalin criticized Lenin, the hero who had turned against him: he even told young Sergo Beria stories about Lenin's affairs with his secretaries. 'At the end of his life', Khrushchev thought he 'lost control over what he was saying.' It was probably after 4 a.m.; the guests were desperately drunk, tired and nauseous but the omnipotent insomniac was awake, vigilant and almost sober.

There was a short rest to wash their hands, another opportunity to roll their eyes at Stalin's latest peccadillo: the magnates chuckled at the ever-increasing number of locks on the doors and whispered about another of Stalin's boasts of his drinking exploits: 'You see, even in youth, he'd drink too much!' Then it was back to the dinner which now sank to the level of a Neanderthal stag night.

Sometimes Stalin himself 'got so drunk he took such liberties,' said Khrushchev. 'He'd throw a tomato at you.' Beria was the master of practical jokes along with Poskrebyshev. The two most dignified guests, Molotov and Mikoyan, became the victims as Stalin's distrust of them became more malicious. Beria targeted the sartorial splendour of the 'dashing' Mikoyan. Stalin teased him about his 'fancy airs' while Beria delighted in tossing Mikoyan's hat into the pine trees where it remained. He slipped old tomatoes into Mikoyan's suits and then 'pressed him against the wall' so they exploded in his pocket. Mikoyan started to bring spare pairs of trousers to dinner. At home, Ashken found chicken bones in his pockets. Stalin smiled as Molotov sat on a tomato or Poskrebyshev downed a vodka full of salt that would make him vomit. Poskrebyshev often collapsed and had to be dragged out. Beria once wrote 'PRICK' on a piece of paper and stuck it on to Khrushchev's back. When Khrushchev did not notice, everyone guffawed. Khrushchev never forgot the humiliation.

Sometimes Svetlana popped in during dinner but could not hide her embarrassment and distaste. She thought the magnates resembled 'Peter the Great's *boyar*s' who had almost killed themselves with drink to entertain the Tsar at his drunken 'Synod'.

After dinner, 'Stalin played the gramophone, considering it his duty as a citizen. He never left it,' said Berman. He relished his comic records, including one of the 'warbling of a singer accompanied by the yowling and barking of dogs' which always made him laugh with mirth. 'Well, it's still clever, devilishly clever!' He marked the records with his comments: 'Very good!'

Stalin urged his grandees to dance but this was no longer the exhilarating whirligig of Voroshilov and Mikoyan tripping the light fantastic. This too had become a test of power and strength. Stalin himself 'shuffled around with his arms spread out' in Georgian style, though he had 'a sense of rhythm'.

'Comrade Joseph Vissarionovich, how strong you are!' chirped the Politburo. Then he stopped and became gloomy:

'Oh no, I won't live long. The physiological laws are having their way.'

'No no!' Molotov chorused. 'Comrade Joseph Vissiaronovich we need you, you still have a long life ahead of you!'

'Age has crept up on me and I'm already an old man!'

'Nonsense. You look fine. You're holding up marvellously ...'

When Tito was present, Stalin waved away these reassurances and looked at his guest whose assassination he would later order: 'Tito should take care of himself in case anything happens to him. Because I won't live long.' He turned to Molotov: 'But Vyacheslav Mikhailovich will remain here.' Molotov squirmed. Then, in a bizarre demonstration of his virility, Stalin declared: 'There's still strength in me!' He slipped both arms around Tito's arms and thrice lifted him off the floor in time to the Russian folk song on the gramophone, a *pas-de-deux* that was the tyrannical equivalent of Nureyev and Fonteyn.

'When Stalin says dance,' Khrushchev told Mikoyan, 'a wise man dances.' He made the sweating Khrushchev drop to his haunches and do the *gopak* that made him look like 'a cow dancing on ice'. Bulganin 'stomped'. Mikoyan, the 'acknowledged dancer', still managed his wild *lezginka*, and 'our city dancer' Molotov immaculately waltzed, displaying his unlikely terpsichorean talent. Ever since the thirties, Molotov's party trick had been gravely slow-dancing with other men to the guffaws of Stalin: his last male partner, Postyshev, had been shot long ago.

Polish security boss Berman was amazed when the Soviet Foreign Minister asked him to slow-dance to a waltz. 'I just moved my feet in rhythm like the woman,' said Berman. 'Molotov led. He wasn't a bad dancer. I tried to keep in step but what I did resembled clowning more than dancing. It was pleasant but with an inner tension.' Stalin watched from the gramophone, grinning roguishly as Molotov and Berman glided across the floor. It was Stalin who 'really had fun. For us,' said Berman, 'these dancing sessions were a good opportunity to whisper to each other things that couldn't be said out loud.' Molotov warned Berman 'about being infiltrated by various hostile organizations', a warning prearranged with Stalin.*

There were rarely women at these dinners but they were sometimes invited for New Year's Eve or on Stalin's birthday. When Nina Beria was at Kuntsevo with her husband, Stalin asked her why she was not dancing. She said she was not in the mood so Stalin went over to a young actor and ordered him to ask Nina to dance. This was to tease the jealous Beria who was furious. Svetlana hated her visits to these orgies. Stalin insisted she dance too: 'Well go on, Svetlana, dance! You're the hostess so dance!'

'I've already danced, Papa. I'm tired.' Stalin pulled her hair, expressing his 'perverse affection in its brutish form'. When she tried to flee, he called: 'Comrade Hostess, why have you left us poor unenlightened creatures without ... direction? Lead us! Show us the way!'

When Zhdanov moved to the piano, they sang religious hymns, White anthems and Georgian folk songs like 'Suliko'. When Georgian actors and directors such as Chiaureli were present, the entertainment was more elevated. Chiaureli's 'imitations, songs,

---

* This male slow-dancing symbolizes the sinister degeneracy of Stalin's dictatorship but it was not unique. In November 1943, at President Roosevelt's Thanksgiving party in Cairo, just before their departure to meet Stalin in Teheran, there was a shortage of female dancers. So Churchill happily danced with FDR's military assistant General Edwin 'Pa' Watson.

anecdotes made Stalin laugh'. Stalin loved singing and was very good at it. The two choirboys, Stalin and Voroshilov, joined Mikoyan, Beria and Zhdanov at the piano.*

It was almost dawn but the haunting nostalgia of these songs from those lost worlds of seminaries and church choirs was instantly shattered by Stalin's explosions of anger and contempt. 'A reasonable interrogator,' said Khrushchev, 'would not behave with a hardened criminal the way Stalin behaved with friends at his table.' When Mikoyan disagreed with Stalin, he flared up: 'You've all got old. I'll replace you all.'

At about 5 a.m., Stalin dismissed his exhausted comrades who were often so drunk they could hardly move. The guards ordered the cars round to the front and the chauffeurs 'dragged away their charges'. On the way home, Khrushchev and Bulganin lay back, relieved to have survived: 'one never knows,' whispered Bulganin, 'if one's going home or to prison.'

The guards locked the doors of the dacha and retired to their guardhouse. Stalin lay on one of his divans and started to read. Finally, drink and exhaustion soothed this obsessional dynamo. He slept. His bodyguards noted the light go out in Stalin's quarters: 'no movement.'

---

* They were so pleased with these sessions that they made a record of this murderous boy band with Voroshilov on lead vocals, backed up by Zhdanov on piano. There one can actually hear the fine voices and tinkling piano of a night at Kuntsevo. This remarkable recording is in the possession of the Zhdanov family.

47

Molotov's Chance:
'You'll Do Anything When You're Drunk!'

'The war,' Stalin admitted, 'broke me.' By October 1945, he was ill again. Suddenly at dinner, he declared: 'Let Vyacheslav go to work now. He's younger.' Kaganovich, sobbing, begged Stalin not to retire. There is no less enviable honour than to be appointed the heir of a murderous tyrant. But now Molotov, the first of a deadly line of potential successors, got his chance to act as proxy leader.

On 9 October, Stalin, Molotov and Malenkov voted 'to give Comrade Stalin a holiday of a month and a half' – and the Generalissimo set off in his special train for Sochi and then Gagra on the Black Sea. Some time between 9 and 15 October, Stalin suffered a serious heart attack. A photograph in the Vlasik family archive shows a clearly ailing Stalin, followed by an anxious Vlasik, probably arriving at Sochi, now a sizeable green two-storey mansion built around a courtyard. Then he headed south to Coldstream near Gagra. This was Stalin's impregnable eyrie, cut out of the rock, high on a cliff over the sea. Rebuilt, by Merzhanov, into a green southern house that closely resembled Kuntsevo, this became his main southern residence for the rest of his life, a sort of secret Camp David. Its studded wooden gates could only be reached by a 'narrow and sharply serpentine road'. It was completely surrounded by a Georgian veranda and there was a large sunroof. A rickety wooden summerhouse perched on the edge of the mountain.*

In this beautiful isolation, Stalin recuperated in a restful and hermetic holiday rhythm, sleeping all morning, walking during the day, breakfasting on the terrace, reading late, receiving a

---

* There was a little villa down the steps on the cliffside for Svetlana. When Stalin saw it, he muttered, 'What is she? A member of the Politburo?' Vasily's cottage adjoined the guardhouse: visitors drove through a long tunnel within the guardhouse to reach Stalin's house.

stream of paperwork, including the two files he never missed: NKGB reports and translations of the foreign press. Perhaps because he so closely supervised the Soviet press, he had surprising faith in foreign journalists.

During his absence, Molotov ran the government with Beria, Mikoyan and Malenkov, the Politburo Four. But Molotov's moment in the sun was soon overshadowed by unsettling rumours that Stalin was dying, or already dead. On 10 October, *TASS*, the Soviet press agency, announced that 'Comrade Stalin has left for a rest.' But this only awakened curiosity and aroused Stalin's vigilance. The *Chicago Tribune* reported that Stalin was incapacitated. His successors would surely be Molotov and Marshal Zhukov – a report sent southwards as 'Rumours in Foreign Press on the State of Health of Comrade Stalin.' Stalin's suspicions deepened when he read an interview with Zhukov in which the Marshal took the credit for victory in the war, only deigning to praise Stalin rather late in the proceedings. Stalin focused on why these rumours had appeared. Who had spread them, and why had Soviet honour, in his person, been desecrated?

Perhaps 'our Vyascheslav' was so thrilled at last to have the responsibility that he did not notice the brooding in Abkhazia. Molotov was at the height of his prestige as an international statesman. He had only just returned from a series of international meetings. There had been tension between them when Stalin had demanded that his Minister put pressure on Turkey to surrender some territory: Molotov argued against it, but Stalin insisted – Soviet demands were rebuffed. In April, Molotov had visited New York, Washington and San Francisco to meet President Truman and attend the opening of the UN. In an unpleasant meeting, Truman confronted Molotov on Soviet perfidy in Poland. 'We live under constant pressure, not to miss anything,' Molotov wrote to 'Polinka my love' but as ever he gloried in his eminence: 'Here among the bourgeois public,' he boasted, 'I was the focus of attention, with barely any interest in the other ministers!' As ever, 'I miss you and our daughter. I shan't conceal sometimes I am overcome with impatient desire for your closeness and caresses.' But the essential thing was that 'Moscow [i.e. Stalin] really supports our work and encourages it.'

In September, Molotov was in London for the Council of Foreign Ministers where he pushed for a Soviet trusteeship in

Italian Libya, joking drily about the Soviet talent for colonial administration. Unlike Stalin who restlessly pushed for radical leaps, Molotov was a realistic gradualist in foreign policy and he knew the West would never agree to a Soviet Libya. He made some gaffes but Stalin forgave him for the conference's failure, blaming it on American intransigence. Molotov again complained to Polina of the 'pressure not to fail'. He hardly left the Soviet Embassy, watching movies like *An Ideal Husband* by Wilde, but 'Once, only once I went to Karl Marx's tomb.' In typically Soviet style, he congratulated Polina on her 'performance of the annual [textiles] plan' but 'I want to hold you close and unburden my heart.'

Now, with Stalin recuperating and Molotov acting slightly more independently, the temperature was rising. Molotov felt the time was right for a deal with the West. Stalin overruled him: it was time to 'tear off the veil of amity'. When Molotov continued to behave too softly towards the Allies, Stalin, using the formal *vy*, attacked him harshly. 'Molotov's manner of separating himself from the Government to portray himself as more liberal ... is good for nothing.' Molotov climbed down with a ritualistic apology: 'I admit that I committed a grave oversight.' It was a telling moment for the magnates: even Stalin and Molotov ceased to address each other informally: no more 'Koba', just 'Comrade Stalin.'

On 9 November, Molotov ordered *Pravda* to publish a speech of Churchill's praising Stalin as 'this truly great man, the father of his nation'. Molotov had not grasped Stalin's new view of the West. He cabled a furious message: 'I consider the publication of Churchill's speech with his praise of Russia and Stalin a mistake,' attacking this 'infantile ecstasy' which 'spawns ... servility before foreign figures. Against this servility, we must fight tooth and nail ... Needless to say, Soviet leaders are not in need of praise from foreign leaders. Speaking personally, this praise only jars on me. Stalin.'

Just as the foreign media was trumpeting Stalin's illness and Molotov's succession, Molotov got tipsy at the 7 November reception and proposed the easing of censorship for foreign media. Stalin called Molotov who suggested treating 'foreign correspondents more liberally'. The valetudinarian turned vicious:

'You blurt out anything when you're drunk!'

Stalin devoted the next three days of his holiday to the crushing of Molotov. By the time the *New York Times* had written about Stalin's illness 'in a ruder way even than has taken place in the French yellow press', he decided to teach Molotov a lesson, ordering the Four to investigate – was it Molotov's mistake? The other three tried to protect Molotov by blaming a minor diplomat but they admitted he was following Molotov's instructions. On 6 December, Stalin cabled Malenkov, Beria and Mikoyan, ignoring Molotov, and attacking their 'naïvety' in trying to 'paper over the affair' while covering up 'the sleight of hand of the fourth'. Stalin was burning at this 'outrage' against the 'prestige' of the Soviet Government. 'You probably tried to hush up the case to slap the scapegoat ... in the face and stop there. But you made a mistake.' Hypocritically referring to the pretence of Politburo government, Stalin declared: 'None of us has the right to act single-handedly ... But Molotov appropriated this right. Why? ... Because these calumnies were part of his plan?' A reprimand was no longer sufficient because Molotov 'cares more about winning popularity among certain foreign circles. I cannot consider such a comrade as my First Deputy.' He ended that he was not sending this to Molotov 'because I do not trust some people in his circle'. (This was an early reference to the Jewish Polina.)

Beria, Malenkov and Mikoyan, who sympathized with poor Molotov, summoned him like judges, read him Stalin's cable and attacked him for his blunders. Molotov admitted his mistakes but thought it was unfair to mistrust him. The three reported to Stalin that Molotov had even 'shed some tears' which must have satisfied the Generalissimo a little. Molotov then wrote an apology to Stalin which, one historian writes, was 'perhaps the most emotional document of his life in politics'.

'Your ciphered cable is imbued with a profound mistrust of me, as a Bolshevik and a human being,' wrote the lachrymose Molotov, 'and I accept this as a most serious warning from the Party for all my subsequent work, whatever job I may have. I will seek to excel in deeds to restore your trust in which every honest Bolshevik sees not merely personal trust but the Party's trust – something I value more than life itself.'

Stalin let Molotov stew for two days, then at 1.15 a.m. on 8 December replied to the Four again, restoring his errant deputy to his former place as First Deputy Premier. But Stalin never spoke of

Molotov as his successor again and stored up these mistakes to use against him.*

* * *

This was only the beginning. Stalin was feeling better but he had mulled angrily over the challenges from abroad, indiscipline at home, disloyalty in his circle, impertinence among his marshals. He was bored and depressed by stillness and solitude but his angry energy and zest for life were stimulated by struggle. He revelled in the excitement of personal puppeteering and ideological conflict. Returning in December with a glint in his yellow eyes and a spring in his step, he resolved to reinvigorate Bolshevism and to diminish his over-mighty *boyars* in a deft sweep of arrests and demotions.

Having shaken Molotov, Stalin turned on Beria and Malenkov. He did not need to invent the scandal. When Vasily Stalin had visited him at Potsdam, he reported the disastrous safety record of Soviet planes: of 80,300 planes lost in the war, 47 per cent were due to accidents, not enemy fire or pilot error. Stalin had mused over this on holiday, even inviting the Aircraft Production Minister, Shakhurin,† to Sochi. Then he ordered the investigation of an 'Aviators' Case' against Shakhurin and the Air Force Commander, Air Marshal Novikov, one of the heroes of the war, whom he had jokingly threatened at de Gaulle's banquet.

On 2 March, Vasily Stalin was promoted to Major-General. On 18 March, Beria and Malenkov, the two wartime potentates, were promoted to full Politburo membership – just as the Aviators' Case nipped at their heels. Then Shakhurin and Air Marshal Novikov were arrested and tortured. Their agonies were carefully directed to kill two birds with one stone: the overlord of aircraft production was Malenkov.

Abakumov, the Smersh boss and Stalin's protégé, arranged the Aviators' Case which was also aimed at Beria. Stalin's old fondness for the Mingrelian had long since turned to a surly disdain. Beria's

---

* Mikoyan too felt his icy disapproval. He sensed his two old comrades were closet Rightists, absurd in Molotov's case. But during the complex arguments about whether to strip Germany of its industry or build the eastern sector as a satellite, and the endless crises of famine and grain, Mikoyan had become a moderating voice. When Mikoyan did not report properly from the Far East, he received another sharp note from Stalin: 'We sent you to the Far East not so you could fill your mouth with water [say nothing], and not send information to Moscow.'

† It was Shakhurin whose son had killed his girlfriend and then himself on Kamenny Most in 1943.

theatrical sycophancy and murderous creativity disgusted Stalin as much as his administrative genius impressed him. Stalin no longer trusted 'Snake Eyes'. His first rule was to maintain personal control over the secret police. 'He knows too much,' Stalin told Mikoyan. Stalin's resentment burned slowly. They were strolling in the Kuntsevo gardens with Kavtaradze when Stalin hissed venomously at Beria in the Mingrelian dialect (which no one except Georgians understood): 'You traitor, Lavrenti Beria!' Then he added 'with an ironic smile': 'Traitor!' When he dined at Beria's house, he was charming to Nina but dismissive of Lavrenti: in his toasts, he damned Beria with the faintest of praise. Beria reminisced about his first meeting with Stalin in 1926:

'I don't remember,' Stalin replied crushingly. Beria's attempt to speak Georgian to him at meetings now irritated Stalin: 'I keep no secrets from these comrades. What kind of provocation is this! Talk the language everyone understands!'

Stalin sensed, correctly, that Beria, the industrial and nuclear magnifico, wanted to be a statesman. 'He's ambitious on a global scale,' he confided in a Georgian protégé, 'but his ammunition isn't worth a penny!' Stalin decided something was rotten in the Organs. During his holiday, he asked Vlasik about the conduct of Beria. Vlasik, delighted to destroy Beria, denounced his corruption, incompetence and possibly his VD. At a dinner in the south, Stalin told a joke about Beria:

'Stalin loses his favourite pipe. In a few days, Lavrenti calls Stalin: "Have you found your pipe?" "Yes," replies Stalin. "I found it under the sofa." "This is impossible!" exclaims Beria. "Three people have already confessed to this crime!"' Stalin relished stories about the power of the Cheka to make innocent people confess. But he became serious: 'Everyone laughs at the story. But it's not funny. The law-breakers haven't been rooted out of the MVD!'

Stalin moved swiftly against him: Beria was retired as MVD Minister in January, but remained *curator* of the Organs with Merkulov as MGB boss. Then Merkulov was denounced by his secretary. Beria washed his hands of him. On 4 May, Stalin, backed by Zhdanov, engineered the promotion of Abakumov to Minister of State Security: his qualifications for the job were his blind obedience and independence from Beria. When Abakumov modestly refused, Stalin jokingly asked if he would 'prefer the Tea Trust'.

Abakumov remains the most shadowy of Stalin's secret-police bosses just as the post-war years remain the murkiest of Stalin's reign, although we now know much more about them. The coming atrocities were Abakumov's doing, not Beria's, even though most histories blame the latter. Beria, who, as Deputy Premier in charge of the Bomb and the missile industry, now moved his office from the Lubianka to the Kremlin, was henceforth 'sacked' from the Organs. He bitterly resented it.

'Beria was scared to death of Abakumov and tried at all costs to have good relations ...' recalled Merkulov. 'Beria met his match in Abakumov.' Like a rat on a sinking ship, Beria's pimp Colonel Sarkisov denounced the sexual degeneracy of the Bolshevik 'Bluebeard' to Abakumov who eagerly took it to Stalin: 'Bring me everything this arsehole will write down!' snapped Stalin.

48

Zhdanov the Heir and
Abakumov's Bloody Carpet

Abakumov, tall with a heart-shaped, fleshy face, colourless eyes, blue-black hair worn *broussant*, pouting lips and heavy eyebrows, was another colourful, swaggering torturer, amoral *condottiere* and 'zoological careerist' who possessed all Beria's sadism but less of his intelligence.* Abakumov unrolled a bloodstained carpet on his office floor before embarking on the torture of his victims in order not to stain his expensive Persian rugs. 'You see,' he told his spy Leopold Trepper, 'there are only two ways to thank an agent: cover his chest with medals or cut off his head.' He was hardly alone in this Bolshevik view.

Until Stalin swooped down to make him his own Chekist, Victor Abakumov was a typical secret policeman who had won his spurs purging Rostov in 1938. Born in 1908 to a Moscow worker, he was a *bon viveur* and womanizer. During the war, he stashed his mistresses in the Moskva Hotel and imported trainloads of plunder from Berlin. His splendid apartment had belonged to a soprano whom he had arrested and he regularly used MGB safehouses for amorous assignations. He loved jazz. The bandleader, Eddie Rosner, played at his parties until jazz was banned.

Abakumov dealt directly with Stalin, seeing him weekly, but never joined the dining circle: 'I did nothing on my own,' he claimed after Stalin's death. 'Stalin gave orders and I carried them out.' There is no reason to disbelieve him. He cultivated Stalin's children. At one Kremlin dinner, 'he suddenly started, jumped up and obsequiously inclined his head before a short and reddish-haired girl' – Svetlana Stalin. Stalin's grandeur was such that people now bowed to his daughter. Abakumov went drinking

---

* Abakumov appears as the consummate cunning courtier, utterly submissive to Stalin's mysterious whims, in Solzhenitsyn's novel of the post-war Terror, *The First Circle*, and as a shrewd and debauched secret-police careerist in Rybakov's *Fire and Ashes*, the last volume of his *Children of the Arbat* trilogy.

with Vasily Stalin. Together, they fanned the Aviators' Case. Vasily purloined Novikov's dacha while the 'father of the Soviet air force' was tortured. Stalin asked for Abakumov's recommendations:

'They should be shot.'

'It's easy to shoot people,' replied Stalin. 'It's more difficult to make them work. Make them work.' Shakhurin received seven years' hard labour, Novikov ten years – but their confessions implicated bigger fish.

On 4 May, Malenkov was abruptly removed from the Secretariat. His family remembered that they had to move out of their dacha. Their mother took them on a long holiday to the Baltic. Malenkov was despatched to check the harvest in Central Asia for several months, but never arrested. Beria tried to persuade Stalin to bring him back, which amused the Generalissimo: 'Why are you taking such trouble with that imbecile? You'll be the first to be betrayed by him.'

* * *

Beria had lost his Organs and his ally, Malenkov, so the success of the Bomb was paramount. Later in the year, he rushed to Elektrostal at Noginsk, near Moscow, to see Professor Kurchatov's experimental nuclear reactor go critical, creating the first Soviet self-sustaining nuclear reaction. Beria watched Kurchatov raise the control rod at the panel and listened to the clicks that registered the neutrons rise to a wail.

'It's started!' they said.

'Is that all?' barked Beria, afraid of being tricked by these eggheads. 'Nothing more? Can I go to the reactor?' This would have been a delicious prospect for millions of Beria's victims but they dutifully restrained him, so helping to preserve the diminished Beria.

* * *

The reversal of fortunes of Beria and Malenkov marked the resurrection of their enemy, Andrei Zhdanov, Stalin's special friend, that hearty, pretentious intellectual who, after the stress of Leningrad, was a plump alcoholic with watery eyes and a livid complexion. Stalin openly talked about Zhdanov as his successor. Meanwhile, Beria could hardly conceal his loathing for Zhdanov's pretensions: 'He can just manage to play the piano with two fingers and to distinguish between a man and a bull in a picture, yet he holds forth on abstract painting!'

'The Pianist' had become a hero in Leningrad where he was apt to boast that the siege had been more important than the battle for Stalingrad. Sent as Stalin's proconsul in Finland in 1945, he mastered Finnish history, displayed an encyclopaedic knowledge of Helsinki politics and even charmed the British representative there. When he pushed to annex Finland (a Russian duchy until 1917), Molotov reprimanded him: 'You've gone too far ... You're too emotional!' But none of this harmed his standing with Stalin who recalled him from Leningrad and promoted him to Party Deputy in charge of both Agitprop and relations with foreign Parties, making him even more powerful than he had been before the war. His family, particularly his son Yury, became close to Stalin again. Indeed, they wrote to him *en famille*: 'Dear Joseph Vissarionovich, we cordially congratulate you on ... the anniversary of Bolshevism's victory and ask you to accept our warmest greetings, Zinaida, Andrei, Anna and Yury Zhdanov.'

Zhdanov had played his cards cleverly since returning in January 1945. He consolidated his triumph over Malenkov and Beria by persuading Stalin to promote his own camarilla of Leningraders to power in Moscow: Alexei Kuznetsov, the haggard, long-faced and soft-spoken hero of the siege, received Malenkov's Secretaryship. Zhdanov understood that Stalin did not wish Beria to control the MGB so he suggested Kuznetsov to replace him as *curator* of the Organs. It was 'naive' of Kuznetsov to accept this poisoned chalice; 'he should have refused,' said Mikoyan, but he was 'unworldly'. Kuznetsov's promotions earned him the undying hatred of the two most vindictive predators in the Stalinist jungle: Beria and Malenkov.

By February 1946, with Stalin in semi-retirement, Zhdanov seemed to have control of the Party as well as cultural and foreign policy matters, and to have neutralized the Organs and the military.* Zhdanov was hailed as the 'second man in the Party', its 'greatest worker', and his staff whispered about 'our Crown Prince'. Stalin toyed with appointing him General Secretary. During 1946, Zhdanov signed decrees as 'Secretary' alongside Stalin as Premier: 'the Pianist' was so important that the Yugoslav

---

* Stalin himself soon retired as Armed Forces Minister, handing this to Bulganin, another ally of Zhdanov who hated Malenkov because he had removed him from the Western Front in 1943. The ruling inner circle of Five (Stalin, Molotov, Mikoyan, Malenkov and Beria) gradually expanded to embrace Zhdanov, Voznesensky, Bulganin and Kuznetsov, regardless of whether they were yet formally Politburo members.

Ambassador noticed how, when a bureaucrat entered his office, he bowed 'to Zhdanov as he was approaching' and then retreated backwards, managing to cover 'six or seven yards and in bowing himself out, he backed into the door, nervously trying to find the doorknob with his hand'. At the November parade, Zhdanov, in Stalin's absence, took the salute with his Leningrad camarilla filling the Mausoleum.

Yet his health was weak.* Zhdanov never wanted to be the successor. During Stalin's serious illnesses, he was terrified at the prospect, telling his son, 'God forbid I outlive Stalin!'

* * *

Stalin and Zhdanov picked up where they had left off before the war, debating how to merge the patriotic Russianness of the war with the Bolshevism of the Revolution in order to eradicate foreign influence and restore morality, pride and discipline. Like two crabby professors, obsessed with the greatness of nineteenth-century culture and repulsed by the degeneracy of modern art and morals, the old seminarist and the scion of provincial intelligentsia reached back to their youths, devising a savage attack on modernism ('formalism') and foreign influence on Russian culture ('cosmopolitanism'). Poring over poetry and literary journals late into the night, these two meticulous, ever-tinkering 'intellectuals', who shared that ravenous Bolshevik appetite for education, cooked up the crackdown on the cultural freedom of wartime.

Steeped in the classics, despising new-fangled art, Zhdanov embarked on a policy that would have been familiar to Tsars Alexander I and Nicholas I. Victory had blessed the marriage of Russianness and Bolshevism: Stalin saw the Russians as the binding element of the USSR, the 'elder brother' of the Soviet peoples, his own new brand of Russian nationalism very different from its nineteenth-century ancestor. There would be no new freedoms, no foreign influences, but these impulses would be suppressed in an enforced celebration of Russianness.

The Leningrad journals were the natural place to start because they published the works of the satirist Mikhail Zoshchenko, whom Stalin had once read to his children, and the poetess Anna

---

* In late 1946, Zhdanov suffered heart trouble and had to rest in Sochi, reporting to Stalin on 5 January 1947, 'Now I feel much better ... I don't want to end the course of treatment ... I ask you to add 10 days to my holiday ... Let me return 25th ... For which I'll be enormously grateful. Greetings! Your Andrei Zhdanov.'

Akhmatova, whose passionate verses symbolized the indestructible dignity and sensitivity of humanity in terror and war. Zhdanov's papers reveal in his own words what Stalin wanted: 'I ask you to look this through,' Zhdanov asked the master, 'is it good for the media and what needs to be improved?'

'I read your report. I think it's perfect,' Stalin replied in crayon. 'You must hurry to publish it and then as a book. Greetings!' But 'there are some corrections' – which expressed Stalin's thinking: 'if our youth had read Akhmatova and been educated in such an atmosphere, what would have happened in the Great Patriotic War? Our youth [has been] educated in the cheerful spirit able to win victory over Germany and Japan ... This journal helps our enemies to destroy our youth.'*

On 18 April, Zhdanov launched his cultural terror, known as the *Zhdanovshchina*, with an attack on the Leningrad journals. In August, the literary inquisitor travelled to Leningrad to demand: 'How weak was the vigilance of those citizens in Leningrad, in the leadership of the journal *Zvezda*, for it to publish, in this journal, works ... poisoned with the venom of zoological hostility to the Soviet leadership.' He castigated Akhmatova as this 'half-nun, half-harlot or rather harlot-nun whose sin is mixed with prayer', a grotesque distortion of her own verses. He followed this up with attacks on film-makers and musicians. At a notorious meeting with Shostakovich and others, 'the Pianist' tinkled on the piano to demonstrate easily-hummed people's tunes, a vision as absurd as Joseph II admonishing Mozart for writing 'too many notes'. Yury Zhdanov went to the theatre with his father and Stalin. When they talked to the actors afterwards, the cast boasted that their show had been acclaimed in Paris:

'Those French aren't worth the soles of your shoes,' replied Stalin. 'There's nothing more important than Russian theatre.'

Bantering playfully, the omnipotent double-act, Stalin and Zhdanov, held *conversazione* to guide writers and film directors. On the night of 14 May 1947, they received Stalin's two favoured literary bureaucrats, the poet Simonov and the hack novelist,

---

* Zhdanov discussed the campaign with his son Yury, who had studied chemistry, taken a master's degree in philosophy – and remained Stalin's ideal young man and his dream son-in-law. Zhdanov explained that 'after the war, with millions dead and the economy destroyed, we have to form a new concept of spiritual values to give a foundation to a devastated country, based on classical culture ...' Zhdanov, raised on nineteenth-century 'authors from Pushkin to Tolstoy, composers like Haydn and Mozart', sought 'an ideological basis in the classics'.

Fadeev, the head of the Writers' Union. Stalin first set the pay for writers:

'They write one good book, build their dacha and stop working. We don't begrudge them the money,' laughed Stalin, 'but this can't happen.' So he suggested setting up a commission:

'I'll join!' declared Zhdanov, showing his independence.

'Very modest!' Stalin chuckled. As they discussed the commission, Zhdanov opposed Stalin thrice before being overruled, another example of how his favourite could still argue with him. Stalin teased Zhdanov fondly. When 'the Pianist' said he had received a pitiful letter from some writer, Stalin joked:

'Don't believe pitiful letters, Comrade Zhdanov!' Stalin asked the writers: 'If that's all, I've a question for you: what kind of themes are writers working on?' He launched into a lecture about 'Soviet patriotism'. The people were proud but 'our middle intelligentsia, doctors and professors don't have patriotic education. They have unjustified admiration for foreign culture ... This tradition comes from Peter ... admiration of Germans, French, of foreigners, of assholes –' he laughed. 'The spirit of self-abasement must be destroyed. You should write a novel on this theme.'

Stalin had a recent scandal in mind. A pair of medical professors specializing in cancer treatment had published their work in an American journal. Stalin and Zhdanov created 'courts of honour', another throwback to the Tsarist officer class, to try the professors. (Zhdanov chaired the court.) Stalin set Simonov to write a play about the case. Zhdanov spent an entire hour giving literary criticism to Simonov before Stalin himself rewrote the play's ending.*

In August, Bolshakov, the cinematic impresario, showed Stalin a new movie, *Ivan the Terrible, Part Two*. Knowing from MGB reports that Eisenstein compared The Terrible with Yezhov, Stalin rejected this 'nightmare', hating its lack of Russian pride, its portrayal of Ivan (and the length of his kisses, and beard). Eisenstein shrewdly appealed to Stalin. At 11 p.m. on 25 February 1947, Eisenstein and his scriptwriter arrived in the Little Corner where Stalin and Zhdanov gave them a master-class on national Bolshevism, a most revealing *tour d'horizon* of history, terror and

---

* 'I have fulfilled the orders according to Comrade Stalin's instructions which I wrote down about the play,' Simonov wrote to Poskrebyshev on 9 February 1949, delivering the work for inspection.

even sex. Stalin attacked the film for making the Tsar's MGB, the *Oprichnina*, resemble the Ku Klux Klan. As for Ivan himself, 'Your Tsar is indecisive – he resembles Hamlet,' said Stalin. 'Tsar Ivan was a great wise ruler ... wise ... not to let foreigners into the country. Peter the Great's also a great Tsar but treated foreigners too liberally ... Catherine, more so. Was Alexander I's Court Russian? ... No, it was German ...' Then Zhdanov gave his own view, with its interesting reflection on Stalin's own nature:

'Ivan the Terrible seems a hysteric in the Eisenstein version!'

'Historical figures,' added Stalin, 'must be shown correctly ... Ivan the Terrible kissed his wife too long.' Kisses, again. 'It wasn't permitted at that time.' Then came the crux: 'Ivan the Terrible was very cruel,' said Stalin. 'You can show he was cruel. But you must show why he *needed to be cruel*.' Then Zhdanov raised the crucial question of Ivan's beard. Eisenstein promised to shorten it. Eisenstein asked if he could smoke.

'It seems to me there's no ban on smoking. Maybe we'll vote on it.' Stalin smiled at Eisenstein. 'I don't give you instructions, I merely give you the comments of a viewer.'*

Zhdanov's campaign to promote Russian patriotism was soon so absurd that Sakharov remembered how people would joke about 'Russia, homeland of the elephant'. More ominously, the unleashing of Russian nationalism and the attacks on 'cosmopolitans' turned against the Jews.

---

* Eisenstein died before he could shorten the beard, cut the kiss and show why The Terrible 'needed to be cruel'. This was a mercy since it seems unlikely he would have survived the anti-Semitic purge of 1951–3.

49

The Eclipse of Zhukov and the Looters
of Europe: the Imperial Elite

Early in the war, Stalin realized the usefulness of Soviet Jewry in appealing for American help but even then the project was stained with blood.* Stalin then ordered Beria to set up the Jewish Anti-Fascist Committee, controlled by the NKVD but officially led by the famous Yiddish actor, Solomon Mikhoels, 'short, with the face of a puckish intellectual, with a prominent forehead and a pouting lower lip', whom Kaganovich had perform *King Lear* for Stalin. When Mikhoels toured America to raise support for Russia in April 1943, Molotov briefed him and Stalin emerged from his office to wave goodbye. The JAFC was supervised by Solomon Lozovsky, a grizzled Old Bolshevik with a biblical beard who was the token Jew in the highest echelons of Molotov's Foreign Commmissariat.

The ghastly revelations of the Nazi Holocaust, the Mikhoels tour and the attractions of Zionism to give the Jewish people a safe haven, softened the stern internationalism of even the highest Bolsheviks. Stalin tolerated this but encouraged a traditional anti-Semitic reaction. When casting *Ivan the Terrible, Part Two*, Bolshakov openly rejected one actress because 'her Semitic features are clearly visible'. Anyone too Jewish-looking was sacked.

When the advancing Soviet Army exposed Hitler's unique Jewish genocide, Khrushchev, the Ukrainian boss, resisted any special treatment for Jews staggering home from the death camps. He even refused to return their homes, which had meanwhile been occupied by Ukrainians. This habitual anti-Semite grumbled that 'Abramoviches' were preying on his fiefdom 'like crows'.

This sparked a genuine debate around Stalin. Mikhoels complained to Molotov that 'after the Jewish catastrophe, the local authorities pay no attention'. Molotov forwarded this to Beria who, to his credit, was sympathetic. Beria demanded that Khrushchev

---

* The first two candidates to lead this wartime PR campaign, Polish leaders of the Bund (Jewish Socialist Party), V. Alter and G. Ehlich, demanded too much and were arrested, respectively being shot and committing suicide in prison.

help the Jews who 'were more repressed than any others by the Germans'. In this he was taking a risk since Stalin had decreed that *all* Soviet citizens suffered *equally*. Stalin later suspected Beria of being too close to the Jews, perhaps the origin of the rumour that Beria himself was a 'secret' Jew. Molotov forwarded Beria's order. Khrushchev agreed to help his 'Abramoviches'.

Encouraged by this growing sympathy, Mikhoels and his colleague Fefer, a poet* and MGB plant, suggested a Jewish republic in the Crimea (now empty of Tartars), or in Saratov (now empty of the Volga Germans) to Molotov and his deputy in charge of the JAFC, Lozovsky. Molotov thought the Volga German idea ridiculous, 'it's impossible to see a Jew on a tractor', but preferred the Crimea: 'Why don't you write a memorandum to me and Comrade Stalin, and we'll see.'

'Everyone,' recalls Vladimir Redens, 'believed Jewish Crimea would happen.' Molotov, showing more independence than before, may have discussed this with Beria but his judgement almost cost him his life. Most of those involved were dead within five years.

On 2 February 1944 Mikhoels delivered his letter to Molotov, copied to Stalin who now decided that the actor had moved from Soviet to Jewish propaganda. Stalin, with his acute awareness of anti-Semitism, sent Kaganovich to pour cold water on the idea of this 'Jewish California': 'Only actors and poets could come up with such a scheme,' he said, that was 'worth nothing in practice!' Zhdanov supervised the making of lists of Jews in different departments and recommended closing down the JAFC.† Like Molotov in 1939, Zhdanov loosed his hounds against Jews in the *apparat* which, he said, had become 'some kind of synagogue'.

Stalin's anti-Semitism remained a mixture of old-fashioned prejudice, suspicion of a people without a land, and distrust, since his enemies were often Jewish. He was so unabashed that he openly told Roosevelt at Yalta that the Jews were 'middlemen, profiteers and parasites'. But after 1945, there was a change: Stalin emerged as a vicious and obsessional anti-Semite.

* Fefer was the author of an absurd poem during WW2 called 'I a Jew' in which he praised the great Jewish Bolsheviks from King Solomon to Marx, Sverdlov and 'Stalin's friend Kaganovich' which no doubt enormously embarrassed the latter.
† Zhdanov's chief ideological anti-Semite was the tall, thin and ascetic CC Secretary Mikhail Suslov, who had played a key role in the Caucasian deportations and then served as Stalin's proconsul in the Baltics which he brutally purged after the war. Working alternately under both Zhdanov and Malenkov, he became one of Stalin's youngish protégés.

Always supremely political, this was partly a pragmatic judgement: it matched his new Russian nationalism. The supremacy of America with its powerful Jewish community made his own Jews, with their US connections restored during the war, appear a disloyal Fifth Column. His suspicion of the Jews was another facet of his inferiority complex towards America as well as a symptom of his fear of the new self-assertive confidence of his own victorious people. It was also a way to control his old comrades whose Jewish connections symbolized their new cosmopolitan confidence after victory. Equally, he loathed any people with mixed loyalties: he noticed the Holocaust had touched and awakened Soviet Jewry even among the magnates. His new anti-Semitism flowed from his own seething paranoia, exacerbated when Fate entangled the Jews in his family.

Yet he still played the internationalist, often attacking people for anti-Semitism and rewarding Jews in public, from Mekhlis to the novelist Ehrenburg. Soon this malevolent whirlpool threatened to consume Molotov, Beria and his own clan.

* * *

'As soon as hostilities end,' Stalin said at Yalta, 'the soldiers are forgotten and lapse into oblivion.' He wished this was so but the prestige of Marshal Zhukov had never been higher. The Western press even acclaimed him as Stalin's successor. Stalin liked Zhukov but 'didn't recognize personal ties' and he probed to see if this idea had any support.

'I'm getting old,' he casually told Budyonny, his old pal and Zhukov's friend. 'What do you think of Zhukov succeeding me?'

'I approve of Zhukov,' he replied, 'but he's a complicated character.'

'You managed to govern him,' said Stalin, 'and I can manage him too.'

Stalin 'managed' Zhukov by using the 'Aviators' Case' against him, torturing Air Marshal Novikov to implicate him.* 'Broken morally, brought to desperation, sleepless nights, I signed,'

---

* Churchill himself had bouts of jealousy of his generals: 'Monty wants to fill the Mall when he gets his baton! And he will not fill the Mall,' Churchill told Sir Alan Brooke on his way back from Moscow in October 1944. 'He will fill the Mall because he is Monty and I will not have him filling the Mall!' It was, wrote Brooke, 'a strange streak of almost unbelievable petty jealousy on his part ... Those that got between him and the sun did not meet his approval.' There was a great tradition of rulers jealous of, and threatened by, brilliant but overmighty generals: Emperor Justinian humiliated Belisarius; Emperor Paul did the same to Suvorov.

admitted Novikov later. Abakumov tortured seventy other generals to get the necessary evidence. In March, Zhukov was recalled to Moscow. Instead of reporting directly to the Generalissimo, he was summoned by Stalin's deputy as Armed Forces Minister, Bulganin, 'the Plumber' (as Beria called him) who was in high favour. Zhukov grumbled at Bulganin's arrogance and Bulganin grumbled that Zhukov had pulled rank on him, resisting orders from the Party. Stalin ordered 'the Plumber' to prepare a kangaroo court against Zhukov. Abakumov searched Zhukov's homes which turned out to be an Aladdin's cave of booty:

'We can simply say,' Abakumov reportedly gleefully to Stalin, 'that Zhukov's dacha is a museum', filled with gold, 323 furs, 400 metres of velvet and silk. There were so many paintings, some even hung in the kitchen. Zhukov even went so far as to hang over his bed a huge canvas depicting two naked women … we did not find a single Soviet book.' Then there were 'twenty unique shotguns from Holland & Holland'. They left the trophies (returning for them in 1948) but for now they bizarrely confiscated a doll of one of the Marshal's daughters, and his memoirs:

'Leave history writing to the historians,' Stalin warned Zhukov.

In early June, Zhukov was summoned to the Supreme Military Council. Stalin strode in 'as gloomy as a black cloud'. Without a word, he tossed a note to Shtemenko.

'Read it,' he snapped. Shtemenko read out Novikov's testimony that Zhukov had claimed credit for the Soviet victory, criticized Stalin and created his own clique. He had even awarded a medal to the starlet Lydia Ruslanova, with whom he may have been having an affair.

This was 'intolerable', declared Stalin, turning to the generals. Budyonny (who had been coached by Bulganin) vaguely criticized his friend but not damningly. Zhukov's rival, Koniev, called him difficult but honest. Only Golikov, whom Zhukov had removed from the Voronezh Front in 1943, really denounced him. But Molotov, Beria and Bulganin attacked the Marshal for 'Bonapartism', demanding that Zhukov 'be put in his place'. Zhukov defended himself but admitted to having inflated his importance.

'What shall we do with Zhukov?' asked Stalin who, typically, had expressed no opinion. The potentates wanted him repressed, the soldiers did not. Stalin, seeing this was not 1937, suggested demoting Zhukov to the Odessa Military District. The Terror against the victors was a deliberate policy, with Admiral Kuznetzov, among others, arrested (though also only demoted). Ex-Marshal Kulik was bugged grumbling on his telephone that politicians were stealing the credit from the soldiers. This was heresy: he was quietly shot in 1950. Zhukov himself was expelled from the CC, his trophies confiscated, friends tortured, and then further demoted to the Urals. He suffered a heart attack but Stalin never let Abakumov arrest him for planning a Bonapartist coup:

'I don't trust anyone who says Zhukov could do this. I know him very well. He's a straightforward, sharp person able to speak plainly to anyone but he'll never go against the CC.'

Finally Stalin demonstrated the subordination of the generals by writing this note to the Politburo:

'I propose Comrade Bulganin be promoted to Marshal for his distinction in the Patriotic War.' In case anyone wished to query 'the Plumber's' utterly undistinguished war – and civilian – record, Stalin added: 'I think my reason requires no discussion – it's absolutely clear.'

* * *

Zhukov was not alone in his 'museum' of gold and paintings. Corruption is the untold story of Stalin's post-war Terror: the magnates and marshals plundered Europe with the avarice of Göring, though with much more justification after what the Germans had done to Russia. This imperial élite cast aside much of their old 'Bolshevik modesty'. Yet 'Comrade Stalin', foreign visitors were told, 'cannot endure immorality' though he had always believed that conquerors could help themselves to some booty and local girls. He laughed about the luxuries of his generals with their courtesans and batmen yet his archives overflow with denunciations of corruption which he usually filed away for later.

The marshals benefited from the feudal etiquette of plundering whereby officers stole their booty and then paid a sort of tribute to their superiors. Some needed no such help: Air Marshal Golovanov, one of Stalin's favourites, dismantled Goebbels' country house and flew it back to Moscow, an exploit that ruined his career.

The soldiers reached the treasures first but it was the Chekists who enjoyed the best swag. At Gagra, Beria pursued and impressed female athletes in a fleet of plundered speedboats. Abakumov drove around Moscow in Italian sports cars, looted Germany with Göringesque extravagance, sent planes to Berlin to commandeer

Potemkinesque quantities of underwear, assembling an antique treasure-trove like a department store. He flew in the German film star and international woman of mystery, Olga Chekhova, for an affair. When actress Tatiana Okunevskaya (already raped by Beria) refused him, she got seven years in the Gulags. Stalin's staff were mired in corruption. Vlasik, the *vizier* who ran a luxurious empire of food, drink and mansions, entertained his courtesans at official rest homes with a crew of raffish painters, thuggish Chekists and sybaritic bureaucrats. Limousines delivered the 'concubines' who received apartments, caviar, tickets to Red Square parades and football games. Vlasik seduced his friends' wives by showing them his photographs of Stalin and maps of Potsdam. He even pilfered Stalin's own houses, stripping his villa at Potsdam, stealing 100 pieces of porcelain, pianos, clocks, cars, three bulls and two horses, transported home in MGB trains and planes. He spent much of the Potsdam Conference drinking, fornicating, or stealing.

Then there was the massive wastage of food at Stalin's dachas. Vlasik was soon denounced for selling off the extra caviar, probably by Beria whom he had denounced in turn. In 1947, he was almost arrested but, instead, Stalin let him explain his sins: 'Every time, the mealtime was changed by [Stalin], part of the dishes were not used. They were distributed among the staff.' Stalin forgave him – and ordered less food than before. Vlasik kept his job.

Yet Vlasik's mistresses, like Beria's pimps, informed on him to Abakumov who in turn was denounced by his MGB rival, General Serov, who wrote to Stalin about the Minister's corruption and debauchery. Stalin stored the letters for later use. Serov himself was said to have stolen the crown of the King of Belgium. By now courtesans, procurers and MGB generals were informing on each other in a merry-go-round of sexual favours and betrayals.

* * *

Stalin's potentates now existed in a hothouse of rarefied privilege, their offices bedecked with fine Persian carpets and broad oil paintings.* Their houses were palatial: the Moscow boss now occupied the whole of Grand Duke Sergei Alexandrovich's palace.

---

* The size and quality of their Stalin portrait was as much a mark of rank as the stars on an officer's shoulder-boards: a life-size oil original by a court artist like Gerasimov was the sign of a potentate. Budyonny and Voroshilov also boasted life-size portraits of themselves in military splendour on horseback with sabre by Gerasimov. These 'grandees' were now so pompous, recalled Svetlana, that they made 'authoritative speeches' on 'any pretext', even at lunch in their own homes while their families 'sighed with boredom'.

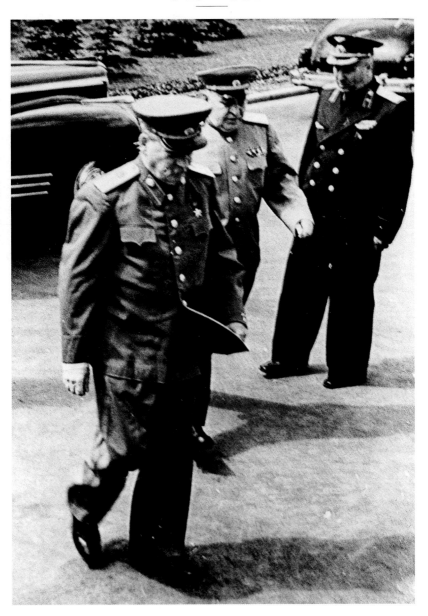

After victory, Stalin fell ill with a series of minor strokes or heart attacks. Here, the clearly ailing Generalissimo arrives to rest, accompanied by the porcine Vlasik.

On 12 August 1945 Generalissimo Stalin cheerfully leads his magnates for the parade – Mikoyan, Ukrainian viceroy Khrushchev, Malenkov, Beria in Marshal's uniform, Molotov (with Vlasik behind him).

Zhdanov, in Colonel-General's uniform, was Stalin's heir apparent and cultural supremo who attacked the arts after the war. Stalin promoted his son Yury and wanted him as his own son-in-law. But the charlatan geneticist Trofim Lysenko (far left) proved the nemesis of the Zhdanovs.

Opposite page The exhausted Stalin gloomily leads Beria, Mikoyan and Malenkov through the Kremlin to the Mausoleum for the 1946 May Day parade. In this nest of vipers, they walked arm in arm, but their friendships were masks: each would liquidate the others. Stalin now loathed Beria and mocked Malenkov for being so fat he had lost his human appearance. When Beria tormented dapper Mikoyan at Stalin's dinners by hiding tomatoes in his well-cut suits and squashing them, Mikoyan started bringing a spare suit.

Top As the struggle for the succession builds up, Stalin leads the mourning at Kalinin's funeral in 1946. (Front row, from left): Beria, Malenkov, Stalin and Molotov. Behind Molotov stands the ill and frail Zhdanov at the height of his power. Zhdanov's two protégés, Voznesensky and Kuznetsov, are both to the right behind Malenkov's shoulder. Kaganovich is behind Molotov.

Bottom The death of Zhdanov, Stalin's friend and favourite, here in an open coffin, unleashes the vengeance of Beria and Malenkov against his faction. Stalin, Voroshilov and Kaganovich follow the coffin. That night, at the funeral supper, Stalin became drunk: with Zhdanov gone, he had lost his only intellectual equal.

Here, in late 1948, Stalin sits with the older generation, Kaganovich, Molotov and Voroshilov, while an intrigue is being prepared behind them amongst the younger. After ten years without a single top leader being shot, Beria (second row, far left) and Malenkov (second row, second from left) helped Stalin murder his two appointed successors, Kuznetsov (second row between Molotov and Stalin) and Voznesensky (second row between Stalin and Voroshilov) in the 'Leningrad Case'.

Left Summertime chez Stalin: natty Mikoyan in whites with 'young handsome' and doomed Kuznetsov, Molotov and Poskrebyshev in uniform.

Bottom At his seventieth birthday gala on stage at the Bolshoi, Stalin stands between Mao Tse-tung and Khrushchev, whom Stalin summoned from Ukraine to offset Malenkov and Beria.

Opposite page STALIN'S RESTLESS LAST HOLIDAY IN 1952.

He effectively ruled Russia for months on end from his new house at New Athos in the late forties – this was his favourite *(top)*. He also returned to a house where he had enjoyed a happy holiday with Nadya after Vasily's birth in 1921 – the Likani Palace, which once belonged to Tsar Nicholas II's brother Grand Duke Michael *(middle)*. When Khrushchev and Mikoyan visited, they had to share a room. He spent weeks in this remote house at Lake Ritsa *(bottom)*. He was now so frail that his guards built these green metal boxes (inset) containing special phones so that Stalin could call for help if he was taken ill on his daily strolls.

All his life, Stalin slept on the big divans that were placed in virtually every room of all his houses. This is the sofa at Kuntsevo on which he died on 5 March 1953.

Left Plotting the destruction of Molotov and Mikoyan, the aging but determined Stalin watches Malenkov give the chief report at his last public appearance at the Nineteenth Congress in 1952. While organising the anti-semitic Doctors' Plot, he ordered his secret police to torture the doctors: 'Beat, beat and beat again!' he shouted. But he still found time to play with his grandchildren...

The fight for power began over the deathbed. On the right Khrushchev and Bulganin (alongside Kaganovich and Mikoyan) face Beria and Malenkov (alongside Molotov and Voroshilov) across Stalin's body. Beria seemed to have won the struggle for succession, but he fatally underestimated Khrushchev.

Stalin at the 1927 Congress: unshaven, pockmarked, sardonic, sarcastic and utterly vigilant, the supreme politician, the messianic egotist, fanatical Marxist, and superlative mass-murderer, in his prime.

Stalin himself fostered this new imperial era when, after Yalta, he took a fancy to Nicholas II's Livadia and Prince Vorontsov's Alupka Palaces: 'Put these palaces in order,' Stalin wrote to Beria on 27 February 1945. 'Prepare for responsible workers.' He so liked Alexander III's Palace at Sosnovka in the Crimea that he had a dacha built there which he only visited once. Henceforth, the magnates and their children booked these palaces through the MGB 9th Department: Stepan Mikoyan honeymooned at Vorontsov's palace; Stalin himself holidayed at Livadia. The families flew south on a special section of the state airline – Sergo Mikoyan remembers flying home on this with Poskrebyshev. The children enjoyed their privileges but had to set an example and follow Party dictums: when Zhdanov denounced jazz, Khrushchev broke his son's beloved jazz records in a temper.

Svetlana Stalin noticed how the dachas of the Mikoyans, Molotovs and Voroshilovs were 'crammed with gifts from workers … rugs, gold Caucasian weapons, porcelain' which they received like 'the medieval custom of vassals paying tribute'. The magnates travelled in armoured ZiS limousines, based on the American Packards, on Stalin's orders, followed by another 'tail' of Chekists, with sirens blaring. Muscovites called this procession 'a dog's wedding'.

An entire detachment, commanded by a colonel or a general, was assigned to each leader, actually living at their dachas, half an extended family, half MGB informers. There were so many of them that each Politburo member was able to form a volleyball team, with the Berias playing the Kaganoviches. But Kaganovich refused to play on his own team: 'Beria always wins and I want to be on the winning side,' he said. In MGB vernacular, the magnate was called 'the subject', their house 'the object' and the guards 'attachments to the subject', so the children used to laugh when they heard them say, 'The subject's on his way to the object.' Malenkov often walked to the Kremlin from Granovsky Street surrounded by a phalanx of 'attachments'.

The Politburo ladies now had their own haute couture designer. All the 'top ten families' went to the *atelier* on Kutuzovsky Prospekt, controlled by an MGB department where Abram (Donjat Ignatovich according to Nina Khrushcheva) Lerner and Nina Adzhubei designed the men's suits and the women's dresses. Lerner was a traditional Jewish tailor who designed uniforms including Stalin's Generalissimo extravaganza. If he was the

Politburo's Dior, Nina Adzhubei, 'short, round, pug-nosed and very strong', trained by 'monks in a monastery', was its Chanel. Heaps of *Harper's Bazaar* and *Vogue* lay around. She would either copy fashions from Dior, from *Vogue* or *Harper's* or design her own, 'but she was as good as Chanel', says her client Martha Peshkova, Beria's daughter-in-law. 'You didn't have to pay if you didn't ask the price,' explains Sergo Mikoyan. 'My mother always paid but Polina Molotova didn't.' This practice was finally denounced, like everything else, to Stalin who reprimanded the Politburo: Ashken Mikoyan threw the bills in Anastas's face, proving she always paid. Adzhubei 'made Svetlana Stalin's first dress'.*

The dressmaker was discovered by Nina Beria but Polina Molotova, the grand 'first lady', was her best client. Once the grandees of Victorian Europe had taken the waters at the Bohemian resort of Carlsbad. Now Zinaida Zhdanova and Nina Beria held court there. 'Lavishly dressed and covered in furs', with her daughter in a 'mink stole', Polina often arrived at the same spa in an official plane with an entourage of fifty. Her daughter Svetlana, a 'real Bolshevik princess', was chauffered daily to the Institute of Foreign Relations, where many of the élite studied, arriving in a cloud of Chanel No. 5, 'wearing a new outfit every day'.

Stalin retained his control of these privileges, continuing to choose the cars for every leader so that Zhdanov received an armoured Packard, a normal Packard and a ZiS 110, Beria got an armoured Packard, a ZiS and a Mercedes, while Poskrebyshev got a Cadillac and a Buick. He consoled the family of Shcherbakov, the Moscow boss who died of alcoholism, with a shower of cash.†
Stalin specified: 'Give them an apartment with a dacha, rights to the Kremlin Hospital, limousine ... NKVD special staff ... teacher for children ...' He awarded Shcherbakov's widow 2,000 roubles a

---

* Nina Adzhubei joined the élite herself when her son married Khrushchev's daughter, Rada. When Khrushchev became Soviet leader, Alexei Adzhubei became powerful as the leader's adviser and *Izvestiya* editor.
† Although Stalin was cynical about the renaming of places after his late magnates, he decided to build a statue and rename a region, street and factory after Shcherbakov. The original draft suggested naming a town after him, too, but Stalin crossed that out, scribbling: 'Give his name to a cloth factory.' On 9 December 1947, the Politburo set annual salaries of the Premier and President at 10,000 roubles; Deputy Premiers and CC Secretaries 8,000 roubles. Stalin's salary packets just piled up, unspent, in his desk at Kuntsevo.

month, his sons 1,000 a month until graduation, his mother 700 a month, his sister 300. His wife also received a lump sump of 200,000 roubles and his mother 50,000 roubles – sums of unthinkable munificence for the average worker. Here was Stalin's new imperial order.

* * *

'Crown Prince' Vasily set a new standard for corruption, debauchery and caprice. Even when officers complained about him to Stalin, they used a special formula to define Vasily's sacred place: 'He is close to the Soviet people because he is your son.' Yet beneath the arrogance, Vasily was the most terrified of all the courtiers: Stalin scoffed that he would 'walk through fire' if he ordered it. Vasily especially feared the future:

'I've only got two ways out,' he told Artyom. 'The pistol or drink! If I use the pistol, I'll cause Father a lot of trouble. But when he dies, Khrushchev, Beria and Bulganin'll tear me apart. Do you realize what it's like living under the axe?'

He callously abandoned his wife, Galina, taking their son Sasha to live with him at the House on the Embankment. She so longed to see Sasha that the nanny secretly met her so she could play with him. But Galina was too frightened to demand a flat or housekeeping from him. Vasily then married Marshal Timoshenko's daughter Ekaterina, 'a pretty Ukrainian'. His apartment was not grand enough for the scions of the Generalissimo and the Marshal so he demanded General Vlasik's elegant villa on Gogolevsky. He flew back from Germany with a plane filled with 'loot': 'golden ornaments, diamonds, emeralds, dozens of carpets, lots of lady's lingerie, a huge number of men's suits, overcoats, fur coats, fur wraps, astrakhan' until Vasily's house was 'bursting with gold, German carpets and cut glass'. There was so much that his wife Timoshenka gradually sold it and pocketed the money. When his marriage to Timoshenka collapsed, he married a swimming star, the statuesque Kapitolina Vasileva, with whom he was happiest. Svetlana thought he was looking for his mother in his wives because he called her 'mama' and she even wore her hair in a bun like Nadya.

Vasily commanded the Air Force in the Moscow Military District, a job beyond his capabilities. He demanded that his strutting entourage call him *Khozyain* like his father. 'Vasily drank heavily almost every day,' testified his adjutant later, 'didn't turn up for work for weeks on end and couldn't leave the women alone.'

Once Crown Princes proudly drilled their own regiments. Now, like a Western millionaire's son, Vasily was determined to make his own VVS (Air Force) football team top of the league. He immediately sacked the football manager, having decided to rescue Starostin, Russia's pre-eminent soccer manager exiled by Beria, for plotting to assassinate Stalin, from the Gulag. Starostin was called into his camp commandant's office and handed the *vertushka*: 'Hello, Nikolai, this is Vasily Stalin.' General Stalin's plane arrived and flew Starostin back to Moscow where Vasily hid him while he tried to get his sentence reversed.

Abakumov, now boss of the Dynamo team, was furious. The MGB kidnapped Starostin. Vasily, using Air Force intelligence officers, grabbed him back. Abakumov kidnapped him again. When Vasily phoned the Minister, he denied any knowledge of the footballer but Starostin managed to get a message to Vasily who despatched the head of Air Force security to bring him back yet again. That day, Vasily attended the Dynamo game in the government box, with Starostin beside him. The MGB brass were foiled. Vasily called Abakumov's deputy and shouted: 'Two hours ago you told me you didn't know where Starostin was ... He's sitting here right beside me. Your boys abducted him. Remember, in our family, we never forgive an insult. That's told to you by General Stalin!'*

When he visited Tiflis, he got drunk, took a fighterplane up over the city and caused havoc by swooping over the streets. If he did not get his way, he denounced officers to Abakumov or Bulganin. The only escape was to denounce him to Stalin himself:

'Dear Joseph Vissarionovich, I ask you to tell Vasily Josephovich not to touch me,' wrote the air-force officer N. Sbytov, who had spotted the first German tanks approaching Moscow. 'I could help him.' Sbytov revealed that Vasily was constantly name-dropping: 'When my father approved this job, he wanted me to have an independent command,' he whined.

---

* When Starostin was finally returned to his camp (where he ran the soccer team), Vasily hired the famous coach of Dynamo Tiflis and managed to make it to fourth place in 1950 and the semi-finals of the USSR Cup. He favoured Stalinist punishments and plutocratic incentives: when his team lost 0–2, he ordered their plane to dump them in the middle of nowhere, far from Moscow, as a punishment; when the team won, a helicopter landed on the field filled with gifts. When he bothered to turn up to his Air Force command, he ruled there too with wild generosity and grim terror. Thanks to Zurab Karumidze for these anecdotes of his father-in-law, Vasily's football manager.

Vasily certainly behaved like a boy brought up by Chekists: when some 'Enemies' were found in his command, he set up an impromptu torture-chamber in his own apartment and started 'beating the soles of the man's feet with a thin rod' until this *ersatz*-Lubianka broke up into a party.

* * *

Days after Zhukov's exile, President Kalinin, who was ill with stomach cancer, started to deteriorate. Stalin was fond of Papa Kalinin, personally arranging to send him down to recuperate in Abkhazia, calling the local boss to demand 'maximum care', and later ordering his bodyguards to look after him tenderly. Yet he also tormented the half-blind Kalinin, remembering 'Papa's' dissent in the twenties for which he had excluded him from active government for two decades. When Tito offered Kalinin some cigarettes at a banquet, Stalin quipped:

'Don't take any of those Western cigarettes!' Kalinin 'confusedly dropped them from his trembling fingers'.

The 71-year-old Kalinin lived with his housekeeper and two adopted children while his adored wife festered in the camps. Emboldened by his imminent death, Kalinin appealed to Stalin:

'I look calmly on the future of our country ... and I wish only one thing – to preserve your power and strength, the best guarantee of the success of the Soviet State,' he started his letter. 'Personally I turn to you with two requests – pardon Ekaterina Ivanovna Kalinina and appoint my sister to bring up the two orphans living with me. With all my soul, a last goodbye. M. Kalinin.' Stalin, Malenkov and Zhdanov voted to pardon Kalinin's wife after she had admitted her guilt, the usual condition for forgiveness:

'I did bad things and was severely punished ... but I was never an enemy to the Communist Party – pardon me!'

'It's necessary to pardon and free at once, and bring the pardoned to Moscow. J Stalin.'

Before he died, on 24 June, Kalinin wrote an extraordinary but pathetic letter to Stalin, inspired by his bitter need of Bolshevik redemption:

'Waiting for death ... I must say that during all the time of the oppositions, no one from the opposition ever proposed hostility to the Party line. This might surprise you because I was friendly with some of them ... Yet I was criticized and discredited ... because Yagoda worked hard to imply my closeness to the oppositions.' Now he revealed a secret he had kept for twenty-two years: 'In the year after Lenin's death, after the row with Trotsky, Bukharin invited me to his flat to admire his hunting trophies and asked – would I consider "ruling without Stalin?"; I replied I couldn't contemplate such a thing. Any combination without Stalin was incomprehensible ... After the death of Lenin, I believed in Stalin's policy ... I thought Zinoviev most dangerous.' Then he again requested that Stalin care for his sister and the orphans, and 'commit this letter to the archive'.

At the funeral, when photographers hassled Stalin, he pointed at the coffin, growling: 'Photograph Kalinin!'

* * *

On 8 September, Stalin headed off on his holiday while Molotov shuttled around the world to attend meetings with the Allies to negotiate the new Europe. In Paris, he defended Soviet interests in Germany while still trying to win a protectorate over Libya, against the ever-hardening opposition of the Western allies. It seems that Stalin still hoped to consolidate his position by negotiations with his former allies.

Stalin, writing in code as 'Druzhkov' or *Instantsiya*, praised Molotov's indomitable defiance. Molotov was very pleased with himself too. When he found himself relegated to the second row at a French parade, he stormed off the podium but then wrote to Stalin for approval: 'I'm not sure I did the right thing.'

'You behaved absolutely correctly,' replied Stalin. 'The dignity of the Soviet Union must be defended not only in great matters but in minutiae.'

'Dear Polinka honey,' the vain Molotov wrote exultantly. 'I send greetings and newspaper pictures as I left the parade on Sunday! I enclose *Paris-Midi* which shows the three pictures of 1. me on the tribune. 2. I start to leave; and 3. I leave the tribune and enter my car. I kiss and hug you warmly! Kiss Svetusya for me!' Molotov flew on to another session in New York, which Stalin again supervised from Coldstream in Gagra: Stalin cared less about the details of Italian reparations than about Soviet status as a great power. Molotov was in favour again: on 28 November, Stalin wrote tenderly: 'I realize you are nervous and getting upset over the fate of the Soviet proposal ... Behave more calmly!' But faced with Ukrainian famine and American rivalry, the cantankerous *Vozhd* sensed dangerous weakness, corruption and disloyalty around him.

* * *

While Molotov was triumphant at having signed the peace treaties with the defeated nations, Stalin contrived another humiliation. Stalin was already a member of the Academy of Sciences and now Molotov was offered the same honour, with the *Vozhd's* blessing. Molotov dutifully sent the Academy a grateful cable, upon which Stalin swooped with aquiline spite: 'I was struck by your cable ... Are you really so ecstatic about your election as an honorary Academician? What does this signature "truly yours, Molotov" mean? I never thought you could become so emotional about such a second-rate matter ... It seems to me that you, a statesman of the highest type, must care more about your dignity.'

Stalin continued to seethe about the inconvenience of his people starving, Hungry Thirty Three all over again.* First he tried to joke about it, calling one official 'Brother Dystrophy'. Then, when even Zhdanov reported the famine, Stalin blamed Khrushchev, his Ukrainian viceroy as he had done in 1932: 'They're deceiving you ...' Yet 282,000 people died in 1946, 520,000 in 1947. Finally he turned on the Supply maestro, Mikoyan. He ordered Mekhlis, resurgent as Minister of State Control, to investigate:

'Don't trust Mikoyan in any business because his lack of honest character has made Supply a den of thieves!'

Mikoyan was clever enough to apologize:

'I saw so many mistakes in my work and surely you see it all clearly,' he wrote to Stalin with submissive irony. 'Of course neither I nor the rest of us can put the issue as squarely as you can. I will do my best to study from you how to work as necessary. I'll do everything to learn lessons ... so it will serve me well in my subsequent work under your fatherly leadership.' Like Molotov, Mikoyan's old intimacy with Stalin was over. Khrushchev too fell into disfavour about his attitude to the famine: 'Spinelessness!' Stalin upbraided him and, in February 1947, sacked him as Ukrainian First Secretary (he remained Premier). Kaganovich, who now resembled 'a fat landowner', replaced him and arrived in Kiev to batter him into shape. Stalin's disfavour always brought debilitating stress to his grandees: Khrushchev collapsed with

---

* Not only could Stalin not feed his civilians but his correspondence with Beria and Serov (in Germany) shows that the Soviets were anxious that they could not feed their army in Germany, let alone the East Germans.

pneumonia. His name vanished from Ukrainian newspapers, his cult withered. But Kaganovich ordered doctors to treat Khrushchev with penicillin, one of the western medicines of which Stalin so disapproved. Even if he recovered, was Stalin's 'pet' doomed?

50

'The Zionists Have Pulled One Over You!'

In 1947, the American Secretary of State, George Marshall, unveiled a massive programme of economic aid to Europe that initially sounded attractive to the shattered Imperium. Molotóv was immediately despatched to Paris to find out more. At first the leaders thought of the Plan like Lend-Lease with no strings attached, but Stalin soon grasped that it would resuscitate Germany and undermine his East European hegemony. Molotov initially favoured the Plan and still leaned towards a negotiated settlement but Stalin rejected Marshall.

Stalin and Zhdanov resolved to tighten their control over Eastern Europe. Simultaneously, Stalin supported the foundation of the Jewish state, which he hoped would become a Middle Eastern satellite. On 29 November, he voted for it at the UN and was the first to recognize Israel. He gave Mikhoels the Stalin Prize. But it soon became clear Israel was going to be an American ally, not a Russian one.

In the cauldron of Stalin's irrational prejudices, razor-sharp political instincts and aggressively Russian sensibilities, Mikhoels's dream of a Jewish Crimea became a sinister Zionist/American Trojan horse,* a Hebraic Marshall Plan. Zionism, Judaism and America became interchangeable in Stalin's mind. He was obviously supported by his magnates: even after Stalin's death, Khrushchev sympathetically explained to some Polish Communists, 'We all know Jews; they all have some connection with the capitalistic world because they have relatives living abroad. This one has a granny ... The Cold War began; the imperialists were

---

* Like so many of Stalin's febrile fears, there was substance here: the Ottoman Sultans had controlled the Black Sea through their control of Crimea. Catherine the Great and Prince Potemkin annexed the Crimea in 1783 for the same reason, just as the Anglo-French armies landed there in 1853 to undermine Russia. Khrushchev controversially donated Crimea to Ukraine in 1954, a decision that almost caused a civil war in the 1990s between Ukrainians and those who wished to be ruled by Russia.

plotting how to attack USSR; then the Jews want to settle in the Crimea ... here's the Crimea and Baku ... Through their connections, the Jews had created a network to carry out American plans. So he squashed it all.' This view was not only held in Stalin's councils: his nephew, Vladimir Redens, agreed with complaints that 'the Committee was giving off terrible Zionist propaganda ... as if the Jews were the only people who suffered.' Stalin's anti-Semitism dovetailed with his campaign of traditional nationalism. Even his prejudices were subordinate and complementary to *realpolitik*.

Stalin ordered Abakumov to gather evidence that Mikhoels and the Jewish Committee were 'active nationalists orientated by the Americans to do anti-Soviet work', especially through Mikhoels's American trip when 'they made contact with famous Jewish persons connected with the US secret service'. Mikhoels played into Stalin's hands.

Mikhoels, the Yiddish actor out of his depth in this duel with the Stalinist *Golem*, wanted to appeal to Stalin. He called the second most influential Jew after Kaganovich, Polina Molotova, to ask whether to appeal to Zhdanov or Malenkov.

'Zhdanov and Malenkov won't help you,' replied Polina. 'All power in the country's in Stalin's hands alone and nobody can influence him. I don't advise you write to Stalin. He has a negative attitude to Jews and won't support us.' It would have been unthinkable for her to speak in such a way before the war.

Mikhoels made the tempting but spectacularly ill-timed decision to reach Stalin through Svetlana. Stalin was already brooding about Svetlana's taste for Jewish men. After Kapler, there was Morozov whom she had married on the rebound from Sergo Beria. Stalin had nothing against Morozov personally, 'a good fellow', he said, but he had not fought in the war, and he was Jewish. 'The Zionists have pulled one over you,' Stalin told her. Malenkov's daughter Volya had just married the Jewish grandson of Lozovsky, who ran Mikhoels' Jewish Committee. Molotov proposed Mikhoels' Jewish Crimea letter and his wife Polina's brother was a Jewish American businessman. These American agents were everywhere. Now it got worse.

Mikhoels, frantic to protect the Jewish community, asked Zhenya Alliluyeva who mixed with the Jewish intelligentsia, if he could meet Svetlana. The élite children were wary of suitors using them for their connections: 'One of the unpleasant things of being daughter of a *chinovnik* was that I couldn't trust young people around me,' says Volya Malenkova. 'Many wanted to marry me. I didn't know if they wanted me or my father's influence.'

The Alliluyevs warned Zhenya against meddling in dangerous Jewish matters: 'All stirred together in this pot,' says Vladimir Redens. 'We knew it wasn't going to end well.' But it seems that Zhenya did introduce Mikhoels to Svetlana and Morozov. Stalin heard about this immediately* and erupted in a rage: the Jews were 'worming their way into the family'. Furthermore, Anna Redens was once again irritating Stalin, publishing a tactless memoir of his early days and nagging Vasily who complained to Stalin. Thus Mikhoels innocently stumbled into a hornets' nest.

Stalin ordered Abakumov to investigate the Alliluyev connection to American-Zionist espionage, muttering to Svetlana that Zhenya had poisoned her husband Pavel in 1938. Shrewd people began to divorce their Jewish spouses. Svetlana Stalin divorced Morozov: every history book repeats that Stalin ordered this and Svetlana's cousin Leonid Redens also claims that he did. But she herself explained, 'My father never asked me to divorce him', adding in more recent interviews that she had not been in love with Morozov: 'We divorced because I wasn't in love with him.' This rings true as far it goes: Leonid Redens adds that 'there were many men in Svetlana's life; she'd had enough of Morozov.' But Stalin himself told Mikoyan that 'if she doesn't divorce Morozov, they'll arrest him'. She left Morozov: 'No one would have left me,' said this Tsarevna. It seems that Stalin got his son to fix the matter. 'Vasily took Morozov's passport,'† says Redens, 'and brought him a new one without the wedding stamp.'

Abakumov started to arrest the Alliluyevs' Jewish circle. On 10 December, he arrested Zhenya Alliluyeva, once so intimate with Stalin, accusing her of 'disseminating foul slander about the Head of the Soviet Government'. Zhenya's husband, her vivacious actress daughter Kira, and Anna Redens joined her. Prominent Jews were pulled in.

The *Instantsiya*, that dread euphemism for the sacred eminence

---

* It was not long before Zhenya learned that her own husband was an MGB agent who had informed on her ever since their marriage, but every élite family had its informer. She divorced him.

† Grigory Morozov, who became a respected Soviet lawyer and always behaved with great discretion and dignity, refused to be interviewed for this book, saying, 'I never want to relive 1947 again.' He died in 2002.

in the Kremlin, believed the Jewish/Alliluyev set had 'expressed interest in the personal life of the Head of the Soviet Government, backed by foreign intelligence'. Stalin permitted 'methods of persuasion' to implicate Mikhoels. The 'French wrestling', as the torturers called it, was led by Komarov, a vicious anti-Semitic psychopath, who announced to his victims: 'Your fate's in my hands and I'm not a man, I'm a beast,' adding, 'All Jews are lousy bastards!' Abakumov supervised this diabolical sadist, ordering the prisoners 'a deadly beating!'

Goldshtein, who had introduced Mikhoels to the Alliluyevs, testified later how 'they started to beat me with a rubber baton on the soft parts of my body and my bare heels ... until I couldn't sit or stand.' They beat his head so hard 'my face was swollen terribly and my hearing affected. Exhausted by day and night-time interrogations, terrorized by beatings, curses and threats, I fell into a deep depression, a total moral confusion and began to give evidence against myself and others.'

'So you say Mikhoels's a swine?' Abakumov shouted.

'Yes he is,' replied the broken Goldshtein who admitted that Mikhoels had asked him to 'notice all the small details of the relationship between Svetlana and Grigory ... [to] inform our American friends.' When Stalin read this, it confirmed his worst fears about Mikhoels.

Vladimir Redens, at twelve, had now lost both mother and father. His young cousins, Zhenya's boys, had lost their parents and sister. Vladimir rushed to tell Olga, his grandmother, who had continued to live in the Kremlin after the death of her husband Sergei in 1946. To his amazement, she had never forgiven Zhenya for marrying so fast:

'Thank God!' she said on hearing about Zhenya's arrest, and crossed herself. But she called Stalin about Anna's arrest:

'They were used by the Enemy,' replied Stalin. When the family wished 'someone would tell Stalin', the old lady replied, 'nothing happened without him knowing.' They naïvely blamed Beria, not realizing that Abakumov reported only to Stalin.

Svetlana tried to intercede for the 'Aunties' but Stalin warned her 'they talked too much. You make anti-Soviet comments too.' Kira Alliluyeva, Svetlana's first cousin also arrested, claims that Stalin warned his daughter: 'If you act as their defender we'll also put you in jail.' Both she and Vasily cut dead the Alliluyev children.

* * *

Now that Svetlana was single again, Stalin started to talk about whom she should next marry, telling his magnates, 'She said she'd marry either Stepan Mikoyan or Sergo Beria.' The Politburo fathers were alarmed. The Tsarevna did not seem to mind that both boys were not only already married but in love with their wives. Stalin told the anxious Mikoyan and Beria:

'I told her neither one nor the other. She should marry Yury Zhdanov.' Simultaneously, this clumsy, tyrannical matchmaker told Yury to marry Svetlana.

On 16 July, Stalin embarked on a road trip to meet the people and see the country, something he had not done since 1933. It was to be a reflective and nostalgic three-month holiday, a mark of his exhaustion and his new style as a distant but paramount leader. He left the indecisive Bulganin in charge.

While Abakumov tortured Jews to create a new 'American' conspiracy and destroy Mikhoels, Stalin and his convoy of armoured ZiS110s headed south, accompanied by Valechka, towards Kharkov.

51

A Lonely Old Man on Holiday

The Generalissimo ordered that there was to be no tedious ceremony and all passed off 'without any sensationalism – which greatly pleased Stalin', wrote Vlasik, who found the expedition exhausting. Stalin himself had only slept for about two hours but he was 'in a good mood which made us all happy'. He inspected everything, muttering that he would not have seen anything 'from my desk'.

He even experienced some aspects of ordinary life: his car broke down near Orel. Stalin got out for a stroll, surrounded by his 'attachments', and came upon some parked trucks whose drivers were struck dumb when he introduced himself. At Kursk, Stalin stayed the night in the flat of a local Chekist. In the morning, he thought they should leave the couple a present so he left a bottle of scent on the lady's dressing table. At Kharkov, Stalin noticed people were still living in dugouts. He told Valechka that this upset him. When out-of-favour Khrushchev arrived, reassuring Stalin that the famine was much exaggerated and presented him with some juicy melons, Valechka was naïvely appalled, grumbling to Svetlana that they deceived 'your father – of all people!'

Finally, the relieved Vlasik loaded Stalin on to the special train that took them down to Yalta where he probably stayed at the Livadia before the cruiser *Molotov* conveyed him to Sochi. The weather was gorgeous, the crew thrilled by their passenger. Vlasik, court photographer, took so many photographs that Stalin, 'always sensitive', noticed:

'Vlasik's doing well but no one photographs him. Someone must photograph him with us.'

In Sochi, Stalin strolled around the town, followed by Vlasik, Poskrebyshev and the frantic bodyguards who struggled to control the campers holidaying on the coast. When some schoolchildren gathered round his car, he offered them a ride to the local café, the Riviera, where a little girl cried because she had not got any sweets. Stalin put her on his knee and told her to choose anything she liked. Porcine Vlasik paid the bill, then turned to the children and cried:

'Now children! A Pioneer Hurrah for Comrade Stalin' – the Soviet version of 'Hip hip hurrah!' One can imagine him punching the air as 'the children shouted a harmonious hurrah!'

* * *

They then drove down to Stalin's spiritual home in these twilight years, Abkhazia, where he believed the air and the food ensured longevity:

'Do you remember how amazed that English writer J. B. Priestley was when he met an Abkhazian peasant aged 150?' he reflected. 'If I lived here, I might live to 150!'* Stalin often told Molotov how he missed his homeland. Stalin had championed the Russian people as the ties that bound his empire; it was they who provided the dynamic power to promote Bolshevism and guaranteed his glory. His destiny was Russian. Hence Vasily said, 'Papa was once a Georgian.' But his personal Russianness has been exaggerated. His lifestyle and mentality remained Georgian. He talked Georgian, ate Georgian, sang Georgian, personally ruled Georgia through the local bosses, becoming involved in parochial politics, missed his childhood friends, and spent almost half of his last eight years in his own isolated, fantasy Georgia.

Stalin based himself at Coldstream but constantly moved to new houses. It is claimed that they were gloomy. Certainly the wood-panelling was sombre but when one visits them in the summer, they are delightful. Stalin usually ate and worked outside on the verandas and all had lush gardens full of flowers where he loved to walk. Above all, the houses were chosen for their vistas: the views from these grave houses are all breathtakingly beautiful.

He now started staying at the white mock-Baroque mansion in the lush gardens of Dedra Park at Sukhumi where Mandelstam had watched Yezhov dance the *gopak*. During the thirties, he had holidayed at a small dacha built by Lakoba, at New Athos; now he had another Cuban-style villa built next to it, all on one floor and

* Stalin had always taken a great interest in longevity. In 1937, he had sponsored Professor Alexander Bogomolov's work into the phenomenon of the extraordinary life-spans of the people of Georgia and Abkhazia. Stalin is said to have believed this was due to water from glaciers and their diet – he therefore drank special glacial water.

with a splendid sea view. There was already a CC sanatorium by the lake at the remote Lake Ritsa which could only be reached by a long drive through a scenic gorge beside a bubbling torrent. In 1948, he ordered a new house to be joined to the old.*

Stalin had access to any of the innumerable state dachas, but there seem to have been about five around Moscow, several in the Crimea, including two imperial palaces, three in Georgia proper, and about five in Abkhazia that he used regularly. At least fifteen were kept staffed. Yet in many ways, he remained the itinerant, restless Georgian revolutionary of his youth. Accompanied by Poskrebyshev, constantly supplied by air with the latest CC papers, summoning his potentates at will, despatching telegrams round the world, he was always the fulcrum of power.

* * *

When he arrived, there was one ritual that was an echo of older times: Stalin had hung Lenin's death-mask on the wall at Kuntsevo where it was illuminated like an icon with a burning lamp. Whenever he went on holiday, the icon would travel with him. He ordered his commandant Orlov 'to hang the face in the most visible place'.

As he moved in, the magnates and the entire Georgian leadership arrived simultaneously at their local houses, waiting to be summoned. Abakumov was ready to fly down at a moment's notice with news of the latest interrogations. If there were Politburo rows, he summoned the magnates for Solomonic judgement. They dreaded having to spend any time with Stalin on holiday, which 'was worse than the dinners', according to Khrushchev who once endured a whole month. Fighting the

---

* Most of Stalin's houses were reached through an archway of the security building (though not Lake Ritsa and New Athos) before emerging in a lush garden with privet hedges and a path that led up to a Mediterranean-style villa surrounded by a veranda. Their biggest room was always the high-ceilinged wood-panelled dining-room that boasted a long table that could be made smaller. All were painted a sort of military green, perhaps to camouflage them from the sky. All were virtually invisible, hidden up narrow lanes, and so concealed within palm and fir trees that it was hard to see them even from their own garden. Virtually all of them had their own jetties and all had summerhouses where Stalin worked and held dinners. All contained the tell-tale billiard room which was usually combined with a cinema, the film being projected out of little wooden windows across the billiard table on to the far wall. All had many bedrooms with divans and vast bathrooms with tiny baths made to fit Stalin's height. All had been built or refashioned for Stalin by his court architect Miron Merzhanov who lived with Martha Beria's mother, Timosha, Gorky's daughter-in-law and Yagoda's love. Merzhanov was arrested in the late forties like all of Timosha's previous lovers.

Ukrainian famine and separatism, Khrushchev remained under a temporary cloud as he recuperated. Stalin ordered Kaganovich to supervise Khrushchev and beat any nationalism out of the Ukrainians, a feat he had formerly achieved in the late twenties. Khrushchev and Kaganovich, long-time allies, lived cheek by jowl, their families going on walks every weekend. Inevitably, they soon became mortal enemies. Both appealed to Stalin who summoned them to Coldstream. Over dinner and a movie, he stoked their hatred, enforced peace and ultimately recalled Kaganovich to Moscow.

His East European vassals, especially Gottwald, Bierut and Hoxha, did not dare resist a summons. But the two favourites were the local chiefs with whom Stalin could relax, partly because both were in their mid-thirties, partly because they were Georgians. Confiding in them more than in his own children, he appeared divine to them but also paternal.

Candide Charkviani, the cultured Georgian First Secretary, visited him 'every second day'. It helped that Stalin had been taught the alphabet by a priest named Charkviani, even though he was no relation to Candide. He trusted Charkviani so much that he not only revealed his sleeping arrangements but when Candide told him about a Georgian prince who changed his underwear daily, Stalin showed him a chest of drawers full of 'white cotton underclothes': 'It's not hard for a prince,' Stalin quipped. 'But I'm a peasant and I do the same.'

The other confidant was Akaki Mgeladze, the ruthless and sleekly handsome boss of Abkhazia, whom Stalin nicknamed 'Comrade Wolf'. Stalin liked Charkviani for his knowledge of literature and Mgeladze for his political intriguing. He sometimes challenged Mgeladze to drive from his Sukhumi office to the dacha in seventeen minutes. Charkviani and Mgeladze hated each other, like their predecessors Beria and Lakoba.*

Valechka, Vlasik and Poskrebyshev, who stayed in nearby dachas, plus a stenographer and cipher officer, were his other regular companions. With his 'sad face, swivelling eyes and cunning', Poskrebyshev sorted out the papers that arrived each

---

* This is based on Charkviani's memoirs. Mgeladze's memoirs, that almost rank alongside Mikoyan's for their intimacy, have only just been published in Georgia. The Georgian and Abkhazian bosses were naturally rivals: in the case of Beria versus Lakoba, the Tbilisi boss destroyed the Sukhumi boss but it worked the other way round with Charkviani and Mgeladze.

day by plane from Moscow and then brought them up to the villa. Poskrebyshev, whom Stalin had lately nicknamed 'the Commander-in-Chief', defended the Generalissimo from unwanted callers. When Mikoyan phoned in October 1947, Poskrebyshev chided him:

'You've already been told you shouldn't bother Comrade Stalin on this question and you do it again.' To outsiders, for whom the Politburo was the holy of holies, this was a shocking display.

Stalin ate his meals outside, on the verandas, in the summer-house or by Lake Ritsa, reading the papers. There were open magazines and books on virtually every surface and piles of papers. Before he set off for the south, he scrawled to Poskrebyshev:

'Order all these books. Stalin. *Goethe's Letters, Poetry of the French Revolution*, Pushkin, Konstantin Simonov, Shakespeare, Herzen, *History of the Seven Years War* – and *Battle at Sea 1939–1945* by Peter Scott.' He still worked late into the evenings, starting his dinners late. Vlasik and Poskrebyshev did not always dine with the Boss but the *chef de cabinet* invited guests with the drear words:

'Stalin awaits you.' When Poskrebyshev shepherded the guests to the door, Stalin joked:

'So how's our Commander-in-Chief?' Sunburnt, grey-haired, with a bald patch, thin-faced with a pot belly and sloping shoulders, Stalin met them on the veranda like an affable Georgian countryman, wearing a civilian suit like a safari costume. When it was very hot, there was a sprinkler on the Coldstream terrace that cooled the air, spraying an arch of water over the roof.

Sometimes, the housekeeper pointed the guests down the garden where they found Stalin wielding a spade, weeding his lemon trees assisted by General Vlasik:

'I'm showing you how to work!' He showed off his lemons and roses: 'he was a romantic about nature,' wrote Mgeladze. But his favourite flower, the mimosa, was an organic metaphor for his own secretive sensitivity for when touched, it closed like a mouth. 'The mimosa's the earliest flower that anticipates the coming of spring,' Stalin told Mgeladze. 'How Muscovites love mimosas, they stand in queues for them. Think how to grow more to make the Muscovites happy!' They often went for walks and sometimes even strolled through Sukhumi where Stalin asked schoolchildren questions like: 'What do you want to do when you're grown up?'

* * *

At the Georgian feast often laid up outside, Stalin genially opened the bottles. The 'endless meals' were agonizing for the magnates but fascinating for the younger Georgians. Maps were brought in, empires admired, characters from the past discussed, jokes told, toasts raised. Poskrebyshev toasted Stalin for destroying Bukharin and Rykov:

'You were right, Comrade Stalin – if they'd won ...' Poskrebyshev could afford a certain levity with Stalin who often appointed him '*tamada*'. 'Now you'll drink to my health!' Poskrebyshev ordered. Stalin obeyed. Molotov hailed Stalin elaborately:

'If you weren't Stalin,' Iron Arse toasted, 'the USSR would not have beaten Trotsky, won the war, gained the Bomb or conquered such an Empire for Socialism.' This pleased the host. The drinking often turned nasty when the Politburo or foreign vassals were guests but with the Georgians, it was much more cheerful and nostalgic.

When Stalin sang, Poskrebyshev and Vlasik provided the harmonies like a pair of grotesque choirboys. After dinner the guests usually stayed the night. Stalin could be unsettlingly kind: when Mikoyan's brother Artyom, designer of MiG (Mikoyan-Gurev) aircraft, suffered angina and was put to bed, he was aware of someone coming into his room and tenderly laying a blanket over him. He was amazed to see it was Stalin.

One thing united virtually all his guests: the desire to escape this strange nervy old man with his alternation of vicious, dangerous explosions, self-pitying regrets and excruciatingly boring reminiscences. Their frantic and creative efforts to find excuses to leave their all-powerful but supersensitive host, without causing offence, provide a comical theme to these long nights.

That year, Svetlana was one of the first guests, staying for three weeks in her own smaller house. She found the awkward dinners with Beria and Malenkov tedious. Escape was easier for her but none the less a struggle: once at dinner with Molotov, Mikoyan and Charkviani, she suddenly asked:

'Let me go back to Moscow!'

'Why're you in such a hurry?' replied her hurt father. 'Stay ten days. Is it boring here?'

'Father, it's urgent! Please let me go!' Stalin became angry:

'Stop going on about it! You'll stay!' Then later, Svetlana started again.

'Go if you want!' barked Stalin. 'I can't make you stay!' He could not grasp the extent to which his political murders had sterilized and poisoned his world but perhaps he sensed it when he pathetically told Svetlana: 'You aren't in a stranger's house.' Svetlana was still there when Zhdanov arrived. She managed to depart on good terms, sending 'Father' a warm letter to which he replied:

'Hello Svetka ... It's good you haven't forgotten your father. I'm well ... I'm not lonely. I'm sending you some little presents – tangerines. A kiss.'

Zhdanov came to help work out Stalin's policy for securing his hold over Eastern Europe. Molotov's tendency to negotiate with the West had ended with the rejection of the Marshall Plan. Now Zhdanov seemed to gain ascendancy in foreign as well as domestic policy, or rather he was naturally closer to his master's voice. Their relationship remained almost paternal. Stalin marked Zhdanov's speeches with schoolmasterly notes: 'Must put in Lenin quotations!' he scrawled in brown crayon on one.

Together they created Zhdanov's speech that divided Europe into 'two camps', the ideological basis for the Iron Curtain over the next forty years. To counteract the Marshall Plan and the discomfiting independence of Tito's Yugoslavia, Stalin ordered Zhdanov to create a new Communist International, the Cominform, to enforce Soviet hegemony over Eastern Europe.

Zhdanov, accompanied by his hated rival Malenkov, recently recalled to a lower post, then flew up to the Polish town of Szklarska Poreba where the ruling Communist Parties from Poland to Yugoslavia awaited Moscow's instructions. The conference took place in a secret police convalescent home, with Zhdanov and the rest of the delegates staying upstairs. Apart from giving his 'two camps' speech on 25 September, Zhdanov behaved with all the blustering arrogance of an imperial viceroy. When Berman, one of the Polish leaders (the one who had waltzed with Molotov), expressed doubts about his Cominform, Zhdanov arrogantly replied,

'Don't start throwing your weight around. In Moscow we know better how to apply Marxism-Leninism.' At every stage, 'Comrade Filipov', or Stalin on holiday, instructed 'Sergeev and Borisov' (Zhdanov and Malenkov) on how to proceed. This was the high point of Zhdanov's career and his greatest lasting achievement, if it can be called that. It was appropriate that the meeting was held in a sanatorium because, by the end of it, 'the Pianist' was collapsing from alcoholism and heart failure. He may have triumphed over Molotov, Malenkov and Beria but he could not control his own strength. Zhdanov, only fifty-one but exhausted, knew 'he wasn't strong enough to bear the responsibility of succeeding Stalin. He never wanted power,' asserts his son. He flew back to the seaside to recover near Stalin, where the two called on each other, but then he suffered a heart attack.*

Zhdanov's illness created a vacuum that was keenly filled by Malenkov and Beria who became so close, they even sent their greetings to Stalin jointly that November, writing 'we derive great happiness from working under your rule ... Devoted to you, L. Beria and G. Malenkov.' Yet their friendship was always political: Beria really thought Malenkov 'spineless ... nothing but a billygoat!' None the less, Zhdanov noticed their resurgence, telling his son: 'A faction has been formed.' Resting until December, he was too weak to fight this vicious battle.

* * *

Once Molotov and Mikoyan, fresh from their recent humiliations, had also been to stay, Stalin found himself alone. He longed for the company of young people. Beria, according to his son, thought that Stalin's loneliness was an act. He wanted his associates around him 'to keep an eye on them, not from fear of solitude', but this does not explain his yearning for the companionship of unimportant youngsters. 'While everyone talks about the great man, genius in everything,' Stalin muttered to Golovanov, 'I have no one to drink a glass of tea with.' Zhdanov, on one of his visits, was accompanied by his son Yury, Stalin's ideal son-in-law. Stalin often telephoned him to give career advice:

'People say you spend lots of time on political activities,' he had once told Yury, 'but I want to tell you politics is a dirty business – we need chemists!' Yury qualified as a chemist then took a master's degree in philosophy.

Now twenty-eight, Yury and one of his aunts were driving along by the Black Sea and as they passed the road to the Gagra dacha,

---

* Zhdanov was not the only one: Andreyev, just fifty-two, fell ill in 1947 though he remained an active Politburo member until 1950; he lost his position in 1952.

they were surprised to see a number of guards running towards them:

'Comrade Stalin summons you, Comrade Zhdanov!' they said. Yury sent a message that he was with his aunt and the guard ran back: 'Both invited.' On the enclosed veranda, a suntanned, relaxed Stalin awaited them. After asking about his father's health, Stalin, pouring the wine, came to the point:

'Maybe you should work for the Party.'

'Comrade Stalin,' replied Yury, 'You once told me politics was a dirty business.'

'This is a different era. Times change. You'll do Party work, you'll travel and see the regions. You'll see how we make decisions and how they disagree with them immediately.'

'I'd better consult my mother and father,' said Yury Zhdanov who knew that no magnate wanted their children in the snakepit of Stalin's court. But Zhdanov agreed: Stalin appointed Yury to the important job – for such a young man – of Head of the CC Science Department. Unwittingly, Yury was placing his head inside the jaws of the crocodile at the very moment that the battle for succession was about to burst into blood-letting. 'I didn't fear him,' says Yury now, 'I knew him since childhood. Only later I realized that I *should* have been afraid.'

Yury did not have to stay, but another young man was less fortunate and endured nine days before he managed to escape. That October, Oleg Troyanovsky, a Foreign Ministry interpreter of twenty-six, was sent down to Gagra to interpret for Stalin at a meeting with some British Labour MPs.*

Handsome, brown-haired and erudite, Troyanovsky was another child of the élite. When Stalin first met young Troyanovsky, he liked him so much that he put on the Red Indian accent from *Last of the Mohicans*: 'Send my regards to pale-faced brother from leader of redskins!' When Stalin had seen off the British MPs, he said to Troyanovsky: 'Why don't you stay on and

* Stalin had stayed with Troyanovsky's father Alexander in Vienna in 1913, appointed him first Soviet Ambassador to Washington and protected him during the Terror. Stalin liked but never quite trusted Troyanovsky who was an ex-Menshevik. Once he crept up on him, put his hands over his eyes and whispered, 'Friend or foe?' In 1948, Troyanovsky's career as Stalin's interpreter came to an abrupt end when Molotov suddenly moved him in order to protect him. His father, the old diplomat, had been playing bridge and criticizing the leadership, with the indomitable Litvinov. It was a dangerous time. Later Troyanovsky interpreted for Khrushchev. This account is based on an interview with him.

live with us for a while. We'll get you drunk and then we'll see what sort of person you are.'

This was so unexpected and alarming that Troyanovsky stammered that surely it would be 'a burden to Comrade Stalin', but he insisted. Troyanovsky was understandably uneasy but Stalin summoned him to play billiards a few times, a game he played extremely well without even seeming to aim at the ball. They mainly met at dinner where they were sometimes joined by Poskrebyshev or Politburo members. The host personally served Troyanovsky. The conversation was 'never awkward, no silences', even though Troyanovsky was shrewd enough to ask no questions and proffer few opinions. Stalin did the talking, reminiscing about his stay with Oleg's father in Vienna in 1913, his 'first time with a Western-style family'. Otherwise Stalin just told him to rest but 'it was hardly possible to describe anything to do with Stalin as restful'.

Troyanovsky, like every other guest, fretted about how to escape without offending Stalin. After nine nights, he plucked up the courage to ask Stalin if he could leave. Stalin seemed surprised until Troyanovsky explained that he was returning to Moscow to become a Party member.

'An important event,' said Stalin. 'Good luck.' Presenting Troyanovsky with a basket of fruit, there was an awkward but telling moment as he saw him off: 'It's probably boring for you here. I've got used to loneliness. I got accustomed to it in prison.'

On his return to Moscow on 21 November, this genial old host ordered Abakumov to murder the Yiddish actor, Mikhoels. Nine days later, he supported the UN vote for the creation of Israel.

52

Two Strange Deaths: the Yiddish Actor and the Heir Apparent

The Stalin Prize Committee sent Mikhoels to Minsk to judge plays at Belorussian theatres. When this was reported to Stalin, he verbally ordered Abakumov to murder Mikhoels on the spot, specifying some of the details with Malenkov present. Abakumov gave the task to his deputy, and the Minsk MGB boss, invoking the *Instantsiya*. Abakumov's plan was to 'invite Mikhoels to visit some acquaintances in the evening, provide him with a car ... bring him to the vicinity of [Belorussian MGB boss] Tsanava's dacha and kill him there; then take the corpse to a deserted street, place it across the road leading to the hotel and have a truck run over it ...' The plan has all the hallmarks of the clumsy, gangsterish games that Stalin used to devise with Beria to liquidate those too celebrated to be arrested. Tsanava passed the orders down the line, always dropping the magic word – *Instantsiya*.

On 12 January, Mikhoels and his friend Vladimir Golubov-Potapov, a theatre critic and MGB agent, spent the day meeting actors, then dined at their hotel. At 8 p.m. they left the hotel to meet Golubov's 'friend'. Presumably the MGB car took them to Tsanava's dacha where Mikhoels was probably injected with poison to stun him, another job for the MGB's doctors. Perhaps he fought back. This exuberant artist, the last connection with the intellectual brilliance of Mandelstam and Babel, loved life and must have struggled. He was smashed on the temple with a blunt object, and shot too. Golubov, the duplicitous bystander, was killed as well. The bodies were then driven into town, run over with a truck and left in the snow.*

---

* The man in charge of the operation was Lavrenti Tsanava, black-haired with a dapper moustache, one of the Georgians Beria had brought to Moscow. Like so many in the Cheka, he was a criminal. Those who knew him well could only say that 'he was a beast'. His real name was Djandjugava and he had been convicted of murder until Beria rescued him and he became boss of the Belorussian MGB. He did not prove a particularly loyal protégé since he was now close to Abakumov. After Stalin's death he was arrested and executed.

Stalin was informed of the killings probably before the bodies had been dumped in the street, and just as Svetlana was arriving to visit him at Kuntsevo. Stalin was on the phone, most likely to Tsanava: 'Someone was reporting to him and he listened. Then to sum up, he said, "Well, a car accident." I remember his intonation very well – it was not a question, it was a confirmation ... He was not asking, he was proposing it, the car accident.' When he had put down the phone, he kissed Svetlana and said, 'Mikhoels was killed in a car accident.'

At seven the next morning, two bodies were found sticking out of the snow. Mikhoels's body was returned to Moscow and delivered to the laboratory of Professor Boris Zbarsky, the (Jewish) biochemist in charge of Lenin's mummy: noticing the damaged head and the bullethole, he was ordered to prepare the victim of the 'road accident' for the lying-in-state in the Jewish Theatre, where no one was fooled by his 'broken face' and 'mutilated features made up with greasepaint'.

Mikhoels was an artistic hero to some of Stalin's courtiers as well as to the public: on the 15th, the night before the funeral, Polina Molotova, who had rediscovered her Jewish roots during the war, quietly attended the lying-in-state and muttered, 'It was murder.' After the funeral, Yulia Kaganovich, the niece of Lazar and daughter of Mikhail who had committed suicide in 1941, arrived at the Mikhoels' and led his daughter into the bathroom. Here, with taps running, she whispered: 'Uncle sends his regards,' adding an order from the anxious Kaganovich: 'He told me to tell you – never ask anyone about anything.' The Jewish Theatre was renamed for Mikhoels; a murder investigation was opened. The Jewish Committee continued, and Stalin would be the first to recognize Israel.

However, out of the public eye, Mikhoels's murderer, Tsanava, received the Order of Lenin 'for exemplary execution of a special assignment from the Government'. Zhenya Alliluyeva was sentenced to ten years, her daughter Kira to five years, 'for supplying information about the personal life of [Stalin's] family to the American Embassy'. Anna Redens also got five years. They were placed in solitary confinement.*

The MGB now started to build a case against Deputy Foreign

---

* The 'Aunties' were in Vladimir prison. Zhenya Alliluyeva wanted to commit suicide and swallowed stones but survived. Like so many others, she was kept alive by the kindness of strangers. A Polish prisoner in the neighbouring cell knocked in prison code 'Live for your children.'

Minister Solomon Lozovsky and other prominent Jews: Polina Molotova was quietly sacked from her job. Stalin openly joked about his own anti-Semitism, teasing Djilas about Jews in the Yugoslav leadership:

'You too are an anti-Semite, you too ...'

* * *

Zhdanov, despite his 'red puffy face and lively movements', recovered his heartiness and power: 'I might die at any moment and I might live a very long time,' he told Djilas. At dinners, he tried to resist alcohol and ate nothing but a plate of clear soup.

For a sick man, the next few months could hardly have been less restful: Stalin now encountered his first real opposition for almost twenty years. Marshal Tito was no vassal. His Partisans had fought valiantly against the Germans and not depended on the Red Army to liberate them. Now, the Yugoslavs bitterly denounced Zhdanov's 'dictatorial behaviour' at the Cominform conference. When Stalin read this, he could not believe the impertinence of it, scrawling in brown crayon: 'Very queer information!'

Stalin had agreed to leave Greece to the West, reserving the right to choose when and where to confront America. Tito disregarded his orders and started to supply the Greek Communists. Stalin was determined to test American resolve in Berlin, not in some obscure Balkan village. The final straw was the planned Balkan federation agreed between the Bulgarian leader, Dmitrov, and Tito, without Stalin's permission. As the row heated up, Tito sent his comrades, Milovan Djilas and Edvard Kardelj, to negotiate with Stalin. At grisly Kuntsevo dinners, Stalin, Zhdanov and Beria tried to overawe Yugoslavia with Soviet supremacy. Djilas was fascinated but defiant. So, on 28 January, *Pravda* denounced Dmitrov's plan.

On 10 February, Stalin summoned the Yugoslavs and Bulgarians to the Little Corner to humiliate them, as if they were impudent Politburo members. Instead of opposing the Bulgarian–Yugoslav plan, he proposed a collage of little federations, linking countries that already hated each other. Stalin was 'glowering and doodling ceaselessly'.

'When I say no it means no!' said Stalin who instead proposed that Yugoslavia swallow Albania, making gobbling gestures with his fingers and gulping sounds with his lips. The scowling threesome – Stalin, Zhdanov and Molotov – only hardened Tito's resistance.

Stalin and Molotov despatched an eight-page letter implying that Tito was guilty of that heinous sin – Trotskyism. 'We think

Trotsky's political career is sufficiently instructive,' they wrote ominously but the Yugoslavs did not care. On 12 April, they rejected the letter. Stalin decided to crush Tito.

'I'll shake my little finger,' he ranted at Khrushchev, 'and there'll be no more Tito!' But Tito proved a tougher nut than Trotsky or Bukharin.

* * *

At Kuntsevo dinners, Zhdanov, the heir apparent but increasingly a frail alcoholic with a sick heart, 'sometimes lost the willpower to control himself' and reached for the drink. Then Stalin 'shouted at him to stop drinking', one of the rare moments he tried to restrain the boozing, a sign of Zhdanov's special place. But at other times, the pasty-faced, sanctimonious Zhdanov, sitting prissily and soberly while Stalin swore at Tito and smirked at scatological jokes, outraged him:

'Look at him sitting there like Christ as if nothing was any concern to him! There – looking at me now as if he were Christ!' Zhdanov blanched, his face covered with beads of perspiration. Svetlana, who was present, gave him a glass of water but this was only a routine eruption of Stalin's blazing temper that usually passed as suddenly as it struck. None the less, Stalin was increasingly irritated by Zhdanov's over-familiar smugness and independence of mind. Beria and Malenkov were aided in their vengefulness from a surprising quarter.

Chosen by Stalin, growing closer to Svetlana and, at twenty-eight, Head of the CC Science Department, Yury Zhdanov was cock of the walk. He took his science as seriously as his father took culture. Yury resented the absurd dominance of Trofim Lysenko in the field of genetics: the scientific charlatan had used Stalin's backing during the Terror to purge the genetics establishment of genuine scientists.

'Yury, don't tangle with Lysenko,' Zhdanov jokingly warned his son. 'He'll cross you with a cucumber.' But Zhdanov may have been too ill to stop him.

On 10 April, 1948, young Zhdanov attacked both Lysenko's so-called creative Darwinism, and his suppression of scientists and their ideas, in a speech at the Moscow Polytechnic. Lysenko listened to the lecture through a microphone in a nearby office. This experienced courtier appealed to Stalin, attacking Yury's impudence in speaking for the Party 'in his own name'. Lysenko copied the letter to Malenkov who supported him. Wheels were turning. Malenkov sent the lecture to Stalin who now believed himself the 'Coryphaeus' – the 'choirmaster' – of science. He read Yury's lecture with mounting disdain:

'Ha-ha-ha!' he scribbled angrily. 'Nonsense!' and 'Get out!' The impertinent puppy had contradicted Stalin's views on heredity and evolution, and usurped his personal authority. When Yury claimed that these were his own personal views, Stalin exclaimed: 'Aha!' and forwarded his comments to a delighted Malenkov.

Frustrated by Yugoslav resistance, tension in Berlin, and Zionist intrigues, Stalin had decided this was the moment to challenge America in Europe. He demanded Party discipline; Yury had flouted it. In an Olympian flash that changed Soviet science and politics, Coryphaeus intervened. On 10 June, Stalin held one of his set-piece humiliation sessions in the Little Corner. Andrei Zhdanov humbly took notes at the front, his son lurked at the back while Stalin, pacing 'pipe in hand and puffing frequently', muttered:

'How did anyone dare insult Comrade Lysenko?' Zhdanov miserably noted Stalin's words in his exercise book: 'Report is wrong. ZHDANOV HAS BEEN MISTAKEN.' Then Stalin stopped and asked: 'Who authorized it?'

His gaze chilled the room. 'There was the silence of the grave,' wrote Shepilov, a Zhdanov protégé. Everyone looked down. Shepilov stood up to admit:

'The decision was mine, Comrade Stalin.'

Stalin walked up to him and stared into his eyes. 'I can honestly say,' recalled Shepilov, ' I never saw such a look ... His eyes seemed to possess some incredible force. Their yellow pupils transfixed me like ... a cobra coiled to strike.' Stalin 'did not blink for what seemed eternity'. Then he demanded:

'Why did you do it?' Shepilov tried to explain but Stalin interrupted: 'We'll set up a committee to clarify all the facts. The guilty must be punished. Not Yury Zhdanov, he's still young,' but he pointed his pipe at 'the Pianist': 'It's necessary to punish the fathers.' Then, in a terrible silence, slowly pacing, he listed the members of the committee – Malenkov ... but no Zhdanovs! Stalin deliberatedly waited until the end. Did this mean the *Zhdanovshchina* was over? 'After long thought, Stalin uttered, "And Zhdanov," leaving a long silence before adding, "Senior." '

Yury wrote an apology to Stalin, citing his own 'inexperience':

'I unquestionably committed a whole series of grave mistakes.' Malenkov masterfully manipulated the unintentional impudence of Zhdanov junior to pull himself back into the centre: the apology was published in *Pravda*. But Stalin himself had engineered Zhdanov's eclipse. The humiliation worsened Zhdanov's health: he must have wished he had emulated the Berias and Malenkovs who kept their children far from politics.

On 19 June, an exhausted Zhdanov, accompanied by his rival Malenkov, arrived at the second Cominform meeting in Bucharest to preside over the expulsion of Yugoslavia from the fold. 'We possess information,' Zhdanov declared absurdly, 'that Tito is an Imperialist spy.' The Yugoslavs were excommunicated.

On 24 June, Stalin imposed the Berlin Blockade, challenging the Western Allies and hoping to force them out by closing land supplies to their zone deep in Soviet East Germany. Both these challenges could only accelerate the vicious campaign against Jews in Moscow and the venomous fight for Stalin's succession. It is usually claimed that Zhdanov had supported the Yugoslavs and therefore was blamed for the rift. Zhdanov and Voznesensky had indeed known the Yugoslavs well since 1945 but they not only supported Stalin's stance but accelerated it by bringing Tito's antics to his notice.

The Yugoslav schism was the unnecessary result of Stalin's own obstinacy. While the country worshipped Stalin the God, familiarity bred contempt. By 1948, Djilas believed he was 'showing conspicuous signs of senility', comparing everything to distant memories of his childhood or Siberian exiles: 'Yes I remember the same things ...' then 'laughing at inanities and shallow jokes'. His own men observed his intellectual decline and dangerous unpredictability: 'old and addled, we started to lose respect for him,' said Khrushchev. Beria too had gone through the same 'evolution' – starting with zealous worship and ending with disillusion. But most of the magnates, particularly Molotov, Mikoyan, Kaganovich and Khrushchev, remained fanatical believers in Marxism-Leninism, while virtually all of them, including Malenkov who saw himself as a civil servant *chinovnik*, believed Stalin was still on the side of history, for all his faults.

In June, Zhdanov, back from Bucharest, suffered another cardiac crisis and a minor stroke, resulting in breathing difficulties and paralysis of the right side. 'I've been told to have medical care and rest,' he told a protégé. 'I don't think I'll be away for long.'

On 1 July, Stalin replaced Zhdanov with his nemesis, Malenkov, as Second Secretary. He was a useful scapegoat but, in Stalin's orbit, there was no need to destroy Zhdanov to promote Malenkov: it suited Stalin to run them in parallel. Zhdanov fainted on his way back from Kuntsevo: now, desperately ill, he could no longer perform his duties. Yury explains that his father 'wasn't dismissed – he simply fell ill and couldn't defend his interests', which is confirmed by the doctors: 'Comrade Zhdanov needs two months' rest, one in bed,' Professor Yegorov told Stalin in a Top Secret report on which Stalin wrote: 'Where vacation? Where treatment?'

Stalin, recalls Yury, 'became worried. Father's illness caused a change in the balance of power.' Mikoyan confirmed this. Indeed Zhdanov's allies, Voznesensky and Kuznetsov, remained ascendant. Yury kept his job.

Stalin sent his own doctors to supervise Zhdanov who was moved to a sanatorium at Valdai, near Novgorod. None the less, Zhdanov felt power slipping through his sclerotic fingers: when, on 23 July, Shepilov called to update him on Malenkov's return, Zhdanov shouted into the phone. That night, he had a heart attack. Stalin sent his deputy Voznesensky and his own physician Vinogradov to visit the patient.

Zhdanov's obvious symptoms of arteriosclerosis and heart failure were misdiagnosed. Instead of daily cardiograms and total rest, he was prescribed exercise and harmful massages. On 29 August, he had another severe attack. Once again Stalin sent Vinogradov and ordered Voznesensky and Kuznetsov to check the treatment. Before the politicians arrived, a row broke out over the patient. Dr Lydia Timashuk, the cardiographer, diagnosed a 'myocardial infarction' (a heart attack), and she was almost certainly right, but the distinguished professors made her rewrite her report to specify a much vaguer 'dysfunction due to arteriosclerosis and hypertension' in a typical piece of bureaucratic infighting. The doctors pooh-poohed her grave diagnosis and prescribed walking in the park. Hence, Zhdanov suffered another heart attack.

Timashuk denounced her superiors and had Zhdanov's chief bodyguard deliver the letter to General Vlasik to give personally to Stalin. When nothing happened, Timashuk, an MGB agent, wrote to the secret police. Abakumov forwarded the letter to Stalin that same day. Stalin signed it, wrote 'Into the archive', but did nothing. But he was 'very anxious and sent back Voznesensky to check on Father', says Yury who was already there.

On the 31st, Stalin's fallen favourite got out of bed to visit the lavatory and died of a massive coronary. On Poskrebyshev's orders, the post-mortem was carried out in an ill-lit, shoddy bathroom in Kuznetsov's presence. The professors were terrified that their misdiagnosis and cover-up would be exposed so they sacked and denounced Timashuk who then wrote more damning letters to Stalin and Kuznetsov, MGB *curator*. But this time, Vlasik did not deliver the letter and Kuznetsov ignored his.

Timashuk became the villainess of the Doctors' Plot because her letters were later used by Stalin but this was ironic since she was medically correct. Zhdanov may have been mistreated but the rumours of murder seem unlikely. The Kremlevka was meant to be the finest Soviet hospital but was so ruled by fear of mistakes, scientific backwardness and political competition that incompetent decisions were made by committees of frightened doctors. Famous patients, from Mekhlis to Koniev, were routinely mistreated. Even in democracies, doctors try to cover up silly mistakes. If Stalin had really wanted to murder Zhdanov, it would have not have taken five heart attacks over years but a quick injection. Zhdanov's widow and son were convinced he was not killed: 'Everything was simpler,' Yury recalls. 'We knew his doctors well. Father was very ill. His heart was worn out.'

Yet why did the manically paranoid Stalin ignore the denunciation? Zhdanov's illness was obviously serious and Stalin may well have been content to leave treatment to the top Kremlin doctors: besides he was irritated with Zhdanov. But at a deeper level, these medical squabbles were an opportunity for Stalin. He had used medical murder himself and forced doctors in the thirties to confess to killing Kuibyshev and Gorky. This meticulous opportunist and patient conspirator, older but still a genius for creating complex machinations, would exploit Zhdanov's death when he was ready to create the Terror he was convinced was necessary. A year later, his old comrade Dmitrov, the Bulgarian leader, died while being treated by the same doctor. Walking in the Sochi garden with his Health Minister, Stalin stopped admiring his roses and mused, 'Isn't it strange? One doctor treated them and they both died.' He was already considering the Doctor's Plot but it would take him three years to return to Timashuk's letters.

Stalin helped bear Zhdanov's open coffin at the funeral,

showing kindness to the family. At dinner afterwards, Stalin
became drunk.*

It was said that the Aragvi restaurant was full of Beria's Georgians
that night, toasting Zhdanov's death.

* * *

On 8 September, Stalin, delayed in Moscow by the Berlin crisis
and Zhdanov's funeral, started a three-month holiday, moving
restlessly from Sukhumi to the Livadia, where he entertained the
Czech President Gottwald. At Museri, the old dacha built by
Lakoba, he was visited by Molotov and Mikoyan. At dinner,
Poskrebyshev rose and denounced Mikoyan:

'Comrade Stalin, while you're here resting in the south, Molotov
and Mikoyan have prepared a plot against you in Moscow.'

Mikoyan leapt up, black eyes flashing: 'You bastard!' he yelled,
raising his fist to punch Poskrebyshev.

Stalin caught his hand: 'Why do you shout like that?' he soothed
Mikoyan. 'You're my guest!' Molotov sat 'pale as paper like a statue'.
Mikoyan protested his innocence. 'If so, don't pay any attention to
him,' Stalin added, having inspired Poskrebyshev in the first place.

Stalin declared that these veterans were too old to succeed him.
Mikoyan, just fifty-two, much younger than Stalin, thought this
silly but said nothing. The successor, said Stalin, had to be a
Russian, not a Caucasian. Molotov remained 'the obvious person'
but Stalin was disenchanted with him. Then, in a lethal blessing,
Stalin pointed at the benign, long face of Zhdanov's protégé,
Kuznetsov: 'here's the man' he wanted to succeed him as General
Secretary. Voznesensky would succeed as Premier. Mikoyan sensed
'this was a very bad service to Kuznetsov, considering those who
secretly dreamed of such a role'.

Stalin himself was bound to become suspicious of any anointed
successor, especially given the failure of his Berlin Blockade,
which had to be called off when the West energetically supplied
their zones with a remarkable airlift. This only fuelled Stalin's
seething paranoia, already stimulated by his own illness, Tito's
defiance and Zionist stirrings among Russian Jews. Beria and
Malenkov sharpened their knives.

---

* Perhaps Stalin was affected by Zhdanov's death. He named the dead man's birth-
place, Mariopól on the Black Sea, Zhdanov. According to the bodyguards, after
Zhdanov's funeral, Molotov was worried about Stalin's health and asked them not to
let him garden. When Stalin discovered this interference in his private life, he
mistrusted Molotov all the more.

Part Ten
The Lame Tiger, 1949–1953

53

Mrs Molotov's Arrest

While Stalin anointed successors in the south, the indomitable Envoy Extraordinary of the new State of Israel, Golda Myerson (known to history as Meir) arrived in Moscow on 3 September to tumultuous excitement among Soviet Jews. The Holocaust and the foundation of Israel had touched even the toughest Old Bolshevik internationalists like Polina Molotova. Voroshilov's wife (née Golda Gorbman) amazed her family by saying, 'Now we have our Motherland too.'

On Jewish New Year, Meir attended the Moscow Great Synagogue: jubilant Jews waited outside because the synagogue was full yet it was hardly a riot. Even Polina Molotova, now fifty-three, made an appearance. At Molotov's 7 November diplomatic reception, Polina met Golda Meir, two formidable, intelligent women from almost identical backgrounds.

Polina spoke Yiddish, the language of her childhood, which she always used when she met Mitteleuropeans, though she tactfully called it 'the Austrian language'. Meir asked how she knew Yiddish. '*Ikh bin a yidishe tokhhter,*' replied Polina. 'I'm a daughter of the Jewish people.' As they parted, Polina said, 'If things go well for you, then things will be good for Jews all over the world.' Perhaps she did not know how Stalin resented her pushy intelligence, snobbish elegance, Jewish background, American businessman brother and, as he told Svetlana, 'bad influence on Nadya'. Her sacking in May was a warning but she did not know that Stalin had considered murdering her in 1939.*

* Some Jews were sacked. Kaganovich continued as Deputy Premier and Politburo member but his elder brother Yuli lost his job. Like Polina, Kaganovich's grandson recalls that Lazar too remembered the Yiddish of his childhood: when he met the German Communist Ernest Thalman he tried to use it. The 'second lady of the state', Andreyev's wife Dora Khazan, was sacked as Deputy Minister of Textiles and General Khrulev's Jewish wife was arrested. Mekhlis, like Kaganovich, continued as Minister of State Control and only retired in 1950 after a stroke. The Jewish Boris Vannikov continued to run the First Directorate of Sovmin in charge of the nuclear project.

The synagogue 'demonstration' and Polina's Yiddish *schtick* outraged the old man on holiday, confirming that Soviet Jews were becoming an American Fifth Column. No wonder Molotov had supported a Jewish Crimea. On 20 November, the Politburo dismantled the Jewish Committee and unleashed an anti-Semitic terror, managed by Malenkov and Abakumov. Mikhoels's colleagues were now arrested, together with some brilliant Jewish writers and scientists, from the Yiddish poet Perets Markish to the biochemist Lina Shtern. They also arrested the father of Svetlana's newly-divorced husband: 'The entire older generation's contaminated with Zionism,' Stalin lectured her, 'and now they're teaching the young people too.'

Stalin ordered the prisoners to be tortured to implicate Polina Molotova while spending the steamy evenings over dinner at Coldstream, telling Charkviani folksy tales of his childhood. He suddenly missed his old friends, particularly a priest named Peter Kapanadze with whom he had studied at the seminary. After the Revolution, the priest had become a teacher but Stalin sometimes sent him money. Now he invited Kapanadze and MGB Lieut.-Gen. Sasha Egnatashvili, the Gori family friend whom Stalin called 'the innkeeper's son', to a dinner party. Charkviani hurried back to Tiflis to gather the guests. The seven old friends were soon singing Georgian songs led by the 'host with the sweet voice'. Stalin insisted that some of them stay for a week by which time, like all his guests, they were desperate to escape. Finally one of them displayed considerable ingenuity by singing a folk song at dinner with the refrain: 'Better go than stay!'

'Oh I see,' said Stalin, 'you're bored. You must be missing your grandchildren.'

'No, Soso,' replied the guest. 'It's impossible to be bored here but we've been here almost a week, wasting your time ...' Stalin let them go, returning on 2 December to Moscow, brooding about the dangerous duplicity of Molotov. He had discovered (probably from Vyshinsky) that Molotov had travelled alone in a special railway carriage from New York to Washington when he had perhaps received instructions to undermine the USSR with a Jewish homeland. It was Poskrebyshev, Stalin's alter ego, who 'started to hint' to Molotov:

'Why did they assign you a special car?' Molotov put 'two and two together' but there was nothing he could do.

Amazingly, it was an opera that finally convinced Stalin to

move against the Molotovs. Soon after his return, Stalin saw an Armenian opera, *Almast*, that told the story of a prince whose wife betrays him. 'He saw treason could be anywhere with anyone' but especially among the wives of the great. Stalin, fortified operatically and armed with Abakumov's testimonies, confronted Molotov with Polina's guilt. 'He and I quarrelled about it,' said Molotov.

'It's time for you to divorce your wife,' said Stalin. Molotov agreed, partly because he was a Bolshevik but partly because obedience might save the woman he loved. When he told her the charges against her, she shrieked:

'And you believe them! If this is what the Party needs, we'll divorce,' she agreed. In its queer way, it was a most romantic divorce, with both sacrificing themselves to save the other. 'They discussed how to save the family,' says their grandson. Polina moved in with her sister. They waited nervously but, said Molotov, 'a black cat had crossed our path.'

* * *

Stalin ordered Malenkov and Abakumov to put together the Jewish Case. Malenkov insisted to Beria that he was not anti-Semitic: 'Lavrenti, you know I'm Macedonian. How can you suspect me of Russian chauvinism?'

Since its centrepiece was the plan for the Jewish Crimea, on 13 January 1949 Malenkov summoned Lozovsky, ex-overlord of the Jewish Committee, to Old Square for an interrogation. This was already a matter of life and death for Lozovsky – but it also had its dangers for that punctilious but murderous 'clerk' Malenkov, because his eldest daughter Volya was married to the son of a Jewish official named Shamberg whose sister was married to Lozovsky.

'You sympathized ...' with the Jewish Crimea, said Malenkov, 'and the idea was vicious!' Stalin ordered Lozovsky's arrest.

Malenkov extricated his family from its Jewish connections. Volya Malenkova divorced Shamberg. Every history repeats that Stalin ordered this divorce and that Malenkov enforced it. Volya Malenkova vigorously denies this, claiming that the marriage had not worked because Shamberg had married her for the wrong reasons – and had 'bad artistic taste'. 'My father even discouraged me saying, "Think carefully and seriously. You rushed into the marriage. Careful before rushing out of it."' But this was not how it appeared to Shamberg, who was summoned to Malenkov's office. Just as Vasily Stalin accelerated Svetlana's divorce, so Malenkov's bodyguard fixed Volya's.*

As many as 110 prisoners, most of them Jews, were suffering 'French wrestling' at the hands of the vicious Komarov in the Lubianka. 'I was merciless with them,' boasted Komarov later, 'I tore their souls apart ... The Minister himself didn't scare them as much as me ... I was especially pitiless with (and I hated the most) the Jewish nationalists.' When Abakumov questioned the distinguished scientist Lina Shtern, he shouted at her: 'You old whore ... Come clean! You're a Zionist agent!' Komarov asked Lozovsky which leaders 'had Jewish wives', adding, 'no one is untouchable'. The prisoners were also encouraged to implicate the Jewish magnates, Kaganovich and Mekhlis, but Polina Molotova was the true target. Abakumov told Stalin that she had 'contacts with persons who turned out to be Enemies of the People'; she attended synagogue once, gave advice to Mikhoels, 'attended his funeral and showed concern for this family'.

Five days later, Stalin gathered the Politburo to read out the bizarre sexual-Semitic accusations against Polina. A young man testified about having had an affair and 'group sex' with this Bolshevik matron. Molotov could hardly believe this 'terrible filth' but, as Stalin read on, he realized that 'Security had done a thorough job on her!' Even the iron-bottomed Molotov was scared: 'My knees trembled.' Kaganovich, who disliked Molotov, and as a Jew had to prove his loyalty, viciously attacked Iron-Arse, recalling how 'Molotov couldn't say anything!'

Polina was expelled from the Party for 'close relations with Jewish nationalists' despite being warned in 1939, when Molotov had abstained on a similar vote. Now, remarkably, he abstained again but sensing the gravity of the case, he buckled. 'When the Central Committee voted on the proposal to expel PS Zhemchuzhina ... I abstained which I acknowledge to be politically incorrect,' he wrote to Stalin on 20 January 1949. 'I hereby declare that after thinking the matter over, I now vote in favour ... I

* Shamberg 'was heartbroken', according to his friend Julia Khrushcheva. Both Svetlana Stalin and Volya Malenkova are adamant that they ended unhappy marriages but there can have been no greater incentive to end an unhappy Jewish marriage than the seething anti-Semitic paranoia of Stalin. Stalin did not need to say a word. The young people knew what to do. To Malenkov's meagre credit, he managed to protect the Shambergs themselves, hiding the boy's father Mikhail in the provinces. 'Volya' was a name invented by Malenkov, meaning 'Will' as in the People's Will.

acknowledge I was gravely at fault in not restraining in time a person close to me from taking false steps and from dealings with such anti-Soviet nationalists as Mikhoels ...'

On 21 January, Polina was arrested in her squirrel-fur coat. Her sisters, doctor and secretaries were arrested. One of her sisters and a brother would die in prison. Her arrest was ominous for the other leaders who secretly sympathized with her.

Polina, who was not tortured, denied everything: 'I was not at the synagogue ... It was my sister.' But she also faced more accusations of sexual debauchery: the confrontation with Ivan X reads like a bad farce:

'Polina, you called me into your office [and] proposed intimacy!'

'Ivan Alexeevich!' exclaimed Polina.

'Don't deny it!'

'I had no relationship with X,' she asserted. 'I always regarded Ivan Alexeevich X as unreliable but I never thought he was a scoundrel.' But X appealed to her mercy:

'I remind you of my children and my broken family to make you admit your guilt towards me ... You forced me into an intimate relationship.' Meanwhile Polina continued to play the *grande dame* in the netherworld. Another prisoner heard her shouting,

'Phone my husband! Tell him to send my diabetes pills! I'm an invalid! You've no right to feed me this rubbish!'

No one heard anything more of Polina, who became Object No. 12. Many believed she was dead but Beria, who played little part in the Jewish Case, knew better from his contacts. 'Polina's ALIVE!' he whispered to Molotov at Politburo meetings.

Stalin and Abakumov discussed whether to make her the leading defendant in their Jewish trial but then decided Lozovsky would be the star. Polina was sentenced to five years in exile, a mild sentence considering the fates of her co-prisoners, in Kustanai, Central Asia. She turned to drink but overcame it. 'You need three things' in prison, she told her daughters later, 'soap to keep you clean, bread to keep you fed, onions to keep you well.' Ironically, she was befriended by some deported kulaks so that the innocent peasants, whom she and her husband had been so keen to liquidate, were the kind strangers who saved her life. She never stopped loving Molotov, for during her imprisonment, she wrote:

'With these four years of separation, four eternities have flowed

over my strange and terrible life. Only the thought of you forces
me to live and the knowledge that you may still need the
remnants of my tormented heart and the whole of my huge love
for you.' Molotov never stopped loving her: touchingly, he
ordered his maids to lay a place for her at table every evening as
he ate alone, aware that 'she suffered because of me ...'

Stalin now excluded Molotov from the highest echelons,
scrawling that documents should be signed by Voznesensky, Beria
and Malenkov 'but not Comrade Molotov who doesn't participate
in the work of the Buro of the Council of Ministers'. However he
still trusted Mikoyan just enough to send that worldly Armenian
on a secret mission to size up Mao Tse-tung who was about to
complete his conquest of China.

The Chinese Civil War was in its last throes. Stalin had
miscalculated how quickly Chiang Kai-shek's regime would
collapse. Until 1948, Mao Tse-tung's success was an inconvenience to Stalin's policy of a *realpolitik* partnership with the West
but the Cold War changed his mind. He began to think of Mao as
a potential ally even though he told Beria that the Chairman was
a 'margarine Marxist'.

On 31 January 1949, in great secrecy, Mikoyan reached Mao's
headquarters in Xibaipo in Hopei province where he met Mao
and Chou En-lai and presented Stalin's gifts. One present was
typically venomous: Mikoyan had to tell Mao that an American at
his court was a spy and should be arrested. Stalin (Comrade
Filipov) kept in contact with Mikoyan (Comrade Andreev)
through Mao's Russian doctor, Terebin, who doubled as decoder.
The visit was a success even though Mikoyan admitted that he
had hoped for a rest from Stalin's nocturnal habits, only to find
that Mao kept the same hours.

On his return, Mikoyan found a shock awaiting him. Stalin
sacked Molotov and Mikoyan as Foreign and Foreign Trade
Ministers, though both remained Deputy Premiers. Then he
accused Mikoyan of breaking official secrecy about his Chinese
trip. Mikoyan had only told his son Stepan: 'Did you tell anyone
about my Chinese trip?' he asked him.

'Svetlana,' replied Stepan.

'Don't blab.' An innocent comment by Svetlana to her father
had endangered the Mikoyans. Stalin had not forgotten the arrest
of Mikoyan's children in 1943. They were still under surveillance.

'What happened to your children who were arrested?' Stalin

suddenly asked Mikoyan ominously. 'Do you think they deserve the right to study at Soviet institutions?' Mikoyan carefully did not reply – but he understood the threat, particularly after Polina's arrest. He expected the boys to be arrested, yet nothing happened. Stalin started to mutter that Voroshilov was 'an English spy' and hardly saw him* while the diminished Molotov and Mikoyan just hung on. But now Stalin's chosen successors succumbed to the brutal vendetta of Beria and Malenkov in a sudden blood bath.

* On 22 August 1946, Stalin listened to the weather forecast and was infuriated to hear that it was completely wrong. He therefore ordered Voroshilov to investigate the weather forecasters to discover if there was 'sabotage' among the weathermen. It was an absurd job that reflected Stalin's disdain for the First Marshal who reported the next day that it was unjust to blame the weather forecasters for the mistakes.

54

Murder and Marriage:
the Leningrad Case

The 'two scoundrels' played for only the highest stakes: death. But Stalin himself was always ready to scythe down the tallest poppies – those gifted Leningraders – to maintain his own paramountcy.

Stalin's heir apparent as Premier, Nikolai Voznesensky, 'thought himself the cleverest person after Stalin', recalled the Sovmin manager, Chadaev. At forty-four, the youngest Politburo member distinguished himself as a brilliant planner who enjoyed an unusually honest relationship with Stalin. However, this made him so brash that 'that he didn't bother to hide his moods' or his strident Russian nationalism. Rude to his colleagues, no one made so many enemies as Voznesensky. Now his patron Zhdanov was dead, his enemy Malenkov resurgent. Beria 'feared him' and coveted his economic powers. Voznesensky's arrogance and Stalin's touchiness made him vulnerable.

During 1948, Stalin noticed that production rose in the last quarter of the year but dipped in the first quarter. This was a normal seasonal variation but Stalin asked Voznesensky to level it out. Voznesensky, who ran Gosplan, promised he would. However, he failed to do so and, afraid of Stalin, he concealed the statistics. Somehow this *legerdemain* was leaked to Beria who discovered that hundreds of secret Gosplan documents had gone missing. One night at Kuntsevo, Beria sprung it on Stalin, who, observed Mikoyan, 'was astonished,' then 'furious'.

'Does it mean Voznesensky deceives the Politburo and tricks us like fools?' Beria then revealed the damning secret about Voznesensky that he had treasured ever since 1941: during Stalin's breakdown, Voznesensky had told Molotov,

'Vyacheslav, go forward, we'll follow you!' That betrayal clinched it. Andreyev, that relentless bureaucratic killer, was brought in to investigate. Frantic, Voznesensky called Stalin but no one would receive him. Sacked from the Politburo on 7 March 1949, he spent his days at his Granovsky flat writing an economics treatise. Once again, that dread duo, Malenkov and Abakumov, took over the Gosplan Case.

The other anointed heir was 'young handsome' Kuznetsov, who had helped Zhdanov remove Malenkov in 1946 and replaced Beria as *curator* of the MGB, thus earning their hatred. Sincere and affable, Kuznetsov was the opposite of Voznesensky: virtually everyone liked him. But decency was relative at Stalin's court: Kuznetsov had aided Zhdanov in anti-Semitic matters and forwarded Stalin a report on the sexual peccadilloes of Party officials. He worshipped Stalin, treasuring the note he had received from him during the war – yet he did not understand him. He made the mistake of examining old MGB files on Kirov's murder and the show trials. Kuznetsov's blundering into such sensitive matters aroused Stalin's suspicions.

Simultaneously, Malenkov alerted Stalin that the Leningrad Party had covered up a voting scandal and held a trade fair without Government permission. He managed to connect these sins with a vague plan mooted by Zhdanov to create a *Russian* (as opposed to a Soviet) Party alongside the Soviet one and make Leningrad the Russian capital. These trivialities may hardly sound like crimes punishable by death but they masked the fault lines in the Soviet Imperium and Stalin's dictatorship.* Besides, a Russian Party could not be led by a Georgian. Stalin championed the Russian people as the binding force of the USSR but he remained an internationalist. Voznesensky's nationalism worried the Caucasians: 'For him not only Georgians and Armenians but even Ukrainians aren't people,' Stalin told Mikoyan. Beria must have worried about his future under the Leningraders.

Malenkov had shrewdly amassed a collage of mistakes that touched all Stalin's sensitive places. 'Go there and take a look at what's going on,' Stalin ordered Malenkov and Abakumov who arrived in Leningrad with two trains carrying five hundred MGB officers and twenty investigators from the *Sled-Chast*, the department 'to Investigate Especially Important Cases'. When

---

* These dangers were perfectly demonstrated in 1991 when Boris Yeltsin used his Russian Presidency to demolish Gorbachev's USSR. The moving of the capital back to Leningrad, city of Zinoviev and Kirov, had been a deadly issue in Russian politics ever since Peter the Great. Men died for it in the eighteenth century and they would die for it in 1949. Stalin was also suspicious of the popular heroism of Kuznetsov and the city of Leningrad itself during WW2. It represented an alternative totem of military patriotism to himself and Moscow.

'Stalin orders him to kill one', Beria said, 'Malenkov kills 1,000!' Malenkov attacked the local bosses, stringing together disparate strands into one lethal conspiracy. The arrests began, but Voznesensky and Kuznetsov lingered at their flats in the pink Granovsky block, convinced that Stalin would forgive them: 1937 seemed a long time ago. Even Mikoyan thought blood-letting was a thing of the past.

* * *

He had reason to hope so because his youngest son Sergo, now eighteen, was engaged to Kuznetsov's 'charming, beautiful' daughter Alla. When her father fell, Alla gave Sergo the chance to avoid marrying an outcast:

'Does it change your intentions?' But Sergo loved Alla and his parents had come to adore her 'like our own daughter'. Mikoyan supported the marriage.

'And you allow this marriage? Have you gone crazy?' the pusillanimous Kaganovich whispered to Mikoyan. 'Don't you understand that Kuznetsov's doomed? Stop the marriage.' Mikoyan was adamant. On 15 February, 1949, Kuznetsov was sacked as Party Secretary and accused of 'non-Bolshevik deviation' and 'anti-State' separatism. Three days later, the couple got married. Kuznetsov was cheerfully oblivious, 'a courageous man,' thought Mikoyan, 'with no idea of Stalin's customs.' Mikoyan gave the couple a party at Zubalovo but Kuznetsov, finally realizing his plight, telephoned Mikoyan to say he could not come because he had an 'upset stomach'. Mikoyan would not hear of it:

'We've enough lavatories in the house! Come!'

'I've no car,' answered Kuznetsov. 'You do better without me.'

'It's indecent for a father to miss his daughter's wedding,' retorted Mikoyan who sent his limousine.* At the party, Kuznetsov could not relax. He felt he was endangering his daughter.

'I feel unwell,' he said, 'so let's drink to our children!' Then he left.

* * *

---

* Meanwhile just across the landing, in another apartment at Granovsky, a similar discussion in this tiny world was going on: Rada Khrushcheva, whose father was still in Kiev, was staying with her father's friends the Malenkovs. She wanted to go to the wedding, but Malenkov, who knew how doomed Kuznetsov was, refused to give her the limousine to take her there. 'I won't give you the car – you're not studying well.' But Rada went under her own steam.

That dangerous spring, poor Kuznetsov attended another Politburo marriage that involved the beleagured Zhdanov faction. 'Stalin had always wanted me to marry Svetlana,' recalls Yury Zhdanov, still at the Central Committee. 'We were childhood friends so it wasn't daunting.' But marrying a dictator's daughter was not so straightforward: Yury was not sure to whom he should propose, the dictator or the daughter. He went to Stalin, who tried to dissuade him:

'You don't know her character. She'll show you the door in no time.' But Yury persisted. 'Stalin didn't give any lectures but told me that he trusted me to look after Svetlana,' says Yury.

Stalin now played matchmaker, according to Sergo Beria: 'I like that man,' Stalin told Svetlana. 'He has a future and he loves you. Marry him.'

'He made his declaration of love to you?' she retorted. 'He's never looked at me.'

'Talk to him and you'll see,' said Stalin.

Svetlana still loved Sergo Beria and told him: 'You didn't want me? Right, I'll marry Yury Zhdanov.'

However, she became fond of 'my pious Yurochka' and they agreed to marry. But 'my second marriage was the choice of my father', explained Svetlana, 'and I was tired of struggling so went through with it.'

The Generalissimo did not attend the wedding party at the Zhdanovs' dacha seven miles beyond Zubalovo along the Uspenskoye Road. The guests included another Politburo couple: Natasha, the daughter of Andreyev and Dora Khazan, was there with her husband, Vladimir Kuibyshev, the son of the late magnate. 'There were also schoolmates ... from comparatively ordinary families too,' remembers Stepan Mikoyan who was also a guest. Then there was dancing and a feast: Yury, like his father, played the piano. It was natural that Kuznetsov was there because he had been Zhdanov's closest ally but everyone knew he was under a cloud.

Yury and Svetlana, along with her son Joseph Morozov, now aged four, lived with Zhdanov's widow in the Kremlin. 'I never saw my own father,' Joseph recalled. 'I called Yury "daddy". Yury loved me!'

A few days later, they were visiting Zubalovo when Vlasik called: Stalin was on his way. 'What do you want to move to the Zhdanovs' for?' he asked her. 'You'll be eaten alive by the women there. There are too many women in that house.' He wanted the young couple to move into Kuntsevo, adding a second floor but in his maladroit way he could not ask directly and probably did not want to be bothered.

Svetlana remained with the prissy widows of Zhdanov and Shcherbakov: soon she loathed her mother-in-law Zinaida who combined 'Party bigotry' with 'bourgeois complacency'. Her marriage was not loving: 'the lesson I learned was never to go into marriage as a deal.' Sexually it was, in her words, 'not a great success'. She never forgave Zinaida Zhdanova for telling her that her mother had been 'mad'. However they had a daughter, Katya, though Svetlana was so ill during the birth that she wrote to her father saying she felt abandoned and was delighted to receive his brusque reply.*

Besides, the wedding was not well timed for the Zhdanovs. Kuznetsov and Voznesensky were on the edge of the precipice. Yury sensed the Leningrad Affair 'was undoubtedly aimed at my father' but 'I wasn't afraid then. I discovered later I should have been destroyed ...' He was right: the prisoners were later tortured to implicate Zhdanov.

* * *

Stalin mulled over Kuznetsov's fate. Poskrebyshev invited the Leningrader to dinner at Kuntsevo but Stalin refused to shake his hand: 'I didn't summon you.' Kuznetsov 'seemed to shrink'. Stalin expected a letter of self-criticism from Kuznetsov but the naïve Leningrader did not send one. 'It means he's guilty,' Stalin muttered to Mikoyan.

Yet Stalin had doubts. 'Isn't it a waste not letting Vosnesensky work while we're deciding what to do with him?' he asked Malenkov and Beria who said nothing. Then Stalin remembered that Air Marshal Novikov and Shakhurin were still in jail.

'Don't you think it's time to release them?' But again the duo said nothing, whispering in the bathroom that if they released

---

*'Dear Svetochka,' Stalin wrote to Svetlana in hospital on May 1950. 'I got your letter. I'm glad you got off so lightly. Kidney trouble is a serious business. To say nothing of having a child. Where did you ever get the idea I'd abandoned you? It's the sort of thing people dream up. I advise you not to believe your dreams. Take care of yourself. Take care of your daughter too. The State needs people even those born prematurely. Be patient a little longer – we'll see each other soon. I kiss you my Svetochka. Your "little papa".' He did not devote all his time to the Leningrad Case. During these days, he also supervised the creation of the new Soviet Encyclopaedia, deciding every detail from its quality of paper to its contents. When the editor asked if he should include 'negative persons' such as Trotsky, he joked, 'We'll include Napoleon, but he was a big scoundrel!'

Shakhurin and Novikov, 'it might spread to the others' – the Leningraders. While he considered these matters of life and death, Stalin drove off to his dacha at Semyonovskoe, passing on the way a queue of bedraggled citizens waiting in the rain at a bus stop. Stalin stopped the car and ordered his bodyguards to offer the people a lift but they were afraid.

'You don't know how to talk to people,' growled Stalin, climbing out and ushering them into the limousine. He told them about the death of his son Yakov and a little girl told him of the death of her father. Afterwards Stalin sent her a school uniform and a satchel. Three weeks later, he ordered Abakumov to arrest, torture and destroy the Leningraders who had only recently been his anointed successors.

On 13 August, Kuznetsov was summoned to Malenkov's office. 'I'll be back,' he told his wife and son Valery. 'Don't start supper without me.' The boy watched him head down Granovsky towards the Kremlin: 'He turned and waved at me. It was the last time I ever saw him,' says Valery. He was arrested by Malenkov's bodyguard.

Yet Stalin hesitated about Voznesensky, whose arrest would leave him in the hands of Malenkov and Beria. Stalin still invited him to Kuntsevo for the usual dinners and talked of appointing him to the State Bank. On 17 August, Voznesensky wrote pathetically to Stalin, begging for work: 'It's hard to be apart from one's comrades ... I understand the lesson of Partymindedness ... I ask you to show me trust,' signing it, 'Devoted to you.' Stalin sent the letter to Malenkov. The duo kept up the pressure. The ailing but drear Andreyev exposed all manner of 'disorders in this organization': 526 documents had gone missing from Gosplan. This invented case was one of Andreyev's last achievements. Voznesensky admitted he had not prosecuted the culprits because there were 'no facts ... Now I understand ... I was guilty.' Khrushchev later accused Malenkov of 'whispering to Stalin' to make sure Voznesensky was exterminated. 'What!' Malenkov replied. 'That I was managing Stalin? You must be joking!' Stalin was unmanageable but highly suggestible: he remained in absolute command.

Four months later, Voznesensky was arrested in this sweep of Zhdanovites, joining Kuznetsov and 214 other prisoners who were tortured in a frenzy of 'French wrestling'. Brothers, wives and children followed them into the maw of Abakumov's MGB.

Kuznetsov was thrashed so badly his eardrums were perforated. 'I was beaten until the blood came out of my ears,' one prisoner, Turko, testified after Stalin's death. 'Komarov smashed my head against the wall.' Turko implicated Kuznetsov. The torturers asked Abakumov if they should beat prisoner Zakrizhevskaya who was pregnant:

'You're defending her?' bellowed Abakumov. 'The law doesn't ban it. Get on with your business!' She was tortured and miscarried:

'Tell us everything,' the torturers told her. 'We're the vanguard of the Party!'

The fallen vanguard, Kuznetsov and Voznesensky, were held in a Special Prison on Matrosskaya Tishina Street set up by Malenkov who arrived incognito with Beria and the Politburo to interrogate the prisoners.

The sinisterly genial Bulganin, who was also under threat, was given the duty of interrogating his old friend, Voznesensky's brother, Alexander, who had been Rector of Leningrad University. When the prisoner saw him, he thought he was saved: 'He rushed to me,' Bulganin admitted later, 'and cried, "Comrade Bulganin, my dear, at last! I'm not guilty. It's great you've come! Now Comrade Stalin will learn the truth!"' Bulganin snarled back at his erstwhile friend:

'The Tambov wolf's your friend', a Russian saying that meant 'no friend of yours'. Bulganin felt he had no choice: 'What could I do?' he whined. 'I knew Beria and Malenkov sat in the corner and watched me.' Like all of Stalin's cases, the guilt was elastic and could be extended on his whim: Molotov, who was close to Voznesensky, was vaguely implicated too.

* * *

By the time Kuznetsov's daughter Alla and her new husband Sergo Mikoyan rushed back from their honeymoon, just days later, her father had already been beaten into a signed confession. Anastas Mikoyan received his daughter-in-law in his Kremlin study. 'It was very hard for me to speak to Alla,' wrote Mikoyan. 'Of course I had to tell her the official version.' Alla ran out sobbing.

'I ran to follow,' Sergo recalls, 'afraid she'd kill herself.'* Mikoyan

---

* Sergo and Alla were convinced this was 'an intrigue by Malenkov and Beria who tricked Stalin. It's amazing we believed this,' recalls Sergo. 'But we NEVER ONCE spoke about the case until after Stalin's death.' His father allowed Sergo to see Kuznetsov's son but not his wife because he knew she too would be arrested. As for the Kremlin children who lived in Granovsky Street, they noticed that suddenly their neighbours, the Voznesenskys and Kuznetsovs, had gone. 'But no one mentioned it,' said Igor Malenkov, whose father was responsible. 'I just concentrated on reading about sport.'

called back Sergo and showed him Kuznetsov's confession, which Stalin had distributed. Sergo did not believe the charges.

'Every page is signed,' said Mikoyan.

'I'm sure the case will clear up and he'll return,' replied Sergo.

'I couldn't tell him,' wrote Mikoyan, 'that Kuznetsov's fate was already predetermined by Stalin. He would never return.'

* * *

The Leningrad Case was not Beria's only success: just after Kuznetsov's arrest in late August 1949, Beria set out in a special armoured train for a secret nuclear settlement amidst the Kazakh steppes. Beria was frantic with worry because if things went wrong, 'we would', as one of his managers put it, 'all have to give an answer before the people'. Beria's family would be destroyed. Malenkov comforted him.

Beria arrived in Semipalatinsk-21 for the test of the 'article'. He moved into a tiny cabin beside Professor Kurchatov's command post. On the morning of 29 August, Beria watched as a crane lowered the uranium tamper into position on its carriage; the plutonium hemisphere was placed within it. The explosives and the initiator were in place. The 'article' was then wheeled out into the night on to a platform where it would be raised to the top of the tower. Beria and the scientists left.

At 6 p.m., they assembled in the command post ten kilometres away with its control panel and telephones to Moscow, all behind an earthen wall to deflect the shock wave. Kurchatov ordered detonation. There was a bright flash. After the shock wave had passed, they hurried outside to admire the mushroom cloud rising majestically before them.

Beria was wildly excited and kissed Kurchatov on the forehead but he kept asking,

'Did it look like the American one? We didn't screw up? Kurchatov isn't pulling our leg, is he?' He was very relieved to hear that the destruction at the site was apocalyptic. 'It would have been a great misfortune if this hadn't worked out,' he said. He hurried to the telephone to ring Stalin, to be the first to tell

Julia Khrushcheva 'used to play with Natasha, Voznesensky's daughter. Soon after her father's arrest, I brought her home to our flat. But my mother said nothing.' The etiquette of unpersonage differed from family to family: while Natasha Poskrebysheva went on playing with Natasha Voznesenskaya, Nadya Vlasik 'crossed the road whenever she saw her'. I am especially grateful to Sergo Mikoyan for sharing his account of this story.

him. But when he rang, Stalin replied crushingly that he already knew and hung up. Stalin had his own sources. Beria punched the General who had dared tell Stalin first, shouting, 'You've put a spoke in my wheel, traitor, I'll grind you to pulp.' But he was hugely proud of his 'colossal achievement'. Four years after Hiroshima, Stalin had the Bomb.

Beria had another reason to be happy: he had met a good-looking woman named Drozhdova whose husband worked in the Kremlin. He may have had an affair with her before she introduced him to her daughter, Lilya, only fourteen but already a 'blue-eyed, long-legged paragon of Russian beauty with long blonde plaits', recalls Martha Peshkova. Beria was entranced: 'his last great love.' The mother wanted all the benefits:

'Don't let him do it until you've got a flat, car, dacha,' she said to Lilya, according to Peshkova. Beria set her up in style. Nina Beria tolerated this affair but in the summer when she and Martha were in Gagra, her husband entertained Lilya at the dacha. 'The whole of Moscow knew,' says Martha. Beria and Malenkov were riding high but it turned out that someone else would benefit most from the power vacuum left by the Leningraders.

* * *

Stalin summoned Khrushchev from Kiev. 'I couldn't help but feel anxious,' he admitted, when Kuznetsov and Voznesensky were being tortured. He called Malenkov who comforted him:

'Don't worry. I can't tell you now why you've been called but I promise you've got nothing to fear.' Khrushchev had governed the Ukraine since 1938, ruthlessly purging the kulaks before the war, crushing the Ukrainian nationalists, ordering the assassinations of Uniate bishops afterwards and, in February 1948, organizing the expulsion of 'harmful elements' from villages: almost a million were arrested on Khrushchev's initiative, a colossal crime which approached the deportation of the kulaks in brutality and scale. Small wonder that in retirement, he reflected, 'I'm up to my elbows in blood.' Apart from the short period in 1947 when Stalin sent Kaganovich to replace him in Kiev, Khrushchev, 'vital, pig-headed, jolly' but now bald and almost spherical in shape, was an enduring favourite. His plain speaking made his sycophancy sound genuine. Stalin regarded this dynamic cannonball of a man as a semi-literate peasant – 'Khrushchev's as ignorant as the Negus of Ethiopia,' he told Malenkov. Yet he did not completely underestimate his 'deep naturalness, pure masculinity, tenacious cunning, common sense and strength of character'.

'With him,' Stalin reflected, 'you need a short leash.' When Khrushchev arrived in Moscow, he hurried to Beria's house for further reassurance. There was a growing solidarity among Stalin's courtiers. Beria comforted him too.

Stalin appointed Khrushchev CC Secretary and Moscow boss but confided, 'things aren't going very well ... We've exposed a conspiracy in Leningrad. And Moscow's teeming with anti-Party elements.' He wanted Khrushchev to 'check it out'. As the Leningrad Case showed, the system encouraged Terror entrepreneurialism. The magnates could either douse a case or inflame it into a massacre: it was then up to Stalin to decide whether to protect the victims, save the evidence for later or slaughter them immediately.

'It's the work of a provocateur,' Khrushchev replied. Stalin accepted his judgement. He soon placed him in charge of Agriculture. 'Stalin treated me well.' Having destroyed the Leningrad connection, and undermined Molotov and Mikoyan, the 'two scoundrels' were perfectly placed for the succession. Khrushchev was recalled to balance their power. However, this plan did not quite work because Khrushchev became 'inseparable' from Beria and Malenkov. The Khrushchevs and the Malenkovs* lived close to one another at Granovsky while Beria's limousine seemed to be constantly parked on the street waiting for them. Sometimes he hailed the young Khrushchevs as they went to school:

'Look at you! The very image of Nikita!'

The threesome joked about Stalin's plan while betraying one another to him. After Malenkov had failed to master the impossible job of Agriculture, Andreyev took it over but was then discredited and forced to recant, marking the end of his career. Now Khrushchev was in charge but his plan for gigantic agricultural centres, 'agrotowns', rebounded on him. Stalin, Beria and Malenkov forced him to recant publicly. Molotov and Malenkov wanted him sacked but Beria, who underestimated the 'round-headed fool,' intervened to save him. Stalin protected Khrushchev, tapping his pipe on his head – 'it's hollow!' he joked.

---

* They were now the heart of Stalin's new inner 'quintet' along, with Beria and Bulganin. Kaganovich enjoyed a partial return to favour. On Sundays, those two fat bureaucrat friends, Khrushchev and Malenkov, took bracing walks up Gorky Street, surrounded by phalanxes of secret policemen.

* * *

On 5 September, Stalin began his holiday in Sochi where Beria joined him for a barbecue of *shashlyks* to celebrate the Bomb which, along with the destruction of the Leningraders, had temporarily returned him to favour. But it would not last. Stalin's distrust of the men around him was now overwhelming. He moved south to New Athos, the smallest and cosiest of his houses, where he spent most of his last holidays.

When the Supreme Soviet announced the Soviet Bomb, Stalin mused to his young confidant Mgeladze about the new world order:

'If war broke out, the use of A-bombs would depend on Trumans and Hitlers being in power. The people won't allow such people to be in power. Atomic weapons can hardly be used without spelling the end of the world.' He was so happy that he burst into song, singing 'Suliko' accompanied by Vlasik and Poskrebyshev, in a rendition that hit the notes perfectly, just like Beria's Bomb.

'Chaliapin sang it a little better,' beamed Stalin.

'Only a little bit better,' chorused his companions.

Old Stalin was thinking more and more about Nadya. Walking in the gardens with Mgeladze, Stalin lamented his disasters as a parent. First there was Yasha:

'Fate treated Yakov badly ... but he died a hero,' he said. Vasily was an alcoholic: 'He does nothing, but drinks a lot.' Then Svetlana, his feminine alter ego, 'does whatever she wants'. This most destructive of husbands was sensitive enough about Svetlana's marriages: 'Morozov was a good fellow but for Svetlana, it wasn't love ... It's just fun for her. She walked all over him ... Naturally this made the marriage unsuccessful. Then she got married again. Who knows what next? ... Svetlana can't even sew on a button, the nannies didn't teach her. If her mother had raised her, she'd be more disciplined. You understand, there was always too much pressure on me ... No time for the children, sometimes I didn't see them for months ... The kids didn't get lucky. Ekaterina!' He fondly mentioned his first wife Kato, then 'Oh Nadya, Nadya!' Mgeladze had never seen Stalin so sad. 'Comrade Wolf, I ask you not to say a word about what you've heard.'

55

Mao, Stalin's Birthday
and the Korean War

On 7 December 1949, Stalin arrived back in Moscow in time for two momentous events: the arrival of the new Chinese leader, Chairman Mao Tse-tung, and the celebration of his seventieth birthday. At noon on 16 December, Mao, who had taken Peking in January, arrived at Yaroslavsky Station where he was met by Molotov and Bulganin in his Marshal's uniform.* The visit started as awkwardly as it ended. Mao invited the Russians to a Chinese meal on the train but Molotov refused. Mao sulked, the beginning of a sulk as monumental in its way as the Great Wall itself. Overawed by Stalin's greatness but also contemptuous of his consistent lack of support and misreading of China, the tall, gangling Mao was taken directly to one of Stalin's dachas, Lipki.

At 6 p.m., Mao and Stalin met for the first time at the Little Corner. The two Communist titans of the century, both fanatics, poets, paranoics, peasants risen to rule empires whose history obsessed them, careless killers of millions, and amateur military commanders, aimed to seal America's worst nightmare: a Sino-Soviet treaty that would be Stalin's last significant achievement. Yet they observed each other coolly from the Olympian heights of their own self-regard. Mao complained of being 'pushed aside for a long time'.

'The victors are never blamed,' answered Stalin. 'Any ideas or wishes?'

'We've come to complete a certain task,' said Mao. 'It must be both beautiful and tasty.'

A cantankerous silence followed. Stalin appeared baffled by this enigmatic allusion which meant a treaty that was both symbolic and practical, standing for both world revolution and Chinese

---

* Mao had brought a treasure trove of Chinese gifts and several carriages of rice. The lacquer ornaments still hang on the walls of Molotov's retirement flat on Granovsky and Stalin divided the rice amongst his courtiers. In return, Stalin presented him with the names of his Soviet agents in the Chinese Politburo. Back in Peking, Mao swiftly liquidated them.

national interests. Stalin's first priority was protecting his Far Eastern gains, agreed at Yalta and confirmed in the old Sino-Soviet Treaty. He would sign a new treaty if it did not alter the old one. Mao wished to save face, before signing away Chinese lands. This was stalemate. Mao suggested summoning Chou En-lai, his Premier, to complete the negotiations.

'If we cannot establish what we must complete, why call for Chou?' asked Stalin.

They parted: Mao claimed Stalin refused to see him but he had his own reasons to wait. He remained miserably in Moscow for several weeks before the two sides came together, grumbling bitterly that there was 'nothing to do there but eat, sleep and shit'. The prim Russians were shocked at Mao's scatological jokes both in person and on their bugs.

'Comrades,' said Stalin, 'the battle of China isn't over yet. It's only just beginning.' Beria joked to the others that Stalin was jealous of Mao for ruling a bigger nation.

Mao was not completely ignored: Molotov, Bulganin and Mikoyan visited him at the dacha. Stalin wondered if the Chinese enigma was a 'real Marxist'. Like an abbot testing a novice, Molotov patronizingly tested Mao's Marxist knowledge, deciding the Chairman was a 'clever man, a peasant leader, something like a Chinese Pugachev'* but not a real Marxist. After all, Molotov repeated prissily to Stalin, Mao 'confessed he had never read *Das Kapital*'.

* * *

On 21 December, Mao and the entire Communist world gathered at the Bolshoi to celebrate the birthday of their supreme pontiff. Something between a religious pilgrimage and an imperial triumph, a royal wedding and a corporate junket, the festivities cost 5.6 million roubles and attracted thousands of pilgrims. Stalin, torn between contempt for their worship and craving for it, played the modest curmudgeon as Malenkov, always at the forefront of the basest acts of idolatry, tried to persuade him that 'the people' expected a celebration – and a second Hero of the Soviet Union star.

'Don't even think of presenting me with another star,' he growled.

---

*Emelian Pugachev was the Cossack pretender claiming to be the dead Emperor Peter 111 who led a massive peasant rebellion against Catherine the Great in 1773–4.

'But Comrade Stalin, the people ...'

'Leave the people out of it.' But he finally accepted the second star and happily reviewed the arrangements. The archives contain the extraordinary preparations: President Shvernik headed the 'Committee for Preparations of Comrade Stalin's Birthday' which self-consciously contained 'ordinary workers', magnates, marshals and artists such as Shostakovich, who gravely debated the creation of an Order of Stalin, the guest-list, *placement* – and a Stalin gift-pack. At a total cost of 487,000 roubles, every delegate was to receive a dressing-gown, slippers, razor and a set of Moskva soap, talc and scent (the proudest creation of Polina Molotova, now in jail).

In *Pravda*, Khrushchev hailed Stalin's 'sharp intransigence to rootless cosmopolitans', the Jews. Poskrebyshev praised Stalin's brilliance at growing lemons. The wives of the magnates brought their own presents – Nina Beria made walnut jam 'as a little souvenir ... of your mother', to which Stalin wrote a thank-you letter:

'As I eat your jam, I remember my youth.'

Beria rolled his eyes: 'Now you'll be lined up for this chore every year.'

Famous artistes and élite children rehearsed their tributes. Parents had never been pushier: Poskrebyshev managed to land his daughter Natasha the plum role of reciting an idolatrous ditty, then presenting Stalin (who had ordered the death of her mother) a bouquet. At the Bolshoi, ballerinas practised 'curtsies to the God'.

At the Little Corner, the night before, Stalin changed the *placement* so that he was no longer in the centre but Malenkov insisted he had to be in the front row. He pointedly placed himself between Mao and Khrushchev, the new favourite. Later he felt pressure on his neck, then staggered from a dizzy spell, but Poskrebyshev steadied him. He would not call the doctors. Poskrebyshev prescribed one of his remedies.

The next night, the packed Bolshoi awaited the magnates. Stalin's exotic entourage, including Mao, Ulbricht of Germany, Rakosi of Hungary and Bierut of Poland, mingled in the *avant-loge* until everything was ready. When they trooped out, the audience applauded madly. Stalin sat to the left of centre under a jungle of scarlet banners and a giant portrait of himself. Then the endless speeches started, hailing the birthday boy as a genius. Stalin gestured to General Vlasik and whispered that guests were to speak in their own languages, an internationalist gesture by 'the father of peoples'. Togliatti spoke in Italian which he translated into Russian himself. Mao's address, in his surprisingly high-pitched voice, won a standing ovation. Stalin was exhausted from standing up so often. Then the schoolgirls, in their Pioneer dresses, emerged led by Natasha Poskrebysheva to recite their poem. Poskrebyshev winked at his daughter who scampered up and presented the bouquet of red roses: 'Papa and Stalin both loved red roses,' she says.

'Thanks *ryzhik*, redhead, for the roses!' Stalin said and pointed at his devoted Poskrebyshev who beamed with pride.

The party reassembled for a huge banquet at the Kremlin's Georgievsky Hall and for a concert starring the tenor Kozlovsky, the ballerina Maya Plisetskaya and the soprano Vera Davydova. Vlasik personally checked their dressing rooms for assassins or bombs. When she danced, Maya noticed 'the Emperor's bewhiskered face in the first row at the long festive table facing away from the stage and half turned to me [with] Mao next to him'.

Mao's superlative sulk was wearing thin. Face had been saved. When he tried to call Stalin, he was told he 'was not at home and it would be better to talk to Mikoyan'. Finally, on 2 January, Stalin sent Molotov and Mikoyan to begin negotiations. Chou En-lai* arrived on the 20th and started to negotiate with the new Foreign Minister, Vyshinsky, and Mikoyan. Mao and Chou were invited to the Kremlin only to be reprimanded by Stalin for not signing a critique of US Secretary of State Dean Acheson's recent speech. When Mao grumbled about Stalin's resistance to the treaty, Stalin retorted:

'To hell with that! We must go all the way.' Mao sulked even more. In the limousine out to Kuntsevo, the Chinese interpreter invited Stalin to visit Mao.

'Swallow your words!' Mao hissed in Chinese to the interpreter. 'Don't invite him!' Neither of the titans spoke for the entire thirty-minute drive. When Stalin invited Mao to dance to his gramophone, a singular honour for a visiting leader, he refused. It

---

* Stalin admired Chou and President Liu Shao-chi as the most 'distinguished' of Mao's men but he thought that Marshal Chu-Teh was a Chinese version of 'our Voroshilov and Budyonny'.

did not matter: the game of poker was over. While reserving for himself the supreme priesthood of international Communism, Stalin allowed Mao a leading role in Asia.

At the banquet at the Metropol Hotel on 14 February, after the treaty was signed, Stalin pointedly denounced Titoism – and Mao continued his heroic sulk. The two giants barely spoke: 'sporadic' exchanges subsided into 'endless pauses'. Gromyko struggled to keep the conversation going. Stalin may not have liked Mao but he was impressed: 'Of the Marxist world, the most outstanding is Mao ... Everything in his Marxist-Leninist life shows principles and drive, a coherent fighter.' The alliance was immediately tested on the battlefields of Korea.

* * *

Kim Il Sung, the young leader of Communist North Korea, now arrived in Moscow to ask Stalin's permission to invade South Korea. Stalin encouraged Kim but shrewdly passed the buck to Mao, telling the Korean he could 'only get down to action' after consulting with 'Comrade Mao Tse-tung personally'. In Peking, the nervous Mao referred back to Stalin. On 14 May, Stalin cunningly replied, 'The question should ultimately be decided by the Chinese and Korean comrades together.' He thus protected his dominant role but passed the responsibility. None the less, his magnates were worried by his reckless challenge to America and failing powers of judgement. At 4 a.m., on Sunday, 25 June 1950, North Korea attacked the south. Driving all before them, the Communists were soon poised to conquer.

On 5 August, a weary, ageing Stalin departed by special train for his longest holiday so far. It was to be four and a half months, brooding on his anti-Jewish case, on his anger towards Molotov and Mikoyan, distrust of Beria, and dissatisfaction with the ruthlessness of Abakumov's MGB – while the world teetered on the brink thousands of miles away in Korea.

No sooner had he arrived to rest than disaster struck in the faraway peninsula. Stalin had withdrawn from the UN to protest against its refusal to recognize Mao's China instead of Taiwan as the legitimate government but President Truman called Stalin's bluff by convening the Security Council to approve UN intervention against North Korea. The Soviet Union could have avoided this but Stalin wrongly insisted on boycotting the session, against Gromyko's advice. 'Stalin for once was guided by emotion,' remembered Gromyko. In September, the powerful US counter-attack at Inchon, under the UN flag, trapped Kim's North Koreans in the south and then shattered their army. Once again, Stalin's testing of American resolve had backfired badly – but the old man simply sighed to Khrushchev that if Kim was defeated, 'So what. Let it be. Let the Americans be our neighbours.' If he did not get what he wanted, Russia would still not intervene.

As the Americans advanced into North Korea towards the Chinese border, Mao desperately looked towards Stalin, fearing that if they intervened and fought the Americans, their Sino-Soviet Treaty would embroil Russia too. Stalin replied, with Nero-like nonchalance, that he was 'far from Moscow and some-what cut off from events in Korea'. But on 5 October, Stalin fired off a telegram of blunt *realpolitik* and shameless bluff: America was 'not prepared ... for a big war' but if it came to it, 'let it happen now and not in a few years when Japanese militarism will be restored'. Thus Stalin pulled the sting out of Mao's reservations and pushed his ally one step closer to war.

Mao deployed nine divisions but despatched Chou to Stalin's holiday house, probably New Athos, to discuss the promised Soviet air cover for the Chinese troops. On 9 October, a tense Chou, accompanied by Mao's trusted protégé, the fragile but talented Lin Piao, later his doomed heir apparent, faced Stalin, Malenkov, Beria, Kaganovich, Bulganin, Mikoyan and Molotov.

'Today we want to listen to the opinions and thinking of our Chinese comrades,' Stalin opened the meeting. When Chou stated the situation, Stalin replied that Russia could not enter the war – but China should. None the less, if Kim lost, he offered the North Koreans sanctuary. He could only help with military equipment. Chou, who had been counting on Soviet air cover, gasped. Afterwards, Stalin invited the Chinese to a Bacchanal from which only Lin Piao emerged sober. This was one of the occasions when Beria disagreed with Stalin and, as ever, he was the most daring in expressing himself. When he came out of the meeting on sending Chinese forces into Korea, he found the Georgian boss, Charkviani, waiting outside:

'What's he doing?' Beria, who understood the nuclear threat, exclaimed nervously. 'The Americans will be furious. He'll make them our enemy.' Charkviani was amazed to hear such heresy.

'It's hard for me to trust a man 100% but I think I can rely on him,' Stalin reflected to Mgeladze over dinner, having manoeuvred Mao into fighting the Americans without Soviet air cover.

On 19 October, Mao deployed his waves of Chinese cannon fodder to throw back the surprised Americans. Henceforth, even when the front finally stabilized along the 38th Parallel and the North Koreans begged for peace, Stalin refused to agree: attrition suited him. As he told Chou at a later meeting, in a phrase that illustrates Stalin's entire monstrous career, the North Koreans could keep on fighting indefinitely because they 'lose nothing, *except for their men'*.

* * *

While the old Generalissmo basked in the sun pulling the strings in Korea, he was also killing his own men. On 29 September, Kuznetsov and Voznesensky were tried at the Officers' Club in Leningrad before an MGB audience. Before the trial finally started, the accused were ordered to leave Zhdanov out of their testimony. The main accused were sentenced to death by shooting next day and the Politburo endorsed the sentences. 'He'd sign first,' admitted Khrushchev, 'and then pass it around for the rest of us to sign. We'd sign without even looking ...' Did they sign the death-list over dinner on the veranda?

Kuznetsov defiantly refused to confess, which outraged Stalin and embarrassed Abakumov:

'I'm a Bolshevik and remain one in spite of the sentence I have received. History will justify us.' The accused were said to have been bundled into white sacks by the Chekists and dragged out to be shot. They were killed fifty-nine minutes after midnight on 1 October, their families exiled to the camps. There is some evidence that Stalin marked the lists with symbols specifying how they were to die. Voznesensky may have been kept alive for a while because Stalin later asked Malenkov:

'Is he in the Urals? Give him some work to do!' Malenkov informed Stalin that Voznesensky had frozen to death in the back of a prison truck in sub-zero temperatures. After Stalin's death, Rada Khrushcheva asked what had happened to Kuznetsov:

'He died terribly,' replied her father, 'with a hook through his neck.'

This little massacre consolidated the power of Malenkov, Beria, Khrushchev and Bulganin – the last men standing as Stalin entered his final years – but it was the swansong of Abakumov. That sensuous, flashy sadist would soon roll up his bloody carpet for good. Perhaps it was over-confidence that led him to close the Jewish Case in March 1950: no one was released. The tortures were so grievous that one victim counted two thousand separate blows on his buttocks and heels.

Yet as that main case temporarily subsided, Stalin was orchestrating another anti-Semitic spasm from his holiday. Anti-Semitism now 'grew like a tumour in Stalin's mind', said Khrushchev, yet he himself praised it in *Pravda*. Stalin called in the Ukrainian bosses for a dinner at which he briefed them on orchestrating a similar anti-Semitic campaign in Kiev. The hunt for 'Zionist danger' was pursued through the Government with thousands of Jews being sacked.*

Stalin was particularly fascinated by a case against Jewish managers in the prestigious Stalin Automobile Plant that made his limousines: they had sent Mikhoels a telegram celebrating the foundation of Israel.

'The good workers at the factory should be given clubs so they can beat the hell out of those Jews at the end of the working day,' Stalin told Khrushchev in February.

'Well, have you received your orders?' Beria asked sardonically. Khrushchev, Malenkov and Beria, that inseparable threesome, summoned the Jewish ZiS managers to the Kremlin and accused them of 'loss of vigilance' and complicity in an 'anti-Soviet Jewish nationalistic sabotage group'. The terrified manager fainted. The three magnates had to resuscitate him with cold water. Stalin released the manager but two Jewish journalists, one a woman, who had written about the factory, were executed. His personal intervention made the difference between life and death. Another Jewish manager, Zaltsman, was saved because, during the war, he had sent Stalin a desk-set shaped like a tank with the pens forming the guns.

The Jews were not Stalin's only target: his suspicions of Beria were constantly fanned by the ambitious Mgeladze, his boss in Abkhazia, who shrewdly revealed Beria's crimes and vendettas of the late thirties. Stalin encouraged him and denounced Beria during their chats over dinner. Mgeladze's was only one voice that informed Stalin of how corruptly the Mingrelians ran Georgia. Beria was a Mingrelian, so was Charkviani who had run it since

---

* Even Svetlana's husband was now involved. In the Central Committee machine, Yury Zhdanov, Stalin's son-in-law, that highly qualified paragon of Soviet education, reported to the orchestrator of the anti-Semitic hunt, Malenkov, that some scientists 'had flooded theoretical departments of ... Institutes with its supporters, Jews by origin.'

1938. Stalin ordered Abakumov to check the notoriously venal Georgia, and build a case against the Mingrelians, not forgetting Beria himself: 'Go after the Big Mingrelian.'

On 18 November, towards the end of his holiday, Stalin agreed to arrest the first Jewish doctor. Professor Yakov Etinger, who had treated the leaders, was bugged talking too frankly about Stalin. Etinger was tortured about his 'nationalistic' tendencies by one of Abakumov's officers, Lieut.-Col. Mikhail Riumin, who forced him to implicate all the most distinguished Jewish doctors in Moscow but he somehow failed to please his boss. Abakumov ordered Riumin to desist but the officer tortured Etinger so enthusiastically that he died of 'heart paralysis' – a euphemism for dying under torture. Riumin was in trouble – unless he could destroy Abakumov first.

Abakumov was not guilty of idleness: Stalin was now redoubling the repression. Arrests intensified. In 1950 there were more slaves in the Gulags – 2.6 million – than ever before. But Abakumov knew too much about the Leningrad and Jewish cases. Worse, Stalin sensed the foot-dragging of the MGB – and Abakumov himself. It was Yagoda all over again – and he needed a Yezhov.

The brakes on the Jewish Case, the rumours of corruption, the whispers of Beria and Malenkov, possibly the strutting bumptiousness of the man himself, turned Stalin against Abakumov. There was no sudden break but when Stalin returned from holiday,* just after his seventy-first birthday, on 22 December, he did not summon Abakumov. The weekly meetings ceased, as they had for Yagoda and Yezhov. Within the MGB snakepit, the ebbing of Stalin's favour and the death of Etinger presented Riumin with an opportunity. 'Little Mishka' or, as Stalin nicknamed him, 'the Midget' or 'Pygmy' – the '*Shibsdik*', was the *Vozhd*'s second murderous dwarf.

---

* 'I want to delay my return because of bad weather in Moscow and the danger of flu. I'll be in Moscow after coming of frost,' Stalin wrote to Malenkov in December 1950.

56

The Midget and the Killer Doctors:
Beat, Beat and Beat Again!

Riumin, thirty-eight, plump and balding, stupid and vicious, was the latest in the succession of ambitious torturers who were only too willing to please and encourage Stalin by finding new Enemies and killing them for him. Unlike Yezhov, who had been so popular until he became an inquisitor, Riumin was already an enthusiastic killer even though he had passed eight school grades, qualifying as an accountant. As Malenkov showed, education was no bar to mass murder. He had his own problems. Dismissed for misappropriating money in 1937 – and now in danger for killing the elderly Jewish doctor, the Midget decided to act. Perhaps to his own surprise, he lit the fuse of the Doctors' Plot.

On 2 July 1951, Riumin wrote to Stalin and accused Abakumov of deliberately killing Etinger to conceal a Jewish medical conspiracy to murder leaders such as the late Shcherbakov. This brought together Stalin's fears of ageing, doctors and Jews. It was not Beria but Malenkov who sent Riumin's letter to Stalin. This is confirmed by Malenkov's assistant though he claimed that Riumin wrote the letter 'for his own reasons'. The Doctors' Plot worked against Beria and the old guard like Molotov but this swelling case could threaten Malenkov and Khrushchev too. So often at Stalin's court, a case would start coincidentally, be encouraged by some magnate and then be spun back at them by Stalin like a bloody boomerang. Malenkov sometimes allied himself with Khrushchev, sometimes with Beria, but it was always Stalin making the big decisions. Riumin's allegation of medical murder may have been prompted by Stalin himself – or it may have been the spark that inspired him to reach back to Zhdanov's death and create a maze of conspiracies to provoke a Terror that would unite the country against America outside and its Jewish allies within.

He now ordered Beria and Malenkov to examine the 'Bad Situation at the MGB', accusing Abakumov of corruption, ineptitude and debauchery. Around midnight on 5 July in the

Little Corner, Stalin agreed to Malenkov's suggestion to appoint Semyon Ignatiev, forty-seven, as the new boss. At 1 a.m., Abakumov was called in to hear of his downfall. At 1.40 a.m., Riumin arrived to receive his prizes: promotion to General and, later, Deputy Minister. Serving a short spell as a Chekist in 1920, Ignatiev was an eager, bespectacled CC bureaucrat who was a friend of Khrushchev and Malenkov. Indeed Khrushchev described Ignatiev as 'mild and considerate' though the Jewish doctors would hardly have agreed with him. Beria again failed to regain control over the secret police. Henceforth Stalin himself ran the Doctors' Plot through Ignatiev. Stalin sent Malenkov to tell the MGB that he wanted to find a 'grand intelligence network of the USA' linked to 'Zionists'.

The next day, 12 July, Abakumov was arrested. In the tradition of fallen secret policeman, his corruption was lovingly recorded: 3,000 metres of expensive cloth, clothes, sets of china, crystal vases – 'enough for a shop' – were found in his homes. In order to build his flats Abakumov removed sixteen families and spent a million roubles to make a 'palace' using two hundred workers, six engineers and the entire MGB Construction Department. Yet the downfall of monsters also destroyed the innocent: Abakumov's young wife, Antonina Smirnova, with whom he had a two-month-old son, had received 70,000 roubles-worth of presents, including an antique Viennese pram. So she was arrested: the destiny of the girl and the baby are unknown.*

Abakumov, no longer a Minister but just a number, Object 15, spent three months shackled in the refrigerator cell, being viciously interrogated by his nemesis, the Midget:

'Dear LP,' he wrote pitifully to Beria, 'I feel so terrible … You're the closest man to me, and I wait for you to ask me back … You will need me in the future.' Abakumov had been destroyed for failing to push the Jewish Case. Ignatiev and the egregious

---

* As in 1937, the Terror first destroyed the leadership of the MGB itself which was now arrested. Colonel Naum Shvartsman, one of the cruellest torturers since the late thirties and a journalist expert at editing confessions, testified that he had had sex not only with his own son and daughter, but also with Abakumov himself, and, at night when he broke into the British Embassy, with Sir Archibald Clark Kerr, a momentous diplomatic development in Anglo-Soviet relations that had mysteriously passed unnoticed at the Court of St James. Shvartsman claimed to have been poisoned with 'Zionist soup' – an idea that harks back to the infamous plot by Enemies in the Jewish Autonomous Oblast during the thirties to poison Kaganovich's gefilte. But he also delivered what Stalin wanted, implicating Abakumov, that unlikely Zionist sympathizer.

'Midget' Riumin set about torturing the Jewish officials of the JAFC and the doctors to 'substantiate the evidence of espionage and nationalistic activity'.

* * *

The impresario of this theatre of plots and pain was now ageing fast. He sometimes became so giddy that he fell over in his Kremlin apartment. The bodyguards had to keep a close eye on him because 'he didn't look after himself'. He hardly bothered to read all his papers. Kuntsevo was strewn with unopened boxes. He still corrected Bulganin's speeches like a schoolmaster but then forgot Bulganin's name in front of the rest of the Politburo:

'Look, what's your name?'

'Bulganin.'

'Right yes ... that's what I meant to say.'

Riven by arthritis, diminished by raging arteriosclerosis, dazed by fainting spells, embarrassed by failing memory, tormented by sore gums and false teeth, unpredictable, paranoid and angry, Stalin left on 10 August for his last and longest holiday. 'Cursed old age has caught up with me,' he muttered. He was even more restless than usual, travelling from Gagra to New Athos, Tsaltubo to Borzhomi and back. At Lake Ritsa, the woods, lakeside and paths were peppered with strange green metal boxes, containing special telephones so Stalin could call for help if taken ill on a stroll.

But dizzy spells were not going to stop him cleansing his entourage:

'I, Molotov, Kaganovich, Voroshilov – we're all old ... we must fill ... the Politburo with younger ... cadres,' he ominously told Mgeladze. Yet his paranoia gave him no rest: 'I'm finished,' he told Mikoyan and Khrushchev who, like all the magnates, were on holiday near by so they could visit Stalin twice a week. 'I don't even trust myself.'

At dinner, he surveyed his courtiers and 'puffing out his chest like a turkey', he embarked on that favourite but lethal subject – his successor. It could not be Beria because he 'wasn't Russian', nor Kaganovich, a Jew. Voroshilov was too old. He did not even mention Mikoyan (an Armenian) or Molotov. It could not be Khrushchev because he was a 'country boy' and Russia needed a leader from the intelligentsia. Then he named Bulganin, the very man whose name he tended to forget, as his successor as Premier. None was ideologically qualified to lead the Party but he had not mentioned Malenkov who perhaps took this as an encouraging sign. He ordered books and started frantically studying.

'Well, Comrade Stalin requires me to study political science.' Malanya, caught reading Adam Smith, asked a colleague, 'How long will it take to master?'

The magnates were convinced that Stalin was becoming senile but actually he was never more dangerous, determined and in control. He lashed out in every direction, at his comrades, Jews, Mingrelians, even banana importers. The story of the bananas sums up the governing style of the ageing Stalin.

Vlasik learned a shipment of bananas had just arrived and eager to soothe the bad teeth of the Master, he bought some for Stalin. At dinner at Coldstream with all the magnates, Vlasik proudly presented the bananas. Stalin peeled one and found it was not ripe. He tried two more. They too were not ripe. 'Have you tried the bananas?' he asked his guests. Stalin summoned Vlasik:

'Where did you get these bananas?' Vlasik tried to explain but Stalin shouted: 'These crooks take bribes and rob the country. What was the name of the banana ship?'

'I don't know,' said Vlasik, 'I didn't take an interest ...'

'Take an interest! I'll put you on trial with the rest of them!' bellowed Stalin. Poskrebyshev rushed off to find out the name of the ship and order arrests. Malenkov pulled out his notebook and took notes. Stalin ordered Mikoyan to sack the new Trade Minister. But Beria was eager to beat Mikoyan to the banana, as it were.

The dinner ended at 5 a.m. At 6 a.m., Stalin called Beria to tell him to sack the Minister. When Mikoyan called Moscow just after 6 a.m., he found that Beria had already reprimanded the unfortunate. A few days later, Mikoyan arrived to say goodbye and Stalin was still talking about those bananas. The Minister was sacked. Charkviani wrote that this was typical of Stalin's 'eruptions leading to irrelevant decisions'. Stalin, concluded Mikoyan drily, 'was simply very fond of bananas.'

Stalin's limbs ached but when he took the waters at Tsaltubo, the weather was too hot. He decided to take the waters at Borzhomi and visit a house with special memories. He had stayed at the Likani Palace, a neo-Gothic mansion owned by Grand Duke Michael, Nicholas II's brother, overlooking the Kura River, with Nadya in happier times. It had become a museum and was barely habitable, without bedrooms, which suited Stalin. It suited his magnates less: he ordered Khrushchev and Mikoyan to stay too. They rushed over from Sochi and Sukhumi but, without beds, they had to camp together, sharing a room like boy scouts.

Stalin ate every day at a table laid under a tree by the Kura in idyllic lush countryside. When he went for walks, he cursed at the bodyguards, bumping into them by suddenly changing direction. He decided to visit Bakuriani but the locals mobbed his car, placing carpets and banqueting tables across the road. The supreme curmudgeon had to dismount and join his overexcited fans for a Georgian feast. 'They open their mouths and yell like dunderheads!' he muttered, face twitching. He never made it to Bakuriani and returned to Abkhazia.

At the Palace, where Nadya had rested after Vasily's birth, Stalin brooded on his family. Vasily, now pitifully ill with alcoholism, visited. 'His health's so poor, his stomach's sick, he can't even eat,' Stalin confided in Charkviani. Like a Western millionaire booking his playboy son into the Betty Ford Clinic, Stalin intervened to enrol Vasily in a drying-out programme but here too he searched for a culprit and found one in the banana procurer:

'Vlasik and his friends did it, they turned his drinking into an addiction!' Stalin had been cursing Vlasik's corruption for years. A denunciation letter and Malenkov's investigation into MGB venality revealed Vlasik's orgies and shenanigans. Stalin was upset but felt mired in corruption. He finally sacked his most devoted retainer.*

Svetlana's marriage to Yury was over after just two years. In a letter to her father, she called Yury a 'heartless bookworm' and an 'iceberg'. Stalin told Mgeladze that Svetlana wore the trousers:

'Yury Zhdanov's not the head of that family – he can't insist on anything. He doesn't listen to her nor she to him. The husband should run a family … that's the main thing.' But Yury himself would never dare ask Stalin for a divorce so Svetlana came to see him instead.

'I know what you want to say,' he said. 'You've decided to divorce him.'

'Father,' Svetlana answered in a begging tone. Charkviani, who was present, was embarrassed and excused himself but Stalin insisted he stay.

---

* Vlasik was despatched to be Deputy Commandant of a labour camp in the Urals whence he rashly bombarded Stalin with protestations of his innocence. But this did not place Beria in charge of his bodyguards who remained under Ignatiev's MGB.

'So why're you divorcing him?' Stalin asked.

'I can't live with my mother-in-law. She's impossible!'

'What does your husband say?'

'He supports his mother!'

Stalin sighed: 'If you've decided to divorce him, I can't change your mind, but your behaviour isn't acceptable.' She blushed and left, walking out of the Zhdanov family and moving into a flat in the House on the Embankment with her two children.

'Who knows what next?' muttered Stalin.

'Stalin wasn't too happy when it ended,' admits Yury, but he was not too surprised either. He did not hold it against Yury but invited him to stay at Lake Ritsa where they chatted half the night about Stalin's visit to London in 1907. When they naturally talked about the campaign against cosmopolitanism, Zhdanov, who had played his own role in hunting out Jewish scientists, asked Stalin if he thought it was 'assuming a lopsided national character', meaning it was aimed too much against the Jews.

'Cosmopolitanism's a widespread phenomenon,' replied Stalin. When he finally got up to go to bed in the early hours, he cited a Jewess he admired: 'Maria Kaganovich – there's a real Bolshevik! One should pay attention to social position, not national condition!' and he staggered off to sleep. In the morning the table was laid on the bank of Lake Ritsa and Yury watched Stalin peruse *Pravda*. 'What are they writing about?' he snarled, reading out, 'Long live Comrade Stalin, leader of all nations!' – and he tossed it away in disgust.

After entertaining other old friends, who complained that the Mingrelians were notoriously corrupt, Stalin headed back to New Athos and then dared Mgeladze to be there within seventeen minutes. The ambitious Abkhazian boss, who sensed his hours of chatting with the old man were about to bear fruit, made it in fifteen and finally convinced Stalin that Charkviani was running 'a bordello!'

He furiously summoned the Georgian MGB boss, the crude, barrel-chested Rukhadze. 'The Mingrelians are totally unreliable,' said Stalin, who in old age embraced the parochial hatreds of different regions of Georgia. Thousands of Mingrelians were arrested but Stalin wanted to destroy Beria. Perhaps he suspected that Lavrenti was no Marxist: 'He's become very pretentious ... he's not how he used to be ... Comrades who dine with him say he's utterly bourgeois.'

Stalin was 'afraid of Beria', thought Khrushchev, 'and would have been glad to get rid of him but didn't know how to do it.' Stalin himself confirmed this, sensing that Beria was winning support: 'Beria's so wily and tricksy. He's become so trusted by the Politburo that they defend him. They don't realize he's pulled the wool over their eyes. For example – Vyacheslav [Molotov] and Lazar [Kaganovich]. I think Beria has his eye on a future goal. But he's limited. In his time, he did great work but as for now ... I'm not sure he wouldn't misuse his power.' Then Stalin remembered his closest allies: 'Zhdanov and Kirov thought poorly of him but ... we liked Beria for his modesty and efficiency. Later he lost these qualities. He's just a policeman.'

Ignatiev sent sixty MGB interrogators and a torture specialist carrying a special medical case filled with his instruments, down to Tiflis. Stalin phoned Charkviani, with whom he had spent hours discussing literature and family, and without saying hello, threatened:

'You've closed your eyes to corruption in Georgia ... Things'll go badly for you, Comrade Charkviani.' He hung up. Charkviani was terrified.

The Beria family, Nina and Sergo, sensed this tightening garrotte. Stalin appointed Beria to give the prestigious 6 November address but three days afterwards, he dictated an order about a Mingrelian conspiracy that directly threatened Beria, using his wife Nina's links to the Menshevik émigrés in Paris.

Vasily Stalin naïvely confided to Sergo Beria that relations between their fathers were 'tense', which he blamed on anti-Georgian Russians in the Politburo. Svetlana, who was so close to Nina, warned her that something was afoot. Beria's marriage to Nina was under strain because Lilya Drozhdova had given birth to a daughter by Beria whom they named Martha after his mother. Lilya was now about seventeen and she had lasted as Beria's mistress for a couple of years. The bodyguards told Martha Peshkova that when Lilya was at the dacha, the baby was placed in the same cradles as Sergo's children. Not surprisingly, the arrival of the baby upset Nina. She unhappily decided she needed a separate life and built herself a cottage in Sukhumi.

* * *

On 22 December 1951, Stalin, like a lame, restless and hungry tiger, returned to Moscow, clearly intent on enforcing a new Terror, with specific anti-Semitic features. The torture chambers of

Ignatiev and Riumin groaned with new Jewish and Mingrelian victims to destroy Molotov and Beria. Stalin did know how to 'get rid' of Beria, but the 'master of dosage' had always worked with agonizing patience. But now he was old. Stalin loathed Beria yet Sergo recalls that 'when in a morose mood, he came to see us seeking human warmth'. Stalin admitted to Nina he could barely sleep any more:

'You can't know how tired I am. I have to sleep like a gundog.'

Beria played Stalin well: he shrewdly offered to purge Georgia himself. In March 1952, Beria sacked Charkviani,* replaced him with Mgeladze and publically admitted:

'I too am guilty.'

Stalin and Beria despised each other but were linked by invisible threads of past crimes, mutual envy and complementary cunning. Stalin still discussed foreign policy with Beria, even letting him write a paper proposing a neutral, reunified Germany. Beria could still manipulate the Generalissimo with what Khrushchev called 'Jesuitical shrewdness' but he was too clever by half, riling Stalin. 'You're playing with a tiger,' Nina warned him.

'I couldn't resist it,' replied Beria.

The gap between Beria's dreams and his reality had made him 'a deeply unhappy man', wrote his son. Without the ideological fanaticism that bound the others to Stalin, Beria now questioned the entire Soviet system: 'The USSR can never succeed until we have private property,' he told Charkviani. He despised Stalin, whom he considered 'no longer human. I think there is only one word that describes what my father felt in those days,' wrote Sergo Beria. 'Hatred.' Beria became ever more daring in his denunciations of Stalin: 'For a long time,' he sneered sarcastically, 'the Soviet State had been too small for Joseph Vissarionovich!' Always the most craven and most irreverent, he denounced Stalin but the other leaders were afraid to join in: 'I considered it an attempt to provoke us,' said Mikoyan.

Yet, gradually, their shared fears and Stalin's unpredictability

* Stalin protected Charkviani because the leader had been taught the alphabet as a boy by a Father Charkviani. Stalin moved him to work as a CC Inspector in Moscow. But Beria was powerless to defend himself or his protégés. When the Mingrelian secret policeman Rapava, who was a family friend of the Berias, was arrested, his wife bravely set off secretly to Moscow to ask Nina Beria's help. But when the desperate woman called Beria's house, Nina was too scared to come to the phone. The German housekeeper Ella said, 'Nina cannot come to the phone.' This was how the Mingrelians realized that Beria himself was in trouble.

created a 'sense of solidarity', a support system among ambitious killers who wanted to survive and protect their families. Even Beria became the unlikely avuncular comforter for bruisers like Khrushchev and Mikoyan in these uneasy times. The others revelled in Beria's eclipse – and shared his fears. Malenkov warned him, Khrushchev teased him. Molotov and Kaganovich were so impressed with Beria that even when Stalin criticized him, they defended him. Yet any and all were ready to destroy the others. It was not long before Ignatiev and his MGB torturers were even trying to link Stalin's two obsessions: Beria, they whispered, was secretly Jewish.

That spring, Stalin was examined by his veteran doctor, Vinogradov, who was shocked by his deterioration. He suffered from hypertension and arteriosclerosis with occasional disturbances in cerebral circulation, which caused minor strokes and little cysts in the brain tissue of the frontal lobe. This exacerbated Stalin's anger, amnesia and paranoia. 'Complete rest, freedom from all work,' wrote Vinogradov on the file but the mention of retirement infuriated Stalin who ordered his medical records destroyed and resolved to see no more doctors. Vinogradov was an Enemy.

On 15 February, Stalin ordered the arrests of more doctors who admitted helping to kill Shcherbakov, which in turn led to Dr Lydia Timashuk, the cardiologist who had written to Stalin about the mistreatment of Zhdanov. Stalin called in Ignatiev and told him that, if he did not accelerate the interrogations of the Jewish doctors already under arrest, he would join Abakumov in prison. The MGB were 'nincompoops!'

'I'm not a supplicant of the MGB!' barked Stalin at Ignatiev. 'I can knock you out if you don't follow my orders ... We'll scatter your group!' He now talked more to his bodyguards and Valechka than to his comrades. The death of the Mongolian dictator, Marshal Choibalsang, in Moscow that spring worried him enough to confide in his chauffeur: 'They die one after another. Shcherbakov, Zhdanov, Dmitrov, Choibalsang ... die so quickly!* We must change the old doctors for new ones.' The bodyguards could talk quite intimately to Stalin and Colonel Tukov replied that those doctors were very experienced. 'No, we must change them for new ones ... The MVD insists on arresting them as saboteurs.' Valechka heard

---

*Georgi Dmitrov, the Bulgarian leader, died in 1949.

him say he was not sure about the case. But Stalin was not for turning: he wanted the Jewish Crimea case to be tried imminently. Lozovsky and a distinguished cast of Jewish intellectuals again became the playthings of Riumin and Komarov.

Meanwhile, Vasily Stalin's treatment for alcoholism had failed completely. At the May Day parade, the weather was bad and the planes should not have been allowed to fly but a drunken Vasily ordered the flypast to proceed. Two Tupolev-4 bombers crashed. Stalin watched darkly from the Mausoleum and afterwards sacked Vasily as Moscow Air Force commander, sending him back to the Air Force Academy.

Eight days later, at midday on 8 May, the 'trial of the Jewish poets' starring Solomon Lozovsky, former Deputy Foreign Minister, and the Yiddish poet Perets Markish opened in the Dzerzhinsky Officers' Club at the Lubianka. Stalin had already specified that virtually all the defendants were to be shot.

Lozovsky had been tortured but his pride in his Bolshevik and, more surprisingly, Jewish pedigrees was unbroken. His speech shines out of this primordial darkness as the most remarkable and moving oration of dignity and courage in all of Stalin's trials. He also shredded Riumin's imbecilic Jewish-Crimean conspiracy.

'Even if I had wanted to engage in such activity ... would I have gotten in touch with a poet and an actor? ... After all, there is an American Embassy ... swarming with intelligence officers. The doorman at the Commissariat of Finance would not do such a thing, let alone the Deputy Foreign Minister!'

Lozovsky was so convincing that the judge, Lieut.-Gen. Alexander Cheptsov, stopped the trial, a unique happening which suggests that Stalin was forcing a new Terror onto an unwilling and no longer blindly obedient bureaucracy. Cheptsov complained of its flimsiness to Malenkov in the presence of a rattled Ignatiev – and humiliated Riumin. Malenkov ordered the trial to proceed. On 18 July, Cheptsov sentenced thirteen defendants to death (including two women), sparing only the scientist Lina Shtern, perhaps because of her research into longevity. But Cheptsov did not carry out the executions, ignoring Riumin's shrill orders to do so, and appealed to Malenkov.

'Do you want to bring us to kneel before these criminals?' Malenkov retorted. 'The Politburo has investigated this case three times. Carry out the Politburo's resolution.' Malenkov admitted later that he had not told Stalin everything: 'I did not dare!'

Stalin rejected official appeals. Lozovsky* and the Jewish poets were shot on 12 August 1952.

* * *

Stalin refused to take a holiday that August: instead, unhappy at the dominance of Malenkov and Khrushchev, he decided to call a Congress in October, the first one since 1939, to anoint new, younger leaders and destroy his old comrades.

By September, Ignatiev, assisted by 'Midget' Riumin, had tortured the evidence out of his prisoners to 'prove' that the Kremlin doctors, led by Stalin's own physician, had indeed murdered Zhdanov, Shcherbakov, Dmitrov and Choibalsang. A new crop were arrested but not yet Vinogradov. On the 18th, Stalin told Riumin to torture the doctors. Riumin, who possessed a macabre gift for primitive theatre, designed a special torture chamber at Lefortovo, furnished like a dissection room and operating theatre, to intimidate the doctors. Long before Laurence Olivier played the Nazi dentist in *Marathon Man*, Stalin was torturing his own doctors in a ghastly surgical parody.

'You're acting like a whore! You're an ignoble spy, a terrorist!' Riumin shouted at one of the doctors. 'We'll torture you with a red-hot iron. We have all the necessary equipment for that ...' Stalin's family was included in a bizarre medical melodrama, spawned by Stalin's furious imagination and Riumin's diabolical obedience: the doctors had deliberately subverted Vasily Stalin's treatment for 'nervous disorders' and had failed to prevent toxicosis in Svetlana Stalin after the birth of her child Katya Zhdanov in the spring of 1950. A surreal touch, if any was needed, was added by the case of Andreyev who had been ill since 1947: the doctors prescribed cocaine for his insomnia so it was hardly surprising he was unable to sleep. Andreyev† had become

---

* One of the survivors of Stalin's time, Maxim Litvinov, the Jewish ex-Foreign Commissar, managed to die in his bed on 31 December 1951. He was a perennial target of the MGB's anti-Semitic cases. Molotov admitted that Litvinov should have been shot for his rambunctious indiscretions in the late war years: 'It was only by chance that he remained among the living,' said Molotov chillingly. There was a plan to arrange a road accident à la Mikhoels but finally Litvinov died with his errant English wife by his bedside: 'Englishwoman go home!' were his last words. 'They did not get him,' said Ivy Litvinov who returned to London. Their daughter now lives in Brighton.
† Andreyev had appealed to Malenkov in January 1949 to 'check the treatment ... I don't feel good despite following doctors' orders. My head's dizzy ... I almost fall over. I'm disastrous. I feel the treatment and diagnosis is wrong ...' He was probably right since the cocaine was clearly the wrong medicine. He signed off: 'I'm devilishly unhappy to be out of work.'

dependent on the drug, one of history's more unlikely coke addicts.

Absurd as the details may sound, the Doctors' Plot had the beautiful enveloping symmetry of a panacea, one of Stalin's fantastical masterpieces: working alone, only informing his grandees when he had results, and keeping complete control over all the parallel threads through the 'Midget', he wove a tapestry that sewed together every intrigue and leading victim since the war, in order to mobilize the Soviet people against the external enemy, America, and its internal agents, the Jews, and therefore justify a new Terror. New research shows Stalin would toss into this cauldron various 'murderous' Jews and doctors, Abakumov and his 'unvigilant' Chekist 'nincompoops', and the executed Leningrader, Kuznetsov, who would be the link between the Jews, Zhdanov's death, and the magnates – especially Mikoyan, via their children's marriage. Just as in 1937 a man did not have to be a Trotskyite to be shot as one, so now the victims did not have to be Jewish to be accused of 'Zionism': Abakumov, no philo-Semite, was now smeared with Zionism. As for the sturdily Russian Molotov, Stalin had not nicknamed him 'Molotstein', in the twenties, for nothing.

Did Stalin really believe it all? Yes, passionately, because it was politically necessary, which was better than mere truth. 'We ourselves will be able to determine,' Stalin told Ignatiev, 'what is true and what is not.'

Stimulated by his labyrinth of secret investigations, Stalin did not give up his literary and scientific interests. As his brain atrophied, Stalin still 'swotted like a good pupil', as Beria put it, studying to dominate new fields and solve ideological problems. 'I am seventy yet I go on learning just the same,' Stalin boasted to Svetlana. He read all the entries for the Stalin Prize and chaired the Committee to choose the winners in his office. That year, pacing as usual, he decreed that a novelist named Stepan Zlobin should win. Malenkov however pulled out a file and said,

'Comrade Stalin, Zlobin conducted himself very badly when he was in a German concentration camp …' Stalin walked round the table three times in dead silence then asked:

'To forgive?' He continued pacing the table in silence. 'Or not to forgive? To forgive or not to forgive?' Finally, he answered: 'Forgive!' Zlobin won the prize. Stalin then attacked anti-Semitism: he had lately insisted that Jewish writers must have their Semitic names published in brackets after their Russian pseudonyms. Now he asked the surprised Committee: 'What's this for? Does it give pleasure to someone to underline that this man is Jewish? Why? To promote anti-Semitism?' As usual the old fox was playing several games in parallel.

He had always been interested in the theory of linguistics: the field had been dominated by Professor Marr who had established Stalinist orthodoxy by arguing that language, like class, would ultimately disappear and merge into one language as Communism approached. A Georgian linguistics scholar, Arnold Chikobava, wrote to Stalin to attack the theory. Stalin, keen to buttress his national Bolshevism by overturning Marrism, summoned Chikobava to a dinner that lasted from 9 p.m. to 7 a.m. taking notes diligently like a student. He then held an open debate in *Pravda*, finally intervening with his own article, 'Marxism and the Problems of Linguistics' which immediately altered the entire field of Soviet science and ideology.*

Just before the Congress opened, Stalin proudly distributed the other fruit of his studies, his turgid masterpiece *Economic Problems of Socialism in the USSR*, which declared the 'objectivity' of economic laws and reasserted the orthodoxy that the imperialist states would go to war, but it also leapt some of the stages of Marxism, to claim that Communism was achievable in his lifetime. Faith in ideology was always vital to Stalin but those old believers Molotov and Mikoyan did not agree with this 'Leftist derivation'. When they came to dinner at Kuntsevo, Stalin asked:

'Any questions? Any comments!' Beria and Malenkov, never ideologists, praised it. But even now, in danger of his life, Molotov would not agree with an ideological deviation. He just mumbled and Mikoyan said nothing. Stalin noticed their silence and, later, smiled maliciously at Mikoyan:

'Ah, you've lagged behind! Right now, the time has come!' When they met to discuss the Presidium of the Congress, Stalin said,

---

* Chikobava told Stalin that some of his Armenian colleagues had been sacked for sharing his views so Stalin immediately got the Armenian boss, Arutinov, on the telephone and asked about the professors. 'They were removed from their posts,' replied Arutinov. 'You were in too much of a hurry,' replied Stalin and hung up. The professors were woken up immediately and restored to their positions. His meeting with Chikobava probably took place on 12 April 1950 just as he was discussing the timing of the Korean War; Stalin's article was published on 20 June that year. Chikobava's original letter was sent to Stalin by Candide Charkviani, then Georgian First Secretary, which shows the power of those with direct access to the *Vozhd*.

'No need to enter Mikoyan and Andreyev – they're inactive Politburo members!' Since Mikoyan was immensely busy, the Politburo chuckled.

'I'm not joking,' snapped Stalin. 'I suggest it seriously.' The laughter stopped instantly, but Mikoyan was included. Even at the height of his tyranny, Stalin had to feel his way in this close-knit oligarchy: Mikoyan and Molotov were prestigious Poltiburo titans, respected not only by their colleagues but by the public. Stalin proposed they expand the Politburo into a Presidium of twenty-five members. Mikoyan realized this would make it easier to remove the old Politburo members. 'I thought – "something's happening."' Mikoyan was suddenly afraid: 'I was just knocked off my feet.' They realized Stalin had meant it when he shouted:

'You've grown old! I'll replace you all!'

At 7 p.m. (to suit Stalin's own timetable) on 5 October 1952, the Nineteenth Congress opened. The leaders sat bunched together on the left with the ageing Stalin alone on the right. Stalin himself only attended the beginning and the end of the Congress but giving the major reports to Malenkov and Khrushchev placed them in pole position for the succession.* He only spoke at the end of the Congress for a few rambling minutes but a punch-drunk Stalin boasted to Khrushchev:

'There, look at that! I can still do it!' Khrushchev was ill during the Congress: when an old doctor visited him on Granovsky and treated him kindly, 'I was tormented because I already had the testimony against the doctor. I knew no matter what I said, Stalin would not spare him.' But the real action was on 16 October at the Plenum to elect the Presidium and Secretariat. No one was ready for Stalin's ambush.

---

* Molotov opened the Congress, Kaganovich spoke on the Party rules, and Voroshilov closed it, representing the status quo, which few guessed that Stalin was planning to radically overturn. But there were clues. Significantly Stalin changed the Party's name from Bolshevik to Communist Party. In the new Presidium, Beria slipped from his usual third place after Molotov, and Malenkov to fifth after Voroshilov. Beria's acolytes Merkulov and Dekanozov were dropped from the new CC.

57

Blind Kittens and Hippopotamuses:
the Destruction of the Old Guard

Stalin loped down to the rostrum two metres in front of the pew-like seats where the magnates sat. The Plenum watched in frozen fascination as the old man began to speak 'fiercely', peering into the eyes of the small audience 'attentively and tenaciously as if trying to guess their thoughts'.

'So we held the Party Congress,' he said. 'It was fine and it would seem to most people that we enjoy unity. However, we don't have unity. Some people express disagreement with our decisions. Why did we exclude ministers from important posts ... Molotov, Kaganovich, Voroshilov? ... Ministers' work ... demands great strength, knowledge and health.' So he was bringing forward 'young men, full of strength and energy'. But then he unleashed his thunderbolt: 'If we're talking unity, I cannot but touch on the incorrect behaviour of some honoured politicians. I mean Comrades Molotov and Mikoyan.'

Sitting just behind Stalin, their faces turned 'pale and dead' in the 'terrible silence'. The magnates, 'stony, strained and grave', wondered 'where and when would Stalin stop, would he touch the others after Molotov and Mikoyan?'

First he dealt with Molotov:

'Molotov's loyal to our cause. Ask him and I don't doubt he'd give his life for our Party without hesitation. But we cannot overlook unworthy acts.' Stalin dredged up Molotov's mistake with censorship: 'Comrade Molotov, our Foreign Minister, drunk on *chartreuse* at a diplomatic reception, let the British Ambassador publish bourgeois newspapers in our country ... This is the first political mistake. And what's the value of Comrade Molotov's proposal to give the Crimea to the Jews? That's a huge mistake ... the second political mistake of Comrade Molotov.' The third was Polina: 'Comrade Molotov respects his wife so much that as soon as we adopt a Politburo decision ... it instantly becomes known to Comrade Zhemchuzhina ... A hidden thread connects the

Politburo with Molotov's wife – and her friends … who are untrustworthy. Such behaviour isn't acceptable in a Politburo member.' Then he attacked Mikoyan for opposing higher taxes on the peasantry: 'Who does he think he is, our Anastas Mikoyan? What's unclear to him?'

Then he pulled a piece of paper out of his tunic, and read out the thirty-six members of the new Presidium, including many new names. Khrushchev and Malenkov glanced at each other: where had Stalin found these people? When he proposed the inner Bureau, everyone was astonished that Molotov and Mikoyan were excluded.* Then, returning to his seat on the tribune, he explained their downfall: 'They're scared by the overwhelming power they saw in America.' He ominously linked Molotov and Mikoyan to the Rightists, Rykov and Frumkin, shot long before, and Lozovsky, just shot in August.

Molotov stood and confessed:

'I am and remain a loyal disciple of Stalin,' but the Generalissimo cupped his ear and barked:

'Nonsense! I've no disciples! We're all disciples of Lenin. Of Lenin!'

Mikoyan fought back defiantly: 'You must remember well, Comrade Stalin … I proved I wasn't guilty of anything.' Malenkov and Beria heckled him, hissing 'liar' but he persisted. 'And as for the bread prices, I completely deny the accusation' – but Stalin interrupted him:

'See, there goes Mikoyan! He's our new Frumkin!'

Then a voice called out:

'We must elect Comrade Stalin General Secretary!'

'No,' replied Stalin. 'Excuse me from the posts of General Secretary and Chairman of the Council of Ministers [Premier].' Malenkov stood up and ran forward, chins aquiver, with the desperate grace of a whippet sealed inside a blancmange. His 'terrible expression' was not fear, observed Simonov, but an 'understanding much better than anyone else of the mortal danger that hung over all: it was impossible to comply with Stalin's request.' Malenkov, tottering on the edge of the stage, raised his hands as if he was praying and piped up:

'Comrades! We must all unanimously demand that Comrade

---

* Yet Stalin still remembered his loyalest retainer Mekhlis, who had suffered a stroke in 1949. Now dying at his dacha, all he longed for was to attend the Congress. Stalin refused, muttering that it was not a hospital but when the new CC was announced, he remembered him. Mekhlis was thrilled – he died happy and Stalin authorized a magnificent funeral.

Stalin, our leader and teacher, remain as General Secretary!' He shook his finger, signalling. The whole hall understood and began to cry out that Stalin had to remain at his post. Malenkov's jowls relaxed as if he had 'escaped direct, real mortal danger'. But he was not safe yet.

'One doesn't need the applause of the Plenum,' replied Stalin. 'I ask you to release me ... I'm already old. I don't read the documents. Elect yourselves another Secretary.' Marshal Timoshenko replied:

'Comrade Stalin, the people won't understand it. We all as one elect you our leader – General Secretary!' The cheering went on for a long time. Stalin waited, then, waving modestly, he sat down.

Stalin's decision to destroy his oldest comrades was not an act of madness but the rational destruction of his most likely successors. As Stalin remembered well, the ailing Lenin had attacked his likely successor (Stalin himself) and proposed an expanded Central Committee with none of the leaders as members. It was now that the magnates realized 'they were all in the same boat' because, Beria told his son, 'none of them would be Stalin's successor: he intended to choose an heir from the younger generation.' There was probably no secret heir: only a 'collective' could succeed Stalin.*

Stalin was satisfied by Molotov's ritual submission but asked him to return the secret protocols of the Ribbentrop Pact, clearly to form part of the case against him. As for Mikoyan, Stalin was shocked at his defiance. At Kuntsevo, in the absence of his two bugbears, Stalin grumbled to Malenkov and Beria:

'Look, Mikoyan even argued back!' In the days after the

---

* One of these heirs would probably have been Mikhail Suslov, fifty-one, Party Secretary, who combined the necessary ideological kudos (Zhdanov's successor as CC Ideology and International Relations chief) with the brutal commitment: he had purged Rostov in 1938, supervised the deportation of the Karachai during the war, suppressed the Baltics afterwards and presided over the anti-Semitic campaign. In 1948, he frequently met Stalin. Furthermore, he was personally ascetic. Beria loathed this 'Party rat', bespectacled, tall and thin as a 'tapeworm' with the voice of a 'grating castrate'. Roy Medvedev makes the educated guess that Suslov was 'Stalin's secret heir' in his new *Neizvestnyi Stalin* but there is no evidence of this. Suslov helped overthrow the de-Stalinizing Khrushchev in 1964 and became the éminence grise of the re-Stalinizing Brezhnev regime right up until his death in 1982. At the Plenum, Brezhnev himself was one of the young names elected to the Presidium. On his title, Stalin got his way: afterwards he appeared as the first 'Secretary' but no longer as 'General Secretary', a change that persuaded some historians that he lost power at the Plenum. Until recently, the only account of this extraordinary meeting was Simonov's but now we also have the memoirs of Mikoyan, Shepilov and Efremov.

Plenum, Molotov and Mikoyan continued to play their usual roles in the Government but Stalin was now supervising the climax of his Doctors' Plot, burning with fury against Professor Vinogradov for recommending his retirement. Yet it was typical of this stealthy old conspirator that he had suppressed his anger and waited eleven months to gather the evidence to destroy his own physician. Now it all came bursting out. Ordering Ignatiev to arrest Vinogradov, he shouted:

'Leg irons! Put him in irons!'

On 4 November, Vinogradov was arrested, touching every Politburo family because, as Sergo Beria wrote, he was 'our family doctor'.

* * *

Three days later, Svetlana, now entangled in another dangerous relationship, this time with Johnreed Svanidze, the son of those executed 'spies' Alyosha and Maria, brought over her two children to play with their grandfather. It was the Revolution holiday, the twentieth anniversary of Nadya's suicide. At the height of the Jewish Terror, Stalin really 'hit it off' with his half-Jewish grandson, Joseph Morozov, now seven, with his 'huge shiny Jewish eyes and long lashes'.

'What thoughtful eyes,' said Stalin, pouring the children thimbles of wine 'in the fashion of the Caucasus'. 'He's a smart boy.' Svetlana was touched. He had recently met Yakov's fifteen-year-old daughter, Gulia Djugashvili, whom he delighted by letting her serve the tea.

'Let the *khozyaika* do it!' he said, tousling her hair, kissing her. Gulia, better than anyone, catches his febrile excitement at the great enterprise of a new struggle: 'His face was very tired but he could hardly stay still.'

Stalin was infuriated by Riumin's slowness in beating the evidence out of the doctors, calling the MGB a herd of 'hippo-potamuses'. He shouted at Ignatiev: 'Beat them! What are you? Do you want to be more humanitarian than Lenin who ordered Dzerzhinsky [founder of the Cheka] to throw Savinkov out of the window? … Dzerzhinsky was no match for you but he didn't shirk the dirty work. You work like waiters in white gloves. If you want to be Chekists, take off your gloves.' Malenkov repeated Stalin's orders to use 'death blows'.

On 13 November, a few days after little Joseph's visit, he ordered the petrified Ignatiev to sack Riumin: 'Remove the Midget!' As for the doctors, 'Beat them until they confess! Beat, beat and beat again. Put them in chains, grind them into powder!' Stalin offered Vinogradov his life if he admitted 'the origins of your crimes ... You may address your testimony to the Leader who promises to save your life ... The whole world knows our Leader has always kept his promises.' Vinogradov knew no such thing.

'My situation is tragic,' the doctor replied. 'I have nothing to say.' He tried to name dead people whom his testimony could no longer harm. Stalin then lashed out at Ignatiev himself for his backsliding. Ignatiev suffered a heart attack and took to his bed.*

Now Stalin turned on his dogged retainer, Vlasik, destroying his debauched bodyguard just as he had the colourful Pauker in 1937. Vlasik had been on drinking terms with the homicidal doctors but he also knew too much, particularly that Stalin had been informed of Zhdanov's mistreatment and done nothing about it. Vlasik himself had probably only ignored Timashuk's letters on Stalin's lead. But now he was arrested, brought to Moscow and accused of concealing the evidence with Abakumov. He never betrayed the Boss. But his arrest was a cunning move because Vlasik's 'treason' helped cover Stalin's own role. All his mistresses and drinking cronies were arrested and questioned by Malenkov. Vlasik was tortured: 'My nerves were broken and I suffered a heart attack. I had months without sleep.' Stalin knew that Poskrebyshev, his other devoted old retainer, was best friends with Vlasik: had he played some role in suppressing the evidence against the killer doctors? He had distrusted Poskrebyshev ever since his article on Stalin's lemon-growing skills in 1949: was someone encouraging his grim amanuensis to step out of the shadows? But Stalin also learned that Poskrebyshev had shared Vlasik's orgies. He was mired in 'filthy affairs', said Molotov. 'Women can serve as agents!' Poskrebyshev arrived at Beria's house in a panic: everyone ran to Beria for reassurance but he himself was in equal danger.

Stalin sacked Poskrebyshev (his deputy, Chernukha, replaced him), moved him to be secretary of the Presidium and received

---

* The 'Midget' plunged with the same speed that he had risen to an obscure desk in the Ministry of State Control and was replaced by S. A. Goglidze. Earlier, Stalin turned against his instrument in the Mingrelian Case, Georgian MGB boss Rukhadze, who had boasted of his intimacy with the *Vozhd*. 'The question of Rukhadze's arrest is timely,' Stalin wrote to Mgeladze and Goglidze on 25 June 1952. 'Send him to Moscow where we'll decide his fate!' Riumin, Goglidze and Rukhadze were all shot after Stalin's death.

him for the last time on 1 December. He had removed his two most loyal servants. Stalin now had enough evidence to escalate the hysteria.

After seeing the heart-broken Poskrebyshev, Stalin unveiled the horror of what he called 'the killers in white coats' to the Presidium: 'You're like blind kittens,' he warned them at Kuntsevo. 'What will happen without me is that the country will die because you can't recognize your enemies.' Stalin explained to the 'blind kittens' that 'every Jew's a nationalist and an agent of American intelligence' who believes 'the USA saved their people'. He linked these killer doctors to the medical murderers of Gorky and Kuibyshev and repeated his mantra-like justification for 1937. A Great Terror was again imminent. He turned to the secret police: 'We must "treat" the GPU,' he said. 'They know they're sitting in shit!'

The magnates understood this ominous reference because an anti-Semitic trial was already underway in Prague where the Czech General Secretary, Rudolf Slansky, a Jew, was accused of 'anti-State conspiracy'. Three days later, he and ten other mainly Jewish Communists were hanged. Stalin planned something similar in Warsaw for he asked Bierut about his Jewish lieutenants:

'Who's dearer to you – Berman or Minc?'

Bierut to his credit replied:

'Both equally.'

Stalin ordered more schemes to assassinate Tito.

* * *

The Czech executions brought the noose closer to Molotov and Mikoyan who debated the court etiquette of condemned men. Stalin called them 'American or British spies'. 'To this day,' Molotov reminisced, 'I don't know precisely why. I sensed he held me in great distrust.'

They kept turning up for dinner as if nothing had happened. 'Stalin wasn't glad to see them', noticed Khrushchev. Finally Stalin banned Molotov and Mikoyan: 'I don't want those two coming around any more.' But the staff secretly told them when the dinners were taking place. So Stalin banned the staff from talking to them. Still, they kept turning up because Khrushchev, Beria, Malenkov and Bulganin, the Four, alerted them – a sign of growing sympathy, because they appreciated that 'they were trying to stay close to save themselves ... to stay alive.' Mikoyan asked Beria's advice:

'It would be better if you lay low,' he suggested.

'I'd like to see your face when ... you're sacked,' replied Mikoyan.

'That happened to me years ago,' said Beria.

Molotov and Mikoyan, realizing their lives were in danger, met in the Kremlin to decide what to do. Mikoyan had always trusted Molotov not to repeat his comments – and 'he never let me down or used my trust against me'. Both were hurt, and angry.

'It's practically impossible to rule a country in your seventies and decide all issues at the dinner-table,' Molotov said aloud at a meeting, a risky act of *lèse-majesté* that would have been unthinkable before the Plenum.*

The magnates would all have assisted in the liquidation of Molotov and Mikoyan. Stalin was old, raging, vindictive, paranoid and in a hurry. Yet his sense of the possible, the patience and charm that balanced his cruelty, and his roughness still worked, as he methodically, logically micromanaged the case. The unpredictable fury, frantic hastiness and implacable paranoia ironically drove the magnates closer together. Beria and Khrushchev were against Stalin's changes. Malenkov comforted Beria who comforted Mikoyan; Khrushchev and Beria comforted Molotov. During whispered consultations in the Kuntsevo lavatories, the Four laughed off Stalin's suspicions and mocked the Doctors' Plot.

'We should protect Molotov,' Beria told the other three, 'he's still needed by the Party.'

December 21 was officially Stalin's seventy-third birthday. Molotov and Mikoyan had not missed his birthday for thirty years. He rarely invited anyone – one just arrived for supper. The outcasts discussed what to do. Mikoyan thought that if they did not go, it would 'mean that we had changed our attitude to Stalin'. They phoned the Four, who told them they had to come.

So at 10 p.m. on the 21st, they arrived at Kuntsevo, where Stalin had hung plangent magazine photographs on the walls of children feeding lambs and famous historical scenes like Repin's *Reply of the Zaporozhian Cossacks*, his favourite picture. Svetlana was there too. Stalin was quiet but friendly, proud that he had given up smoking after fifty years. But he was already suffering from breathing difficulties. His face was livid and he had put on

* Voroshilov, sacked and humiliated, seems to have respectfully resented Stalin too. His wife used to whisper that Stalin was jealous of Klim's popularity – another unthinkable heresy.

weight, suggesting high blood pressure. He sipped light Georgian wine. As Svetlana was leaving, Stalin asked her:

'Do you need any money?'

'No,' she answered.

'You're only pretending. How much do you need?' He gave her 3,000 roubles for herself and for Yakov's daughter, Gulia, useful housekeeping money but Stalin thought it was millions. 'Buy yourself a car but show me your driving licence!' Underneath, Stalin was 'angry and indignant' that the Four had invited Molotov and Mikoyan.

'You think I don't realize you let Molotov and Mikoyan know? Stop this! I won't tolerate it,' he warned Khrushchev and Beria. He ordered them to give this message to the outcasts: 'It won't work: he's not your comrade any more and doesn't want you to visit him.' This really alarmed Mikoyan:

'It was becoming clear ... Stalin wanted to finish with us and that meant not only political, but physical destruction.'

The four last men standing decided, according to Beria's son, 'not to let Stalin set them against each other'. Stalin sometimes asked the Four: 'Are you forming a bloc against me?' In a sense they were, but none of them, not even Beria, had the will. Mikoyan discussed, probably with Molotov, the murder of Stalin but, as he later told Enver Hoxha, 'We gave up the idea because we were afraid the people and the Party would not understand.'

* * *

On 13 January 1953, after two, maybe even five, years' patient plotting, Stalin unleashed a wave of hysterical anti-Semitism by announcing the arrest of the doctors in *Pravda*: 'Ignoble Spies and Killers under the Mask of Professor-Doctors', a phrase that he had personally coined and scrawled on to the draft article which he annotated carefully.* On 20 January, Doctor Timashuk, Zhdanov's cardiologist, was called to the Kremlin where Malenkov gave her Stalin's personal thanks for her 'great courage' and the next day, she received the Order of Lenin. But Stalin was still using Ehrenburg as his decoy when a week later, on 27 January, he awarded him

---

* Stalin diligently added the following phrases in his handwriting: 'For a long time, Comrade Stalin warned us our success had shadows ... Thoughtlessness is good for our enemies who sabotage us ...' They were the 'slavemasters and cannibals of USA and England ... What about the people who inspired the killers? They can be sure we'll repay them ... As long as there is wrecking, we must kill thoughtlessness in our people.'

the Stalin Prize. Meanwhile throughout January and February, the arrests intensified.

The article revealed the lack of vigilance in the security services, a signal that Beria himself was a target. Not only were Beria's allies arrested in Georgia; his protégés in Moscow, such as the Chief of Staff, Shtemenko, were sacked. His ex-mistress V. Mataradze was also arrested. He 'expected the death-blow ... at any minute,' wrote his son. Beria 'expressed his disrespect for Stalin more and more boldly', noted Khrushchev, 'insultingly'. He even boasted to Kaganovich that 'Stalin doesn't realize if he tried to arrest me the Chekists would organize an insurrection.'

Apart from their fears for their own lives, the magnates were worried about nuclear war with America: Stalin, who was still stoking the Korean War, inconsistently swung between fear of war and the ideological conviction that it was inevitable. Beria, Khrushchev and Mikoyan feared the effect on America of Stalin's alarming unpredictability.* Stalin ringed Moscow with anti-aircraft missiles. As his own campaign inspired fear of American attack, he even discussed it with his bodyguards:

'What do you think – will America attack us or not?' he asked Kuntsevo's Deputy Commandant, Peter Lozgachev.

'I think they'd be afraid to,' replied the officer, at which Stalin suddenly flared up:

'Clear out – what are you doing here anyway? I didn't call you.' But he was sensitive to the guards in a way that was unthinkable with the politicians. He called in Lozgachev:

'Forget that I shouted at you but just remember: they will attack us. They're Imperialists, and they certainly will attack us. If we let them. That's the answer you should give.'

* * *

Stealing sleep on his sofas like 'a gundog', Stalin calmed himself by repeatedly playing Mozart's Piano Concerto No. 23. Visitors found him 'greatly changed' – a 'tired old man' who 'talked with difficulty' between 'long pauses' – but he managed his Terror tenaciously. Stalin orchestrated the drafting of a letter, to be signed by prominent Soviet Jews, begging for Jews to be deported

---

* After Stalin's death, Mikoyan told his sons that 'if we didn't have war when he was alive, we won't have war now.' This was ironic since for all Stalin's paranoia, inconsistencies and risk-taking in foreign policy, it was the clumsy and impulsive Khrushchev who brought the world closest to nuclear war during the Cuba Missile Crisis.

from the cities to protect them from the coming pogrom. The letter itself has never been found but Mikoyan confirmed that 'the voluntary-compulsory eviction of Jews' was being prepared. Kaganovich was hurt when he was asked to sign it but found a loyal way of refusing.

'Why won't you sign?' asked Stalin.

'I'm a member of the Politburo, not a Jewish public figure, and I'll only sign as a Politburo member.'

Stalin shrugged: 'All right.'

'If it's necessary, I'll write an article.'

'We might need an article,' said Stalin.

Even Kaganovich complained about Stalin, confiding in Mikoyan: 'It's so painful for me that I've always been consciously struggling against Zionism – and now I have to "sign off on it".' Khrushchev claimed that Kaganovich 'squirmed' but signed the letter. (Neither Kaganovich nor Khrushchev is a truthful witness when it comes to their own roles.) However Ehrenburg, who saw it and managed to avoid signing by appealing to Stalin, said it was addressed *to* the Politburo and signed by 'scholars and composers' which suggests that Kaganovich had managed to 'squirm' successfully. The latest evidence shows that two new camps were being built, perhaps for the Jews.

Stalin closely read the testimonies of the tortured doctors, sent daily by Ignatiev. He ordered the likely star in his Jewish Case, Object 12 (otherwise known as Polina Molotova), brought back to Moscow and interrogated. But the Jewish Case was not Stalin's only business during these weeks.

He rarely saw diplomats, but on 7 February, he received the young Argentine Ambassador, Leopoldo Bravo, who thought Stalin 'healthy, well-rested and agile in conversation'. Stalin admired Peron, offering generous loans because, despite his Fascist past, he appreciated Peron's anti-Americanism. But he was most interested in Eva Peron.*

'Tell me,' he asked Bravo, 'did she owe her rise to her character or her marriage to Colonel Peron?' Bravo was the second-last outsider to see Stalin alive.

Seven days later, at 8 p.m. on 17 February, Stalin visited the Little Corner for the last time to receive the Indian diplomat K. P. S. Menon. His mind was on his plots for he spent the

* Evita had died of ovarian cancer on 26 July 1952.

half-hour sketching wolves' heads on his pad, reflecting, 'The peasants are right to kill mad wolves.' At 10.30 p.m. Stalin left with Beria, Malenkov and Bulganin, probably for dinner at Kuntsevo.

He was still working up a case against Beria and his other Enemies: he ordered his new Georgian boss Mgeladze to get Beria to sign an order to attack the MGB, effectively against himself. Beria was not happy but had to agree. One of the Premier's last meetings was to order another assassination attempt on Tito.

At 8 p.m. on 27 February, Stalin arrived alone at the Bolshoi to watch *Swan Lake*. As he left, he asked his 'attachment', Colonel Kirillin, to thank the cast for him, speeding to Kuntsevo where he worked until about 3 a.m. He rose late, read the latest interrogations of the Jewish doctors and the reports from Korea, walked around the snowy garden and ordered Commandant Orlov:

'Brush the snow off the steps.' That afternoon, Stalin may have taken a steam bath. As he got older the heat eased the arthritis in his stiff arm, but Professor Vinogradov had banned *banyas* as bad for high blood pressure. Beria had told him he did not have to believe doctors. Now he threw caution to the winds. In the evening, he was driven into the Kremlin where he met his perennial companions, Beria, Khrushchev, Malenkov and Bulganin, in the cinema. Voroshilov joined them for the movie, noting Stalin was 'sprightly and cheerful'. Before he left, he arranged the menu with Deputy Commandant Lozgachev and ordered some bottles of weak Georgian wine.

At 11 p.m., Stalin and the Four drove out to the dacha for dinner. The Georgian buffet was served by Lozgachev and Matrena Butuzova (Valechka being off duty that night). Bulganin reported on the stalemate in Korea and Stalin decided to advise the Chinese and North Koreans to negotiate. Stalin called for more 'juice'. They talked about the doctors' interrogations. Beria is supposed to have said that Vinogradov had a 'long tongue', gossiping about Stalin's fainting spells.

'Right, what do you propose to do now?' said Stalin. 'Have the doctors confessed? Tell Ignatiev if he doesn't get full confessions out of them, we'll shorten him by a head.'

'They'll confess,' replied Beria. 'With the help of other patriots like Timashuk, we'll complete the investigation and come to you for permission to arrange a public trial.'

'Arrange it,' said Stalin. This is Khrushchev's account: he and Malenkov later blamed Beria for all Stalin's crimes but their own parts in the Doctors' Plot remain murky. It is unlikely that Beria was the only one encouraging Stalin.

The guests were longing to go home. Stalin was pleased with the suave Bulganin but growled that there were those in the leadership who thought they could get by on past merits.

'They are mistaken,' he said. In one account, he then stalked out of the room, leaving his guests alone. Perhaps he returned. The accounts seem contradictory – but then, so was his behaviour. At about 4 a.m., on the morning of Sunday, 1 March, Stalin finally saw them out. He was 'pretty drunk ... in very high spirits', boisterously jabbing Khrushchev in the stomach, crooning 'Nichik' in a Ukrainian accent.

The relieved Four asked the 'attachment', Colonel Khrustalev, for their limousines: Beria as usual shared his ZiS with Malenkov, Khrushchev with Bulganin. Stalin and the guard escorted them to their cars. Indoors, Stalin lay down on a pink-lined divan in the little dining room, with its pale wooden panelling, which was where this old itinerant conspirator had chosen to sleep that night – not helpless, not mad, but a brutal organizer of Terror at the awesome peak of his power.

'I'm going to sleep,' he cheerfully told Khrustalev. 'You can take a nap too. I won't be calling you.' The 'attachments' were pleased: Stalin had never given them a night off before. They closed the doors.

* * *

At midday that Sunday morning, the guards waited for the Boss to get up, sitting in their guardhouse that was linked to his rooms by a covered passageway twenty-five yards long. But there was 'no movement' all afternoon. The guards became anxious. Finally, at 6 p.m. Stalin switched on the light in the small dining room. He was obviously up at last. 'Thank God, we thought,' said Lozgachev, 'everything's all right.' He would call for them soon. But he did not.

One, three, four hours passed but Stalin did not appear. Something was wrong. Colonel Starostin, the senior 'attachment', tried to persuade Lozgachev to go in to check on the old man. 'I replied, "you're senior, you go in!"' recalled Lozgachev.

'I'm afraid,' said Starostin.

'What do you think I am? A hero?' retorted Lozgachev. They were not the only ones waiting: Khrushchev and the others expected the call to dinner. But the call did not come.

58

'I Did Him In!': the Patient and
his Trembling Doctors

At around 10 p.m., the CC mail arrived. The short, burly Lozgachev, gripping the papers, stepped nervously into the house, going from room to room. He was especially noisy because 'we were careful not to creep up on him ... so he'd hear you coming.' He 'saw a terrible picture' in the small dining room. Stalin lay on the carpet in pyjama-bottoms and undershirt, leaning on one hand 'in a very awkward way'. He was conscious but helpless. When he heard Lozgachev's steps, he called him by 'weakly lifting his hand'. The guard ran to his side:

'What's wrong, Comrade Stalin?'

Stalin muttered something, 'Dzhh' but he could not speak. He was cold. There was a watch and a copy of *Pravda* on the floor beside him, a bottle of Narzan mineral water on the table. He had wet himself.

'Shall I call the doctor maybe?' asked Lozgachev.

'Dzhhh,' buzzed Stalin. 'Dzhhh.' Lozgachev picked up the watch: it had stopped at 6.30 when the stroke had hit him. Stalin gave a snore and seemed to fall asleep. Lozgachev dashed to the phone and called Starostin and Butuzova.

'Let's put him on the sofa, it's uncomfortable ... on the floor,' he told them and the three lifted him on to the sofa. Lozgachev kept vigil – 'I didn't leave the Boss's side' – while Starostin telephoned MGB boss Ignatiev, in charge of Stalin's personal security since Vlasik's dismissal in May 1952. He was too frightened to decide anything. He had the power to call doctors himself but he had to act carefully. He ordered Starostin to call Beria and Malenkov. He probably also warned his friend Khrushchev because he needed protection against Beria who blamed him for the Doctors' Plot and the Mingrelian Case, and wanted his head. Beria was probably the last to find out.

Meanwhile the 'attachments' moved Stalin on to the sofa in the main dining room where the famous dinners took place, because it was airier there. He was very cold. They covered him with a blanket and Butuzova rolled his sleeves down. Starostin could not find Beria, probably entangled with his mistress somewhere, but contacted Malenkov who said he would search for him. Half an hour later, he called back:

'I haven't found Beria yet,' he admitted. After another half-hour, Beria called:

'Don't tell anybody about Comrade Stalin's illness,' he ordered, 'and don't call.' Lozgachev sat anxiously beside Stalin. He said his hair went grey that night. Malenkov had also called Khrushchev and Bulganin:

'The Chekists have rung from Stalin's place. They're very worried, they say something's happened to Stalin. We'd better get out there ...' Yet Khrushchev claimed that when they arrived at the guardhouse, they 'agreed' not to enter but to leave this sensitive matter to the guards. Stalin was now sleeping and would not want to be seen 'in such an unseemly state. So we went home.' The guards do not remember this visit. It seems more likely that Khrushchev, Bulganin, and probably Ignatiev, after frantic consultations, sent in Beria and Malenkov to find out if anything was really wrong. Somehow, during the night, the anti-Semitic campaign in *Pravda* was halted by someone – or was it Stalin's deliberate pause?*

At 3 a.m. on the morning of Monday 2 March, this little delegation arrived at Kuntsevo, over four hours after Starostin's first call to Malenkov. Both men acted in character: Beria was the dynamic, keyed-up (possibly drunk) adventurer, Malenkov, Stalin's punctilious, nervous clerk. While Beria marched into the hall, Malenkov noticed to his horror that his shoes were creaking and slipped them off. 'Malanya' tucked his shoes under his arm and tiptoed forward in his socks with the grace of a flabby dancer.

'What's wrong with the Boss?' They looked at the sleeping Generalissimo, snoring under his blanket, and then Beria turned on the 'attachments'.

'What do you mean ... starting a panic?' he swore at Lozgachev. 'The Boss is obviously sleeping peacefully. Let's go, Malenkov.'

'Malanya' tiptoed out in his socks while Lozgachev tried to

* Perhaps the other two waited outside in their ZiS. Ignatiev must also have been present. But already, it seems, Beria had taken control. No one knows who stopped the anti-Semitic media campaign that night. Suslov was the CC Secretary in charge of Ideology but who ordered him to put it on hold? It remains a mystery.

explain that 'Comrade Stalin was sick and needed medical attention'.

'Don't bother us, don't cause a panic and don't disturb Comrade Stalin!' The worried guards persisted but Beria swore:

'Who attached you fools to Comrade Stalin?'

The limousine drove away to meet the waiting Khrushchev and Bulganin. The bargaining for power surely started that night. Lozgachev returned to his vigil while Starostin and Butuzova went to sleep in the guardhouse.

Dawn broke over the firs and birches of Kuntsevo. It was now twelve hours since Stalin's stroke and he was still snoring on the sofa, wet from his own urine. The magnates surely discussed whether to call doctors. It was extraordinary that they had not called a doctor for twelve hours but it was an extraordinary situation. This is usually used as evidence that the magnates deliberately left Stalin without medical help in order to kill him. But in their fragile situation, at a court already bristling with spy-mania against the killer doctors, it was not just hyperbole to fear causing panic. Stalin's own doctor was being tortured merely for saying he should rest. If Stalin awoke feeling groggy, he would have regarded the very act of calling doctors as an attempt to seize power. Furthermore, they were so accustomed to his minute control that they could barely function on their own.

But the Four had those hours to divide power. The decision to do nothing suited everyone. Beria and Malenkov, Stalin's first deputies, in the Government and Party respectively, were legally in charge until a full meeting of the Politburo and then of the Central Committee. If Stalin was dying, they needed time to tie up power. Possibly for the same reasons, it was in the interests of Khrushchev and Bulganin to delay medical help until they had protected their position. They seem to have promised to protect Ignatiev and promote him to the CC Secretariat.

Beria, the only one of the Four fearing for his life at that time, had every reason to hope the hated Stalin would die. (Molotov and Mikoyan did not yet know Stalin was ill.) Yet Beria was never alone with Stalin – he took care that Malenkov was with him. He was not in control of the MGB, nor the Doctors' Plot, nor the bodyguards, hence his comment, 'Who attached you fools to Comrade Stalin?' Even though Beria has always been blamed for the delay, Khrushchev and Ignatiev may actually have been the cause of it.

Whatever their motives, the Four delayed calling a doctor until morning. We will never know if this was medically decisive or not. There was the possibility of an operation to clear the blood clot but doctors agree that it had to take place within hours of the stroke and who would have dared to authorize it? In the fifties, there was a remote chance of such an operation being successful: it was more likely to kill the patient. Melodramatic accounts of Stalin's death, of which there are no shortage, claim that Stalin was murdered. It is most likely that the denial of medical care made not the slightest difference. But Beria clearly thought it had:

'I did him in!' he later boasted to Molotov and Kaganovich. 'I saved you all!'

Recent research has suggested that he perhaps spiked Stalin's wine with a blood-thinning drug such as warfarin, which, over several days, might cause a stroke. Perhaps Khrushchev and the others were accomplices, hence the cover-up suited them all.

The Four now returned home to sleep, saying nothing to their families. At the imperial bedside, Lozgachev was desperate. He awoke Starostin and told him to call the Politburo – 'otherwise he'll die and it'll be curtains for you and me'. The terror that prevented the leaders calling the doctors now made the guards demand them. They phoned Malenkov who told them to send in Butuzova to take another look. She announced it was 'no ordinary sleep'. Malenkov called Beria.

'The boys have rung again from Stalin's place,' Malenkov told Khrushchev. 'They say there really is something wrong with Comrade Stalin. We'll have to go back again. We agreed the doctors would have to be called.' Beria and Malenkov were making all the decisions but which doctors to call? So they asked Tretyakov, Minister of Health, to select some *Russian* (not Jewish) doctors. Khrushchev arrived at Kuntsevo to tell the relieved 'attachments' the doctors were on their way. Colonel Tukov called Molotov, Mikoyan and Voroshilov, another sign that the Four had never approved of their exclusion.

'Call the Politburo. I'm on my way,' Molotov replied. When the phone rang in Voroshilov's home, the old Marshal was transformed: 'He became strong and organized,' wrote his wife in her unpublished diary, 'as I saw him in dangerous situations in the Civil and Great Patriotic Wars ... I understood unhappiness was coming. In great fear through running tears, I asked him, "What happened?" He embraced me. "Don't be afraid!"'

Voroshilov joined Kaganovich, Molotov and Mikoyan at the bedside. Molotov noticed 'Beria was in charge.' Stalin opened his eyes when Kaganovich arrived and looked at his lieutenants one by one – and then closed his eyes again. Unlike the overbearing Beria, Molotov and Kaganovich were deeply moved. Tears ran down their cheeks. Voroshilov reverently addressed the patient:

'Comrade Stalin, we're here, your loyal friends and comrades. How do you feel dear friend?'

Stalin's face was 'contorted'. He stirred but never fully regained consciousness. Khrushchev was 'very upset, I was very sorry we were losing Stalin'. He rushed home to wash and hurried back to Kuntsevo with no one in his family asking any questions. According to his son, Beria called home and told his wife about Stalin's illness: Nina burst into tears. Like most of the Politburo wives, even those about to be killed, she was inconsolable.

At 7 a.m., the doctors, led by Professor Lukomsky, finally arrived but they were a new team who had never worked with Stalin before. They were brought to the patient in the big dining room which must have reeked of stale urine. With their colleagues under torture, they were awestruck by the sanctity of Stalin and petrified by Beria's Mephistophelian presence lurking behind them. Their examination of the powerless, once omnipotent patient was a comedy of errors. 'They were all trembling like us,' observed Lozgachev. First, a dentist arrived to take out Stalin's false teeth but 'he was so frightened, they slipped out of his hands' and fell on to the floor. Then Lukomsky tried to take Stalin's shirt off in order to take his blood pressure. 'Their hands were trembling so much,' noticed Lozgachev, 'that they could not even get his shirt off.' Lukomsky was 'terrified to touch Stalin' and could not even get a grip on his pulse.

'Hold his hand properly!' Beria snapped at Lukomsky.

The clothes had to be cut away with scissors. 'I ripped open the shirt,' recalled Lozgachev. They began to examine the patient 'lying on a divan on his back, his head turned to the left, eyes closed, with moderate hyperaemia of the face ... There had been involuntary urination, [his clothes were soaked in urine.]' His pulse was 78; heartbeat 'faint'; blood pressure 190 over 110. His right side was paralysed while his left limbs quivered sometimes. His forehead was cooled. He was given a glass of 10 per cent magnesium sulphate. A neuropathologist, therapist and nurse stood vigil. The doctors asked the guards who had seen what. The guards now feared for their lives too: 'We thought, this is it then, they'll put us in a car and it's goodbye, we're done for!'

Stalin had suffered a cerebral catastrophe or, in their words, 'middle-left cerebral arterial haemorrhaging ... The patient's condition is extremely serious.' It was official at last. Stalin would not be able to work again.

The bodyguards stepped back and faded into the furniture. There was little the doctors could actually do. They recommended: 'Absolute quiet, leave the patient on the divan; leeches behind the ears (eight now in place); cold compress on the head ... No food today.' When he was fed, it was to be with a teaspoon 'to give liquid when there is no choking'. Oxygen cylinders were wheeled in. The doctors injected Stalin with camphor. They took a urine sample. The patient stirred. 'Stalin tried to cover himself.'

Svetlana, who had celebrated her birthday the night before, was called out of a French class and told, 'Malenkov wants you to come' to Kuntsevo. Khrushchev and Bulganin, both in tears, waved her car to a stop and hugged her.

'Beria and Malenkov will tell you everything.' It was again clear who was in charge. The bustle and noise astonished her: Kuntsevo had always been so quiet. She noticed that the doctors were strangers. When she came to the bedside, she kissed Stalin, realizing 'I loved my father more tenderly than I ever had before'.

When he was summoned, Vasily was so scared of his father that he thought he would have to present his work and pitifully arrived with his air-force maps. He was soon drunk. Throughout the next two days, he lurched in and out of the quiet sickroom, shouting:

'You swine haven't saved my father!' Svetlana was embarrassed to hear him. The leaders wondered whether to remove this loose cannon but Voroshilov took Vasily aside, soothing him:

'We're doing all we can to save your father's life.'

Once it was proved that he was incapacitated, Beria 'spewed forth his hatred of Stalin' but whenever his eyelids flickered or his eyes opened, Beria, terrified that he would recover, 'knelt and kissed his hand' like an Oriental vizier at a Sultan's bedside. When Stalin sank again into sleep, Beria virtually spat at him, revealing his reckless ambition, and lack of tact and prudence. The other magnates observed him silently but they were weeping for Stalin, their old but flawed friend, longtime leader, historical titan, and the supreme pontiff of their international creed, even as they sighed with relief that he was dying. Perhaps 20 million had been killed; 28 million deported, of whom 18 million had slaved in the Gulags. Yet, after so much slaughter, they were still believers.

At about ten, the entire old Politburo, from Beria and Khrushchev, to Molotov, Voroshilov and Mikoyan, headed to the Kremlin where they met at 10.40 a.m. in the Little Corner to agree a plan. Stalin's seat stood empty. They had restored themselves to power. For ten minutes, Dr Kuperin, the new Kremlevka chief, and Professor Tkachev nervously presented the report quoted above to the confused, upset and pent-up magnates. Afterwards, no one spoke, which made Kuperin even more nervous. It was perhaps too early to discuss what would happen next. Finally, Beria, who had already emerged as the most active leader, dismissed the doctors with this ominous order:

'You're responsible for Comrade Stalin's life. Do you understand? You must do everything possible and impossible to save Comrade Stalin!' Kuperin flinched, then withdrew. Malenkov, with whom Beria seemed to be co-ordinating everything, read out a decree for twenty-four hour vigils by the leaders in pairs. Then Beria and Malenkov sped back to Kuntsevo to watch over the patient. Molotov and Mikoyan were not asked to keep vigil: Beria ordered Mikoyan to stay in the Kremlin and run the country.

Back at Kuntsevo, when Malenkov was on vigil with Beria, they requested the doctor's prognosis. Kuperin displayed a chart of the blood circulation:

'You see the clotted blood vessel,' he lectured the Politburo as if to medical students. 'It's the size of a five-kopeck piece. Comrade Stalin would remain alive if the vessel had been cleared in time.'

'Who guarantees the life of Comrade Stalin?' Beria challenged the doctors to operate if they dared.

'No one dared,' said Lozgachev. Malenkov asked for the prognosis:

'Death is inevitable,' replied the doctors. But Malenkov did not want Stalin to die yet: there could be no interregnum.

At 8.30 p.m., the leaders, chaired now by Beria, met again for an hour at the Little Corner. Kuperin's official report did not present Stalin's condition as hopeless but the patient had deteriorated. His blood pressure was now 210 over 120, breathing and heartbeat irregular. Six to eight leeches were applied around his ears. Stalin received enemas of magnesium sulphate, and spoonfuls of sweet tea.

That evening, Lukomsky was joined by four more doctors including the eminent Professor Myasnikov: the Politburo knew the top doctors were all in prison.

At Kuntsevo, Dr Myasnikov found 'a short and fat' Stalin lying there 'in a heap ... His face was contorted ... The diagnosis seemed clear – a haemorrhage in the left cerebral hemisphere resulting from hypertension and sclerosis.' The doctors kept their detailed log, taking notes every twenty minutes. The magnates sat blearily in armchairs, stretching their legs, standing by the bedside, watching the doctors. These endless nights gave them the chance to plan the transfer of power.

'Malenkov gave us to understand,' wrote Myasnikov, 'he hoped that medical measures would succeed in prolonging the patient's life "for a sufficient period". We all realized he had in mind the time necessary for the organization of the new Government.'

There were no more official meetings in the Kremlin until 5 March. While Beria and Malenkov whispered about the distribution of offices, Khrushchev and Bulganin wondered how to prevent Beria grabbing control of the secret police. Beria's plans had been laid long before, probably with Malenkov: since no Georgian could rule Russia again, Malenkov planned to head the Government while remaining Secretary. Beria would seize his old fiefdom, the MGB/MVD.

Late at night, Mikoyan looked in on the dying man. Molotov was ill but he appeared from time to time, thinking of his Polina whom he hoped was alive in exile. He did not know she was being interrogated in the Lubianka. But that evening, on Beria's orders, her interrogations abruptly stopped. The interrogations of the doctors continued, however. The factotum of the Doctors' Plot, Ignatiev, was noticed nervously peering at the prone Stalin from the doorway. He was still terrified of him.

'Come in – don't be shy!' said Lozgachev. The next morning Khrushchev popped home to sleep and told his family that Stalin was ill.

There were moments when Stalin seemed to regain consciousness: they were feeding him with soup from a teaspoon, when he pointed up at one of the mawkish photographs on the wall of a girl feeding a lamb and then 'pointed at himself'. 'He sort of smiled,' thought Khrushchev. The magnates smiled back. Molotov thought it was an example of Stalin's self-deprecating wit. Beria fell to his knees and kissed Stalin's hand fervently. Stalin closed his eyes, 'never to open them again'. At 10.15 a.m. that morning the doctors reported that Stalin had worsened.

'The bastards have killed Father,' Vasily lurched in again. Khrushchev put his arm round this tiny terrified man, guiding him into the next room.

Beria, who went home for some lunch, was open about his relief. 'It will better for him to die,' he told his family. 'If he survives it will be as a vegetable.' Nina was still weeping about Stalin's death: 'You're a funny one, Nina. His death has saved your life.' Nina visited Svetlana daily to comfort her.

Late on the 4th, Stalin started to deteriorate, his breathing becoming shorter and shallower, the Cheyne-Stokes breathing pattern of a patient losing strength. Beria and Malenkov checked up on their Second Eleven of doctors. That night, three surprised prisoners, tortured daily in the Doctors' Plot, were led off for another session. But this time, their torturers was not interested in the Zionist conspiracy but politely asked their medical advice.

'My uncle is very sick,' said the interrogator, and is experiencing 'this Cheyne-Stokes breathing. What do you think this means?'

'If you're expecting to inherit from your uncle,' replied the professor, who had not lost his Jewish wit, 'consider it's in your pocket.' Another distinguished professor, Yakov Rapoport, was asked to name the specialists who should treat this 'sick uncle'. Rapoport named Vinogradov and the other doctors under arrest. But the interrogator asked if Doctors Kuperin and Lukomsky were good too. He was shocked when Rapoport replied, 'Only one of the four's a competent physician but on a much lower level than the men in prison.' The interrogations continued but the investigators had lost interest. Sometimes they fell asleep during the sessions. The prisoners knew nothing.

At 11.30 p.m. Stalin retched. There were long pauses between ragged breaths. Kuperin told the assembled grandees, who watched in awed silence, that the situation was critical.

'Take all measures to save Comrade Stalin!' ordered the excited Beria. So the doctors continued to struggle to keep the dying Generalissimo alive. An artificial respirator was wheeled in and never used but it was accompanied by young technicians who stared 'goggle-eyed' at the surreal things happening all around them.

On the 5th, Stalin suddenly paled and his breathing became shallower with longer intervals. The pulse was fast and faint. He started to wiggle his head. There were spasms in his left arm and leg. At midday, Stalin vomited blood. The latest research has uncovered a first draft of the doctors' medical notes, which reveal that his stomach was haemorrhaging, a detail deleted from the final report. Perhaps it was cut because it might suggest poisoning. Warfarin might well have caused such bleeding, which does indeed look suspicious, but it may just have marked the collapse of a sick old body.

'Come quickly, Stalin's had a setback!' Malenkov told Khrushchev. The magnates rushed back. Stalin's pulse slowed. At 3.35 p.m., his breathing stopped for five seconds every two or three minutes. He was sinking fast. Beria, Khrushchev and Malenkov had received the Politburo's permission to ensure that Stalin's 'documents and papers, both current and archival, are put in proper order'. Now, leaving the other two at the bedside, Beria sped into the Kremlin to begin the process of searching Stalin's safe and files for incriminating documents. First there may have been a will: Lenin had left a testament and Stalin had talked of recording his thoughts. If so, Beria now destroyed it. The files were filled with denunciations and evidence against all the leaders. There would have been evidence of Beria's dubious role in Baku during the Civil War and there would also have been the missing documents that revealed the bloody role of Malenkov and Khrushchev in the Great Terror, the Leningrad Case and the Doctors' Plot. That afternoon, these three began the destruction of documents. This successfully protected the historical reputation of Khrushchev and Malenkov, even if Beria's was already beyond repair.*

Beria returned. The doctors reported on the latest decline. An official meeting of the whole regime, three-hundred senior officials, was set for that evening. Now the magnates gathered informally in one of the other rooms to form the new Government. Beria and his 'billygoat' Malenkov had prearranged the 'collective leadership', taking turns proposing the appointments. Molotov and Mikoyan returned to the Presidium, shrunk

---

* Five telling letters were supposedly found under a sheet of newspaper in Stalin's desk, Khrushchev told A. V. Snegov, who could only remember three of them to the historian Roy Medvedev. The first was Lenin's letter of 1923 demanding that Stalin apologize for his rudeness to his wife, Krupskaya. The second was Bukharin's last plea: 'Koba, why do you need me to die?' The third was from Tito in 1950. It was said to read: 'Stop sending assassins to murder me ... If this doesn't stop, I will send a man to Moscow and there'll be no need to send any more.'

to its previous size. Molotov returned as Foreign Minister, Mikoyan as Minister of Internal and External Trade. Khrushchev remained one of the senior Secretaries but he was excluded from the Government. Beria was dominant, reuniting the MVD and MGB while remaining First Deputy Premier. Malenkov succeeded to both Stalin's posts of Premier and Secretary. Yet the military were also strengthened: Defence Minister Bulganin's new deputies were the old paladins, Zhukov and Vasilevsky. Voroshilov became President. No wonder Beria was exultant.

The illegitimate Mingrelian, trained as an architect but seasoned in the police, was already dreaming of ruling the Imperium, one of the nuclear superpowers, and becoming an international statesman, not just a secret policeman any more. He had survived against all the odds; he was free of fear. He could unleash his loathing of Stalin: 'That scoundrel! That filth! Thank God we're free of him!' He could expose that phoney Generalissimo: 'He didn't win the war!' he was soon telling his confidants. 'We won the war!' Furthermore, 'We would have avoided the war!' He harnessed the phrase 'the cult of personality' to denounce Stalin. He would free the nationalities, open the economy, liberate East Germany, empty the labour camps with a beneficent amnesty and expose the Doctors' Plot. He did not doubt for a moment that his superior intelligence and fresh anti-Bolshevik ideas would triumph. Even Molotov realized 'he was a man of the future'.

If his policies seemed to prefigure Gorbachev's reforms, Beria always remained 'just a policeman', in Stalin's words, for he was itching to avenge himself on those, such as Vlasik, who had betrayed him. He was not the successor, merely the strongman in a 'collective leadership'. But many of the new potentates feared him, his brutality and his bid for popularity by de-Bolshevizing the regime. Beria underestimated Khrushchev and the marshals. None the less, it was a remarkable achievement.

Afterwards, the magnates gathered beside the wheezing patient. Beria approached the bedside and announced melodramatically like a Crown Prince in a movie:

'Comrade Stalin, all the members of the Politburo are here. Speak to us!' There was no reaction. Voroshilov pulled Beria back:

'Let the bodyguards and staff come to the bedside – he knows them intimately.' Colonel Khrustalev stood by the bed and spoke to him. Stalin did not open his eyes. The leaders queued to bid goodbye, forming up in pairs like a crocodile of schoolchildren in order of importance, with Beria and Malenkov first, then Voroshilov, Molotov, Kaganovich and Mikoyan, followed by the younger leaders. They shook his hand ritually. Malenkov claimed that Stalin squeezed his fingers, passing him the succession.

Leaving just Bulganin at the bedside, the potentates then rushed to the Kremlin where the Presidium, Council of Ministers and Supreme Soviet Presidium gathered to rubber-stamp the new Government: they removed Stalin as Premier but strangely left him as a Presidium member. The three hundred or so officials confirmed the prearranged deal. There was a sense of 'relief' among the magnates.*

They expected a call from Bulganin to announce Stalin's death but none came. Stalin was still holding out and they headed back to Kuntsevo. After 9 p.m., he started to sweat. His pulse was weak, his lips turned blue. The Politburo, Svetlana Stalin, Valechka, the guards gathered round the sofa. The junior leaders crowded outside, watching from the doorway.

At 9.30 p.m., Stalin's breaths were forty-eight a minute. His heartbeat grew fainter. At 9.40 p.m. with everyone watching, the doctors gave Stalin oxygen. His pulse virtually disappeared. The doctors proposed an injection of camphor and adrenalin to stimulate his heart. It should have been Vasily and Svetlana's decision but they just watched. Beria gave the order. Stalin gave a shiver after the injection and became increasingly breathless. He slowly began to drown in his own fluids.

'Take Svetlana away,' commanded Beria to prevent her seeing this dread vision – but no one moved.

'His face was discoloured,' wrote Svetlana, 'his features becoming unrecognizable ... He literally choked to death as we watched. The death agony was terrible ... At the last minute, he opened his eyes. It was a terrible look, either mad or angry and full of the fear

---

* Khrushchev and Bulganin did protect Ignatiev who became a CC Secretary but Beria later managed to get him sacked for his part in the Doctors' Plot. Yet he was merely reprimanded and sent to Bashkiria as First Secretary before moving on to run Tataria. Khrushchev presented him as a victim not a monster in his Secret Speech. Most of the top Chekists of the Doctors' Plot, including Ogoltsov, who had commanded Mikhoels's murder, and Ryasnoi, were protected under Khrushchev, and later under Brezhnev. Khrushchev's punishment of Stalin's crimes was highly selective. Ignatiev received medals on his seventieth birthday in 1974. The luckiest of Stalin's MGB bosses, he was the only one to die, respected, in his bed aged seventy-nine in 1983.

of death.' Suddenly the rhythm of his breathing changed. His left hand rose. A nurse thought it was 'like a greeting'. He 'seemed either to be pointing upwards somewhere or threatening us all ...' observed Svetlana. It was more likely that he was simply clawing the air for oxygen. 'Then the next moment, his spirit after one last effort tore itself from his body.' A woman doctor burst into tears and threw her arms around the devastated Svetlana.

The struggle was not over yet. A Brobdingnagian doctor fell on the corpse and started artificial respiration, athletically massaging the chest. It was so painful to watch that Khrushchev felt sorry for Stalin:

'Stop it please! Can't you see the man's dead? What do you want? You won't bring him back to life. He's already dead,' Khrushchev called out, showing his impulsive authority in the first order not given by Beria or Malenkov. Stalin's features became 'pale ... serene, beautiful, imperturbable,' wrote Svetlana. 'We all stood frozen and silent.'

Once again they formed up in that uneasy crocodile: Beria darted forward and ritually kissed the warm body first, the equivalent of wrenching a dead king's ring off his finger. The others queued up to kiss him. Voroshilov, Kaganovich, Bulganin, Khrushchev and Malenkov were sobbing with Svetlana. Molotov cried, mourning Stalin despite his own imminent liquidation and that of his wife. Mikoyan hid his feelings but 'it may be said I was lucky'. Beria was not crying: indeed he was 'radiant' and 'regenerated' – a bulging but effervescent grey toad, glistening with ill-concealed relish. He strode through the weeping potentates into the hall. The sepulchral silence around the deathbed was suddenly 'shattered by the sound of his loud voice, the ring of triumph unconcealed', in Svetlana's words:

'Khrustalev, the car!' he bellowed, heading for the Kremlin.

'He's off to take power,' Mikoyan said to Khrushchev. Svetlana noticed 'they were all terrified of him.' They looked after him – and then with frenzied haste, 'the members of the government rushed for the door ...' Mikoyan and Bulganin remained a little longer but then they too called for their limousines. The *Instantsiya* had left the building. The colossus had vanished, leaving only the husk of an old man on a sofa in an ugly suburban house.

Just the servants and family remained: 'cooks, chauffeurs and watchmen, gardeners and women who waited at table' now emerged out of the background 'to say goodbye'. Many were sobbing, with rough bodyguards wiping their eyes with their sleeves 'like children'. A weeping old nurse gave them valerian drops. Svetlana watched numbly. Some servants started to turn off the lights and tidy up.

Then Stalin's closest companion, the comfort of the cruel loneliness of this unparalleled monster, Valechka, who was now aged thirty-eight and had worked with Stalin since she was twenty, pushed through the crying maids, 'dropped heavily to her knees' and threw herself on to the corpse with all the uninhibited grief of the ordinary people. This cheerful but utterly discreet woman, who had seen so much, was convinced to her dying day that 'no better man ever walked the earth'. Laying her head squarely on his chest, Valechka, with tears pouring down the cheeks of 'her round face', 'wailed at the top of her voice as the women in the villages do. She went on for a long time and nobody tried to stop her.'

Postscript

Stalin was embalmed. On 9 March 1953, Molotov, Beria and Khrushchev spoke at his funeral, after which he was laid in the Mausoleum beside Lenin. Polina Molotova was still in the Lubianka. The next day, Beria invited Molotov to his office there. When Molotov arrived, Beria rushed ahead to greet Polina: 'A heroine!' he declared. Her first question was 'How's Stalin?' She fainted when she learned he was dead. Molotov took her home.

Beria moved to liberalize the regime and arrested those responsible for the Doctors' Plot but his proposal to free East Germany provoked an uprising that alarmed the other magnates. Khrushchev began to plan Beria's destruction. He won over Premier Malenkov and Defence Minister Bulganin. Molotov still admired Beria but agreed to support Khrushchev because of the German crisis. Surprisingly, President Voroshilov supported Beria. When he was consulted, Mikoyan said he distrusted Khrushchev because he was so close to Beria and Malenkov. Khrushchev did not tell Mikoyan the whole story, but he agreed that Beria should be demoted to Petroleum Minister. Kaganovich typically sat on the fence. But Marshal Zhukov and his generals provided the muscle.

On 25 June, Beria was swinging gaily on his hammock at his dacha, singing Georgian songs. He had been called to a special meeting of the Presidium. Nina warned him to be careful but he was not worried because he explained that Molotov supported him. At about 1 p.m. next day, Khrushchev stood up at the meeting and attacked Beria. Bulganin joined in but Mikoyan was surprised to hear that Beria was to be arrested.

'What's going on, Nikita?' Beria asked. 'Why are you searching for fleas in my trousers?' When it was Malenkov's turn to support the coup, he lost his nerve and gave a secret signal to the generals waiting outside. Marshal Zhukov burst in and seized Beria.

Nina Beria, her son Sergo and daughter-in-law Martha Peshkova were also arrested and imprisoned. From his cell, Beria bombarded Malenkov with letters begging for his help and mercy for his family. On 22 December, he, along with Merkulov, Dekanozov and Kobulov, was sentenced to death by a secret political court for treason and terrorism, charges of which these killers were obviously innocent.

Beria was stripped to his underwear; hands manacled and attached to a hook on the wall. He frantically begged to be allowed to live, making such a noise that a towel was stuffed in his mouth. His eyes bulged over the bandage wrapped round his face. His executioner – General Batitsky (later promoted to Marshal for his role) – fired directly into Beria's forehead. He was cremated. His protégé and then rival, Abakumov, was tried for the Leningrad Case and shot in December 1954. Many of Stalin's crimes were blamed on them.

When the new leaders began to release prisoners, their reactions were often similar. Kira Alliluyeva, herself newly released, picked up her mother Zhenya from the Lubianka.

'So finally, Stalin saved us after all!' declared Zhenya.

'You fool!' exclaimed Kira. 'Stalin's dead!' Zhenya admired Stalin up to her death in 1974. Her sister-in-law Anna Redens, like Budyonny's second wife, Olga, had lost her mind in confinement and never recovered. Vlasik returned broken from prison but he and Poskrebyshev remained friends, both dying in the mid-sixties.

Khrushchev emerged as the dominant leader. Malenkov was removed as Premier and replaced by Bulganin. In 1956, Khrushchev, backed by Mikoyan, famously denounced Stalin's crimes in his 'Secret Speech'. Five years later, Stalin's body was removed from the Mausoleum and buried in the Kremlin wall.

In 1957, Molotov, Kaganovich and Malenkov, backed by Voroshilov and Bulganin, managed to overthrow Khrushchev in the Presidium. However Khrushchev mobilized the Central Committee, flying in his supporters in planes organized by Marshal Zhukov.

At a Plenum, Stalin's murderous magnates scrambled to blame one another for their crimes: 'Sleeves rolled up, axe in hand, they lopped off heads,' Zhukov accused them – and Khrushchev himself. Khrushchev attacked Malenkov who replied: 'Only you are completely pure, Comrade Khrushchev!' Kaganovich insisted 'the whole Politburo signed' the death lists. Khrushchev accused

him back but Kaganovich roared: 'Didn't you sign death warrants
in Ukraine?' Finally Khrushchev shouted: 'All of us taken together
aren't worth Stalin's shit!' As a recent historian has written, 'this
was certainly no Nuremberg' but it was the 'closest Stalin's
henchmen came to a day of reckoning'. Molotov, Kaganovich
and Malenkov were sacked. Kaganovich and Malenkov were
despatched to run a potash factory and powerstation respectively
in distant regions. Malenkov's daughter says her father found this
minor job a calming relief; Kaganovich's grandson reports that
'Iron Lazar' immediately discarded his notorious temper and
never shouted again, becoming a cosy grandfather.

Molotov became Soviet Ambassador to Mongolia and then, in
1960, Soviet Representative at the UN Atomic Agency in Vienna
so that he was present, ignored in the background, when President
Kennedy and Khrushchev met there with their delegations in
June 1961.

Khrushchev, like Stalin before him, became Premier as well as
First Secretary. Marshal Zhukov became Defence Minister as a
reward for his help but his pugnacity and fame threatened the
increasingly vainglorious Khrushchev who sacked him for
'Bonapartism'. By 1960, when the senile Voroshilov retired as
President, Khrushchev and Mikoyan were the last of Stalin's
magnates in power. During the Cuba Missile Crisis, it was
Mikoyan who flew to Havana, accompanied by his son Sergo, to
persuade Castro to agree to Khrushchev's compromise, and then
on to Washington to talk to Kennedy. Mikoyan, who had helped
carry Lenin's coffin, also attended JFK's funeral.

After the scare of the Missile Crisis and the autocratic folly of
his agricultural panaceas, Khrushchev was overthrown in 1964 by
a cabal of Stalin's young stars, Brezhnev, Kosygin and their
éminence grise, Suslov, who ruled until their deaths in the eighties.
Mikoyan survived even this upheaval and became President,
retiring in 1965.

The old magnates found it hard to cope with their fall. They
had expected to be arrested so were all relieved to be alive. When
they left their apartments in the Kremlin in 1957, Kaganovich
and Andreyev found they did not even own their own towels or
sheets. Many of them were granted apartments in the palatial
Granovsky buildings where the shrewd Molotov managed to secure
two apartments as well as a dacha. Kaganovich and Malenkov
retired to spartan but large apartments in another building on the

Frunze Embankment but avoided each other. These famous and blood-spattered old pensioners spent their retirements writing their memoirs, receiving Stalinist admirers, avoiding the hostile stares of former victims they encountered in the street, applying for readmission to the Party, and shuffling through papers in the Lenin Library: they were non-people but spotting them became a thrilling form of living archaeology.

Happily and lovingly reunited, Molotov and Polina remained unapologetic Stalinists: Svetlana wrote that visiting them was like entering a 'palaeontological museum'. The prickly disdain between Molotov and Kaganovich lasted until their deaths but was as nothing compared to their loathing for Khrushchev. He admitted being 'up to his elbows' in the blood of his victims and 'that burdens my soul'. He defied his successors by dictating his selectively honest memoirs, dying in 1971. Despite his illnesses, Andreyev died the same year: the commemorative plaque on the wall outside Granovsky makes him the last of Stalin's butchers to be celebrated. Mikoyan wrote frank but equally selective memoirs until his death in 1978.

Three others survived into another era: while Polina died in 1970, Molotov left his remorseless reminiscences, to posterity, in conversations with a sympathetic journalist. He survived to see the accession of Gorbachev, passing away in 1986. Malenkov remained a Stalinist but enjoyed the poetry of Mandelstam and rediscovered the Christian faith of his childhood that may have been a sort of repentance. In 1988, he was buried beneath a cross and the (utterly inappropriate) statue of the 'lion of justice', sculpted by his grandson. Kaganovich, ever the most cautious and pusillanimous, outlived everyone to witness the beginning of the end of the Soviet Union that he had helped build, dying in 1991.

Their families have enjoyed mixed fortunes and take very different views of Stalin and their parents' roles: most became editors, architects or scientists. Vasily Stalin was sent to prison, released, remarried and finally died tragically of alcoholism in 1962. His son Alexander, who uses his mother's name, is a respected theatrical designer in Moscow, but his two children by Marshal Timoshenko's daughter both died young – of alcoholism. Svetlana Alliluyeva defected and returned to Russia and then left again, married an American by whom she had a daughter, lived in Harvard and Cambridge, made and lost a fortune with her beautifully written memoirs, finally found herself without means in sheltered housing in Bristol and is now living alone in obscurity in the American Midwest. Having embraced liberalism and rejected Stalinism, she has displayed both her father's intelligence and his paranoia. Her Russian children, Joseph Morozov and Katya Zhdanova, are both doctors in Russia.

Yury Zhdanov remarried and returned to academia, becoming Rector of Rostov-on-Don University where he still lives as an honoured professor emeritus, admirer of Stalin and defender of his father. Artyom Sergeev remained in the military, rose to Lieutenant-General and lives outside Moscow. The rest of the Alliluyev family remains close: Kira Alliluyeva worked as an actress and is as as irrepressible today as she was when she refused to climb under Stalin's billiard table in 1937.

Stepan Mikoyan flourished as a test pilot and also rose to Lieutenant-General. His younger brother Sergo edited a magazine on Latin America. Both live in Moscow. Kaganovich's daughter Maya married and had children and cared for her father in old age, only outliving him for a few years.

Sergo Beria and Martha Peshkova were released and moved to Kiev with Beria's widow Nina, who never stopped loving her husband. In 1965, Martha divorced Sergo who continued to work as a missile scientist under his mother's name, Gegechkori. Shortly before his death in 2000, he published his memoirs and appealed to the Russian Supreme Court to rehabilitate his father. The Court upheld the trumped-up charges against Beria. Martha, who has kept her looks, still lives in her large dacha on the old estate of her grandfather, Gorky. Beria's charming grandchildren, who use the Peshkov name, are an interior decorator, an art academic and an electronics expert.

Lilya Drozhdova, Beria's 'last love', never betrayed him. She lives in Moscow and, in her early sixties, remains beautiful.

Budyonny's third wife still lives in his apartment on Granovsky filled with life-sized paintings of the Marshal on horseback. The apartments there are now worth over a million dollars so that the Molotovs rent out theirs to American investment bankers, perhaps proving right Stalin's suspicions of Vyacheslav's 'Rightist' tendencies. Molotov's grandson Vyacheslav Nikonov was one of the leading liberals of 1991, who helped open up the KGB archives and became one of President Yeltsin's top advisers, serving on his re-election team in 1996. He now runs one of Moscow's most respected political think-tanks and is writing his grandfather's biography.

Perhaps Stalin was right about the Mikoyans too: Anastas's grandson Stas became a Soviet rock star, set up his own record label during the nineties and is now the leading Russian rock impresario, their Richard Branson. Beria's hope that his grandchildren would study at Oxford was not realized but his great-grandson has just left the English public school, Rugby. Malenkov's daughter Volya, an architect, followed her father's later religious journey to become a builder of churches in her old age: her business cards feature pictures of the churches she has built. She and her brothers, both professors of science, remained convinced of their father's innocence.

Stalin's confidant Candide Charkviani survived to see an independent Georgia in 1991 and wrote his unpublished memoirs. His son Gela served as the chief political adviser to former President Shevardnadze since 1993.

To this day, the friendships and feuds of Stalin's reign survive among the children of the magnates. The families of the grandees who remained in power, Mikoyans, Khrushchevs and Budyonnys, are regarded as a Soviet aristocracy even now. Nina Budyonny, still a Stalinist, is best friends with Julia Khrushcheva, who is not. The friendship of Marshals Budyonny and Zhukov is not only enjoyed by their daughters but by their grandchildren too. Stepan Mikoyan remains friends with Natasha Andreyeva even though the former is a liberal, the latter a diehard Stalinist. Artyom Sergeev remains in contact with those close pals, Nadya Vlasik and Natasha Poskrebysheva. But the Malenkovs and Andreyevs still despise Khrushchev.

It is only natural that all defend their fathers' parts in the Terror. The Khrushchevs and Mikoyans have the courage and decency to admit the truth, reflecting their fathers' attempts to correct the worst of Stalin's (and their own) atrocities. None the less, many of the magnates' children still enthusiastically defend the Terror and many prefer to blame Beria for Stalin's own crimes.

Martha Peshkova, who was brought up with Gorky in Sorrento, who still believes her grandfather and father were murdered, who as a child played with Stalin, reflects that 'Stalin was as clever as he was cruel. Politics in Stalin's time was like a closed jar with intriguers fighting one another to the death. What a frightening time! But if Beria had had his way after Stalin, he'd have improved the lifestyle of the country and we'd probably have avoided the destruction and poverty of today!'

Vladimir Alliluyev (Redens), whose father was shot on Stalin's orders and whose mother lost her mind in his prisons, insists he was a 'great man with good and bad sides'. Natasha Poskrebysheva, whose mother was shot by Stalin, admires him enormously and claims to be his daughter. Natasha Andreyeva, who lives in straitened circumstances in an apartment filled with her father's art deco Kremlin furniture, remains the most aggressively Stalinist. 'I have inherited my mother's intuition,' she warned this author during his interview for this book. 'I can see an Enemy by their eyes. Are you an Enemy? Are you afraid of the Red Flag?' She still supports the Terror: 'We had to destroy spies before the war.' Despite the bulging file chronicling her father's murderous spree in 1937, she asserts his innocence and claims, 'Khrushchev's dirty hands killed far more in Ukraine!' The 'system', not Stalin, were to blame for any 'mistakes', Andreyeva concludes. 'But you Western capitalists have killed many more in Russia with your AIDS than Stalin ever did!'

Those who lived the extraordinary, terrible and privileged life as a child of Stalin's grandees remain linked together and it is no surprise that their attitudes defy time – and the fate of their own families. The passionately optimistic ideals of Marxism-Leninism-Stalinism and the imperial triumphs of the Generalissimo's armies remain as potent and persuasive as the presence of Stalin himself, of whom they are never free. Old Molotov was asked if he dreamed about Stalin: 'Not often but sometimes. The circumstances are very unusual. I'm in some sort of destroyed city and I can't find a way out. Afterwards, I meet HIM ...'

Source Notes

The full and extremely extensive references for this book are available in the hardback edition and also on the author's website at:

http://www.simonsebagmontefiore.com

Many of the sources for this work are totally new. However, to make the paperback a manageable and readable size, the author and publisher have decided not to include them in the paperback. We hope the readers will agree that, for most, the balance of convenience is best served by this policy.

Select Bibliography

Primary

Antipenko, N. A. 'Tyl Fronta', *Novy Mir*, no. 8, 1965

Alanbrooke, Viscount, *War Diaries 1939–45*, London 2001

Alexandrov, G. V. *Epokha I kino*, Moscow 1983

Alliluyeva, Svetlana, *Twenty Letters to a Friend*, London 1967

Alliluyeva, Svetlana, *Only One Year*, London 1971

Alliluyev, Sergei, *Proidennyi put*, Moscow 1946

Alliluyeva, Anna S., *Vospominaniya*, Moscow 1946

Alliluyev, Sergei, and Anna Alliluyeva, (ed. David Tutaev), *The Alliluyev Memoirs*, London 1968

Babel, Isaac, *1920 Diary*, New Haven, CT 1990

Babel, Isaac, *Collected Stories*, London 1994

Baibakov, N. K., *Delo zhizni: zapiski neftyanika*, Moscow 1984

Bazhanov, Boris, *Bazhanov and the Damnation of Stalin*, Athens, OH 1990

Berezhkov, Valentin, *Kak ia stal perevodchikom Stalina*, Moscow 1963

Berezhkov, Valentin, *History in the Making, Memoirs of WW2 Diplomacy*, Moscow 1983

L. P. BERIA:

Beria, L. P., 'Lavrenty Beria: Pizma iz tyuemnogo bunkera', *Istochnik*, no. 4, 1994

Beria, L. P., *On the History of Bolshevik Organizations in Transcaucasia*, Moscow 1949

Beria, Nina, 'Letters to LP Beria', *Istochnik*, no. 2, 1994

Beria, Nina, 'Letter to Members of Presidium 7 January 1954', *Vlast*, no. 34, 2001

Beria, Sergo, *Beria My Father: Inside Stalin's Kremlin*, London 2001

The Beria Affair, The Meetings Signalling the End of Stalinism, (ed. D. M. Sickle), New York 1992.

Beria Affair, CC Plenum 12–7 July 1953, *Izvestiya TsK KPSS*, nos. 1 and 2, 1991

Bessedovsky, G., *Revelations of a Soviet Diplomat*, London 1931

Birse, A. H., *Memoirs of an Interpreter*, London 1967

Bohlen, Charles E., *Witness to History*, London 1973

Bolshakov, I. G., 'Letter to AN Poskrebyshev on film Tarzan', *Istochnik*, no. 4, 1999

Bukharin, Nikolai, *How It All Began*, New York 1998

Budyonny, S. M., *Proidennyi put*, Moscow 1968

Budyonny, S. M., (ed. Nina Budyonny), *Notes*, unpublished

Cadogan, Alexander, *The Diaries of Sir Alexander Cadogan*, London 1971

Charkviani, Candide, *Memoirs on Stalin*, unpublished

Chikobava, Arnold, 'Kogda ix kak eto bylo', *Ezhegodnik iberiysko-kavkazskogo yazykoznaniya*, vol. 12, 1985

W. S. CHURCHILL:

Churchill, Winston S., *Second World War*, London 1951

Churchill and Stalin, documents from British Archives, FCO Historians

Dan, Lydia, 'Bukharin o Staline', *Noviy Zhumal*, 75 (Mar. 1964).

Davies, Joseph E., *Mission to Moscow*, London 1942

Dedijer, V., *Tito Speaks*, London 1953

Dekanozov, Reginald, *Some Episodes of the History of Soviet–German Relations Before the War*, unpublished

Deriabin, Peter, *Inside Stalin's Kremlin*, Dulles, VA 1998

Dmitrov, Georgi (ed. Ivo Banac), *The Diary of Georgi Dmitrov 1933–49*, New Haven, CT 2003

Dobrynin, Anatoly, *In Confidence: Moscow's Ambassador to Six Cold War Presidents*, Washington DC 2001

Djilas, Milovan, *Conversations with Stalin*, NY 1962

Djilas, Milovan, *Wartime*, London 1980

Djugashvili, Gulia, *Ded, Otets, Mat i Drugie*, Moscow 1993

Eden, A., *Memoirs, Facing the Dictators*, London 1962

Efimov, Boris, *Mikhail Koltsov, Kakim On Byl*, Moscow 1965

Efremov, L. N., Memoir of Plenum, *Dosye Glastnosty, Spetsvypusk* 2001

Ehrenburg, Ilya, *Men, Years, Life*, London 1966

Eisenhower, D. D., *Crusade in Europe*, London 1948

Fedorenko, N. T., 'Zapiski diplomata. Rabota s Molotovym', *Novaya i Noveishaya Istoriya*, no. 4, 1991

Gaulle, Charles de, *Memoires de Guerre*, Paris 1959

Gaulle, Charles de, *Complete War Memoirs of Charles de Gaulle 1940–46*, NY 1964

Ginsburg, Eugenia S., *Journey into the Whirlwind*, NY 1967

Gnedin, E. A., *Katastrofa I vtoroe rozhdenie*, Amsterdam 1997

Gromyko, Andrei, *Memoirs*, London 1989

Gromyko, Andrei, *Pamyatnoye*, Moscow 1990

Grossman, Vasily, *Life and Fate*, London 1985

Grossman, Vasily, 'Mama', *Znamya*, vol. 5, 1989

Guinzburg, S. Z., *O proshlom, dlya budushchego*, Moscow 1984

Gunther, John, *Inside Russia Today*, NY 1962

Harriman, Averell W., and Elie Abel, *Special Envoy to Churchill and Stalin, 1941–6*, NY 1975

Hilger, Gustav and Alfred Mayer, *Incompatible Allies: A Memoir History of German–Soviet Relations 1918–41*, NY 1953

Hoxha, Enver (ed. Jon Halliday), *Artful Albanian: the Memoirs of Enver Hoxha*, London 1986

Iskander, Fasil, *Sandro of Chegem*, London 1979

L. M. KAGANOVICH:

Kaganovich, L. M. (ed. Felix Chuev), *Tak Govoril Kaganovich*, Moscow 1992

Kaganovich, L. M., *Pamiatniye Zapiski*, Moscow 1997

Kennan, George, *Memoirs*, Boston 1967

Kamov, B., 'Smert Nikolaia Yezhova', *Iunost*, no. 8, 1993

Kavtaradze, Sergo, *Memoirs*, unpublished

Kavtaradze, Sergo, Interview, *Literaturnaya Rossiya*, no. 12, 1989

N. S. KHRUSHCHEV:

Khrushchev, N. S. (Jerrold Schecter and Vyacheslav Luchkov, eds), *Khrushchev Remembers: the Glasnost Tapes*, NY 1990

Khrushchev, N. S., *Khrushchev Remembers*, London 1971/London 1974

Khrushchev, N, S. 'Memuary Nikity Sergeevicha Khrushcheva', *Voprosy Istorii* 1990–95

Khrushchev, Sergei, *Nikita Khrushchev and the Creation of a Superpower*, Pennsylvania 2001

Koniev, I. S., *Sorok pyatyi*, Moscow 1966

Koniev, I. S., *Zapiski kommanduushchego frontom*, Moscow 1991

Kopelev, Lev, *No Jail for Thought*, London 1977

Krivitsky, Walter, *I Was Stalin's Agent*, London 1940

Kravchenko, Victor, *I Chose Freedom*, NY 1946

Krementsov, Nikolai, *Stalinist Science*, Princeton, NJ 1997

Kuznetsov, N. G., Memoirs, *Voprosy Istorii*, no. 4–5, 1965

Larina, Anna, *This I Cannot Forget, The Memoirs of Nikolai Bukharin's Widow*, London 1993

Lunghi, Hugh, *Minutes of Meeting between Generalissimo JV Stalin and Admiral Mountbatten at Babelsberg, Germany, 25 July 1945 at 12.45 hours*, unpublished

Lunghi, Hugh, *Tribute to Sir Winston Churchill at Churchill Memorial Concert*, Blenheim Palace 1 March 1997

Lunghi, Hugh, *Meeting Stalin*, European Service, General News Talk, BBC, 1 March 1963

Maisky, Ivan, *Memoirs of a Soviet Ambassador*, London 1967

Malenkov, Andrei, *O moem otse Georgie Malenkove*, Moscow 1992

Malyshev, V. A., Notes, *Istochnik*, no. 5, 1997

Mandelstam, Nadezhda, *Hope Against Hope*, London 1999

Meretskov, K. A., *Na sluzhbe narodu*, Moscow 1970

Mgeladze, Akaki, *Stalin, kakim ya ego znal*, Tbilisi 2001

A. I. MIKOYAN:

Mikoyan, Anastas, *Tak bylo*, Moscow 2000

Mikoyan, N., 'A Month at Beria's Dacha', *Forum*, no. 3, 1995

Mikoyan, Stepan, *Memoirs of Military Test-flying and Life with the Kremlin's Elite*, London 1999

V. M. MOLOTOV:

Molotov, V. M. (ed. Felix Chuev), *Molotov Remembers*, Chicago 1993

Molotov, V. M. (ed. Felix Chuev), *Sto Sorok Besed s Molotovym*, Moscow 1991

Muratov, E., '6 Chasov s I V Stalinym na Prieme v Kremle', *Neva*, no. 7, 1993

Myasnikov, A. I., Medical notes on JV Stalin's Illness, *Literaturnaya Gazeta*, 1 March 1989

Nutsibidze, Ketevan and Shalva, *Nakaduli*, Tbilisi 1993

Okunevskaya, Tatiana, *Tatianin den*, Moscow, 1998

Orlov, Alexander, *Secret History of Stalin's Crimes*, London 1954

Ortenberg, David, 'U Zhukova v Perkbushkogo', *Krasnaya Zvezda*, 30 Nov. 1991

Ortenberg David, *Stalin Shcherbakov Mekhlis i Drugie*, Moscow 1995

Pahlavi, HIM Mohammed Reza, *Mission for My Country*, London 1961

Parrott, Cecil, *The Serpent and the Nightingale*, London 1977

Patolichev, N. S., *Ispytanie na zrelost*, Moscow 1977

Pavlov, V. N., Avtobiographicheskie Zametki', *Novaya i Noveishaya Istoriya*, 2000, no. 4

Plisetskaya, Maya, and Tim Scholl, *I, Maya*, New Haven, CT 2001

Platonov, Andrei, *The Foundation Pit*, London 1996

Pronin, Vasily P., 'Gorod u linii fronta', in *Moskovskie Novosti*, no. 21, 26 Mar./2 Apr. 1995, p. 14

Pronin, Vasily P, *Gorod-voin, Bitva za Moskvu*, Moscow 1966

Pirozhkova, A. N., *At His Side, The Last Ten Years of Isaac Babel*, VT 1996

Putin, Vladimir, *First Person*, NY 2000

Rapoport, Yakov, *The Doctors' Plot, Stalin's Last Crime*, London 1991

Razgon, Lev, *Plen v svoem otechestve*, Moscow 1994

Roberts, Frank, *Dealing with Dictators*, London 1991

Rokossovsky, K., *Soldatskiy dolg*, Moscow 1968

Romanov, A. I., *The Nights are Longest There*, Boston 1972

Rosliakov, K., *Ubiistvo Kirova. Polititcheskie i ugolovnye prestupleniya v 1930 godakh*, Leningrad 1991

Rybin, A. G., *Stalin v Oktyabre 1941*, Moscow undated

Rybin, A. T., 'Ryadom s IV Stalinym', *Soziologicheskie Issledovaniya*, no. 3, 1988

Rybin, A. T., *Stalin i Zhukov*, Moscow 1994

Rybin, A. T., *Ryadom Stalinym v Bolshom Teatre*, Moscow undated

Rybin A. T., *Kto Otravil Stalina?*, Moscow undated

Rybin, A. T., *Next to Stalin: Notes of a Bodyguard*, Toronto, 1996

Rzhevskaya E., 'B tot den pozdhnei oseniu' in SS Smirnov, *Marshal Zhukov: kakim my ego pomnim*, Moscow 1988

Sakharov, Andrei, *Memoirs*, NY 1992

Sbornik zakonodatelnykh i normativnykh actov o repressiyakh i reabilitatsii, Moscow 1993

Serge, Victor, *From Lenin to Stalin*, London 1937

Shakhurin, A., 'Memoirs' *Voprosy Istorii*, no. 3, 1975

Shepilov, D., *Neprimknuvshii*, Moscow 2001

Shepilov, D., Vospominaniya, *Voprosy Istoriii*, 1998, vols 3, 4, 5, 6

Shreider, M., *NKVD iznutri. Zapiski chekisti*, Moscow 1995

Sholokhov, Mikhail, *Virgin Soil Upturned*, London 1988

Shostakovich, Dmitri, *Testimony The Memoirs of Dmitri Shostakovich As related to and edited by Solomon Volkov*, London 1981

Shtemenko, S. M., *Generalnyi shtab v gody voiny*, Moscow 1981

Simonov, K., 'Glazami cheloveka moego pokoleniya', *Znamya*, no. 3, 1988

Simonov, K., 'Conversations with Admiral IS Isakov,' *Znamya*, no. 5, 1988

Simonov K., 'Zametki k biografii GK Zhukova', *Voprosy Istorii*, nos. 6, 7, 8, 9, 10, 12, 1987

Simonov, K., *Diaries*, RGALI, Moscow

Smith, Walter Bedell, *My Three Years in Moscow*, NY 1948

Smirnoff, S. S., *G. K. Zhukov: Kakim My Ego Pomnium*, Moscow 1988

J. V. STALIN:

Lih, Lars T., Oleg V. Naumov, and Oleg V. Khlevniuk (eds), *Stalin's Letters to Molotov*, New Haven, CT 1995

O. V. Khlevniuk, R. W. Davies, L. P. Kosheleva, E. A. Rees, and L. A. Rogovaya, *Stalin i Kaganovich Perepiska 1931–36*, Moscow 2001

Stalin, J. V., *Sochineniya*, Moscow 1946–1952

Stalin, J. V., *Ekonomicheskiye problemy socializma v SSSR*, Moscow 1953

Stalin, *Vystuplenie na prieme v Kremle v chest kommanduyushchikh voiskami Krasnoi Armii* in *Works* (ed. Robert McNeal), vol. II 1941–5, Stanford, CA 1967

'Stalin, Molotov Zhdanov o vtoroy serii filma Ivan Grozny', *Moskovskie Novosti*, no. 37, 7 Aug. 1988

'Josif Stalin v obiatiiakh semyii: iz lichnogo arkiva', *Istochnik*, Moscow 1993

Starostin, Nikolai, *Futbol skvoz gody*, Moscow 1992

Sudoplatov, Pavel, and Anatoli Sudoplatov, with Jerrold I. and Leona Schecter, *Special Tasks, the Memoirs of an Unwanted Witness, a Soviet Spymaster*, London 1994

Sukhanov, N. N., *The Russian Revolution 1917. A personal record*, London 1955

Sukhanov, D. M., *Memoirs*, Library of Congress

Timashuk, Lydia, 'Tsel byla spasti zhizn bolnogo. Pisma Lidii Timashuk', *Istochnik*, no. 1, 1997

Trotsky, Leon, *My Life*, NY 1930

Trotsky, Leon, *Stalin*, London 1968

Trail, Vera, *Memoirs of Yezhov*, unpublished

Trifinov, Yury, *House on the Embankment*, Evansto, IL 1999

Troyanovsky, Oleg, *Cherez godiy rasstoyaniya*, Moscow 1997

Valedinsky, I., 'Vospominaniya o vstrechah s tov. Stalinym IV, *Muzei Revolutsii*, vol. 23, bk. 2, Moscow 1992

Vaschchenko, N., *Za Grani Istorii*, Moscow 1998

Vasilevsky, A. M., *Delo Vsey Moey Zhizni*, Moscow 1978

Vishnevskaya, Galina, *Galina, Russian Story*, London 1984

N. S. VLASIK:

Vlasik, N. S., 'Moya Biografiya', *Shpion*, vols 8, 9

'Vlasik Case: Interrogations', *VIZh*, no. 12, 1989

Voronov, N.V., *Memoir of NV Voronov*, Volkogonov Collection, Reel 8, 6 June 1994

K. E. VOROSHILOV:

Voroshilov, K. E., *Stalin and the Armed Foces of the USSR*, Moscow 1951

Voroshilov, K. E., *Razzkaz o zhizni. Vospominaniya*, Moscow 1968

Werth, Alexander, *Year of Stalingrad*, London 1946

Werth, Alexander, *Russia at War*, London 1964

G. YAGODA:

Litvin, A. L., (ed.), *Genrikh Yagoda Narkom vnutrennikh del SSSR, Generalnyi kommissar gosudarstvennoy besopastnosti*, Kazan 1997

Yakovlev, A. S., *Tsel zhizni*, Moscow 1970

Yerofeev, Vladimir, 'Ten Years of Secretaryship', *International Affairs*, vol. 9, 1991

Zakharov, M. V., *Generalnyi shtab v predvoennye gody*, Moscow 1989

Zbarsky, Ilya, and Samuel Hutchinson, *Lenin's Embalmers*, London 1998

A. A. ZHDANOV:

A. A. Zhdanov, 'Doklad Zhdanova o zhurnalakh Zvezda i Leningrad', *Bolshevik*, nos. 17–18, September 1946

Zhdanov, Yury, 'O kritie i samokritike v nauchnoy rabote', *Bolshevik*, 1951, no. 21. pp. 28–43

Zhdanov, Yury, 'Vo mgle protivorechii,' *Voprosy Filosofii*, 1993, no. 7, p. 74

G.K. ZHUKOV:

Zhukov, G. K., *Vospominaniya i razmyshleniya*, 10th edn, Moscow 1990

Zhukov, G. K., 'Korotko o Staline', *Pravda*, 20 January 1989

Zhukov, G. K., 'Na Kurskoy Duge', *VIZh*, Aug. 1967

Secondary

Antonov-Ovseenko, Anton, *The Time of Stalin: Portrait of a Tyranny*, NY 1980

Antonov-Ovseenko, Anton, *Beria*, Moscow 1999

Applebaum, Anne, *GULAG: A History of the Soviet Concentration Camps*, London 2003

Aptekov, Pavel, and Olga Dudorova, 'Peace and statistics of losses: Unheeded Warning and the Winter War', *Slavic Military Studies*, vol. 10, no. 1, March 1997

Avtorkhanov, Abdurakhman, *Stalin and the Soviet Communist Party*, London 1959

Axell, Albert, *Stalin's War Through the Eyes of his Commanders*, London 1997

Babichenko, D., and M. Sidorov, 'Nevelika pobeda', *Itogi*, no. 31 (269), 2001

Barsukov, N., 'Mart 1953. Stranitsy Istorii KPSS', *Pravda*, 27 Oct. 1989

Barbosa, Adalberto Zelmar, *El Federalismo Bloquista: Bravo o el pragmatismo politico*, Buenos Aires 1988

Beevor, Antony, *Stalingrad*, London 1998

Beevor, Antony, *Berlin The Downfall 1945*, London 2002

Biagi, Enzo, *Svetlana: The Inside Story*, London, 1967

Bialer, Seweryn (ed.), *Stalin and his Generals*, NY 1969

Bloch, Michael, *Ribbentrop*, London 1994

Blotsky, Oleg, *Vladimir Putin The Story of My Life*, Moscow 2002

Bobrenov, V., and V. Wiazantsev, 'Marshal protiv Marshala', *Armia*, 1993 nos 8, 9, 10

Bortoli, Georges, *Death of Stalin*, London 1975

Bos, W. H., and E. M. Farber, 'Joseph Stalin's Psoriasis: Its Treatment and the Consequences', *Cutis*, vol. 59, Apr. 1997

Brackman, Roman, *The Secret File of Joseph Stalin*, London 2001

Brent, Jonathan, and Vladimir P. Naumov, *Stalin's Last Crime: The Doctors' Plot*, London 2003

Briukhanov, B. B., and E. N. Shoshkov, *Opravdaniyu ne podlezhit: Ezhov I ezhovshchina*, St Petersburg 1998

Bromage, Bernard, *Molotov*, London 1956

Brooks, Jeffrey, *Thank You Comrade Stalin*, Princeton 2000

Burleigh, Michael, *The Third Reich, A New History*, London 2000

Carlton, David, *Churchill and the Soviet Union*, London 2000

Carr, E. H., *What is History?* London 1964

Carswell, John, *The Exile, the Life of Ivy Litvinov*, London 1980

Chase, William J., *Enemies Within the Gates? The Comintern and the Stalinist Repression 1934–39*, New Haven, CT 2001

Chinsky, Pavel, *Staline archives inedites*, Paris 2001

Chisholm, Anne, and Michael Davie, *Beaverbrook: A Life*, London 1992

Chubariyan, Alexander O., and Vladimir O. Pechatnov, '"Molotov the Liberal": Stalin's 1945 Criticism of his Deputy', *Cold War History*, vol. 1, no. 1, Aug. 2000

Clark, Alan, *Barbarossa*, London 1996

Cohen, Stephen, *Bukharin and the Bolshevik Revolution, A Political Biography 1888–1938*, London 1973

Cohen, Y., 'Des lettres comme action: Stalin au début des années 1930 vu depuis les fonds Kaganovich', *Cahiers du Monde russe*, no. 3, vol. 38, July–September 1997

Conquest, Robert, *The Great Terror, Stalin's Purge of the Thirties*, London 1968

Conquest, Robert, *The Nation Killers*, London 1972

Conquest, Robert, *Inside Stalin's Secret Police: NKVD Politics 1936–1939*, Stanford, CA 1985

Conquest, Robert, *Harvest of Sorrow: Soviet Collectivization and the Terror/Famine*, London 1986

Conquest, Robert, *Stalin and the Kirov Murder*, Oxford 1989

Conquest, Robert, *Stalin: Breaker of Nations*, London 1991

Coox, Alvin D, 'L'affaire Liushkov: Anatomy of a Defector', *Soviet Studies*, 1967, vol. 8, no. 3

Coox, Alvin D., 'The Lesser of Two Hells: NKVD General GS Lyushkov's Defection to Japan 1938–45', *Slavic Military Studies*, vol. 11, no. 3, Sept. 1998

Curtis, J. A. E. , *Manuscripts Don't Burn: Mikhail Bulgakov A Life in Letters and Diaries*, London 1991

Dallin, Alexander, and F. I. Firsov (ed.), *Dmitrov and Stalin 1934–1943*, New Haven CT 2000

Davies, R. W. 'The Sypsov/Lominadze Affair', *Soviet Studies*, 33, no. 1, Jan. 1981

Easter, Gerald, *Reconstructing the State: Personal Networks and Elite Identity in Soviet Russia*, Cambridge 2000

Ebon, M., *Malenkov*, London 1953

Erickson, John, *Soviet High Command A Military/Political History 1918–41*, London 1962

Erickson, John, *The Road to Stalingrad*, London 1983

Erickson, John, *The Road to Berlin*, London 1996

Fairbanks, C. H., 'Clientilism and higher politics in Georgia 1949–1953', *Transcaucasia*, Ann Arbor, MI 1983

Fay, Laurel, *Shostakovich, A Life*, Oxford 2001

Figes, Orlando, *A People's Tragedy: The Russian Revolution 1891–1924*, London 1996

Figes, Orlando, *Natasha's Dance, A Cultural History of Russia*, London 2002

Fitzpatrick, Sheila, *The Cultural Front, Power and Culture in Revolutionary Russia*, Ithaca, NY 1992

Fitzpatrick, Sheila, *Everyday Stalinism, Ordinary Life in Extraordinary Times: Soviet Russia in the 1930s*, Oxford 1999

Fitzpatrick, Sheila, *Stalinism: New Directions*, London 2000

Garros, V., N. Korenevskaya, and T. Lahusen, *Intimacy and Terror: Soviet Diaries of the 1930s*, New Press 1995

Gazur, Edward P., *Secret Assignment: The FBI's KGB General*, NY 2001

Gendlin, L., *Confession of Stalin's Lover*, Moscow 1991

Getty, J. A., and R. T. Manning (eds), *Stalinist Terror. New Perspectives*, Cambridge 1993

Getty, J. Arch, *Origins of the Great Purges: the Soviet CP Reconsidered 1933–1938*, Cambridge 1985

Getty, J. Arch, and Oleg V. Naumov, *The Road to Terror: Stalin and the Self-Destruction of the Bolsheviks 1932–9*, New Haven, CT 1999

Gilbert, Martin, *Churchill: A Life*, London 1991

Glantz, David, 'The Kharkov Operation May 1942', *Slavic Military Studies*, vol. 5, Sept 1992, Dec 1992

Glantz, David, *Zhukov's Greatest Defeat: the Red Army's Epic Disaster in Operation Mars 1942*, Manchester 2000

Glantz, David, *Barbarossa: Hitler's Invasion of Russia 1941*, London 2001

Glantz, David, 'Forgotten Battles of German Soviet War – the Winter Campaign: the Crimean Counter-Offensive', *Slavic Military Studies*, vol. 14, March 2001

Gleason, Abbott, *Totalitarianism: The Inner History of the Cold War*, Oxford 2001

Gobarev, Victor, 'Soviet Military Plans and Actions During the First Berlin Crisis', *Slavic Military Studies*, vol. 10, Sept. 1997

Gobarev, Victor, 'Khrushchev and the Military: Historical and Psychological Analysis', *Slavic Military Studies*, vol. 11, 1998

Goncharov, Sergei N., John W. Lewis, and Xue Litai, *Uncertain Partners: Stalin, Mao and the Korean War*, Stanford, CA 1993

Gorlizki, Yoram, *Stalin's Cabinet: the Politburo and Decision-Making in the Post-War Years*, in Christopher Read, *The Stalin Years: A Reader*, London 2003

Gorlov, S. A., 'Peregovory VM Molotova v Berline v Noiabre 1940 goda', *VIZh*, vols. 6, 7, 1992

Gorodetsky, Gabriel, *Stafford Cripps' Mission to Moscow 1940–2*, London 1984

Gorodetsky, Gabriel, *Grand Delusion; Stalin and the German Invasion of Russia*, New Haven, CT 1999

Gromov, E., *Stalin: Vlast I Iskusstro*, Moscow 1998

Hahn, Werner, *Postwar Soviet Politics: the Fall of Zhdanov and the Defeat of Moderation 1946–53*, Ithaca, NY 1982

Harris, Jonathan, 'The Origins of the Conflict between Malenkov and Zhdanov 1939–1941', *Slavic Review*, vol. 35, no. 2, 1976

Holloway, David, *Stalin and the Bomb: the Soviet Union and Atomic Energy 1939–1956*, New Haven, CT 1994

Hosking, Geoffrey, *A History of the Soviet Union 1917–1991*, London 1992

Ivanov, S. P., *Shtab armeiskii, Shtab frontovoi*, Moscow 1990

Y. Izumov, 'Why Khrushchev took revenge on Stalin', *Dosye Glasnost*, no. 12, 2001

Jansen, Marc, and Nikita Petrov, *Stalin's Loyal Executioner: People's Commissar Nikolai Ezhov 1895–1940*, Stanford, CA 2002

Jeffery, Inez Cope, *Inside Russia: Life and Times of Zoya Zarubina*, Austin TX 1999

Jenkins, Roy, *Truman*, London 1986

Karpov, Vladimir, 'Tainaya rasprava nad marshalom Zhukovym', *Vestnik Protivovozdushnoy Oborony*, no. 7, 8, 17 and 19 August 1991

Karpov, Vladimir, 'Rasprava Stalina nad Marshalom Zhukovym', *Vestnik Protivovozdushnoy Oborony*, 7–8, 1992

Karpov, Vladimir, *Marshal Zhukov: Opala*, Moscow 1994

Karpov, Vladimir, *Rastrelyanniye Marshaly*, Moscow 2000

'Career of Communications Worker Vladimir Kazakov', *Nezavisimoe Voennoe Obrozenie*, vol. 19, 2002, p. 5

Kahan, Stuart, *Wolf of the Kremlin*, NY 1987

Kemp-Welch, A., *Stalin and the Literary Intelligentsia*, London 1991

Kenez, Peter, *Cinema and Soviet Society from the Revolution to the Death of Stalin*, London 2001

Khlevniuk, Oleg, *Stalin NKVD i sovetskoe obshchestvo*, Moscow 1993

Khlevniuk, Oleg, *In Stalin's Shadow, the Career of Sergo Ordzhonikidze*, NY 1993

Khlevniuk, Oleg, *Stalinskoe Politburo v 1930 gody. Sbornik dokumentov*, Moscow 1995

Khlevniuk, Oleg, *Le Circle du Kremlin, Staline et le bureau politique dans les années 30: les jeux du pouvoir*, Paris 1996

Khlevniuk, Oleg, Y. Gorlizki, A. I. Miniuk, M. Y. Prozymenshikov, L. A. Rogovaya, and S. V. Somonova (eds), *Politburo TsK BKP i Sovet Ministrov SSSR 1945–53*, Moscow 2002

Kirilina, A. A. *L'Assassinat de Kirov*, Paris 1995

Amy Knight, *Beria: Stalin's First Lieutenant*, Princeton, NJ 1993

Amy Knight, *Who Killed Kirov? The Kremlin's Greatest Mystery*, NY 1999

Kojevnikov, Alexei, *Games of Stalinist Democracy, Ideological discussions in Soviet sciences 1947–1952* in Sheila Fitzpatrick, *Stalinism: New Directions*, London 2000

Kotkin, Stephen, *Magnetic Mountain: Stalinism as a Civilization*, University of California, 1995

Korol, V. E., A. I. Sliusarenko, and I. U., Nikolaenko, 'Tragic 1941 and Ukraine: New Aspect of Problems', *Slavic Military Studies*, vol. 11, no. 1, March 1998

Kostyrchenko, Gennadi, *Out of the Red Shadows, Anti-Semitism in Stalin's Russia*, NY 1995

Kulikov, E., M. Miakgov, and O. Rzheshevsky, *Voina 1941–1945*, Moscow 2001

Kun, Miklos, *Stalin: An Unknown Portrait*, NY 2003

Kuznetsov, I. I., 'Stalin's Minister VI Abakumov', *Slavic Military Studies*, vol. 12, no. 1, March 1999

Kuznetsov, I. I., 'KGB General Naum Isakovich Eitingon 1899–1991', *Slavic Military Studies*, vol. 14, no. 1, Mar. 2001

Lakoba, S., *Ocherki po politicheskoy istorii Abkhazii*, Sukhumi 1990

Lastours, S. de, *Toukhatchevski*, Paris 1996

Lebedeva, N. S., *Katyn*, Moscow 1994

Levashov, Viktor, *Mikhoels: Ubiystvo Mikhoelsa*, Moscow 1998

Lewis, Jonathan, and Phillip Whitehead, *Stalin: Time for Judgement*, London 1990

Leyda, Jay, *Kino: History of Russian and Soviet Film*, London 1973

Likhanov, D., and V. Nikonov, 'La pochistil OGPU', in *Sovershenno sekretno* 1992, 4

Loguinov, V., *Taini Stalina, General Vlasik i yego soratniki*, Moscow 2000

Malia, Martin, *The Soviet Tragedy: A History of Socialism 1917–2000*, NY 1994

Marcucci, L., *Il Commissario di Ferro di Stalin*, Turin 1997

Mariamov, Grigory, *Kremlevskiy tsenzor: Stalin smotrit kino*, Moscow 1986

McLoughlin, Barry, and Kevin McDermott, *Stalin's Terror: High Politics and Mass Repression in the Soviet Union*, London 2002

Medvedev, Roy, *Let History Judge*, London 1976

Medvedev, Roy, *On Stalin and Stalinism*, Oxford 1979

Medvedev, Roy, *Khrushchev*, NY 1983

Medvedev, Roy, *All Stalin's Men: Six Who Carried the Bloody Purges*, NY 1985

Medvedev, Roy, *Neizvestnyi Stalin*, Moscow 2001

Medvedev, Roy and Zhores, *Politicheskiy dnevnik*, Amsterdam 1975

Medvedev, Zhores, *The Rise and Fall of T. D. Lysenko*, NY 1969

Mee, Charles L. Jr, *Meeting at Potsdam*, London 1975

Merridale, Catherine, *Night of Stone, Death and Memory in Russia*, London 2000

Merridale, C., *Moscow Politics and the Rise of Stalin: the Communist Party in the Capital 1925–32*, Basingstoke/London 1990

Morgan, Ted, *FDR*, London 1985

Munn, Michael, *John Wayne: the Man Behind the Myth*, London 2003

Naumov, V., *1941 god, Dokumenty*, Moscow 2000

Nekrasov, V. F., *Beria: Konets kariery*, Moscow 1991

Nekrasov, V. F., *Zhelezni Narkomy*, Moscow 1995

Nenarakov, A, 'Shatbs/Kapitan, Marshall, Vrag Naroda, Yegorov', *Rodina*, no. 10, 1989

Nevakivi, Jukka (ed.), *Finnish-Soviet Relations 1944–1948*, Helsinki 1994

Nevezhin, V. A., 'Stalin's 5th May Address: the experience of Interpretation', *Slavic Military Studies*, vol. 11, no. 1, March 1998

Nove, Alex (ed.), *The Stalin Phenomenon*, New York 1993

Overy, Richard, *Russia's War*, London 1997

Papkov, S. A., *Stalinsky Terror v Sibiri 1928–1941*, Novosibirsk 1997

Parrish, Michael, *The Lesser Terror: Soviet State Securiy 1939–1953*, London 1996

Parrish, Michael, 'The Last Relic: Serov', no. 3, *Slavic Military Studies*, vol. 10, Sept. 1997

Parrish, Michael, 'Downfall of the Iron Commissar NI Yezhov 1938–1940', *Slavic Military Studies*, vol. 14, no. 2, June 2001

Pavlenko, N. G., 'GK Zhukov: Iz neopublikovanykh vospominaniy', *Kommunist*, vol. 14, Sept. 1988

Pavlenko, N. G., 'Razmyshleniya o sudbe polkovodtsa', *VIZh*, nos 10, 11, 12, 1988

Pechatov, Vladimir O., 'The Allies are pressing on you to break your will ...' *Foreign Policy Correspondence between Stalin and Molotov and other Politburo members, September 1945/December 1946*, Working Paper 26, Cold War International History Project, Woodrow Wilson International Centre for Scholars, Washington DC

Perrie, Maureen, *The Cult of Ivan the Terrible in Stalin's Russia*, London 2001

Perlmutter, Amos, *A Not So Grand Alliance 1943–45*, Columbia, MO 1994

Petrov, N. V., and K. V. Scorkin, *Kto Rukovodil NKVD 1934–41: Spravochnik*, Moscow 1999

Pipes, Richard, *The Formation of the Soviet Union: Communism and Nationalism 1917–1923*, Harvard 1954

Pipes, Richard, *Russia Under the Bolshevik Regime*, London 1994

Polianski, A., *Yezhov: Istoriya zheleznogo stalinskogo narkoma*, Moscow 2001

Pope, Arthur Upham, *Maxim Litvinov*, London 1943

Popov, B. S., and V. G. Oppokov, 'Berievshchina', *VIZh*, 1990, no. 3

Porter, Cathy, *Alexandra Kollantai*, London 1980

Povartsov, S. *Prichina smerti-rastrel*, Moscow 1996

Raanan, Gavriel D., *International Policy Formation in the USSR Factional 'Debates' during the Zhdanovshchina*, Hamden, CT 1983

Radosh, R., M. R. Habeck and G. Sevostianov (eds), *Spain Betrayed the Soviet Union in the Spanish Civil War*, New Haven, CT 2001

Radzinsky, Edvard, *Stalin*, London 1996

Read, Christopher, *The Stalin Years: A Reader*, London 2003

Read Anthony, and David Fisher, *The Deady Embrace: Hitler, Stalin and the Nazi-Soviet Pact 1939–1941*, London 1988

Rees, E. A., *Stalinism and Soviet Rail Transport 1928–1941*, London 1995

Reese, R. R., *Stalin's Reluctant Soldiers: A Social History of the Red Army*, Kansas 1996

Richardson, Rosamond, *The Long Shadow: Inside Stalin's Family*, London 1993

Rieber, Alfred J., 'Stalin Man of the Borderlands', *American History Review*, vol. 106, no. 5, December 2001

Riehl, Nikolaus, and Frederick Seitz, *Stalin's Captive Nikolaus Riehl and the Soviet Race for the Bomb*, London 1996

Rigby, T. H., 'Was Stalin a Disloyal Patron?', *Soviet Studies*, vol. 38, no. 3, July 1986

Rigby, T. H., *Political Elites in the USSR*, Aldershot 1990

Ritterspoon, G. T., *Stalinist Simplifications and Soviet Complications. Social Tensions and Political Conflicts in the USSR 1933–53*, Philadelphia 1991

Roberts, Andrew, *The Holy Fox: A Biography of Lord Halifax*, London 1991

Roberts, Geoffrey, 'Beware Greek Gifts: the Churchill/Stalin Percentages Agreement of October 1944', *Churchill and Stalin, FCO Historians' Conference 2002*

Rogovin, Vadim Z., *1937: Stalin's Year of Terror*, Oak Park, MI 1988

Rosenfeldt, N. E., *Knowledge and Power: the Role of Stalin's Secret Chancellery in the Soviet System of Government*, Copenhagen 1978

Rubenstein, Joshua, *Tangled Loyalties: the Life and Times of Ilya Ehrenburg*, London 1996

Rubenstein, Joshua, and Vladimir P. Naumov, *Stalin's Secret Pogrom, The Postwar Inquisition of the Jewish Anti-Fascist Committee*, New Haven, CT 2001

Rubtsov, Y., *Alter Ego Stalina: Stranitsy politicheskoi biografi LZ Mekhlisa*, Moscow 1999

Rubtsov, Y, *Marshay Stalina*, Rostov 2000

Rybakov, Anatoli, *Children of the Arbat*, Boston 1988

Rzheshevsky, O. A., *Vtoraya Mirovaya Voina*, Moscow 1995

Rzheshevsky, O. A. (ed.), *War and Diplomacy: the Making of the Grand Alliance*, NY 1996

Rzheshevsky, O. A., 'Winston Churchill in Moscow 1942', *Churchill and Stalin, FCO Historians' Conference 2002*

Sainsbury K., *The Turning Point*, London 1986

Salisbury, Harrison, *900 Days, The Siege of Leningrad*, London 1969 (r/p: 2000)

Seaton Albert, *Stalin as Military Commander*, Conshohocken, PA 1998

Service, Robert, *The Bolshevik Party in Revolution: A Study in Organizational Change 1917–23*, London 1979

Service, Robert, *A History of 20th Century Russia*, London 1997

Service, Robert, *Joseph Stalin, the Making of a Stalinist*, John Channon (ed.), *Politics, Sociey and Stalinism in the USSR*, London 1998

Service, Robert, *Lenin*, London 2000

Service, Robert, 'Architectural Problems of Reform: from Design to Collapse', *Totalitarian Movements and Political Religions*, vol. 2, no. 2, autumn 2001

Shapiro, Leonard, *The Communist Pary of the Soviet Union*, London 1970

Sheinis, Z, *Maxim Maksimorich Litvinov*, Moscow 1989

Shentalinsky, Vitaly, *The KGB's Literary Archive*, London 1995

Shentalinsky, Vitaly, 'Okhota v revzapovednike', *Novy Mir*, 1998, no. 12

Shukman, Harold (ed.), *Stalin's Generals*, London 1993

Shukman, Harold (ed.), *Stalin and the Soviet–Finnish War 1939–1940*, London 2002

Siegelbaum, Lewis, and Andrei Sokolov (eds), *Stalinism as a Way of Life, A Narrative in Documents*, New Haven, CT 2001

Smith, Edward Ellis, *Young Stalin*, New York 1967

Soyfer, Valery, *Lysenko and the Tragedy of Soviet Science*, NJ 1994

Spahr, William J, *Zhukov, The Rise and Fall of a Great Captain*, Novato, CA 1995

Spahr, William J., *Stalin's Lieutenants, A Study of Command under Duress*, Novato, CA 1997

Starr, S. Frederick, *Red and Hot, The Fate of Jazz in the Soviet Union 1917–80*, Oxford 1983

Stoliarov, K. A., *Golgofa*, Moscow 1991

Sukhomlinov, A., *Vasily: Syn Vozhdya*, Moscow 2001

Sulianov, Anatoli, *Arrestovat v Kremle. O zhizni i smerti marshala Beria: Povest*, Minsk 1991

Suny, Ronald Grigor, *The Making of the Georgian Nation*, Stanford, CA 1988

Suvenirov, O. F., *Tragediya RKKA 1937–8*, Moscow 1998

Taubman, William, *Khrushchev, The Man and His Era*, London 2003

Taubman, William, Sergei Khrushchev, and Abbott Gleason, *Nikita Khrushchev*, New Haven, CT 2000

Taylor, A. J. P., *Beaverbrook*, London 1972

Thomas, Hugh, *Armed Truce, The Beginnings of the Cold War 1945–6*, London 1986

Thurston, Robert W., *Life and Terror in Stalin's Russia 1934–41*, New Haven, CT 1996

Trepper, L., *Bolshaya igra*, Moscow 1990

Tolstoy, Nikolai, *Stalin's Secret War*, London 1981

Tolstoy, Nikolai, *The Tolstoys*, London 1983

Torchinov, B. A., and A. M. Lentiuk, *Vokrug Stalina*, St Petersburg 2000

Toranska, Teresa, *Oni, Stalin's Polish Puppets*, London 1987

Tucker, Robert, *Stalin as Revolutionary*, NY 1974

Tucker, Robert, *Stalin in Power: the Revolution from Above*, New York 1990

Tucker, Robert, *Stalinism: Essays in Historical Interpretation*, New Brunswick, NJ 2000

Ushakov, S., and A. A. Stukakov, *Front Voennykh Prokurorov*, Moscow 2000

Uspenski, V. D., *Taynyi Sovetnik Vozhdya*, Moscow 1992

Vaksberg, Arkady, *Stalin's Prosecutor, The Life of Andrei Vyshinsky*, NY 1991

Vaksberg, Arkady, 'Delo marshala Zhukova: nerazorvavshayasya bomba', *Literaturnaya Gazeta*, no. 32, 5, Aug. 1992

Vaksberg, Arkady, *Stalin Against the Jews*, NY 1995

Vasilieva, Larissa, *Kremlin Wives*, London 1994

Vasilieva, Larissa, *Kremlevskie Zheny*, Moscow 2001

Vasilieva, Larissa, *Deti Kremya*, Moscow 2001

Veiskopf, Mikhail, *Pisatel Stalin*, Moscow 2001

Volkogonov, Dmitri, *Stalin: Triumph and Tragedy*, London 1991

Volkogonov, Dmitri, *The Rise and Fall of the Soviet Empire*, London 1998

Watson, Derek, 'The Early Career of VM Molotov', *CREES Discussion Papers, Soviet Industrialisation Project Series*, Univ. of Birmingham, vol. 26, 1986

Watson, Derek, *Molotov and Soviet Government: Sovnarkom 1930–41*, Basingstoke 1996

Wheatley, Dennis, *Red Eagle. The story of the Russian Revolution and of Klimenty Efremovitch Voroshilov, Marshal and Commissar for Defence of the USSR*, London 1938

Yakovlev, Alexander, *A Century of Violence in Soviet Russia*, New Haven, CT 2002

Yakovlev, A. N., R. Pikhoya, and A. Geishtor, *Katyn*, Moscow 1997

Yakovlev, N. N., *Zhukov*, Moscow 1992

Young, Gordon, *Stalin's Heirs, Who's Who in Soviet Russia*, London 1953

Zenkovich, N. A., *Marshaly I genseki*, Smolensk 1997

Zhavoronkov, G., 'I snitsya nochyu den', *Sintaksis*, no. 32, 1992

Zhirnov, E., 'Gornichnyh Predstavit k Nagradam', *Vlast*, vol. 16, 2000

Zhirnov, E, 'Conversation with Office Manager of USSR Council of Ministers Mikhail Smirtukov', *Vlast*, vol. 11 (Molotov), vol. 7 (Bulganin), vol. 5 (Malenkov), vol. 25 (Stalin), 2000

Zhukov, Y. N., 'Borba za vlast v rukovodstve SSSR v 1945–1952', *Voprosy Istorii*, no. 1, 1995

Zhukov, N. Y., 'Tainy Kremlevskogo dela 1935 goda I sudba Avelia Yenukidze', *Voprosy Istorii*, no. 9, 2000

Zubkova, Elena, 'Obshchestvennaya atmosphera posle voiny (1945–1946)', *Svobodnaya Mysl*, no. 6, 1992

Zubok, Vladislav, and Constantine Pleshakov, *Inside the Kremlin's Cold War, From Stalin to Khrushchev*, Harvard 1996

Index

386   Index

Artemev, General P.A., 105, 108, 109
Arutinov, G.A., 249n
Astor, Nancy, Viscountess, 124
atomic bomb: developed by USA, 203,
    209; Soviet development of, 209–11,
    249, 309–10, 312
Attlee, Clement, 207
Aviators' Case see Novikov, Air Marshal
    A.A.

Babel, Antonina, 27n
Babel, Isaac, 28, 34n; arrested and shot,
    26, 27 & n; and Mikhoels, 284
Bagirov, M.D., 119
Bagramian, I.Kh., 84
Baibakov, Nikolai, 111, 129–30, 130n,
    142
Balandin, V.P., 85
Baltic states: in Nazi-Soviet pact, 13, 16,
    18; JS occupies, 38
Bashtakov, M.I., 37
Batitsky, Marshal A., 363
Beaverbrook, William Maxwell Aitken,
    1st Baron, 93–4
Belgorod, 163
Belomor see Baltic–White Sea Canal
Belorussia, 25
Berezhkov, Valentin, 41, 101, 171n
Beria, Lavrenti Pavlovich: womanizing
    and sex life, 189, 211, 212–15, 213n,
    229, 259, 260; enmity with Lakoba,
    277; relations with Poskrebyshev, 22;
    and sacking of Litvinov, 3; meetings
    with diplomats, 5; disparages
    Kaganovich, 6; discusses alliance with
    France and Britain, 9; and Nazi-Soviet
    pact, 12n; drinking habits, 17, 228–9;
    on JS's attitude to women, 19–20; and
    Bronka Poskrebysheva's arrest and
    disappearance, 21; and Kavtaradzes,
    23; and death of Yezhov, 27; JS
    questions Terror campaign, 28; and
    invasion of Finland, 32; orders arrest
    of Kira Kulik, 35; arrested, indicted
    and executed, 35–6, 37n, 212, 213n,
    362–3; opposes massacre of Polish
    officers, 37; and killing of Polish
    officers, 37n; and reorganization of
    NKVD, 38n; and German invasion
    threat, 39, 59–61; and accusations
    against Mikhail Kaganovich, 49; dines
    at Zubalovo, 52; enmity with
    Voznesensky, 54, 111, 236, 302;
    rivalry with Malenkov, 54; meets JS
    after German invasion, 69, 71;
    activities in war, 69–70, 75, 81, 83,
    117, 121, 136, 162, 163; and JS's
    despair at early wartime setbacks,
    78–80; proposes wartime State

Defence Committee, 78; and wartime
    proposals to Germans, 83; increases
    Terror in war, 85, 97; declines to arrest
    Zhdanov, 89; and German threat to
    Moscow, 94–5; JS requests to consider
    separate peace with Germany, 95;
    urges abandonment of Moscow, 98,
    104; evacuated from Moscow, 100;
    and JS's move to Semyonovskoe, 103;
    in wartime Moscow, 108–9; and JS's
    proposed offensive, 111;
    organizational power in war, 111–12;
    ordered to defend Caucasus, 129–30;
    works with JS, 141–5, 147; threatens
    Voronov, 145; wartime authority,
    145–6; and formation of Smersh, 149;
    retains overall control of security
    organs, 149n; informs JS of Svetlana's
    romance with Kapler, 154; provides
    slave labour for Kursk battle, 157; and
    new national anthem, 165, 166;
    attends Teheran conference, 168–71,
    176; JS rebukes, 168; arrests and
    deportation of nationalities, 178–9; at
    Yalta conference, 186, 189; sends Nazi
    correspondence to JS, 197; gathers
    evidence against Zhukov, 198; and JS's
    honours, 201; supports renaming
    Moscow after JS, 201; at Potsdam
    conference, 202, 203; promoted
    Marshal, 202; reports US atom bomb
    to JS, 204; in charge of development of
    atom bomb, 204, 208, 209–11;
    manner and style, 209–10, 217; JS
    loathes, 211, 329; private life and
    interests, 211–14; vegetarianism, 212,
    233; wounding mockery, 212, 233;
    illegitimate children, 214n; relations
    with son, 215–16; as JS's companion,
    223; comments on films, 224, 226;
    shares car with Malenkov, 227; bored
    by JS's stories, 228, 234; builds
    greenhouse for JS, 230; proposes
    shooting quail, 230–1; delivers turbots
    to JS, 232; threatens Bierut, 232;
    manipulates JS, 233, 236; enmity with
    Zhdanov, 236, 249, 287; JS's campaign
    against Molotov, 244, 341–2; JS turns
    against, 245–6, 317, 320, 342; made
    full Politburo member, 245; demoted,
    246, 247; and Malenkov's demotion,
    250; hatred of Kuznetsov, 250; sets up
    Jewish Anti Fascist Committee, 255;
    sympathy for Jewish cause, 255–6; and
    JS's anti-Semitism, 257; attacks
    Zhukov, 258; Vlasik denounces, 260;
    plays volleyball, 262; privileges, 262;
    and post-war food shortages, 267n; on
    JS's loneliness, 281; relations with